THE
THEORY
OF THE
NOVEL

THE
THEORY
OF THE
NOVEL
NEW ESSAYS

Edited by
John Halperin

University of Southern California

New York
Oxford University Press
London 1974 Toronto

To the three kind and inspiriting men
who made this book possible:
Howard Schultz, J. Hillis Miller, and A. Walton Litz

ACKNOWLEDGMENTS

In putting together this volume I have been fortunate enough to have had the help, advice, and encouragement of a number of good people. I should like to take this opportunity to thank each of the following for his kindness, patience, and wise counseling: Professors Alfred Kazin and Homer Goldberg of the State University of New York at Stony Brook; Professor A. Walton Litz of Princeton University; Professor J. Hillis Miller of Yale University; Professor Max F. Schulz of the University of Southern California; Professor Irving H. Buchen of Fairleigh Dickinson University; Professor Alan Warren Friedman of the University of Texas; and John W. Wright of the Oxford University Press, New York City.

Manhattan Beach, California   J.H.
November 1973

CONTENTS

THE
GENRE
TODAY

THE
THEORY
OF THE
NOVEL
A CRITICAL
INTRODUCTION

JOHN HALPERIN

Christ left home at the age of twelve. Poetry's age, at the time, was in the thousands of years, and drama's in the hundreds. It was not until a millennium and a half later that the gestation period of the novel began. Thus it is not surprising, three-quarters of the way through the twentieth century, that we find ourselves with a growing but still relatively small body of critical *theory* pertaining to the novel, while poetic and dramatic theory exists, and has existed for centuries, in a multiplication of varieties.

In the last fifty years or so a greater interest has been taken by practitioners and critics of the novel in some of the theoretical bases of the genre. What began in the eighteenth and nineteenth centuries as tentative theoretical groping has begun to blossom, in our century, into a gradually recognizable body of critical novel-theory. It is the purpose of the present volume to reflect and hopefully to deal with some of the more radical issues of contemporary novel-theory that have emerged along with the steady growth of interest in this century in the novel as a *form*. Novel-criticism is beginning to reach not only a degree of sophistication and virtuosity comparable with that of the other genres, but also a measure of searching inquiry that exceeds that of older bodies of theory. This collection, containing original essays of a theoretical cast written especially for this volume by some of the most distinguished critics of our time, hopefully will be a major addition to the growing corpus of theoretical approaches to fiction.

It is my intention in this introductory essay to give the reader a general and, I fear, a kaleidoscopic overview of novel-theory before the twentieth century. A full-scale survey is impossible here; I aim only to provide a flavoring, an indication of what modern trends in theoretical novel-criticism are built on, where they have come from, what they are reacting against.

The earliest theoretical novel-criticism, that of the eighteenth century, tended to concern itself only with the moral implications of technique. Thus Dr. Johnson on fiction:

> It is therefore not a sufficient vindication of a character that it is drawn as it appears; for many characters ought never to be drawn: nor of a narrative that the train of events is agreeable to observation and experience; for that observation which is called knowledge of the world will be found much more frequently to make men cunning than good. . . . In narratives where historical veracity has no place, I cannot discover why there should not be exhibited the most perfect idea of virtue; of virtue not angelical, nor above probability (for what we cannot credit, we shall never imitate), but the highest and purest that humanity can reach, which, exercised in such trials as the various revolutions of things shall bring upon it, may, by conquering some calamities and enduring others, teach us what we may hope, and what we can perform.[1]

Such criticism is concerned less with theoretical aspects of novelistic form than with the moral function of art. Johnson is arguing here not against literary realism *per se* but rather against fiction, such as Fielding's, which for him is corrupt in that it does not adequately distinguish between virtue and vice. This is not an endorsement of unrestricted idealization, for the excessively idealized is too remote to teach us anything ("what we cannot credit, we shall never imitate"); rather it is an invitation to emphasize the virtues of those who are essentially good and whom it is appropriate to imitate. Such emphasis puts into greater relief the model meant to instruct us and thus more effectively appeals to our higher nature. Like Aristotle in sections of the *Poetics,* Johnson is concerned here with art as moral instructor and the artist as instrument of moral instruction. He admired the fiction of Richardson, in whose books the moral pattern is always abundantly clear. Richardson's method uses the letter as the record of consciousness, of the mind at work. If we are exposed to the psychological processes of the ordinary person, Richardson believed, we can compare his private experience to our own—which means that we can identify and sympathize more easily with that person, and, in learning more about him through our aroused interest, we may also learn more about ourselves. This, as we shall see, is also the method of George Eliot a century later; indeed the idea of sympathetic identification for the purpose of moral enlightenment is a tenet as central to mid-nineteenth-century thought about the novel as to that of the Augustan age. In Defoe, to take another example, life is seen as a perpetual moral struggle. Every item of personal experience, as Ian Watt points out, is seen by the novelist as morally important in some way, and thus formal realism—the transcription of real life—in effect has the purpose of alerting us to the moral importance of everything we do.[2] Such, of course, is also the concern of George Eliot: "The evil consequences that may lie folded in a single act of selfish indulgence, is a thought so awful that it ought surely to awaken some feeling less presumptuous than a rash desire to punish."[3]

Despite Johnson's reservations, Fielding, though perhaps less attentive than some of his contemporaries to the didactic functions of literature, is explicit about his moral aims as a novelist. He is interested less in individuals than in types, and his approach to character is in the main external. His desire as a novelist, as he makes clear in the opening paragraphs of *Joseph Andrews* (1742), is the improvement of his reader, an expansion of sympathy through moral education:

> It is a trite but true observation, that examples work more forcibly on the mind than precepts; and if this be just in what is odious and blameable, it is more strongly so in what is amiable and praiseworthy. Here emulation most effectually operates upon us, and inspires our imitation in an irresible manner. A good man therefore is a standing lesson to all his acquaintance, and of far greater use in that narrow circle than a good book.
>
> But as it often happens that the best men are but little known, and consequently cannot extend the usefulness of their examples a great way; the writer may be called in aid to spread their history farther, and to present the amiable pictures to those who have not the happiness of knowing the originals; and so, by communicating such valuable patterns to the world, he may perhaps do a more extensive service to mankind than the person whose life originally afforded the pattern.

The critics have not as yet decided how seriously Fielding is to be taken here,[4] but his concern with the comparative effects of positive and negative examples in fiction is apparent everywhere in his writings. In an essay written two years before *Joseph Andrews,* he says: "We are much better and easier taught by the example of what we are to shun, than by those which would instruct us what to pursue. . . . [T]he reason . . . may be, that we are more inclined to detest and loathe what is odious in others, than to admire what is laudable."[5] If the opening of *Joseph Andrews* seems to contradict this, the fact remains that Fielding in both places is concerned with the moral effect of literature upon its readers. And despite his professed reservations, Johnson's *Rambler* essays in many ways echo the moral precepts for literature suggested by the author of *Joseph Andrews.*

It is interesting to note that the idea expressed in the quoted passage from *Joseph Andrews*—that of the novelist as a provider of moral examples of the good and useful lives often led by the ungreat, the uncelebrated—is also a generating impulse in George Eliot's story of Dorothea Brooke. In the Finale to *Middlemarch,* George Eliot says of Dorothea: "The effect of her being on those around her was incalculably diffusive: for the growing good of the world is partly dependent upon unhistoric acts; and that things are not so ill with you and me as they might have been, is half owing to the number who lived faithfully a hidden life, and rest in unvisited tombs." The Victorian novelists, despite the distance of years between them and their Augustan predecessors, differed in no serious way in their mutual preoccupation with the pedagogical value of art.

Both Augustan and nineteenth-century novel-theory (before Flaubert and James, at any rate) are primarily interested in the relationship between the reader and the text. The nature of that relationship, determined by the mimetic adequacy of the fiction itself, signals some sort of moral value—that is, the spiritual level of a novel is seen as determined as much by the reader's relationship to it as by the moral nature of the writer himself. The moral writer will produce fiction sufficiently "realistic" to teach the reader to be good. The emphasis on the mimetic adequacy of the fiction is really an emphasis on its effect upon the reader. Literary realism, based on a satisfactory imitation of nature, was held to have a particular spiritual effect; for the more "realistic" a novel, the greater was considered its capacity for exercising that effect (both for good and ill). The more moral the writer, the more likely that the effect would be salutary.

In the late eighteenth and early nineteenth centuries, as Ian Watt points out in *The Rise of the Novel*, writers as diverse as Sterne, Fanny Burney, and Jane Austen concern themselves in their novels with the mental life of their characters—sometimes, as in the case of Sterne, to parody the form of the novel itself, but more often, as in the novels of Jane Austen, to teach us about ourselves through the depiction of a psyche which may not be far removed from our own. In general, however, eighteenth-century writers of fiction gave little thought to the theoretical bases of their genre:

> It is true that both Richardson and Fielding saw themselves as founders of a new kind of writing, and that both viewed their work as involving a break with the old-fashioned romances; but neither they nor their contemporaries provide us with the kind of characterisation of the new genre that we need; indeed they did not even canonise the changed nature of their fiction by a change in nomenclature—our usage of the term "novel" was not fully established until the end of the eighteenth century.[6]

By then, however, the Gothic novel and the novels of "sensibility" were in full bloom, and serious speculations upon the form of fiction were more or less in limbo.

Dickens, in his preface to the 1839 edition of *Oliver Twist*, voices a complaint and enunciates a principle remarkably similar to Johnson's in the passage from the *Rambler* essay quoted above. Vice and virtue, says Dickens, have become so inextricably mixed in contemporary fiction that one may often be unable to tell them apart. Reacting strongly against the widely popular "Newgate" novels of the time—many of which, such as the early tales of Bulwer-Lytton, and those of Harrison Ainsworth, had criminals as their heroes—Dickens has, he says, written *Oliver Twist* both to show "the principle of Good surviving through every adverse circumstance, and triumphing at last" and to define the thanklessly tortuous setting in which the criminal mind must pass its existence. For Anthony Trollope, who was no admirer of Dickens, the novel was no less a vehicle for the presentation of a lesson in conduct. Even Hardy comments, some years later, to the effect that the "true object" of reading fiction "is a lesson in life, mental enlargement from elements essential to the narratives themselves and from the reflections they engender."[7] Neo-classic attitudes toward the novel, then, did not disappear in the Victorian age.[8]

George Henry Lewes, surely the most brilliant English-speaking theoretician of the novel before James, echoes what is sometimes implied in Augustan novel-criticism when he asserts that the novel should avoid depicting the sordid and the ugly because otherwise it will be unable to engage the sympathies, and thus enlarge the sensibilities, of its readers. Art, says Lewes, should not attempt to deal with the unreal; but it should idealize reality to some extent in order to inspire and enlarge man's highest faculties—the mere imitation of nature will not impress the human soul with any sense of beauty. In his *Principles of Success in Literature* (1865), Lewes argues that whereas a surface realism is concerned only with achieving verisimilitude in relation to the outward aspect of things, idealism attempts to reveal *inner* as well as external truths. Idealism, then, is a kind of realism; it is "the basis of all Art, and its antithesis is not Idealism, but Falsism."[9] Lewes's insistence that fiction reveal inner as well as external truths leads to his emphasis upon the importance of psychological characterization. His favored method in this context is dramatic representation, or what he calls "dramatic ventriloquism," the means by which the writer makes the character reveal himself.[10] The most immediate fruits of Lewes's theories were of course the novels of George Eliot, who adopted his doctrines of sympathetic engagement and modified realism through psychological characterization (though she is a more intrusive presence in her novels than Lewes's theory of "dramatic ventriloquism" would seem to allow for). Late in her life George Eliot told Cross that she had been taught by Lewes that dramatic representation was the highest quality of fiction.[11] Throughout her career as a novelist, essayist, and reviewer, George Eliot insisted upon the necessity of dramatic representation as the most efficient means of achieving the spiritual enlargement, through example, of her audience (the most obvious place to see this is the famous seventeenth chapter of *Adam Bede*). She admired Stendhal for employing the scenic method.[12] Implicit in an essay on Charles Reade published in 1856 is George Eliot's belief that the successful novelist must possess both the negative capability of a Keats in creating character and the imagination of a Coleridge in shaping his material.[13] But for her, as for Meredith in the 1850's, realism is the only basis of art. Her later novels, like his, are less mimetic, more a softening of reality. Both writers in their later years attempted to steer a middle course between idealism and naturalism.[14]

Another brilliant and unfortunately much-forgotten nineteenth-century critic and theoretician of the novel is David Masson. In his monumental *British Novelists and Their Styles* (1859), a nineteenth-century *Aspects of the Novel*, Masson carries on the attack upon pure realism by arguing that novels are or can be prose epics; for Masson, the novel ought to deal with "elemental" subjects rather than merely with daily life and its comedies of manners. More important, however, are Masson's opinions that novels "give a more various interpretation of passing life" than poems do, that the novel is therefore a form capable of as much high seriousness as poetry, and that the kind of criticism poetry is used to enjoying ought also to be applied to the novel. Masson's well-known essay on Dickens and Thackeray, which is primarily an identification of the differences separating romance from realism in fiction, employs "poetic" criticism in its close analysis of the *styles* of the two writers. Masson's emphasis remains typically upon the connections between mimesis and the moral elements of fiction on the one hand and the moral nature of the novelist himself on the other. For Masson, as for many of his Augustan predecessors, the moral nature of the novelist inevitably colors the moral nature of the fiction he writes:

> The novelist, as the creator of his mimic world, is also its providence; he makes the laws that govern it; he conducts the lines of events to their issue; he winds up all according to his judicial wisdom. It is possible, then, to see how far his laws of moral government are in accordance with those that rule the real course of things, and so, on the one hand, how deeply and with what accuracy he has studied life, and, on the other, whether, after his study, he is a loyal member of the human commonwealth, or a rebel, a cynic, a son of the wilderness.[15]

In his obsession with the connections between morality and realism, Masson is clearly typical of his times; but in his insistence that fiction deserves the sort of criticism usually accorded only to poetry, Masson is bucking a popular view of the novel—which held, following the expressed opinions of such diverse but important writers as Scott, Thackeray, Trollope, Ruskin, and Mill, that the novel was an inferior art form. The cavalier attitude toward fiction of such influential men of letters began to give way in the 1860's, however, before the more serious treatment of the novel as a genre by men like Masson, Lewes, and Charles Kingsley, who emphasized the importance of the drama's unities in fiction, renewed the attack upon "Falsism," and raised the debate over the subject matter of the novel to a higher level of seriousness. Much of this is due, by the 60's, to the rise of French realism and the reactions it was beginning to inspire.

The contrary tendencies toward romance and realism apparently were often at war within Flaubert. Clearly, despite his intense interest in reality itself, he disliked pure realism, the mere imitation or copying of the external. As he says: "The artist must raise everything up."[16] The novel, for him as for George Eliot, creates beauty primarily in its treatment of the internal. *How* it does this is for Flaubert of paramount importance; he is obsessed with questions of *form,* and even more passionately than Masson he believes that the techniques of fiction deserve as much aesthetic and analytic attention as those of poetry. It is *style,* he says, that gives value and beauty to art:

> You tell me that I pay too much attention to form. Alas! it is like the body and the soul; form and the idea, for me, are one and the same thing, and I don't know what the one is without the other. The more beautiful an idea is, the more melodious is the language, make no mistake about that. Precision in thought makes (and is in itself) that of the impression.[17]

For Flaubert, as for James, subject and style are symbiotic, even identical. Maupassant says of Flaubert:

> For him the form was the work itself, in the same way as, in human beings, the blood nourishes the flesh and determines even its shapes, its literal appearance, according to his race and family, thus, with him, the work, the inner meaning of it, inevitably imposes the unique and correct expression, the measure, the rhythm, the whole finish of the form.[18]

Flaubert believed that the author's language should be universal in its clarity—that it should contain nothing that would tie it to any particular locale or class or period.[19] One way to achieve this stylistic neutrality is to avoid becoming the partisan of any particular idea or creed or belief.[20] Art must be as impersonal as science (here, perhaps, are the beginnings of naturalism). And yet Flaubert felt that prose, even in its necessary objectivity, has the capacity to be as musical and harmonious as poetry: "A good sentence of prose must be like a good line of verse, that is to say, impossible to change, and with as much rhythm, melodious."[21] Flaubert believed that fiction, no less than poetry, should use linguistic constructs appropriate to particular artistic situations.

The ideal artistic situation could well be, for Flaubert, "a book about nothing, a book without external attachments of any sort, which would hold of itself, through the inner strength of its style . . . a book with almost no subject. Or at least an almost invisible subject, if possible."[22] Annette Michelson has quite rightly identified Flaubert's questioning of art as mimesis as the moment when the literary aspiration "toward a work of total autonomy, self-referring, self-sustaining and self-justifying" first expressed itself systematically and coherently:

> The dissolution of the subject or figure, the contestation of art as Mimesis, of Realism itself, is grounded in the problematic consciousness of a reality no longer assumed as pre-defined or pre-existent to the work of the imagination. Art now takes the nature of reality, the nature of consciousness in and through perception, as its subject of domain [and becomes] an exploration of the conditions and terms of perception. . . .[23]

The idea of art as "consciousness," as "perception," is peculiar to much modern autonomy-oriented fiction-theory.[24]

In this connection, it should be pointed out that Flaubert was an early advocate of the dramatic representation in fiction of the human mind; he was always a staunch enemy of didacticism, the heavily plotted romance, and "local color." To paint what is universally true, he says, the artist need not tell an elaborate story, nor need he, as we have just seen, have a story to tell at all; he need only be as unobtrusive as possible in his undidactic representation of human psychology. One way of remaining unobtrusive is to refrain from parading one's knowledge or opinions of topical or local conditions and other details. One of the first to enunciate the "disappearing author" principle, Flaubert as early as 1852 expressed his feeling that an author must be completely absent from his work—that we should know no more of what he thinks of his creations than we know of what God thinks of *his* creations: "The author, in his work, must be like God in the universe, present everywhere but visible nowhere."[25] The novelist "must imitate God in the midst of his creation, that is to say act and remain silent [faire et se taire]."[26] The author should keep his opinions to himself; if the reader does not draw the proper moral, it is because he is stupid or the book itself is *"false* from the point of view of truth."

(In his 1868 preface to the second edition of his first novel, *Thérèse Raquin* [1867], Zola takes Flaubert's theory of authorial neutrality one step further and enunciates what was to become a rallying cry of European naturalism: the doctrine of "pure scientific curiosity." As a writer, says Zola, he has "simply done on living bodies the work of analysis which surgeons perform on corpses." Later Zola added to this first compositional principle another seminal idea: the social utility of naturalism.[27])

Flaubert's theories of fiction, like those of Henry James, are original primarily in their departure from the tone and substance of earlier nineteenth-century novel-theory. Flaubert is the first writer to expound a systematic and widely applicable theory of the novel which is less concerned with the moral function of art than with the relationships of the component parts of the aesthetic creation to each other and to the work as a whole. He is thus the first "modern" theorist of the novel. Modern novel-theory, if one dare generalize about it, is notable for its autonomous, sometimes phenomenological, occasionally eclectic approach to form, and it is usually less concerned with moral qualities of structure than with abstract principles of composition. "Realism" here becomes more often the representation of mental states than the imitation of the action of the exterior world. For Flaubert, as for Gautier, the autonomous existence of perfection itself is sufficient moral justification for literature. Roland Barthes puts it this way: "Flaubert . . . finally established Literature as an object, through promoting literary labour to the status of a value; form became the end-product of craftsmanship, like a piece of pottery or a jewel. . . . [T]he whole of Literature, from Flaubert to the present day, became the problematics of language."[28] Barthes here, like Annette Michelson in her essay, views Flaubert as a kind of dividing-line between the old (mimetic) writing and the new (autonomous) writing. The first part of his statement may be applied as well to James, whose theories of fiction and principles of form are too comprehensive to receive anything but superficial treatment here. We may note in passing, however, how many of James's cardinal principles are also Flaubert's. Like Flaubert, James insists on psychological representation of characters through the dramatic method; on the avoidance of philosophical partisanship in art; on the unobtrusiveness of the artist in his work. He too regulates his style carefully in accordance with the subject at hand. Style, for James as for Flaubert, is inseparable from conception:

> since in proportion as the work is successful the idea permeates it, informs and animates it, so that every word and every punctuation-point contributes directly to the expression, in that proportion do we lose our sense of the story being a blade which may be drawn more or less out of its sheath. The story and the novel, the idea and the form, are the needle and the thread, and I never heard of a guild of tailors who recommended the use of the thread without the needle, or the needle without the thread.[29]

This sounds remarkably like Flaubert's letter to Mlle. Leroyer de Chantpie. There are, however, differences. Both writers are more interested in the relationship of the text to the ideas it expresses than in the relationship of the text to the reader. But Flaubert writes about the relation of style (diction, syntax, etc.) to idea (subject)— a version of the traditional Horatian *res/verba* dialectic. James, while alluding to the importance of style, is analyzing the matter somewhat differently—in terms of the relation of story (plot-germ, event) to novel (full realization of story in a narrative presentation). It is clear, however, that both writers, in their preoccupation with aesthetic rather than moral problems of composition, are more concerned with artistic autonomy than mimetic adequacy, and it is here that perspectives upon the novel that I have been defining as "modern" begin.

James's pronouncements on the novel, of course, sometimes echo other earlier writers. For example, his idea that the novelist must consider himself a genuine historian, must not admit that what he is writing is fiction, is a sentiment expressed by Bulwer-Lytton as early as 1838.[30] Meredith had frequently articulated his belief that narrative description and dramatic scene must be alternated, with the dramatic scene used as sparingly as possible. James observes this rule in most of his fiction from the 80's onward, and makes it doctrine later on his preface to *The Ambassadors*. James is most original in his many fascinating discussions of point of view, and in his insistence on the advantages for fiction of the limited perspective of a single sentient consciousness.

The generating source of James's literary theories, then, is not moral intention, but rather constant speculation about the aesthetic bases of the art of narrative. This is not to say that James is indifferent to morality or reality. But in his search for the best means of reproducing the texture of psychological life, his consideration of novelistic form tends to be less moral than aesthetic. James uses his aesthetic to produce moral discriminations, but in its overriding preoccupation with the processes of artistic creation that aesthetic is, like Flaubert's, essentially amoral. George Eliot believes in psychological realism because close, sympathetic concern with the lives of ordinary men and women is the method she considers most likely to engage the sensibilities of her readers and thereby enlarge them. James's belief in psychological realism is a result less of any purely pedagogical desire to enlarge the sympathies of his readers than of his feeling that the novel reaches its highest artistic expression when such a method is used and such enlargement occurs. While James is of course concerned in his fiction with the concrete particularity of human life, as an artist he is obsessed with the abstract truths of literary perfection. As such he anticipates, as does Flaubert, the tone of most twentieth-century novel-theory. His essays and critical prefaces bulge with his own problems as a striving, creating artist; George Eliot's comments on the novel usually reflect her intense desire to improve the lives of her fellow men through mimetic art. If the novels of George Eliot and James have a great deal in common, as indeed they do, the impulses behind their creation are often quite different. James absorbed a great deal from George Eliot, of course, as anyone can see, for example, from the many similarities between *Middlemarch* or *Daniel Deronda* and *The Portrait of A Lady*. But what interested James most in George Eliot's fiction were the expanding possibilities for *the artist* which her kind of fiction represented. Thus we find him, in a characteristic comment, saying of the story of Dorothea Brooke in *Middlemarch* that "the situation seems to us never to expand to its full capacity."[31] The artistic problem always interests him most. And so he writes *The Portrait of A Lady* not only because

George Eliot's theme of the progressive revelation of inner being (in *Daniel Deronda* as in *Middlemarch*) fascinates him, but also because he wants to see how much farther he can take it.[32]

By the end of the century (and for some years beforehand), novel-criticism was feeling the revivalist effects of the so-called Romantic Decadence. Gautier's "l'art pour l'art" was not its only cry. On the contrary: the reaction in England against European naturalism—with the notable exceptions of Gissing, Moore, James, Hardy, Gosse, and some others—led to a pallid resurgence of the kind of literary idealism advocated half a century earlier by Bulwer-Lytton, who had suggested that novelists soften the hard edges of reality in their novels in order to keep their readers amused. The revival of interest in plot, which had begun earlier with Bagehot, Wilkie Collins, and their followers, attained to a degree of legitimacy once again in the writings of Kipling, Stevenson, Saintsbury, and others. The new popularity of escapist literature brought attacks on Trollope, George Eliot, Howells, and James in the 90's, and the storming of the fortress of realism reached perhaps its highest expression in the literary essays of Leslie Stephen, who among other things exhorted novelists to follow the lead of Disraeli in fusing together in their novels the exotic and the mundane.[33] It was during these years that Hardy (and others) complained that "what is called the idealization of characters is, in truth, the making of them too real to be possible."[34] The idealists, Hardy suggested, dwelt so long and lovingly upon their good characters that they left nothing to the imagination of the reader, who soon lost interest in characters whose over-exposure extinguished any possibility of surprising behavior. And yet Hardy himself was no partisan of pure realism. In 1890 he wrote the following in his notebook: "Art is a disproportioning—(i.e. distorting, throwing out of proportion)—of realities, to show more clearly the features that matter in those realities, which, if merely copied or reported inventorially, might possibly be observed, but would more probably be overlooked. Hence, 'realism' is not Art."[35] In the midst of the ongoing battle, however, one could still from time to time hear the mingled voices of the traditional realists and the new autonomy-oriented aestheticians of the novel. In the 90's, the most important voice to be heard was that of "Vernon Lee."

Vernon Lee (Violet Paget) is another unsung but important theorist of the novel. Writing after the publication in the 80's of James's first important essays, Vernon Lee deals with, among other things, some of the crucial literary issues James was to take up later in the New York Edition prefaces—especially the question of point of view.[36] Vernon Lee favors authors who somehow intuit and mysteriously give "birth" to characters over authors whose personages are more consciously evolved and become "illustrations of life in general." In the latter case the author must commit himself to an external point of view, while in the former case the author will usually employ an alternating point of view of "straightforward narrative" which moves from one figure to another and which denotes in turn, through a sense of love or hatred, the total identification of the author with each major character. In this type of narration, which for Vernon Lee is the most effective, the author *becomes* in turn, participates in, each of the important personages, and his own point of view then seems to disappear entirely. This, for Vernon Lee, is the supreme triumph of fiction, and she finds it most often in Tolstoy. Like Flaubert and James, she believes that the highest form of narration is that from which the author seems most to be absent. And when she speaks of the problem of narrative *angle,* she anticipates some of the specific questions taken up by James in his critical prefaces to the New York Edition and later by the Jamesian Percy Lubbock in *The Craft of Fiction:*

> This supreme constructive question in the novel is exactly analogous to that question in painting; and in describing the choice by the painter of the point of view, I have described also that most subtle choice of the literary craftsman: choice of the point of view whence the personages and action of a novel are to be seen. For you can see a person, or an act, in one of several ways, and connected with several other persons or acts. You can see the person from nobody's point of view, or from the point of view of one of the other persons, or from the point of view of the analytical, judicious author.[37]

The question of *whose* point of view the writer should adopt and the reader encounter often occupied James in the last decade of his life. Like James, Vernon Lee often uses, as she does here, analogies to painting in her discussions of the art of narrative. She is not really a "Jamesian" critic, however, even though she discusses some of the same problems James was soon to discuss. On the contrary, she attacks the scenic or dramatic method of construction. A novel, she says, may approach to naturalism, but it should not attempt to imitate the methods of drama. She objects to characters being presented dramatically because, among other things, such presentation often is at odds with the impression of them given in narrative portions. She agrees with James and Meredith that "scenes" should be used infrequently and that they should be dependent on "the force of accumulated action."

In her discussion of the perfectibility of form, Vernon Lee sounds sometimes like Flaubert. The novel, she says, should be written like a symphony or an opera, with interesting leitmotifs producing related effects in the reader. A diagram illustrating the progress of the novel's various ideas and facts and words should be a perfect circle, demonstrating the organic inevitability of form. Thus she insists that every word be weighed carefully, and that those outside the perimeter of the circle be abandoned: "The construction of a whole book stands to the construction of a single sentence as the greatest complexities of counterpoint and orchestration stand to the relation of the vibrations constituting a single just note."[38] Like Flaubert, Vernon Lee believes that it is style that gives beauty to art. And in her preoccupation with the relationships of interior aspects of fiction to one another, she too anticipates the autonomy-oriented fiction-theory of the twentieth century.

We have seen that theoretical novel-criticism before Flaubert and James was generally mimetic in direction and moral in tone; mimesis was the means to morality as an end. Literature could improve man's morals, but only by first convincing him that the world of the novel he was reading bore some relation to the world in which he lived.

The idea that art is mimetic, that it imitates the action of the real world, is after all a premier theory of art from the time of Aristotle to the middle of the eighteenth century. The symbiotic relationship between formal realism and mimesis only begins to break down as writers become increasingly interested in mental processes;[39] such interest usually has as a concomitant an artistic form less mimetic than organic—that is, "autonomous," self-sufficient. This breakdown in theoretical perspectives occurs in the novel somewhat later than in poetry. Organic or autonomous theories of poetry were being voiced as early as the 1760's (in some of Bishop Hurd's writings, for example) and later by some of the English Romantics (most notably Coleridge). But it is not until the mid nineteenth century, in the critical writings of Flaubert and later of James, that novel-theory begins seriously and systematically to entertain aesthetic alternatives to mimesis. And it is not until this later period that autonomy rather than mimesis begins to be looked upon as the chief agent of formal realism. Twentieth-century novel-theory, taking its tone to some extent from the Continental critics, is concerned less with the relationship between reader and text than it is with the relationships among the various structural elements within the work of fiction itself. Modern theoretical novel-criticism, in other words, is occupied less with the novel as a mimetic and moral performance than with the novel as an autonomous creation independent of or at least not wholly dependent on the real world. The world of the autonomous novel may inevitably resemble our own, but it is not created as a conscious representation of anything outside itself. The modern view emphasizes the structure of the work and the symbiosis of its component elements rather than the fiction itself as representative or nonrepresentative of moral or mimetic "reality." Clearly there are other strands which one could pick up for purposes of discussion and comparison, but it seems to me that they are more likely to obfuscate than to illuminate the important distinctions to be made here between Augustan and Victorian novel-criticism on the one hand and pre-twentieth-century "modern" criticism on the other. What has happened in novel-theory in our own century may be suggested by the contents of this volume.

NOTES

1. *The Rambler,* No. 4 (Saturday, March 31, 1750).
2. See *The Rise of the Novel: Studies in Defoe, Richardson, and Fielding* (1957), the early sections of which are particularly helpful to anyone interested in Augustan views on fiction.
3. *Adam Bede,* Book Fifth, Chapter XLI.
4. For two diverse readings of the opening paragraphs of *Joseph Andrews,* both recent, one regarding the novelist as serious and the other seeing him as ironic, consult Sheldon Sacks, *Fiction and the Shape of Belief* (1961) and Homer Goldberg, *The Art of Joseph Andrews* (1969).
5. *The Champion* (June 10, 1740).
6. *The Rise of the Novel,* pp. 9-10.

7. "The Profitable Reading of Fiction," *The Forum* (March 1888).

8. A related concern was the continuing argument over the extent to which literary realism may be diluted by muted idealism and the proper role of romance in the novel. This question is implicit in much of nineteenth-century novel-theory until European naturalism, the short-lived Romantic revival, and the critical writings of Flaubert and Henry James put the question more or less to rest, finally, around the turn of the twentieth century.

For two excellent discussions of this and of English attitudes in general toward the novel in the middle and later decades of the nineteenth century, see Richard Stang, *The Theory of the Novel in England 1850-1870* (1959), and Kenneth Graham, *English Criticism of the Novel 1865-1900* (1965). My view of nineteenth-century attitudes toward the novel, here and subsequently, has been shaped substantially by these two extremely informative studies.

9. *Westminster Review*, LXX (1858), 493-94.

10. *Ibid.*, 499. In this he resembles Flaubert, who was advocating a similar method in letters written during the 50's and 60's. See my discussion of Flaubert, below.

11. See J. W. Cross (ed.), *George Eliot's Life as Related in Her Letters and Journals* (1885), Vol. I, pp. 336-37.

12. *Westminster Review*, LXV (1856), 642.

13. *Ibid.*, 574. See below for my discussion of a later critic, Vernon Lee, who is concerned in part with the role of "negative capability" in narrative point of view. For more detailed discussions of George Eliot and G. H. Lewes in these contexts, see Alice R. Kaminsky, "George Eliot, George Henry Lewes, and the Novel," *PMLA*, LXX (1955), 997-1013, and Richard Stang, "The Literary Criticism of George Eliot," *PMLA*, LXII (1957), 953-61. My argument in this paragraph derives substantially from information provided in these two excellent essays.

14. Meredith discusses this stance explicitly in *Diana of the Crossways* (1885).

15. *British Novelists and Their Styles*, p. 23.

16. Flaubert, *Correspondance*, Vol. III, p. 249, letter to Louise Colet, June 1853. Here, as subsequently, I am indebted both to English translations and summaries of the novelist's views provided by Enid Starkie in her *Flaubert: The Making of the Master* (1967).

17. *Correspondance Supplément*, Vol. IV, p. 243, letter to Mlle. Leroyer de Chantpie, December 1857.

18. *Nouvelle Revue* (January 1881).

19. Nevertheless, Erich Auerbach includes a discussion of Flaubert in his *Mimesis: The Representation of Reality in Western Literature* (1946), in which he finds that Flaubert's style is the incarnation of contemporary reality.

20. Here Flaubert is clearly a precursor of subsequent autonomy-oriented fiction-theory (see, for example, my discussion of Ortega and Robbe-Grillet in "Twentieth-Century Trends in Continental Novel-Theory," pp. 375-88). He also demonstrates the debt he and many of his followers owe to Gautier, who maintained in his famous preface to *Mlle. de Maupin* (1835) and elsewhere that great art is consciously neither didactic, topical, nor mimetic—that art is its own end and that criticisms of society in it are irrelevant.

21. *Correspondance*, Vol. II, p. 469, letter to Louise Colet, July 1852.

22. *Ibid.*, Vol. II, p. 231, letter to Louise Colet, January 1852. See my essay on modern Continental novel-theory (especially notes 19 and 21) for some of the ways in which Flaubert at times sounds remarkably like Robbe-Grillet,

who often compares his views on fiction to Flaubert's and who also talks about making, in fiction, "something out of nothing," and about art that "expresses nothing but itself." This is only one shred of evidence indicating that Flaubert is one of the first writers to anticipate in his theories of fiction the stance and mood of "modern" novel-theory.

23. "Bodies in Space: Film as 'Carnal Knowledge,'" originally published in *Artforum* (February 1969), and reprinted in *The Discontinuous Universe: Selected Writings in Contemporary Consciousness,* ed. Sallie Sears and Georgianna Lord (1972), pp. 313-32. The passages quoted appear on pp. 319-20, *passim.*

24. As my essay on modern Continental novel-theory points out, for example, many of the Russian Formalist critics, and in particular Victor Shklovsky, see art's value as residing in large measure in its capacity to enlarge the *perceptions* of its audience. This, of course, is a simplification of a larger and more complex issue. For a fuller discussion, see my essay.

25. *Correspondance,* Vol. III, pp. 61-62, letter to Louise Colet, December 1852. Ortega expresses a somewhat similar sentiment—see my discussion of him in "Twentieth-Century Trends in Continental Novel-Theory." Also, of course, this becomes the slogan of Stephen Dedalus, the artist of Joyce's *Portrait.*

26. *Ibid.,* Vol. V, pp. 227-28, letter to Amélie Bosquet, August 1866. It is interesting to place Flaubert's attitude in this matter next to that of Joseph Conrad, who expresses in a letter to his friend John Galsworthy a conviction not unlike Flaubert's: "In a book you should love the idea and be scrupulously faithful to your conception of life. There lies the honour of the writer, not in the fidelity to your personages. You must never allow them to decoy you out of yourself. As against your people you must preserve an attitude of perfect indifference, the part of creative power." And like Flaubert once again (and like his friend Henry James as well), Conrad believed in the sacredness of the artist's calling: "A man who puts forth the secret of his imagination to the world accomplishes, as it were, a religious rite." Both quotations are taken from G. Jean-Aubry's *Joseph Conrad: Life and Letters,* 2 vols. (1927), I, 301, and II, 89.

27. See George J. Becker's *Documents of Modern Literary Realism* (1963), a volume of readings in which Professor Becker provides an excellent selection (and skillful summaries) of naturalism-oriented essays. Zola's *Le Roman expérimental,* first published in 1880, is of course the fullest expression of his critical theories.

28. Introduction to *Writing Degree Zero* (1953), reprinted in *The Discontinuous Universe* (see n. 23, above), pp. 3-6. This passage appears on pp. 4-5. The translation is by Annette Lavers and Colin Smith. It is interesting to note that a similar shift from mimesis to autonomy occurs around Flaubert's time in painting—a shift, that is, from paintings which in their faithful representation of perspective direct our attention to the scenes they depict to paintings which force themselves on our attention as objects to be considered in their own right.

29. "The Art of Fiction," originally published in *Longman's Magazine* (September 1884), reprinted in *Partial Portraits* (1888), and widely thereafter.

30. "Art in Fiction," in the *Monthly Chronicle.* James expresses this view often, but most notably in his essay "Anthony Trollope," originally published in *Century Magazine* (July 1883), also reprinted in *Partial Portraits* (1888),

and widely thereafter. James says there in part: "It is impossible to imagine what a novelist takes himself to be unless he regard himself as an historian and his narrative as history. . . . [H]e must relate events that are assumed to be real." The idea of the novelist as historian, of course, did not originate with Bulwer-Lytton and James. Cervantes and Scarron both adopted this stance in their works, as did Fielding in his imitation of them (though sometimes admitting, as Trollope does, that what he is writing is fiction). In a different tradition (the Puritan), both Defoe and Richardson pretend that their works provide "authentic accounts" of the action they describe.

31. Unsigned review of *Middlemarch* in *The Galaxy* (March 1873).

32. This is made abundantly clear by James on several occasions. His preface to *The Portrait* echoes from end to end with references to George Eliot's novels, and he is even more explicit about some of the *données* provided him by George Eliot in his "*Daniel Deronda: A Conversation*," first published in the *Atlantic* in 1876. There are a number of critical discussions of George Eliot's influence on James with particular reference to *The Portrait of A Lady*. Among the most helpful are F. R. Leavis's chapter on James in *The Great Tradition* (1948); Q. D. Leavis's "A Note on Literary Indebtedness: Dickens, George Eliot, Henry James," in the *Hudson Review*, VIII (1955), 423-28; Oscar Cargill's "'The Portrait of A Lady': A Critical Reappraisal," in *Modern Fiction Studies*, III (1957), 11-32; George Levine's "Isabel, Gwendolen, and Dorothea," in *ELH*, XXX (1963), 244-57; Cornelia Pulsifer Kelley's discussion in *The Early Development of Henry James* (1965), especially pp. 293-95; and my own discussion of James and George Eliot in *The Language of Meditation: Four Studies in Nineteenth-Century Fiction* (1973).

James, of course, was not the only writer of his period after Gautier and Flaubert to insist upon the autonomous properties of art. I have simply had to omit others—such as Oscar Wilde, who said that art is independent of real life and everything else except beauty, that life imitates art (see "The Decay of Lying," first published in *Nineteenth Century*, XXV [1889], 35-56, and reprinted widely thereafter); and the unpredictable H. G. Wells, who observed in a 1902 letter to Arnold Bennett that successful art "has its excellence in something which is not commensurable with anything outside itself." Neither Wilde nor Wells, in this context at least, is far from the concept of "l'art pur" articulated by Gautier. For an interesting parallel, see the discussion, in my essay on modern Continental novel-theory, of Roland Barthes, for whom "life can only imitate the book."

33. See *Hours in A Library* (1904), a collection of Stephen's essays published during the preceding thirty or so years. The essay on Disraeli, entitled "Mr. Disraeli's Novels," was first published in 1876. Once again, in my discussion of late nineteenth-century views on the novel, I am indebted to Graham's *English Criticism of the Novel 1865-1900* (n. 8, above).

34. Quoted from "The Profitable Reading of Fiction" (see n. 7, above). The new Romanticism, of course, concentrated its critical fire on literary naturalism, which it was very much in reaction against. The attacks themselves are relatively unimportant except for the vigorous defenses of naturalism they provoked, which are often interesting and are of crucial importance in the history of literary realism. In the 90's a typical defense of the *roman expérimental* against the encroachments of the Romantic Decadence is that by Edmund Gosse in "The Limits of Realism in Fiction" in *The Forum* for June

1890; another is that by Vernon Lee (see below) in an essay entitled "The Moral Teaching of Zola," published three years later. A good selection of essays dealing with this controversy and with the theoretical grounds of literary realism generally may be found in *Documents of Modern Literary Realism* (see n. 27, above), whose editor also provides helpful commentaries on some of these issues.

35. See the second Mrs. Hardy's *Life of Thomas Hardy,* originally in two volumes, published in one in 1962, from which I am quoting here (p. 229). Hardy's principle of "disproportioning" bears some interesting resemblances to Ortega's theories of character portrayal (as in his discussion of Dostoevski) and to Victor Shklovsky's concept of literary "defamiliarization"—see my discussion of both critics, pp. 375-77 and 379-81.

36. See her essay "On Literary Construction" in the *Contemporary Review,* LXVIII (1895), 404-19, which is a central expression of her convictions about literary form. I am indebted to Kenneth Graham's interesting discussion of her work in *English Criticism of the Novel 1865-1900,* which first alerted me to her importance in the history of theoretical novel-criticism.

37. Vernon Lee, "The Craft of Words," *Nouvelle Revue,* XI (1894), 571-80.

38. *Ibid.*

39. For a more detailed discussion, see Elliott B. Gose, Jr., *Imagination Indulged: The Irrational in the Nineteenth-Century Novel* (1972).

THE
GENRE
TODAY

WHAT
IS
EXPOSITION?

AN ESSAY IN
TEMPORAL DELIMITATION

MEIR STERNBERG

As the whole of anything, in James's phrase, is never told, the writer of fiction is necessarily confined to presenting his characters in action within the limits of a certain fictive period of time. It is thus unavoidable that he should intersect the lives of his dramatis personae at a given hour. His problem is only to decide which hour it shall be, and in what situation they shall be discovered: "There is no more reason why they should not first be discovered lying in a bassinette—having just been deposited for the first time in it—than that the reader should make their acquaintance in despairing middle age, having just been pulled out of a canal."[1] In either case, the reader as a rule has no idea as to what is going to happen next, nor does he know anything about the characters figuring in the story. Consequently, he is at a loss as to what has driven the poor middle-aged protagonist to suicide, and must be provided with the necessary information if he is to make anything of the narrative. And even the smiling little cherub has not been born into a vacuum but into a complex of pre-existing circumstances that act upon him and have some influence (at times even a crucial or conditioning effect) on his future career or ultimate fate. In this instance too, therefore, there are antecedents of various kinds with which the reader must be made acquainted.

It is the function of the exposition to introduce the reader into an unfamiliar world, the fictive world of the story, by providing him with the general and specific background information indispensable to the understanding of what happens in it. There are some pieces of information, the number and nature of which varies from one work to another, that the reader cannot do without. He must usually be informed, for instance, of the time and place of the action; of the nature of the peculiar fictive world projected by the work, or, in other words, of the canons of probability operating in it; of the history, the appearance, the traits and habitual behavior of some of the dramatis personae; and of the relations between them. This expositional information the author is obliged to communicate to the reader in one way or another.

In some instances it may indeed seem (though I shall argue this is not the case) that a certain amount of prior information—about the characters and the fictive world—that is not fully contained or is merely hinted at in the work itself may be assumed beforehand. In Greek drama, for example, the dramatists, restricted to a well-defined field of material, repeatedly told and re-told a number of myths with which their audience was familiar. Sophocles did not invent the story of Oedipus, nor Euripides that of Iphigenia and Orestes. Whenever the characters and narrative materials are derived from history, it may likewise seem safe to assume that the reader will not be wholly ignorant of them. It may seem therefore that in both instances the communication of at least part of the expositional information may be dispensed with on the assumption that the author takes for granted his reader's possession of a certain amount of common knowledge. In this respect it may appear that in such cases the author has an easier time of it than most writers of modern times, who, rarely contenting themselves with re-treating familiar or hackneyed material, are accordingly obliged to devote a great deal of space and energy to their expositional duties.

It should be noted, however, that even a number of modern writers may seem to share the expositional privileges or exemptions of their ancient predecessors. I am referring especially to novelists celebrated for their progressive creation or evocation of the same private, full-fledged fictive world of their own—Trollope's Barchester, Balzac's nineteenth-century France, or Faulkner's Yoknapatawpha County—in work after work; and also to the authors of any series of works, notably detective stories, in which at least one central character recurs (e.g. Agatha Christie's Hercule Poirot), though the setting of the fictive world may vary. In the former, extreme case, Balzac and Faulkner not only repeatedly employ the same general or particular setting but also carry over whole casts of characters and clusters of incidents from one work to another of the same cycle.

The question accordingly arises whether in all these cases at least part of the expositional material may indeed be taken as known or be required to be obtained by the reader outside the limits of the single work; whether, that is, the author can be exempted from imparting this information on the strength of the assumption of the reader's acquaintance either with the myths, historical events, or personages treated in the work or with other fictional works by the same author.

Many critics work on the implicit, and sometimes even on the explicit assumption, that this question must be answered in the positive, particularly with reference to different works of the same cycle, which they regard as a single work.[2] A close examination of the literary evidence, however, shows this assumption to be untenable. In their contempt for the fatal futility of Fact, writers usually have no scruples about supplementing, modifying or even distorting historical evidence or tradition to suit their artistic purposes. Shakespeare is notorious for the free use he made of his sources. In *Julius Caesar,* for instance, he simplifies drastically the history of events between Caesar's triumphant return to Rome and the decisive battle of Philippi which took place two years later. He does not feel the slightest hesitation, for example, in telescoping the month between the Lupercalia (celebrated on February 15) and the ides of March (March 15) into a single day; nor in inventing Antony's celebrated funeral speech; nor in collating and freely selecting from different, and even conflicting, traditional conceptions of the traits and merits of the main agents in this Roman drama. He turns various historical controversies to artistic account by embodying all the versions in his work, and leaving them undecided in order to project the theme of the "conflict of images," thus reconciling them *artistically,*[3] though not historically.

Similarly, when a character, a situation, or both, are carried over from one work to another, the writer feels no less free to introduce in them any changes dictated by the distinctive artistic conception of the new work. The Antony of *Julius Caesar,* the libertine turned demagogue, is altogether incompatible with the monumental figure of *Antony and Cleopatra,* and any reader who attempts to reconcile the two will soon find himself in trouble. A totally new expositional presentation of his character is consequently required, and indeed provided, right at the beginning of the play. Likewise, as Cowley himself admits, "as one book leads into another, Faulkner sometimes falls into inconsistencies of detail. . . . Henry Armstid is a likable figure in *As I Lay Dying* and *Light in August;* in *The Hamlet* he is mean and half-demented"; and the list of changes goes on and on.[4] Trollope's Archdeacon Grantly, on the other hand, is a hard worldling, a bully, and something of a hypocrite in *The Warden;* but when he reappears in *Barchester Towers* his weaknesses are softened and his character, hot-tempered but affectionate, is by no means unattractive. Whether we are to shrug such changes off as "inconsequential errors,"[5] as Cowley does, or, as can be established, take them to be frequently major, and as a rule deliberate and significant, deviations from previous thematic and structural conceptions,[6] it is evident, at any rate, that they constitute or call for new expositional material different from that imparted in previous works of the same cycle. In other words, the fact that the author makes use of previously existing materials, whether historical or fictional, does not exempt him from the need for exposition, since the reader cannot be expected to know beforehand the particular principles of selection and combination, of supplementation and modification, that have guided the author in the composition of a particular work. On the contrary, in such cases it may be claimed that unusually careful expositional measures are called for in order to prevent any possible confusions or misunderstandings and to clarify beyond any doubt the principles of selection and combination that are peculiar to the work.

Moreover, notwithstanding general *ex cathedra* declarations to the contrary, writers as a rule take the necessary precautions to render each of their works as expositionally autonomous as possible, even when the resuscitation or carrying over of characters and fictive world involves no deviation from previous conceptions of them. In the second chapter of Trollope's *Barchester Towers,* for instance, the narrator informs the reader that "it is hardly necessary that I should here give to the public any lengthened biography of Mr. Harding up to the period of the commencement of this tale. The public cannot have forgotten how ill that sensitive gentleman bore the attack that was made on him in the columns of *The Jupiter,* with reference to the income which he received as warden to Hiram's Hospital, in the city of

Barchester. Nor can it yet be forgotten that a lawsuit was instituted against him," and so on. In other words, though Trollope ostensibly professes to assume that the ordeal undergone by Mr. Harding, and formerly narrated in *The Warden*, must by now be a matter of common knowledge, he in fact cunningly recapitulates the occurrences expositionally relevant to *Barchester Towers* (in which Mr. Harding plays but a secondary role), in order to render the latter work as independent as possible of the former. What was there the core of the action proper is here telescoped into a number of expositional passages; and some additional sentences then bring the account up to date and effect the necessary transition to "the commencement of this tale." Little Huck Finn, in *The Adventures of Huckleberry Finn*, opens his narrative with a similar statement ("you don't know about me without you have read a book by the name of *The Adventures of Tom Sawyer*; but that ain't no matter. . . . Now the way that the book winds up is this: Tom and me found the money that the robbers hid in the cave, and it made us rich. . . . Judge Thatcher, he took it and put it out at interest," etc.), by which he likewise frees his story from any dependence on Twain's previous novel by selecting from it and summarizing for the reader's benefit those events that are expositionally relevant to his own tale. The same tendency is displayed even in such works as Robert Graves's *Claudius the God*, a *direct* sequel to his *I, Claudius*, to which it is strongly related by both historic and narrative continuity (the same narrator, Claudius, goes on with his autobiography). Here too Claudius first briefly "reminds" us of various antecedents represented at length in *I, Claudius*, and only then does he proceed to "[pick] up the thread just where I dropped it."

In other words, although writers may choose to make use of historical sources or to revert again and again to the fictive world of their own creation, the works themselves reveal their awareness of the fact that, in Coleridge's phrase, each work must contain within itself the reason why it is so and not otherwise. They are conscious that though the reader may possess some previous knowledge about the characters or the initial situation, such expositional information must not be taken for granted but must be worked into each individual story. Apart from the purely theoretical grounds I have mentioned above, it is well to remember that novelists are much more realistic people than we sometimes like to think. Trollope, for instance, frankly admits that he worked on the assumption that though *Phineas Finn* (1867) and its sequel *Phineas Redux* (1873) "are, in fact, but one novel," he "had no right to expect that novel-readers would remember the characters of a story after an interval of six years."[7] And elsewhere he perhaps overstates his case when he goes so far as to claim that he never labored under the illusion that his reader was likely to see such progressively created characters as the Duke of Omnium in the round: their delineation is spread over so wide a canvas that he "cannot expect that any lover of such art should trouble to look at it as a whole," nor that his public should retain in memory a series of novels, "each of which will be forgotten by the most zealous reader almost as soon as read."[8]

Furthermore, these quotations from Trollope, Twain, and Graves seem to imply not only this awareness but also a positive warning to the reader not to drag into a story any associations that are artistically irrelevant to it. In these opening remarks the author seems to caution the reader somewhat as follows: "This is all you need keep in mind for the purposes of the present narrative. If you are possessed of more information than this, all the better, but, in spite of the recurrence of Mr. Harding, do not drag the whole conflict to which *The Warden* is devoted into *Barchester Towers* or you will throw the latter work out of focus." Or, as Percy Lubbock puts it, in any single story by Balzac "such of [the] people as appear by the way, incidentally, must for the time being shed their irrelevant life; if they fail to do so, they disturb the unity of the story and confuse its truth."[9]

In conclusion, it should be noted that these admonitions are perfectly compatible with the dream of such writers to have their work seen as a whole. The limits of a literary unit cannot be fixed *a priori* but are dynamic in that they vary according to the kind of questions the critic poses. Where concerned with the description or evaluation of an author's figure in the carpet or of his output as a whole, he may find it of great interest to trace the evolution of a certain character or situation from work to work, to examine the different traits or aspects selected for intense treatment in each work and even the discrepancies between their presentation in different works. On the other hand, when the critic is concerned (as I am here) with the problems involved in the analysis of a single work, in all its uniqueness of norms and structure, he cannot but regard all extraneous information about its characters and setting as external evidence. This evidence may indeed prove useful for the construction of hypotheses about the work, or for calling the reader's attention to some of its hidden aspects; and as such it is part of the business of criticism to bring as much as possible of it to bear upon the text. But it is to be regarded as strictly external unless it is adequately corroborated by internal evidence and thus established as relevant to the particular work. Exposition, therefore, can in no case be dispensed with with impunity; and the peculiar problems it raises must be confronted and solved by every writer, in every work afresh.

THE LOCATION OF EXPOSITION

So far I have discussed the *function* of the exposition. The question arises, however, whether, bearing in mind this function, we can point to any specific part or parts, segment or segments, of a narrative work that can be called "the exposition." What is the location of the expositional sections or elements? Is it fixed or variable? And, finally, how are the expositional sections or elements to be distinguished from the other, non-expositional, elements in the work?

The most detailed and widely accepted theory of exposition is the time-honored view first proposed by Gustav Freytag, of whose conception of dramatic structure exposition forms an integral part. According to Freytag, "the drama possesses . . . a pyramidal structure. It arises from the *introduction* with the entrance of the exciting forces to the *climax,* and falls from there to the *catastrophe.* Between these three parts lie (the parts of) the *rise* and the *fall.*"[10] An important effect called by Freytag the exciting moment or force "stands between the introduction and the rise": "The beginning of the excited action (or complication) occurs at a point where, in the soul of the hero, there arises a feeling or volition which becomes the occasion of what follows; or where the counter-play resolves to use its lever to set the hero in motion. . . . In *Julius Caesar* this impelling force is the thought of killing Caesar, which by the conversation with Cassius, gradually becomes fixed in the soul of Brutus" (pp. 115, 121). Accordingly, in terms of what has come to be called "Freytag's pyramid,"

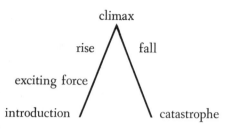

the introduction or exposition—with Freytag, the latter concept is sometimes synonymous with and sometimes subsumed by the former, but in any case their limits are invariably identical[11]—is clearly marked off from the rest of the play by the exciting force, which "always forms the transition from the introduction to the ascending action" (p. 124). This primary delimitation, made in terms of the movement of the action or what I should call the continuum of projected events, is later supplemented by another that is not only looser and less essential but also applies to quite another level—to the continuum of the text. In a typical five-act play, Freytag claims, "each act includes one of the five parts of the older drama; the first contains the introduction; the second, the rising action; the third, the climax; the fourth, the return; the fifth, the catastrophe" (p. 195). According to this purely formal mode of delimitation, then, the exposition is always contained within the boundaries of the first act, preceding the rising action.

However, Freytag's theory, plausible and tidy-looking as it is, seems to me untenable. Its fatal weakness does not consist so much in its narrowness or limited range of applicability as in its internal inconsistency and its failure to stand up to the facts even when tested against works that are constructed more or less "pyramidally." If the function of the exposition is, in Freytag's own words, "to explain the place and time of the action, the nationality and life relations of the hero" (pp. 117-18), it is hardly possible to prescribe or determine *a priori* that all authors must invariably choose to locate the expositional information within the first act or before the "rising action." And, in fact, writers seldom impose on themselves any limitations of this kind, as can be demonstrated even with reference to the plays Freytag himself cites in illustration of his theory. He maintains, for instance, that in *Julius Caesar* the exciting force "is the thought of killing Caesar, which, by the conversation with Cassius [i.e. Act I, scene 2], gradually becomes fixed in the soul of Brutus" (p. 121). As a matter of fact, however, the exposition is not concentrated within the limits of the first act and only a small part of it precedes the impelling moment. Most of the expositional material is widely distributed: one important aspect of Brutus's expositional "life relations," his relation with his wife Portia, is "explained" only in Act II, scene 1, after Brutus has already assumed the leadership of the conspiracy; Julius Caesar's marital "life relations" with Calpurnia are dramatically conveyed even later, in Act II, scene 2; while the full disclosure of Antony's expositional relations with Caesar is delayed until his famous soliloquy in Act III, scene 1; and so on. These various antecedents ("life relations"), in other words, all of them indisputably expositional according to Freytag's definition of the *function* of exposition, turn out to be as indisputably non-expositional according to his description of its location; and as Freytag's definition of the function of exposition is essentially sound, we cannot but conclude that his prescriptive conception of its location must be wrong. And it is even more obvious that Freytag's definition fails to cover such cases as Ibsen's *Ghosts*, a drama where the exposition is distributed throughout the play and new, vital facts concerning the antecedents of the agents keep cropping up as late as the last act.

In view of its patent weaknesses, it is perhaps surprising to discover what a tremendous influence this theory has had on criticism for the last hundred years; but it is a fact that one finds it applied time and again not only to plays[12] but to narrative works as well. In a recent article, for example, Robin H. Farquhar starts by arguing that Hemingway has patterned his novels upon what is "generally accepted as a schematic model of tragic structure in drama. This is the five-part inverted 'V' which represents the movement from an introduction 'up' through rising action to a climax, and thence 'down' through falling action to a catastrophe, or dénouement."[13] And having applied this scheme to *The Sun Also Rises, A Farewell to Arms, For Whom the Bell Tolls,* and *The Old Man and the Sea,* Farquhar concludes that they "all conform to its basic requirements, structural and functional."[14] But Farquhar's discussion too is vitiated, among other things, by his conception of exposition as invariably placed at the beginning of the work ("the introduction typically provides any necessary exposition and establishes the setting, tone, main plot, and chief characters"[15]). In *The Sun Also Rises,* for instance, where according to him the introduction is confined to Book I, the second, middle Book not only presents as many major characters as the preceding one (Bill Gorton, Mike Campbell, and Pedro Romero) but also conveys previously withheld information about the others—Jake's deep interest in bull-fighting, his religious struggles, his literary ambitions, etc. And in *The Old Man and the Sea,* which is interspersed almost to the end with reminiscential anecdotes or dreams evoking the old fisherman's past exploits, the distribution of exposition beyond what Farquhar considers the introductory stage is even more conspicuous.

It would be unprofitable, I believe, to go on illustrating the invalidity of this thesis. It applies neither to works, dramatic or narrative, whose general structure is not "dramatic" or "pyramidal" (and to which, indeed, it does not purport to apply), nor to those which plunge *in medias res,* nor even to those in which, though indeed containing some expositional information in the first act or chapters, the author keeps back a certain number of major expositional facts, disclosing them only later on. The weakness of Freytag's theory of exposition stems, in fact, from one of the main flaws in his general conception of structure. He purports to describe the structure of the action as a movement in time, in a definite direction and through definite stages, or, in other words, in the temporal order in which the reader or audience learns of the developments of the action; but in fact Freytag describes not the movement of the action but the structure of the *conflict.* He divorces this from the actual temporal movement of the action, presenting a structure that is viewed by the reader only when he retrospectively looks back on the action and rearranges or reassembles it chronologically in his mind. To put it differently, Freytag and his followers fail to take into account that the chronological order in which events happen does not necessarily have to coincide with the order in which they are imparted to the reader. Consequently, the "absolute" chronological order of occurrence (in which exposition, or "life relations," is indeed preliminary in point of time) does not necessarily correspond with the actual temporal movement or order of presentation of the same events in an actual work, in which expositional information may even be deferred to the last scene or chapter, as it is in Gogol's *Dead Souls* or in the detective story.

To sum up: as innumerable literary works in which the exposition or part of it is either delayed or distributed cannot be fitted into Freytag's Procrustean scheme, it is evident that his assertion as to the fixed location of exposition must be rejected. The only acceptable theory of exposition will be one flexible enough to hold good equally for all kinds of structure or presentational modes and to cut across the boundaries of genre.

EXPOSITION, *Fabula* AND *Sujet*, STORY AND PLOT

It seems to me it is possible to define exposition satisfactorily only in terms of *fabula, sujet,* and scenic norm or fictive present. The important distinction between *fabula* and *sujet* was first proposed by the Russian Formalists,[16] but is still amenable to further discrimination and development. A narrative work is composed of myriads of motifs, that is, basic and irreducible narrative units.[17] Examples of such motifs in *The Ambassadors,* for instance, would be "Strether reached the hotel at Chester," "He told Waymarsh all about it that very evening," "Strether sat alone in the great dim church," "Waymarsh made a sudden dash into a shop," etc. The *fabula* of the work is the chronological, or chronological-causal, sequence in which these motifs may be arranged; while the *sujet* constitutes the actual arrangement or presentation of these motifs in the work itself. The *fabula* is the aggregate of all the motifs that appear in the narrative work, the raw material which the artist molds and artistically deforms in constructing his work, while the *sujet* is the actual disposition of the motifs in the work before us, as their order and coloring was finally decided on by the author. To put it as simply as possible, the *fabula* involves what happens in the work as arranged in the order of occurrence, while the *sujet* involves what happens in the order of presentation actually encountered by the reader. Suppose an author wishes to compose a narrative which is to consist of three motifs: a_1, a_2, a_3. These motifs, arranged in an order in which a_2 follows a_1 in time and a_3 follows a_2, will form the *fabula* of his story. He can present them, however, in any of the six following sequences, or, in other words, can turn them into any of the six following *sujets:*

$$(1) \quad a_1, a_2, a_3$$
$$(2) \quad a_1, a_3, a_2$$
$$(3) \quad a_2, a_1, a_3$$
$$(4) \quad a_2, a_3, a_1$$
$$(5) \quad a_3, a_2, a_1$$
$$(6) \quad a_3, a_1, a_2$$

Apart from this—to supply a crucial omission of the Formalists'—one must also take into consideration that the *fabula* is equally amenable to manipulations of point of view, a form of artistic deformation which frequently coincides with and sometimes even accounts for temporal displacements. The author can, for example, postulate an omniscient narrator, or compose an epistolary story, or employ any of the characters as the narrator, or record the action as it passes through the consciousness of any or all of them: in each case the order of presentation of the motifs, their significance, weight, or coloring will of course vary. Henry James used to maintain that there are five million ways of telling a story. He meant, of course, that out of a given, basically similar *fabula*, five million *sujets* can be moulded, each with its own order of presentation of motifs, with its own point of view, and consequently with its own peculiar effect on the reader. James's own Notebooks afford some fascinating illustrations of his acute consciousness of this fact. In his first Notebook entry on "The Friends of the Friends," for instance, we find him soliloquizing as follows: "There would be various ways of doing it, and it comes to me that the thing might be related by the 3d person, according to my wont when I want something—as I always do want it—intensely objective. . . . Or if I don't have the third person narrator, what effect would one get from the impersonal form—what peculiar and characteristic, what compensating, effect might one get from it? . . . I might 'impersonally' include the 3d person and his (or her) feelings—tell the thing even from his or her point of view."[18] Similarly, in *The Ambassadors*, while employing the same fundamental aggregate of motifs, James could have postulated Strether as the narrator of his own adventure[19] or might have projected the action through the consciousness of Chad Newsome, for instance, or Madame de Vionnet, or Maria Gostrey. And even with Strether as the center of consciousness, James could have started the novel with Strether still in America or with Strether already in Paris. In any of these cases *The Ambassadors* would have turned out quite a different novel, with different effects on the reader, but the change would have involved not a different *fabula* but only a different *sujet*. In *The Ambassadors* as James actually composed it, the beginning of the *fabula* is the earliest event in Strether's history that we learn about in the course of the novel (namely, his marriage); while the beginning of the *sujet* coincides, of course, with the beginning of the first chapter of the novel (Strether's arrival at Chester).

Lemon and Reis, in their English translation of Tomashevsky's essay, consistently render the Russian terms *fabula* and *sujet* into "story" and "plot," thus clearly suggesting that the distinction made by the Formalists is identical with that proposed by E. M. Forster in *Aspects of the Novel* (1927). At first glance it may indeed appear that the two pairs of concepts (particularly story and *fabula*) overlap. The chronological factor, for instance, is conspicuous in Forster's definitions too. "Story" is "a narrative of events arranged in their time sequence—dinner coming after breakfast, Tuesday after Monday, decay after death and so on. *Qua* story, it can only have one merit: that of making the audience want to know what happens next"; while "plot" is "also a narrative of events, the emphasis falling on causality. 'The king died and then the queen died,' is a story. 'The king died and then the queen died of grief,' is a plot."[20] A close examination of Forster's influential account will, however, reveal that these sets of concepts should be sharply distinguished.

The first radical disparity between the structural principles Forster has in mind and those discussed here relates to what may be called their mode of existence. While the *sujet* is the finished artifact before us, the narrative as actually molded by the artist, the *fabula* is essentially both an abstraction and a reconstitution. It is an abstractive pattern in that it does not contain all the elements that make up the *sujet*—for instance, such atemporal authorial interpolations as the prefatory chapters in *Tom Jones,* or such structural modes as analogy that mainly turn not on linear but on spatial development and integration. And it is also reconstitutive in that it involves the reader's reconstruction of *sujet* components according to a preconceived, "natural," logical-chronological frame of reference, the deviations from which in the *sujet* highlight the modes of presentation peculiar to the work. But there is no corresponding difference between story and plot. Both of them are primarily abstractions—the story is also a re-constitution—denoting different organizing principles that may co-exist in isolation from each other in a single work (or *sujet*). It is pre-cisely in this that Forster's observations on narrative sequences differ from those of Aristotle, whom he curiously fails to mention. The distinction between temporally and causally propelled sequences originates in the *Poetics,* where it is insisted time and again that "it makes all the difference whether any given event is a case of *propter hoc* or *post hoc.*"[21] But while Aristotle's application of this insight is confined to the differentiation between episodic and "properly artis-tic" *sujets,* Forster acutely realizes that both story and plot may well coexist as distinct "aspects" of the same work—the more so (one may add) since every causal sequence necessarily subsumes a temporal-chronological dimension.

And this leads us to another difference in mode of existence. A nar-rative must necessarily have a story as its compositional backbone; but it may do without a plot or have only scattered causal elements (as in most picaresque novels). No narrative, on the other hand, can fail to have both a *fabula* and a *sujet* of its own.

Second, Forster is not interested in the various possibilities of artis-tically "deforming" a given aggregate of motifs through different or-ders of presentation or differently refractive points of view or both. He is chiefly concerned with two different modes of concatenation or kinds of linkages, distinguishing the temporally additive linkage ("and then?") that characterizes the story from the tighter causal linkage ("why?") peculiar to the plot. In Forster's first two illustra-tions, cited above, it is not the different order or angle of presentation of the motifs that distinguishes the story combination from that of the plot: the distinction is made exclusively in terms of mode of linkage, while the order of presentation remains identical. As Forster himself comments on the plot instance, "the time sequence is preserved, but the sense of causality overshadows it" (pp. 93-94). And if plot is, like *sujet,* a high artistic form, it is not owing to its "deformity" but to its superior tightness in comparison with the atavistic principle inform-ing the story.

Let us now proceed to Forster's third, and more complicated, illus-trative combination of the two motifs: " 'The queen died, no one knew why, until it was discovered that it was through grief at the death of the king.' This is a plot with a mystery in it. . . . It suspends the time-sequence, it moves as far away from the story as its limitations will allow" (p. 94). In the light of this example it might seem that plot is after all equivalent to *sujet,* for it may involve "suspensions" of time-sequence too. But this plausible conclusion would be wrong, because according to Forster it is not the deformation of chronology that turns this combination of motifs into a plot but again the *sine qua non* causal linkage, the "logical intellectual aspect" (p. 103). Given the causal concatenation, any complex of motifs is a plot, whether it involves a suspension of the time-sequence or not; but a suspended time-sequence by itself, lacking this linkage, is definitely not a plot, though it may form an important element in some plots. Thus, for instance, the sentence "The queen died twenty years after the king had died," though involving an inverted time sequence, would not be regarded by Forster as a plot;[22] but on the other hand it is beyond doubt a *sujet,* an arrangement of motifs in an artistically deformed order of presentation. In short, as Forster himself concludes with reference to the death of the queen: "If it is in a story we say 'and then?' If it is in a plot we ask 'why?' That [i.e. the additive as opposed to the causal linkage] is the fundamental difference between these two aspects of the novel" (p. 94). But this is not the fundamental difference between *fabula* and *sujet.* Plot cannot then be equated with *sujet* in this respect either, for in the former, given the distinctive causal sequence, everything else (including temporal displacement) is dispensable; whereas in the latter, given the artistic deformation of the *fabula*—and the more deformed it is the more of a *sujet* it is—everything else (including causal sequence) is dispensable.

Nor can story be equated with *fabula,* though both presuppose an abstraction and a chronological reconstruction of events. For the second defining property of story is its purely additive sequence, while *fabula* may, and often does, involve causal concatenation. As Tomashevsky explicitly states, "il faut souligner que la fable exige non seulement un indice temporel, mais aussi l'indice de causalité. . . . Moins ce lien causal est fort, plus le lien temporel prend d'importance."[23] From this viewpoint, in other words, *fabula* is frequently identical not with story but with plot.

The differences between the quartet of terms may accordingly be summarized in the following table:

	story	*fabula*	plot	*sujet*
mode of existence	abstractive and reconstitutive	abstractive and reconstitutive	abstractive	actual (and object of abstraction and reconstitution)
	indispensable	indispensable	dispensable	indispensable
order of presentation	chronological	chronological	chronological or deformed	highly variable, essentially anti-chronological
mode of linkage	additive	additive and/or causal	causal	additive and/or causal and/or spatial
point of view	irrelevant factor	objective (i.e. impersonal)	irrelevant factor	highly variable, usually different from that of *fabula*
conclusion no. 1: possible correspondence with other concepts	with *fabula*	with story and plot, rarely with *sujet*	with *fabula*	rarely with *fabula*
conclusion no. 2: necessary correspondence with other concepts	——	——	——	——

To conclude, the concepts story versus plot and *fabula* versus *sujet* are not interchangeable but complementary, and to translate "*fabula* and *sujet*" into "story and plot" is not only to mislead the reader but to blur a number of very useful theoretical distinctions. For if the precise properties of each of the four concepts are strictly distinguished and kept in mind, the critic may find their complementary nature of great help. When we wish, for instance, to refer to a narrative work that is actually arranged in an essentially temporal-additive sequence (the episodic sequence of a picaresque novel, for instance), we may call it a "story-type *sujet*." But when this sequence does not exist as an ordered whole in the artistically deformed *sujet* itself but has been reconstituted by us during the reading process—as is often the case with a stream-of-consciousness novel, for instance—we had better designate it as a "story-type *fabula*." On the other hand, we should refer to a deformed causal disposition of motifs as a "plot-type *sujet*" (Aristotle's ideal *mythos*, as devised in *Oedipus Rex*, for example), thus distinguishing it from the "plot-type *fabula*"—the same aggregate of motifs, reassembled in a chronological-causal sequence and considered from the viewpoint of its amenability to various artistic dislocations. The critic's having at his disposal eight terms instead of two or even four will make for greater precision and intelligibility. In a critical discussion of a "story," to cite one instance, we shall no longer be at a loss to determine (as we sometimes are with Forster) whether the speaker is referring to an actual arrangement of motifs or merely to one aspect of the work, the purely chronological sequence, as abstracted and divorced from the actual temporal-causal sequence. The critic can make his meaning absolutely unambiguous by designating the former as "story-type *sujet*" and the latter simply as "story."[24]

Of the two pairs of terms, at any rate, only one is by definition related to the order of presentation of motifs; and it is accordingly in terms of the distinction between *fabula* and *sujet* alone that I can now re-formulate my main objection to Freytag's theory. When Freytag and his followers assert that the first act of any play (or the first few chapters of a novel) contains the exposition, they confuse the beginning of the *sujet* and that of the *fabula*. The exposition always constitutes the beginning of the *fabula*, the first part of the chronologically ordered sequence of motifs as reconstructed by the reader; but it is not necessarily located at the beginning of the *sujet*. The beginning of the *fabula* coincides with that of the *sujet* only when the author presents his tale in a straight chronological sequence (as the tale is, more or less, narrated in the Book of Job, or in Balzac's *La Cousine Bette*, or in James's *Washington Square*, for instance). The author, however, may as legitimately choose to plunge *in medias res* or to distribute the expositional material throughout the work; and in these cases, though the exposition is still located in the beginning of the *fabula*, its position in the *sujet*, in the order in which the motifs are actually presented to the reader, radically varies.

REPRESENTED TIME AND
REPRESENTATIONAL TIME:
THE QUANTITATIVE INDICATOR

So far I have defined exposition as the beginning or first part of the *fabula*. This definition, however, though it firmly establishes the expositional *terminus a quo* and though it flexibly covers all the innumerable possibilities of combining and ordering a given number of motifs into different *sujets,* may nevertheless be regarded as seriously incomplete unless we can determine exactly up to *what point* in the *fabula* the motifs are expositional. In order to discover this *terminus ad quem* we must first briefly consider some of the time values of fiction and the important role they play in guiding the reader in his interpretation of the work.

A work of fiction presents characters in action during a certain fictive period of time. In most cases, however, one finds that the author has not treated the whole of the fictive period with the same degree of minuteness or attention. This period falls naturally or is artificially divided into different sub-periods, or time-sections. Some of these are rendered at great length, some galloped through or summarized rapidly, some dismissed with a perfunctory sentence or two; while others are even passed over unmentioned. In other words, even within the framework of a single *sujet* we can generally discover different ratios of *represented time* (i.e. the duration of a projected period in the life of the characters) to *representational time* (i.e. the time that it takes the reader, by the clock, to peruse that part of the work projecting this fictive period).

The question of the amount of representational time (manifested, of course, in terms of narrative space) to be allotted to each of the different time-sections of which the total fictive period or represented time consists is indeed, in James's words, "always there and always formidable." Most writers have dealt with this central aspect of the general problem of selection in an essentially intuitive fashion. Others, however, almost obsessed by it, have grappled with it boldly and consciously and have left behind them valuable hints as to the principles that guided them in their selective procedure. Fielding, for instance, belongs to the second category:

> We intend in [our work] rather to pursue the method of those writers who profess to disclose the revolutions of countries than to imitate the painful and voluminous historian, who, to preserve the regularity of his series, thinks himself obliged to fill up as much paper with the detail of months and years in which nothing remarkable happened as he employs upon those notable eras when the greatest scenes have been transacted on the human stage. . . .
> Now, it is our purpose in the ensuing pages to pursue a contrary

method. When any extraordinary scene presents itself (as we trust will
often be the case), we shall spare no pains nor paper to open it at
large to our reader; but if whole years should pass without producing
anything worthy his notice, we shall not be afraid of a chasm in our
history, but shall hasten on to matters of consequence and leave such
periods of time totally unobserved.

These are indeed to be considered as blanks in the grand lottery of
time. . . .

My reader, then, is not to be surprised if in the course of this work
he shall find some chapters very short, and others altogether as long;
some that contain only the time of a single day, and others that comprise years; in a word, if my history sometimes seems to stand still and
sometimes to fly (*Tom Jones*, II, 1).

Fielding indeed adheres to this principle of selection in all his novels, taking his cue from the historian tracing the revolutions of countries and from the ingenious traveler, "who always proportions his
stay at any place to the beauties, elegancies, and curiosities which it
affords," rather than from the painful and voluminous chronicler or
the various offspring of wealth and dullness, who jog on "with equal
pace through the verdant meadows or over the barren heath" (*Tom
Jones*, XI, 9). His contemptuous disdaining to keep even pace with
time is most conspicuously displayed and drawn attention to in *Tom
Jones*, where sixteen out of the eighteen Book-headings significantly
contain nothing but information concerning the time span (or represented time) that is to be covered by the book. And the striking disparity in treatment that this procedure involves will be duly appreciated if we compare, for instance, the time ratio of Book III with that
of Book IX. The amount of space (in my edition, about thirty pages—
say, about an hour of reading time), or representational time, allotted
to each of these Books is approximately identical; but since the represented time of the former Book (five years) is no less than 3650 times
as long as that of the latter (twelve hours), it is certainly no wonder
that in one the action should comparatively seem to fly and in the
other to stand still.

The differentiation between what I call representational time and
represented time dates back, in fact, to the Renaissance and the neo-
classical age, during which it was exclusively employed as a normative tool for checking the adherence of dramatists to the so-called
unity of time, falsely attributed to Aristotle. Thus, for instance,

Castelvetro distinguishes "perceptible time" from "intellectual time";[25] and Dryden denounces the practice of "mak[ing] too great a disproportion betwixt the imaginary time of the play, and the real time of its representation."[26] The concern with time-ratios, has, moreover, been revived in modern criticism. Various German scholars distinguish between *Erzählzeit* and *Erzähltezeit*;[27] and A. A. Mendilow elaborates a similar distinction between "the chronological duration of the novel" and "the chronological duration of the reading."[28] I believe, however, that these various pairs of terms have not been sufficiently exploited. They have been employed mainly to indicate the ratio between the representational time and the represented time of the work *as a whole,* "the time it takes to read a novel" as against the length of time covered by the content of the novel,"[29] as well as the disparities between different works in point of time-ratios, but only seldom to investigate the variations in time-ratios within a single work. And even where such variations have been pointed out, this has usually been done in order to discuss their implications for the tempo of the work or its narrative rhythm. I certainly agree that a comparison of the time-ratios in different works may yield highly significant results. (The fact that a great many modern novelists have reverted to the ancient unity of time is, for example, a striking feature of their revolt against their predecessors and is intimately correlated with their new conception of life and consequently with some of their dominant compositional principles.) It seems to me, however, that it is at least equally important to trace the variations in time-ratios within the limits of a single work as well; for these variations not only lead the reader to various "formal" conclusions (e.g. as to tempo) but at the same time play a central role in the interpretation of the work.

The reader is always confronted and frequently baffled by such problems as: Who is the protagonist or center of interest in the work? What is the relative importance of the various characters, incidents, and themes represented in it? Which of them is crucial or indispensable to the meaning of the work and which incidental? He is obliged to pose and answer dozens of questions of this sort if he is to construct, or reconstruct, the structure and hierarchy of meaning in the work and to compose a fully integrated picture of its art. However, these questions are never settled explicitly and satisfactorily by the text itself, even when overt rhetoric is employed—even when the author, for example, refers to one of the characters as "my hero" or "our heroine" or openly calls our attention to the role played by a certain incident or character. The reader is therefore forced to follow the multifarious implications of the text (its dramatized rhetoric) as to the nature and functions of its peculiar principles of selection and combination in order to arrive at adequate answers. The *quantitative indicator*, revealing the principles of selection operating in the text, forms in general one of the reader's indispensable guides in the interpretation of the work and one of the decisive factors which enable him to determine its general tendency ("intention") and its particular structure of meaning. For owing to the selectivity of art, there is a logical correlation between the amount of narrative space devoted to an element and the degree of its aesthetic relevance or centrality, so that the reader can very often infer the latter from the former.

As the variations in time-ratios in any particular text form one of the manifestations of the quantitative indicator, it can be determined that, *mutatis mutandis,* the time-ratio of a fictive period generally stands in direct proportion to its contextual relevance: a projected time-section or incident whose representational time approximates its represented time is implied to be more central to the *sujet* in question than another in which these two time factors are incommensurate. I have said "implied" because even in Fielding's novels, which abound in comments on this indicator more than the work of any other novelist I know, only few of the references to it are explicit. The explicit references only serve to heighten the reader's consciousness of the significance of the temporal manipulations and impress on him the necessity of applying the quantitative indicator whenever he comes up against interpretative problems related to the structure of meaning in the work: "Bestir thyself, therefore . . . for though we will always lend thee proper assistance in difficult places, as we do not, like some others, expect thee to use the arts of divination to discover our meaning, yet we shall not indulge thy laziness where nothing but thy own attention is required" (*Tom Jones,* XI, 9).

Illuminating as Fielding's critical asides are, they may be misleading in one important respect. They often seem to suggest that incidents possess an intrinsic, objective, and universally prevalent narrative interest or importance, and that the author stands still or flies according to the varying degrees of interest inherent in the different episodes. Fielding's comments may seem to imply, for instance, that the author will invariably represent at great length any fictive time-section containing "revolutions of countries," "great scenes," "extraordinary scenes," all of which are intrinsically "matters of true importance" or "great prizes"; while, on the other hand, he will as invariaably dismiss cursorily all humdrum domestic occurrences as not "worthy a place in this history" or beneath "the reader's notice": "As the tea-table conversation, though extremely delightful to those who are engaged in it, may probably appear somewhat dull to the reader, we will here put an end to the chapter" (*Amelia*, IX, 3).

A conclusion of this sort is utterly unwarrantable. The question whether any occurrence is "worthy of notice" or "of no consequence," whether it belongs to the class of "beauties, curiosities, elegancies" or is a "barren and gloomy heath," can never be determined *a priori* because the conception of its artistic significance or relevance may vary not only from one century to another or from one author to another but even from one.work to another. This conception varies according to writers' different artistic goals, which dictate different principles of selection. Henry James, holding that "it sounds almost puerile to say that some incidents are intrinsically more important than others," rightly refuses to evaluate *a priori* the different degrees of intrinsic interest adhering to different incidents, "for this will depend on the skill [and, we might add, the artistic goal] of the painter";[30] though his own ideal is to demonstrate "what an exciting *inward life* may do for the person leading it even while it remains perfectly normal" and that these seemingly mild adventures can be converted "into the stuff of drama or . . . of 'story.' "[31] His delight in Stevenson's *Treasure Island,* a novel that "treats of murders, mysteries, islands of dreadful renown, hairbreadth escapes, miraculous coincidences and buried doubloons" is, therefore, perfectly compatible with his singling out as the best thing in *The Portrait of a Lady* Isabel Archer's minutely evoked meditative vigil, when "she sits up by her dying fire, far into the night, under the spell of recognitions on which she finds the last sharpness suddenly wait . . . motionlessly *seeing."* Given the particular line of interest of the latter novel, this quiet vigil of searching criticism, "though it all goes on without her being approached by another person and without her leaving her chair," does indeed "throw the action forward more than twenty 'incidents' might have done," and is doubtless "as 'interesting' as the surprise of a caravan or the identification of a pirate."[32]

It is quite understandable that different writers, each with his own views of life and of art, should disagree as to what fields of material are intrinsically valuable and therefore worthy of being treated at length. The reader, however, finds himself in an altogether different situation. *Qua* reader he has no private artistic axe to grind. His only business, when reading a novel, is to endeavor to grasp the nature and functions of the compositional principles operating in it, so that he may comprehend as fully as possible its structure of meaning. In order to accomplish this he cannot apply to the work any scale of intrinsic interest (including his own) because, as shown above, there is no single one that is universally valid and can be automatically carried over from one work to another. He must, therefore, measure the value of narrative elements not in terms of intrinsic but of contextual significance, largely suggested by the quantitative indicator. And the more revolutionary a work is in its conception of the scale of significance, the more does it depend on the operation of the sharply enclosed, value-determining context of the whole work. For in such revolutionary works it is mainly the quantitative indicator that draws the reader's attention to the modification or even inversion of the conventional hierarchy of significance; or in other words, it is these works that most fully exploit the fact that what is conventionally regarded as trivial can be contextually invested with artistic importance by extensive treatment. Laurence Sterne, for instance, displays his acute awareness of the functionality of his seemingly bizarre selective procedure when he claims, "I am persuaded that the happiness of the Cervantic humour arises from this very thing—of describing silly and trifling Events, with the Circumstancial Pomp of great Ones."

Fielding himself was, in fact, well aware of the value-determining aspect of the variations in time-ratios, though in his polemical impetus against what seemed to him Richardson's petty psychological preoccupations he at times tended to overstate his plea for selecting only incidents of high intrinsic interest. Irrespective of the overt motivation of his selective decisions, his procedure is based, in fact, not on the ostensible criterion of intrinsic interest versus intrinsic dullness but on that of artistic relevance versus irrelevance, as he himself is driven to admit openly immediately after the representation of the muff incident in *Tom Jones*:

> Though this incident will probably appear of little consequence to many of our readers, yet trifling as it was, it had so violent an effect on poor ones that we thought it our duty to relate it. In reality, there are many little circumstances too often omitted by injudicious historians, from which events of the utmost importance arise. The world may indeed be considered as a vast machine in which the great wheels are originally set in motion by those which are very minute and almost imperceptible to any but the strongest eyes.
>
> Thus, not all the charms of the incomparable Sophia, not all the dazzling brightness, and languishing softness of her eyes, the harmony of her voice and of her person; not all her wit, good humour, greatness of mind or sweetness of disposition had been able so absolutely to conquer and enslave the heart of poor Jones as this little incident of the muff (V, 4).

EXPOSITION, QUANTITATIVE INDICATOR, SCENIC NORM, AND FICTIVE PRESENT

The quantitative indicator is an indispensable factor in the delimitation of the boundaries of the exposition within the *fabula*, that is, in the determination of the precise point in the *fabula* which marks the end of the expositional section.

As argued above, the literary author generally exploits the possibilities of varying the time-ratios for the purpose of throwing the contextual centrality of certain fictive periods into high relief against the background of other periods belonging to the total time span of the *sujet*. In other words, it is the approximation of representational to represented time that draws the reader's attention to some subperiods constituting "discriminated occasions" in the fullest sense of the word.[33] And vice versa: the very disparity between the different time ratios (and the wider it is the more conspicuously significant it becomes) suggests that the cursorily treated time-sections are nondiscriminated, that they occupy but a relatively minor or marginal position in the structure of meaning characteristic to this particular work.

Moreover, in most fictional and dramatic works we find not only variations in time-ratios but also a basic similarity between the time-ratios of the various scenes or discriminated occasions. In other words, every narrative establishes as a rule a certain scenic time-norm of its own. This scenic norm may, of course, vary from one writer to another, and even from one work to another. And even within a particular work certain scenes may turn out to deviate to some extent from the basic time-norm established by the majority of the discriminated occasions. But these deviations (say, a ratio of 1 : 3 or even 1 : 5 where the norm is 1 : 2), which may indeed appear to be considerable when examined in isolation, generally prove to be insignificant when considered, as they must be, in the context of the whole work, that is, in the light of all the time-ratios in the work, the nonscenic as well as the scenic. As in the non-scenically treated time-sections of the same narrative the time-ratio usually turns out to be something like 1 : 10,000 or 1 : 50,000 or even 1 : 500,000, the enormous disparity between the scenic and the non-scenic time-ratios clearly points out the comparative slightness of the occasional divergence from the basic scenic norm of the work.

At any rate, in the light of the fact that every work does establish a scenic time-norm and that scenic treatment accorded to a fictive time-section strongly indicates its high aesthetic importance, the first scene naturally assumes in every work a special conspicuousness and significance. The author's finding it to be the first time-section that is "of consequence enough" to deserve full scenic treatment turns it, implicitly but clearly, into a conspicuous signpost, signifying that this is precisely the point in time which the author has decided, for whatever reason, to make the reader regard as the beginning of the action proper. This "occasion," the text strongly suggests, is the first to have been "discriminated" in this way because it constitutes the first stage of the action. In some instances, moreover, this implicit indication is both accounted for and further reinforced by overt references to the extraordinary contextual significance of the first scene. Towards the end of the short preliminary exposition in Henry James's *Washington Square,* for instance, the narrator prefaces the representation of the party at which Catherine Sloper is to meet Morris Townsend with the comment that this occasion "was the beginning of something very important" (chap. 3); and he later intrudes upon this scene in order to point out again that the present "entertainment was the beginning of something important for Catherine" (chap. 4). If, therefore, the first discriminated occasion is the beginning of what Trollope happily calls "the real kernel of [the] story,"[34] it follows that any motif that antedates it in point of time (i.e. precedes it in the *fabula*) is expositional—irrespective of its position or order of presentation in the *sujet*.

The expositional information, always antedating the first discriminated occasion, may precede it in point of its actual location in the *sujet*. In this case, the significant disparity between the time-ratio of the expositional period and that of the first scene (a disparity concomitant with several other indicators, to be soon discussed) clearly exposes the preparatory nature of the section preceding the temporal signpost. The communication of the expositional material, however, may also be delayed, so that it will succeed the first discriminated occasion in point of its actual presentation in the *sujet*. In this case, the expositional information will retrospectively throw light on the first scene, that is, add to, modify or even drastically change the reader's understanding of it; for, within the sharply circumscribed, enclosed world of the literary text, almost every motif or occurrence antedating another tends to illuminate it in some way, no matter what its order of presentation in the *sujet*. The point marking the end of the expositional part in the *fabula* thus coincides with that point in time which marks the beginning of the *fictive present* in the *sujet,* that is, the beginning of the first time-section that the work regards as important enough to be worthy of such full treatment as will involve, according to the scenic norm of the work, a close approximation or correspondence between its representational time and the clock-marked time we employ in everyday life.

It will be noticed that I dissociate my use of the term "fictive present" from any dependence on dramatic or fictive illusion, with which it is usually thought to be interchangeable. The prevalent view of the fictive present as identical with the illusion of presentness has been ably and consistently put forward by A. A. Mendilow, who claims that:

> There is as a rule one point of time in the story which serves as the point of reference. From this point the fictive present may be considered as beginning. In other words, the reader if he is engrossed in his reading translates all that happens from this moment of time onwards into an imaginative present of his own and yields to the illusion that

he is himself participating in the action or situation, or at least is witnessing it as happening, not merely as having happened. Everything that antedates this point, as for instance exposition, is felt as a fictive past, while all that succeeds it, as for instance those premonitions and anticipatory hints that novelists find so useful for directing the attention forward to the climax or evoking a feeling of suspense, are felt as future.[35]

Mendilow's view of exposition is thus by no means Freytagean. He does not deal with Freytag's theory at all, but his passing comments mark a considerable advance over it because they reflect an awareness that the location of the expositional material is not fixed but variable. And for this he must be given full credit. What basically vitiates Mendilow's references to the problem, ultimately reducing them to little more than a series of shrewd insights, however, is the lack of some indispensable theoretical tools and the inefficacy of those employed in their stead. The absence in his account of a distinction comparable to that between *fabula* and *sujet* might perhaps prove less fatal if the concept he proposes as a delimiting temporal signpost, namely the "fictive present," were not so vague as to become useless as a critical tool. The similarity between his conception of the fictive present and mine is primarily terminological: his approach, as implicit in this passage, and that which I have so far outlined necessarily differ since the term we both use denotes for us radically divergent concepts or literary phenomena.[36] While I certainly maintain that the beginning of the fictive present is indeed an important point of reference, I strongly doubt whether "any imaginative shift of the reader from his own chronological present to the fictional past in which novels are written" (pp. 63-64) takes place at all; whether the reader actually identifies himself with the hero and even *is* the hero in imagination (p. 96); whether the reader is ever "cheated" of his reason (pp. 109-10), forgetting his own present and by an effort of the imagination losing or immersing himself in or projecting himself into the fictive present of the story, so that "the reader's actual present, his own time-locus, [is] absorbed into the fictive present of the action" (pp. 97-98). I for one hold that Dr. Johnson's view that "the spectators are always in their senses, and know, from the first act to the last, that the stage is only a stage and the players are only players" is far closer to the truth. The point, however, is that both views, the illusionist as well as the anti-illusionist, are not only equally undemonstrated but undemonstrable by literary critics *qua* literary critics. This psychological crux, therefore, should be relegated to the discipline of psychology, where it properly belongs.

But even if we assume for the sake of argument that the illusion of presentness does operate, the question that immediately arises is, what are the objective elements or factors in the text itself that give rise to or bring about this psychological transfer and that establish the point of reference? This crucial question has never been satisfactorily answered by the proponents of the illusionist theory.

It is here that my definition of the fictive present may come in useful even for the purposes of the illusionist view. If we take "fictive present" as a descriptive metaphor denoting an indisputably objective relationship or ratio between representational time and represented time, a ratio that involves an approximation of the two times; and if this approximation is interpreted as aiming to achieve (to adopt Mendilow's own phrase in another context) a "closer correspondence between the pace of living, or more truly, of thinking and feeling, and [the] depiction of it" (p. 73), we shall be able to account for the possiblity that a temporal transfer takes place at such a point by referring to the objective compositional elements that may produce it.

THE TEXTURE OF EXPOSITION,
SCENIC TEXTURE,
AND MODES OF PRESENTATION

A closer analysis of particular narratives will, I believe, not only confirm the conclusions reached so far but also throw light on some aspects of the texture of exposition as opposed to scenic texture, a most important problem that I have not hitherto treated. I propose to consider first the case of preliminary and concentrated exposition, that is, to examine some narratives that actually start by presenting a continuous block of expositional information—the Book of Job, for instance:

> 1. There was a man in the land of Uz, whose name *was* Job; and the man was perfect and upright, and one that feared God, and eschewed evil. 2. And there were born unto him seven sons and three daughters. 3. His substance also was seven thousand sheep, and three thousand

camels, and five hundred yoke of oxen, and five hundred she asses, and a very great household; so that this man was the greatest of all the men of the east. 4. And his sons went and feasted *in their* houses, every one his day; and sent and called for their three sisters to eat and to drink with them. 5. And it was so, when the days of *their* feasting were gone about, that Job sent and sanctified them, and rose up early in the morning, and offered burnt offerings *according* to the number of them all; for Job said, It may be that my sons have sinned, and cursed God in their hearts. Thus did Job continually. 6. Now there was a day when the sons of God came to present themselves before the Lord, and Satan came also among them. 7. And the Lord said unto Satan, Whence comest thou? Then Satan answered the Lord and said, From going to and fro in the earth, and from walking up and down in it. 8. And the Lord said unto Satan, Hast thou considered my servant Job, that *there is* none like him in the earth, a perfect and an upright man, one that feareth God, and escheweth evil? 9. Then Satan answered the Lord, and said, Doth Job fear God for nought? 10. Hast not thou made an hedge about him, and about his house, and about all that he hath on every side? thou hast blessed the work of his hands, and his substance is increased in the land. 11. But put forth thine hand and touch all that he hath, and he will curse thee to thy face. 12. And the Lord said unto Satan, Behold, all that he hath *is* in thy power; only upon himself put not forth thy hand. So Satan went forth from the presence of the Lord (chap. I, 1-12).

Every reader will instinctively "feel" that this chronologically ordered sequence of motifs "falls naturally" into two parts (namely, verses 1-5 and verses 6-12), the first of which serves to "prepare" us for the second and more "essential" part. The question, however, is whether it is possible to isolate and point out objectively the particular devices employed by the text in order to accomplish this effect and in order to give rise to this "feeling" as to the different roles of the two passages.

To say that the difference between verses 1-5 and 6-12 corresponds to that between "summary" and "action" is merely to beg the question, for what, in fact, is summary and what is action? The best manner of accounting for the disparity in effects is to start with an examination of the different time ratios to be found in the two parts. They are both of about equal length, but whereas the first swiftly flies over several decades in the history of Job and his family, the second restricts itself to the evocation of a very brief time-section containing the colloquy between God and Satan. It is the striking disparity[37] between the two represented time-sections, and consequently between the two time-ratios, that indicates that these two passages occupy very different positions and fulfill different functions within the context of this particular narrative. The quantitative indicator clearly implies, in other words, that the discriminated occasion marking the beginning of the fictive present constitutes the beginning of this particular story about Job; while the preceding passage, which antedates it in the *fabula,* is intended to communicate to the reader the expositional antecedents indispensable to the comprehension of the action proper. Any doubts the reader may entertain as to the possibility of such a short passage constituting a full-fledged discriminated occasion are soon dispelled by the series of discriminated occasions immediately following it, all of them conforming to, and thereby confirming, the basic scenic time-norm established in the first scene.[38]

Moreover, this radical disparity between time-ratios involves or logically correlates with the no less significant differences in point of *texture* between the two passages—texture being defined here in terms of "specificity," "concreteness," and "dynamics." Such a very short passage as the first, with its meager quantity of representational time in relation to a very long span of represented time, can only touch briefly upon some of the occurrences referred to and/or summarize some of their habitual, recurrent features. In other words, the texture of such a passage cannot be *specific,* for, the passage being short and having a long period to cover, the narrator cannot afford to go into the details of the events that took place in the course of the represented time, but is compelled to resort to very broad, generalized strokes of summary. Neither can it be *concrete,* that is, it cannot restrict itself to the representation of incidents that existed only once in time and space, but, having to telescope a long fictive period into a confined space, the writer is constantly forced to summarize the fixed or recurrent traits of characters, incidents, or situations.

And verses 1-5 do indeed concentrate only on the broadest and most typical or habitual features of the character, life, and behavior of Job and his household. The non-specificity of this passage, its generalized texture, is very marked: the names of Job's children, for instance, are not mentioned; about Job's environment the reader can only infer that it is rural rather than urban; and even the account given of the protagonist himself consists of highly generalized character traits such as "perfect," "upright," or "the greatest of all men of the east." The texture, moreover, clearly lacks concreteness as well as specificity, being composed not only of very broad, drastically foreshortened facts but also of habitual occurrences or features, as the grammar of the passage indicates: the feasts of Job's sons, for instance, and their father's offerings are evidently not concrete but customary and recurrent events in their lives. And the narrator himself explicitly points out this fact, when looking back over the whole passage: "Thus did Job continually."

The texture of verses 6-12, however, is quite different. In this discriminated occasion, which restricts itself to a brief period of represented time, the role of summary is minimized. First of all, the narrator no longer chooses to ignore the multifarious details of which every occurrence is composed, or at most telescope them into a generalized epithet or a broad statement, but goes into a relatively minute evocation of what took place on the occasion, quoting the speeches made by the two characters in all their specificity of wording.

This scene is, moreover, not only more specifically treated, but is composed of concrete incidents or motifs. This is not a situation with fixed, habitual features which manifest themselves again and again during a long period of time, but one that existed only once in time and space, one that took place on a particular day, at a particular place, and during a particular short period of time, and is never to recur again. In the narrator's own words, the difference in point of concreteness between the two passages precisely corresponds to that between "Thus did Job continually" and "Now there was a day."

The reader is thus led to the conclusion that verses 1-5 are expositional by a combination of three complementary indicators—two textual and one chronological. The pronounced *quantitative* difference in point of specificity, produced by the manipulation of time-ratios, draws the reader's attention to the secondary position occupied by the opening part within the context of Job's story. And so at the same time does the no less conspicuous *qualitative* difference in point of concreteness, since the "real kernel" of a narrative must necessarily consist of a concrete action, while the de-concretized opening section might equally have paved the way for any number of stories about Job. Given these indications, the fact that this section chronologically antedates the first discriminated occasion leaves no doubt in our minds that its function is preparatory or expositional.

One must, moreover, take into account another consideration which is closely related to, indeed based on, the opposition in point of concreteness. In the first section the narrator portrays a state of affairs that is essentially static or stable, as is indicated by the fact that it is mainly composed of static or recurrent motifs. By itself, therefore, the initial situation can lead to nothing but a repetition of the same habitual events. On the other hand, the second part, the discriminated occasion, is not only concrete but also essentially dynamic or developmental, introducing into the once stable state of affairs the first disturbing, de-stabilizing element (Satan's challenge and God's taking up the glove), which causally leads, by necessary or probable sequence, to the next stages of the action. In other words, the group of concrete discriminated occasions, all of them composed of essentially dynamic and developmental motifs, is closely unified by a causal chain into a network of cause and effect which forms the particular story of Job and which qualitatively distinguishes it from the first static group of motifs. The only way the reader can integrate these static motifs into the structure of meaning of the narrative is to grasp them as what Balzac called "les prémisses à une proposition" or, in other words, as expositional elements which introduce us into the fictive world, establish its canons of probability, and serve as the groundwork on which the particular narrative edifice is to be erected.

It is these objective features of the text that unambiguously mark off the preliminary exposition from the non-expositional sections of the story and establish the point in time at which the action proper starts. As I have demonstrated, this point in time in the *fabula* is seen to coincide with the beginning of the first discriminated occasion in the *sujet*. And once this temporal point of reference is established, the reader has no difficulty in determining what motifs are expositional, no matter what their position in the *sujet*. Thus, for instance, the circumstance that Job has a number of friends, though its disclosure is subsequent to the beginning of the fictive present, turns out to be as unmistakably expositional as the motifs contained in the opening section, for its position in the *fabula* equally precedes the point of reference fixed by the first scene.

All preliminary expositions in fiction and drama are marked off from the "story proper" in an essentially similar fashion. Jane Austen's *Emma*, for instance, opens with an introductory section which telescopes into a few pages the twenty-one years Emma has lived "in the world with very little to distress or to vex her." The disparity in point of time-ratios between this section (twenty-one years of represented time to which the author allots about five minutes of representational time) and the following discriminated occasion (covering a small part of a single evening to which about fifteen minutes of representational time are devoted) immediately strikes the reader. This significant disparity involves again marked differences in texture. The discriminated occasion is both specific (minutely reporting Emma's thoughts and the conversation between Emma, her father, and Mr. Knightley during this evening) and concrete temporally and spatially. In contrast, the opening account is both highly generalized (consisting of a broad summary of Emma's history, her traits of character and those of her father, their general situation, etc.), and de-concretized. Moreover, again as in the Book of Job, the reader perceives that the first discriminated occasion has not been chosen at random. It coincides with that point in time when the static, peaceful situation at Hartfield has just been disturbed and de-stabilized: "Miss Taylor married . . . it was on the wedding day of this beloved friend that Emma first sat in mournful thought of any continuance. The wedding over, and the bride-people gone, her father and herself were left to dine together, with no prospect of a third to cheer a long evening." This change thus marks a crucial turning-point—no less than the beginning of a new era in Emma's history. It is during this scene, when Emma has just been thrown for the first time on her own resources, that she announces her match-making plans, which are strongly objected to by Mr. Knightley but lead to the first phase of her humiliating ordeal. The strongly developmental nature of the chain of events, all of them causally connected, that is set into motion by the de-stabilizing elements contained in the first scene, is again contrasted with the static nature of the opening section, which can be integrated with them only as exposition. In other words, the same features of the preliminary exposition (its priority in point of time, its reduced time-ratio which involves a generalized and de-concretized texture, and the static nature of its motifs) as opposed to those of the first discriminated occasion again clearly establish the coincidence of the beginning of the first scene in the *sujet* with that temporal point marking the end of the expositional section in the *fabula*.

The point at which the preliminary exposition comes to an end and the fictive present starts is sometimes noted explicitly by the narrator himself. In Balzac's *La Cousine Bette,* for example, after informing the reader at length about the history of the family of baron Hulot d'Ervy, about the other main characters, and about the baron's meeting with the fatal Madame Marneffe, the narrator observes that "ici se termine en quelque sort l'introduction de cette histoire. Ce récit est au drame qui le complète, ce que sont les prémisses à une proposition, ce qu'est toute exposition à toute tragédie classique."[39] Similarly, at the end of the fourth chapter of Trollope's *The Eustace Diamonds,* the reader is informed that "dramatists, when they write their plays, have a delightful privilege of prefixing a list of their personages; and the dramatists of old used to tell us who was in love with whom, and what were the blood relationships of all the persons. In such a narrative as this, any proceeding of that kind would be unusual, and therefore the poor narrator has been driven to expand his four first chapters in the mere task of introducing his characters. He regrets the length of these introductions, and will now begin at once the action of his story." The narrators in these novels thus mark the *terminus ad quem* of the exposition both in terms of the continuum of the text (e.g. the end of the fourth chapter) and that of events. In some cases, the narrator does not point out explicitly the end of the exposition in the *sujet,* but only the temporal signpost in the *fabula* at which the "action proper" starts. In Charles Reade's *It Is Never Too Late to Mend,* for instance, the time of the first discriminated occasion is referred to as "the morning of our tale," in Trollope's *Barchester Towers* as "the time at which this history is supposed to commence," and in Singer's "Short Friday" as "the Friday on which this story took place."[40] In other cases, the preliminary exposition is delimited by the narrator's emphasizing the point of transition from it to the first scene in terms of concreteness, prefixing to the latter such tell-tale opening phrases as *"one* day" in order to distinguish it from the preceding, de-concretized events. In Singer's *Short Friday and Other Stories,* for instance, the first discriminated occasion in "Taibele and Her Demon" opens with the words "one moonless summer evening"; in "Big and Little" with "Now listen to this. One day . . ."; in "Blood" with "One morning"; and in "Esther Kreindel the Second" with "One night."[41] And in still other cases, the first scene is overtly indicated to de-stabilize or to have de-stabilized a hitherto static state of affairs. In *The Warden,* for example, the narrator comments that owing to John Bold's words, "the first shade of doubt now fell into [Mr. Harding's] mind, and from this evening, for many a long, long day, our good, kind, loving warden was neither happy nor at ease" (chap. 3). Similarly, the second and third chapters of *Eugénie Grandet* abound in observations on the significant transformation undergone by Eugénie from the moment she meets her cousin: "More ideas had poured into her mind in a quarter of an hour than had ever before occurred to her in her whole life"; "for the first time in her life . . . Eugénie dreamed of love"; or "desiring for the first time in her life to look her best, she felt the satisfaction of having a new dress." The temporal point which "revealed to Eugénie the meaning of things here below" is thus powerfully established.

In most narratives, however, the reader's attention is not explicitly drawn to the point marking the end of the preliminary exposition; he is left to discover it by himself, with the aid of the set of implicit indicators, quantitative and qualitative, formal and thematic, discussed above. Even when a signpost is explicitly provided, the reader should check whether the textual evidence bears out the authorial statement; but in other cases the careful application of these criteria is evidently imperative.

A perfunctory application of these criteria, or an application of some of them only, moreover, will not do, because the author often complicates the reader's task of delimiting the preliminary exposition by considerably varying—usually towards the end of the introductory section—the expositional time-ratio in such a way as to make it approximate the scenic norm of the story. The author may choose to do this for a number of reasons. After a highly generalized introductory summary of the initial state of affairs, he may wish to concentrate more fully on a number of expositional points, occurrences or character traits, that are more directly or immediately relevant to the sequel. He may, therefore, understandably wish to present these at greater length or with a higher degree of specificity than the more general points, or even to dramatize them to some extent. He may wish to recapitulate, vivify, or re-emphasize dramatically some of the expositional motifs merely mentioned before. He may at the same time, wishing to avoid an abrupt shift to the fictive present, prefer a more gradual and therefore less discernible transition from purely stated or "told" exposition to fully dramatized "showing" or scene. In other words, he may also increase the expositional time-ratio towards the end of the preliminary account so as to dissimulate to some extent the stark expositional nature of his opening section. In all these instances, a careful awareness of *all* the *differentia specifica* of discriminated occasion versus concentrated exposition is particularly necessary.

A case in point is the two last verses (4-5) of the opening of the Book of Job, which raise the difficult problem of the illustrative scene. It is clear that as far as the ratio of representational time to represented time is concerned, the feasts projected in these lines are accorded a treatment conspicuously different from that of the other motifs. The time-ratio of this brief complex of incidents, to which about half of the introductory section is devoted, sufficiently diverges from the preceding one of three verses to four decades and sufficiently approximates that of the first discriminated occasion to prove troublesome to a reader who attempts to determine whether it is expositional or not by the blind application of the quantitative criterion by itself. However, if the reader brings the whole set of indicators to bear on the occurrence, he will soon arrive at the conclusion that these verses form an integral part of the exposition. For, though from the viewpoint of degree of specificity this incident indeed approaches the scenic norm as established on the first discriminated occasion, it qualitatively differs from this norm in point of concreteness, being essentially as habitual and recurrent in the life of Job's family as the other expositional motifs. This recurrent incident will then be viewed as no more than a final semi-dramatic highlighting of the central expositional feature, Job's perfect piety, which has been merely "stated" before but which it is so important to impress on the reader that it is dramatically recapitulated, enlarged on, and re-emphasized by way of illustration. Furthermore, just like the other expositional motifs, the incident is in no way dynamic or developmental.

When the reader perceives the de-concretized, habitual, or illustrative nature of the incident, he also understands that its increased degree of specificity is illusory. As soon as its *recurrent* nature is noticed, it becomes clear that the nominal represented time of this incident, the few days of the feast, should be multiplied by a hundred or a thousand so as to cover as much represented time as the other expositional motifs. When this is done, the illustrative incident may still be regarded as more specifically treated than the other antecedents, but the disparity between its time-ratio or degree of specificity and that of the scenic norm is great enough to prevent this semi-dramatized event from being confused with a full-fledged discriminated occasion.

In other instances of thoroughly treated occurrences that are intercalated into the preliminary exposition or round it off, we similarly discover that while the application of the quantitative indicator by itself may mislead us, the criteria of concreteness and development lay bare the illustrative, preparatory nature of these "scenes." The operation of the indicator of concreteness may, however, vary, since there is more than one way of de-concretizing a scene. At the start of Part I, chap. 4 of Dostoevsky's *The Devils*—to cite an interesting case in point—the narrator, having presented different aspects of the relationship between Verkhovensky and Mrs. Stavrogin, stops the flow of exposition in order to enact two events. One is concerned with Mrs. Stavrogin's anger at Verkhovensky's enthusiastic response to the confirmation of the rumors about the emancipation of the serfs, the other with the abrupt way she put an end to their romantic meetings in the summer-house. Each of these events not only diverges significantly from the preceding expositional blocks in point of specificity but, unlike verses 4-5 in Job, also appears to be fully concrete as well —the first opening with the tell-tale words "One day," and the second with "It took place in 1855, in springtime, in the month of May."

Each of these scenes may accordingly seem to sound in turn the gong of first discriminated occasion. But they are nevertheless purely expositional. Though when torn out of context they may pass for concrete, in fact their concreteness is only illusory. What de-concretizes these occasions is neither their tenor nor their "grammar" but the wider narrative framework in which they are set. For the narrator has prefaced the representation of the two incidents with the revealing comment that in return for her patronage Mrs. Stavrogin "demanded a great deal from [Verkhovensky], sometimes even the obedience of a slave. And it was incredible how unforgiving she was. I may as well tell you two stories about that." The context thus leaves no doubt in our minds that the two scenes have been interpolated merely as dramatic illustrations of a central character-trait of the lady's and of the nature of the relations between her and her protégé. Both stories are even linked to the authorial generalization that they exemplify, and to each other, by the fact that in spite of their wholly different tenor they both terminate in an identical whisper hissed by Mrs. Stavrogin: " 'I shall never forgive you for this!' " Consequently, though these anecdotes are concrete in themselves whereas the corresponding incident in Job is not, all three scenes are equally de-concretized in that each ultimately serves to highlight an habitual state of affairs characterizing the expositional period or to drive home an engrained trait. From the viewpoint of development, moreover, these scenes are even more starkly expositional, if possible, than the feasts in Job since they have no sequel and lead us nowhere. Once the narrator has done with them, he resumes his expositional summary: "She even designed the clothes he wore all his life herself," etc.

To conclude, the various indicators which combine to form the set of criteria by which the reader can mark off the preliminary exposition from the action proper are usually concomitant and interdependent. The reader should not apply any of them or judge by any of them without reference to the others. It may sometimes be convenient to start with the quantitative criterion and sometimes with the qualitative criteria, but any attempt to apply only one of these indicators may lead to serious confusions between summary and scene in general[42] and between condensed preliminary exposition and the fictive present in particular.

On the other hand, the systematic application of this set of indicators confirms our conclusion that all the motifs in the *fabula* that antedate the point at which the fictive present begins in the *sujet* are expositional. In other words, we have to compare the presentation of motifs in the *fabula* with that in the *sujet* and note the temporal point in the *fabula* at which the fictive present begins in the *sujet*. All the motifs from the beginning of the *fabula* up to this point are expositional; this point marks the *terminus ad quem* of the exposition. We have already examined the case of works of fiction in which the order or arrangement of the introductory motifs in the *sujet* is identical with or at least similar to that in the *fabula*. In such narratives—and in plays that start with a prologue—the exposition or part of it both antedates (in point of time) and precedes (in point of actual order of presentation) the beginning of the fictive present, while the rest of the work succeeds it both chronologically and structurally.

Whenever the author refrains from opening his work with a block of preliminary exposition, he considerably reduces the difficulty of spotting the point in time which constitutes the end of the expositional section in the *fabula*. For in this case the work generally plunges into a full-fledged discriminated occasion, thus indicating to the reader right at the beginning the point of reference at which the fictive present and the "action proper" start, and delaying for some time the communication of the expositional material which is to explain what is happening at the present moment and why it is happening. In other words, in this case the author prefers a retrospective to a preliminary or anticipatory illumination of the occurrences taking place from the first scene on. However, the problem of spotting the expositional motifs in the *sujet* here is solved in essentially the same manner. By keeping in mind the temporal point in the *fabula* at which the fictive present starts in the *sujet*, the reader can easily identify the expositional motifs as they crop up later in the work.

In *Vanity Fair*, for example, which opens "on one sunshiny morning in June" with the memorable scene representing the departure of Amelia and Becky from Miss Pinkerton's academy, the flow of the fictive present is stopped twice, right after the beginning. This happens first in chapter one, in order to impart to the reader some important information about Amelia (her appearance, character traits, circumstances, and relations with various people); this retrospectively throws light on the concrete events that we have just witnessed: "But as we are to see a great deal of Amelia, there is no harm in saying, at the outset of our acquaintance, that she was a dear little creature," etc. After this doubling back into the expositional past, the novel proceeds to represent further the events of the previously established scene, but stops again, soon after Becky's sacrilegious rejection of the precious dictionary, in order to devote about half of the second chapter to a thorough account of Becky's character and history up to the point of the beginning of the fictive present. This evocation of the past illuminates, retrospectively again, Becky's behavior during the opening scene.

Both blocks of information about the antecedents of these heroines are as expositional from the point of view of their function (accounting as they do for the diametrically opposed conduct of the two girls in the first scene), their position in the *fabula,* their time-ratios and texture, and their mode of integration with the other, scenically rendered, and dynamic narrative elements, as those opening the Book of Job or *Emma.* They differ from the latter only in their location in the *sujet:* these expositional blocks have merely been placed in the *sujet* so as to follow the point of reference, whereas the others precede as well as antedate it. All of them, however, are located at the beginning of their respective *fabulas,* before the temporal point at which the fictive present starts in their respective *sujets.*

In other cases the story also plunges into the fictive present right from the start, thus immediately establishing the temporal point of reference, but prefers to impart the necessary expositional material to the reader in a radically different way, that is, by weaving it into the action proper itself. The author may choose, for instance, to break up what is in the *fabula* a continuous expositional section into a large number of small units or isolated motifs, which are made to crop up at different points in the course of the fictive present, or, in other words, to emerge naturally out of scenes or incidents that are themselves essentially non-expositional. These discontinuous expositional units or motifs, unobtrusively located in standard scenes, consequently do not form separate narrative blocks exclusively concerned with the expositional past, with an individual texture of their own that is perceptibly different from the scenic. They are made to constitute, on the contrary, an integral part of the texture of the discriminated occasions themselves and may be made to fulfill important functions in them. Thus, at the beginning of *The Ambassadors* Strether meets Maria Gostrey, with whom he holds several colloquies. These meetings form perfectly concrete and specific discriminated occurrences, which are part and parcel of the novel's action, theme, and line of interest, namely, Strether's adventure in Europe. However, in the course of these conversations a large number of the relevant details concerning Strether's past naturally come up, and are thereby indirectly relayed to the reader. So the expositional picture slowly unfolds without the author's stopping the flow of the fictive present even for a moment. While in *Vanity Fair* the communication of the expositional blocks necessitates a pause in the action, here the communication of the discontinuous expositional motifs propels the action forward.

Despite all these differences it is clear that the distributed expositional motifs in *The Ambassadors* essentially fulfill the same function as the solid expositional blocks in *Vanity Fair*. They too all belong to that part of the *fabula* that is anterior to the first discriminated occasion in the *sujet*, namely Strether's arrival at Chester; and this occasion is again indicated to be of extreme importance in that it destabilizes a hitherto static state of affairs. The first chapter is interspersed with suggestions that this scene forms a landmark foreshadowing a transformation. Strether experiences "such a consciousness of personal freedom as he had not known for years; such a deep taste of change"; he refers to his encounter with Maria as the most extraordinary thing that has ever happened to him; he feels that it marks his "introduction to things" and that "he was launched in something of which the sense would be quite disconnected from the sense of his past, and which was literally beginning there and then." There is no doubt, in short, that here too the opening scene constitutes the beginning of the action proper. And therefore, though in one novel the exposition is concentrated while in the other it is distributed, though in one novel it is presented explicitly as immutable past while in the other it is cunningly woven into the present, though in one novel it retards the flow of the action while in the other it feeds this flow, in both cases the motifs belonging to the first part of the *fabula* retrospectively throw light on and account for the dynamic chain of occurrences that starts with the first discriminated occasion, and are therefore equally expositional.

To sum up, when we call expositions preliminary or delayed, concentrated or distributed, we refer, in fact, to the order or manner of presentation of the expositional materials in the *sujet*, for in the *fabula* the exposition is always concentrated at the beginning. No normative value can be automatically ascribed either to the position of the exposition in the *sujet* or to its form and texture; but the location and the form of exposition are always worth inquiring into because they are usually indicative of and often integral to the structure and compositional principles of the work as a whole. For instance, as the straight chronological order of presentation of the narrative motifs

composing a story is the most logical, and hence natural, arrangement, it is clear that any deviation from it is a significant indication
of artistic purpose. I believe it is always instructive to inquire why an
author has chosen to make the beginning of the *sujet* coincide with
that of the *fabula,* or why he has decided to make temporal shifts;
why he presents the expositional material (or parts of it) in independent, solid blocks of fictive past or why he weaves it into the fictive present. We usually find, for instance, that the latter procedures
involve an endeavor to move away from a concern with exposition
as such and to make the expositional material serve a number of functions apart from the merely referential, such as the manipulation of
narrative interest or the control of aesthetic distance.

All this may be put in a more general way. A literary work is the
sum of a vast number of selective and combinational decisions which
determine the particular structure of the work, both as regards its
pattern of meaning and its rhetoric, the complex of devices which
bring the meaning of the work home to the reader and manipulate
his reactions. I have already suggested that the reconstruction of the
selective procedures embodied in the work can provide us with important clues to its artistic intentions. The combinational decisions
and procedures, however, are no less significant, and can often be reconstructed and accounted for in as precise a manner as the selective
ones. The broad combinational principles actually operating in narrative works, though their variations in particular texts are infinite,
fall into a number of clear patterns and are meant to fulfill a number
of definite functions or to give rise to a number of definite effects;
and I hope to show elsewhere that this claim can be substantiated
through a study of that part of the narrative work that I have defined
as the exposition. As the location of exposition is fixed in the *fabula*
but highly variable in the *sujet,* the study of the variety of expositional techniques and their functions may give us some idea of the
principles of combination and distribution of materials in the narrative text as a whole. I believe it can be demonstrated that, given a selected number of motifs, the possibilities of presenting the narrative
material called exposition and of combining it with the other narrative materials can be classified into several recognizable and definable
structural patterns, each with its own artistic aims or functions and
each arising out of different overall artistic intentions, either specifi-

cally connected with the aims of the particular work or related to more general conceptions of fiction and literature.

Finally, these distributive and combinational procedures often derive from an acute consciousness on the part of writers that literature is a time-art, in which the continuum of the text is grasped by the reader in a continuum of time and in which events are necessarily communicated not simultaneously but successively, and from their realization that these conditions may be exploited and manipulated in order to produce various artistic effects on the reader. As my definition of it clearly implies, exposition is a time problem *par excellence*.

NOTES

1. V. Sackville-West, *The Edwardians* (New York, 1930), p. 1.
2. Thus Malcolm Cowley claims that all of Faulkner's "books in the Yokoapatawpha saga are parts of the same living pattern. It is this pattern, and not the printed volumes in which part of it is recorded, that is Faulkner's real achievement. Its existence helps to explain one feature of his work: that each novel, each long or short story seems to reveal more than it states explicitly and to have a bigger subject than itself." *The Portable Faulkner* (New York, 1954), pp. 7-8.
3. See Ernest Schanzer, *The Problem Plays of Shakespeare* (London, 1966), chap. 2.
4. *The Portable Faulkner*, pp. 7-8.
5. *Ibid.*, p. 8. Cowley, significantly enough, adds in the same sentence that these inconsistencies are "afterthoughts rather than oversights."
6. Thus, for instance, on taking leave of Archdeacon Grantly in the last but one chapter of *The Warden*, Trollope regrets "that he is represented in these pages as worse than he is," and twice repeats the explanation that in the present novel "we have had to do with his foibles, and not with his virtues." What he, in fact, does here is to account and lay the ground for the different presentation of the Archdeacon in *Barchester Towers*.
7. *An Autobiography* (London, 1961; first published 1883), p. 275.
8. *Ibid.*, pp. 159, 309-10.
9. *The Craft of Fiction* (New York, 1963; first published 1921), p. 210. Cf. Felicien Marceau, *Balzac and His World*, trans. Derek Coltman (London, 1967), pp. 3-6.
10. Gustav Freytag, *Technique of the Drama*, trans. Elias J. MacEwan (Chicago, 1908; first published 1863), pp. 114-15.
11. See, for example, pp. 119-21 in his treatise; note particularly that his definition of the function of the exposition ("its task, to prepare for the action," p. 120) largely overlaps with that of the introduction (pp. 115, 117-18).
12. To cite a single example: Vladimir Nabokov's claim that in Gogol's *The Government Inspector* "there is no so-called 'exposition.' Thunderbolts do not lose time explaining meteorological conditions" (*Nikolai Gogol* [New York, 1961], p. 42) is also based on the preconception that exposition must neces-

sarily be preliminary. The exposition in this play is only delayed and distributed; it is clearly there.

13. "Dramatic Structure in the Novels of Ernest Hemingway," *Modern Fiction Studies,* XIV [1968], p. 272.

14. *Ibid.,* p. 282.

15. *Ibid.,* p. 272.

16. See especially Boris Tomashevsky's "Thématique," in *Théorie de la littérature,* ed. Tzvetan Todorov (Paris, 1965), pp. 240-42; the essay is also partly reprinted in *Russian Formalist Criticism: Four Essays,* eds. Lee T. Lemon and Marion J. Reis (Lincoln, Neb., 1965). It is interesting to note that Tomashevsky himself gives but an indifferent account of exposition, neither fully exploiting the terms he himself suggests nor taking into account the time-problems involved (e.g. the fictive present).

17. The term "motif," as used here, primarily designates not a recurrent and sometimes migratory thematic unit, very often reducible to smaller units, but an irreducible narrative unit, which may or may not recur. Cf. "Thématique," *loc. cit.,* pp. 268-69.

18. *The Notebooks of Henry James,* eds. F. O. Matthiessen and Kenneth B. Murdock (New York, 1961), p. 231. See also p. 55.

19. See Henry James, *The Art of the Novel,* ed. R. P. Blackmur (New York, 1962), pp. 320-21.

20. *Aspects of The Novel* (Harmondsworth, Eng., 1962; first published 1927), pp. 35, 93.

21. *Poetics,* 1452a, 20-22; trans. S. H. Butcher.

22. Nor is it a story, though clearly a narrative: Forster's categories also cover less ground than the other pair.

23. Todorov, p. 267. It should be emphasized that at this point my definition of *fabula* diverges from Tomashevsky's. I see no reason for postulating causality as a necessary condition for *fabula.* This additional condition seems to me gratuitous, since the distinction between *fabula* and *sujet* is designed to differentiate not between linkages but between the logical-chronological sequence in which the motifs might have been arranged and the order in which they are actually presented to the reader. In this context, the additive series of motifs is as much of a *fabula* as the causal, for the chronological framework common to both renders them equally amenable to the artistic deformation distinctive of the *sujet.* I see no justification, therefore, for Tomashevsky's lumping together purely descriptive books and episodic narratives as works equally devoid of a *fabula.* At any rate, while Tomashevsky would hold that story can never be equated with *fabula,* I content myself with indicating that the two concepts fail to overlap in a large number of cases, namely, whatever the *sujet* is causally concatenated as a whole or even in parts: the process of abstraction producing the story will then be markedly more drastic than that producing the *fabula,* since it will necessarily involve the elimination of the causal links too.

24. Similarly, for example, what R. S. Crane actually does in his essay on *Tom Jones* ("The Concept of Plot and the Plot of *Tom Jones,*" in *Critics and Criticism,* ed. R. S. Crane [Chicago, 1952], pp. 616 ff.) is first to reconstitute the plot-type *fabula* of this novel (pp. 624 ff.) and then to consider the functions of its deformation into a plot-type *sujet.* The use of such terms would spare the reader some quite unnecessary confusion.

25. See Bernard Weinberg's "Castelvetro's Theory of Poetics," in *Critics and Criticism*, ed. R. S. Crane (Chicago, 1952), p. 365.
26. *Essays of John Dryden*, ed. W. P. Ker (New York, 1961), Vol. I, p. 131.
27. See, for example, Günter Müller's "Aufbauformen des Romans," in *Zur Poetik des Romans*, ed. Volker Klotz (Darmstadt, 1965), pp. 285-86.
28. *Time and the Novel* (London, 1952), p. 65.
29. *Ibid.*, pp. 65, 71. See also Müller, p. 285.
30. Henry James, "The Art of Fiction" (1884), in *The Future of the Novel*, ed. Leon Edel (New York, 1956), p. 16.
31. *The Art of the Novel*, pp. 56-57 (emphasis mine).
32. *The Future of the Novel*, p. 23; *The Art of the Novel*, p. 57.
33. James shrewdly describes a "discriminated occasion" or "scene" as "copious, comprehensive and accordingly never short, but with its office as definite as that of the hammer on the gong of the clock, the office of expressing *all that is in* the hour" (*The Art of the Novel*, p. 323).
34. *Is He Popenjoy?*, chap. 1.
35. *Time and the Novel*, pp. 96-97.
36. The point that most troubles me, however, in Mendilow's statement "Everything that antedates that point, as for instance exposition, is felt as a fictive past" is how to interpret the words "for instance." What else can antedate the fictive present—even according to Mendilow's conception of it—besides exposition? Is this a mere slip of the pen or does it suggest that had Mendilow offered a formal definition of exposition we would have found ourselves disagreeing even more than it seems to me we do?
37. As hinted above, it is often difficult to arrive at an exact computation of time-ratios. However, even a rough estimate of them in the present instance will prove highly suggestive. Suppose the reading or representational time of each of the passages is one minute. It will not be unreasonable to assume that the fictive time-section covered by the first passage is no less than forty years, while that of the second is at most an hour. The first time-ratio would then be 1:21,024,000, while the second only 1:60. It is obvious that no variation in the speed of reading or in the calculation of the represented time-sections can seriously affect the size of this disparity.
38. I wish to emphasize again that the scenic norm can be determined only contextually. Therefore, for instance, James's assertion that a scene is by definition "copious, comprehensive and accordingly never short" (*The Art of the Novel*, p. 323), is indeed valid for his own scenic norm and that of most modern authors, but does not apply to the scenic norm of biblical narrative.
39. Honoré de Balzac, *La Cousine Bette* (Verviers, n.d.), p. 109.
40. Charles Reade, *It Is Never Too Late to Mend* (London and Glasgow, n.d.), p. 6; Anthony Trollope, *Barchester Towers* (New York, 1963), p. 23; Isaac Bashevis Singer, *Short Friday and Other Stories* (New York, 1965), p. 216.
41. *Ibid.*, pp. 10, 23, 33, 64.
42. Phyllis Bentley, for instance, frequently confuses scene with summary as a result of her awareness of only one criterion that distinguishes between them. She claims: " 'There drove up a coach'—we are being told of a specific action at a specific time in a specific place; that is a scene" (*Some Observations on the Art of Narrative* [London, 1946], p. 19). According to her, then, the only *differentia specifica* of a scene is its "specificity" (what I call "concrete-

ness"). This single criterion, however, is, by itself, inadequate for distinguishing "scene" from "summary," as can be concluded even from an examination of Bentley's own illustrations. She maintains, for instance, that the sentence "Elisabeth passed the chief of the night in her sister's room" (p. 9) is definitely not a scene but a summary. But according to her own criterion, she should have pronounced this to be a scene, for here too the reader is "being told of a specific [i.e. non-recurrent] action at a specific time in a specific place." It is, in fact, summary because of its lack not of concreteness but of specificity (in my sense of the words), which is revealed by the striking disparity between its representational time (only a sentence) and its represented time (a whole night). In other words, a scene must be both specific and concrete. A narrative passage that lacks either of these defining properties is summary. Most expositional summaries, however, lack both in varying degrees.

NOTES TOWARD
A COMIC FICTION

ROBERT BERNARD MARTIN

The title of this essay is intended literally, for I do not propose a complete theory of either comedy or the comic novel—only some possible ways of looking at them. I am aware that most writers on comedy present themselves at the outset as totally flexible, then gradually reveal their unwillingness to consider more than one aspect of it; suffice it to say that I know only too well that I have not covered all, or even very many, of the aspects of comic fiction, and that what I have to say is often directly applicable only to that kind of comedy usually defined as "wit," although I want to suggest that it is intimately related to other forms.

To look at even a part of so enormous a topic as the comic novel necessarily involves sketchiness and some local discontinuity. To lessen the effects of the latter, let me say that I first want to emphasize the distinctions between the intention of the writer, the comic work itself, and the effect upon the audience. Then, in what may seem contradictory fashion, I want to suggest that there has been too much hair-splitting expended upon the naming and isolation of various kinds of comedy, to the detriment of understanding it as a whole. Finally, I want to consider the likeness in effect between some rhetorical devices and the characters and structure of comedy.

In this kind of investigation, it is manifestly impossible to confine ourselves to the novel for either theory or example. The novel is a newcomer, and centuries of comic theory antedate its birth. More importantly, comedy is a fundamental attitude of the human mind, transcending such differences as those between narrative, dramatic, or lyric forms. And we must be prepared to think of comedy as only part of a work as well as the whole; there may be comedy in otherwise non-comic novels, precisely as comedy occurs in much great tragedy. If these remarks seem to tend toward denying the existence of a discrete entity known as The Comic Novel, the impression is correct, for it is my belief that the importance of comedy lies in its likeness to other forms of art, not in its differences from them.

Comedy has had a mixed press for a long time, in part, no doubt, because of its phallic origins, more immediately because of its connections with the stage and with laughter and immoderate behavior. It is not a mode that has conspicuously flourished under the aegis of puritanism.

We often think of the Renaissance as holding both its sides, but that impression is seldom borne out by the literature of the period. Sir Philip Sidney had a distinct lack of faith in comedy; with St. Paul he deplored laughter as "only a scornful tickling," and trusted comedy only when it mixed with laughter "that delightfull teaching whiche is the end of *Poesie*." Ben Jonson fretted about the presence in comedy of laughter, "a kind of turpitude, that depraves some part of a mans nature." We may even wonder how much Shakespeare consciously trusted what he so brilliantly practiced. To be sure, we have his comedies and large sections of the tragedies and histories, but it is perhaps worth remembering that Hamlet, Cleopatra, Jaques, Falstaff, Edmund, even Iago, all have the amused, detached kind of perception associated with comedy, and we may reasonably suspect that Shakespeare felt some distrust of such characters.

Jeremy Collier's *Short View of the Immorality and Profaneness of the English Stage* in 1698 embodied rather than created an attitude so strong that most of the next century was spent in apology for comedy. Novelists and playwrights usually know better than critics (even when, like Jonson, they are the same person), and distrust of the mode did not mean a diminution in its production. Nor did it in the nineteenth century, although the official view of the Victorians might be represented by that rather priggish young Rugbeian, the grave Tyrian trader, whom Matthew Arnold represents as flying the unseemly laughter coming to his ears from the merry Grecian coaster.

And it is in a century not a million miles from our own that the solemnities of Lawrence have been promoted to a position in a Great Tradition that excludes Fielding and admits Jane Austen only for her "moral preoccupation." An indication of how often comedy is regarded with suspicion as something apart from the mainstream of literature is found in the way that one speaks of poetry as distinct from comic poetry, of the novel contrasted to the comic novel. (Whoever spoke of The Tragic Novel?) To many persons it is so clear as to call for no remark that comedy does not treat serious subjects, and hence is not to be taken as more than frivolous. To such low seriousness comedy remains an aberration, mawkish earnestness the norm.

But puritans will accept anything so long as they are sufficiently assured both that it is good for one and that it is not enjoyable. Like most defensive actions, the defense of comedy has too often been an implicit acceptance of defeat, justifying it by an appeal to the very principles of the puritans, saying that it does not lead to laughter and that it serves as a corrective in a naughty world—like a quintessential Trabb's boy, derisively imitating one's pretensions down the centuries.

What has been too frequently lacking is the simple statement that the purpose of comedy is that of all great art, the enlightenment of the mind by any examination of the meaning of symbolic experience. "We dare not contemplate an Atlantis," wrote Charles Lamb in a passage too often derided without comprehension, "a scheme, out of which our coxcombical moral sense is for a little transitory ease excluded. We have not that courage to imagine a state of things for which there is neither reward nor punishment. We cling to the painful necessities of shame and blame. We would indict our very dreams." Lamb was writing of a specific kind of comedy, but his words have wider application than he intended and than many critics have seen. Comedy is neither more nor less moral than other art, but certainly, as I hope will be clear from what follows, I do not think it is any more didactic than others.

To justify comedy by appeal either to the writer's intentions or to its effect upon the audience is the result of a basic misunderstanding of what art is about, for it is to substitute for the work that which precedes it and that which follows from it. Purpose and effect are obviously most intimately related to art, but they differ from it both temporally and in kind. Any sensible critic will take into account the author's intention and the effect upon an audience, but they are both separate from art, precisely as they are separate from one another.

It ought to be no longer necessary to insist much upon the error of judging a work largely or wholly by the purposes of the author, for one of the most significant developments in twentieth-century criticism has been the investigation by aestheticians of what Professor Wimsatt has called "the intentional fallacy." Nonetheless, much modern criticism, although perhaps no longer feeling the need of justifying comic writing, still slips back into description of the author's intentions as definition of the work, almost as if it were a reversed form of intellectual biography of the writer.

At the other end of the scale, taking the effects of comedy as definition has led to other kinds of imprecision, notably in the consideration of laughter. There are many volumes on its physiology, meaning, and causes without any appreciable agreement among the writers, and from the somewhat unrewarding investigation of laughter many writers have veered gradually off into a consideration of the nature of comedy without apparent awareness that they were changing their grounds of consideration. Bergson, for instance, called his study of comedy by the generally inappropriate title of "Le Rire." In *The Secret of Laughter* Anthony M. Ludovici proceeds from a belief that laughter is concealed aggression (he actually substitutes "show teeth" for "laugh") to a condemnation of comedy. But, as most writers have noticed, laughter is not produced by comedy alone, and it is not the only effect of it, either. Although we all know (unless we set out to write about comedy) that laughter is the *typical* result of comedy, it is obvious that we cannot work backwards and say that comedy is that which produces laughter. This would be to suggest that the test of a work of art is a physical response, thus reducing it to the level of cookery and the production of gastric juices. Music is not judged by whether it sets the toes to tapping, nor sculpture by whether it stimulates the viewer to touch it, although either of them may produce such a physical response. Laughter is the province of the psychologist, perhaps of the physiologist, and comedy is the critic's territory.

Nor can we say that comedy is that which produces any other specific result in its audience, even if a less physical result than laughter—whether sympathy, moral reform, or elevation ("sudden glory," as Hobbes called it in his inspired phrase). Nothing producing a profound impression upon the mind can be said to be without effect, but the effect is unpredictable, and it is certainly incapable of use as definition. Least of all is a particular lesson or moral the certain result of comedy or any other form of art. "Henceforth I learn that to obey is best," Adam is made to say, but if that is all that he has taken away from the events of *Paradise Lost*, there has been a mountain of verse to produce a very small mouse of a lesson. And if the reader of *Northanger Abbey* gains nothing from it save the injunction that Gothic novels are not adequate handbooks for the behavior of weekend guests in large country houses, Jane Austen has been uneconomical, to say the least. Any member of an audience believing that the right true end of comedy is instruction is like the lover described by Donne who goes to sea for nothing but to make him sick.

In *Feeling and Form* Susanne K. Langer addresses the problem: "When we say that something is well expressed, we do not necessarily believe the expressed idea to refer to our present situation, or even to be true, but only to be given clearly and objectively for contemplation."[1] If what is expressed need not be true, then surely we are not being taught in any simple way in comedy; and if we cannot bring our own attitudes to bear on art, then, conversely, the author's attitudes cannot be imposed upon us as readers. Contemplation is not the same as being taught, although it may have much to do with the illumination that flashes upon the inward eye, as those daffodils of Wordsworth's did. It is a hard saying, but a true one, that art, literal truth, and didacticism are not necessarily coincident.

The concert scene in *Howards End* is Forster's terse commentary upon the relationship between audience and work of art. Mrs. Munt waits for a tune to which she can surreptitiously tap her feet; Fräulein Moseback thinks how German it all is; Helen loses herself in dreams of heroes and goblins and gods and elephants and shipwrecks. Only Margaret hears the music. Each of the others is absorbed with his own reactions, not the music itself. Even Tibby, intent upon form, is more interested in self-congratulation than he is in the symphony. Between them Beethoven has slipped away. To judge a work by one's own response, whether it be laughter, moral reform, or mere reverie, is a sin of judgment precisely parallel to that of judging it by the intentions of the author.

Writing of opera, Ferruccio Busoni startlingly reminded us of the necessity to remove our own personalities from art: "Just as an artist, if he is to move his audience, must never be moved himself—lest he lose at that moment, his mastery over the material—so the auditor who wants to get the full operatic effect must never regard it as real, if his artistic appreciation is not to be degraded to mere human sympathy."[2] What he is suggesting is, of course, what Edward Bullough named "psychical distance," that constant awareness of the fact that art is composed of symbols and not literal reality. And of all arts comedy is most dependent upon psychical distance.[3] As part of the audience we can never afford to believe that comedy is directly relevant to us; we do not, for instance, condescend as individuals to Mr. Collins, however clearly we see his foolishness, for we know that the plane in which we exist is quite different from Jane Austen's symbolic plane in which he draws his breath. Nor can we really be instructed *directly* by comic action, for—once more—our own world is simply not that of fiction.

Susanne Langer, in talking about music, has summarized what should be our response to all art: "The content has been *symbolized* for us, and what it invites is not emotional response, but *insight*."[4]

One of the complaints of undergraduates in recent years with which I have most sympathy is that learning often appears to be a form of classification, and that the teaching of literature frequently degenerates into unimportant distinctions. The very teachers and critics who would slit their own throats before committing themselves to the "meaning" of a work will happily take the same razor and slice the work into ever-thinner slices of species, phase, or genre. George Meredith, who knew something of comedy from personal experience, found that one of the easiest ways to get into the subject when he came to write "An Essay on Comedy" was to begin dividing the topic, making distinctions between satire, humor, irony, comedy, and so on. The usefulness of his essay is in what he has to say about comedy as a whole, not as mutually exclusive types. Meredith the novelist fortunately knew too much to put up with the postulations of Meredith the critic, and even if his own novels (with the possible exception of *The Egoist*) are seldom distinguished by the silvery laughter that he proposed as the end of comedy, they are uninhibited by a tedious worry about what category they should fit into.

It would be easy to cite plenty of this kind of criticism for hundreds of years before Meredith and for a century after. Let me offer only two examples from the recent work of a competent aesthetician who finds herself slipping into the comfortable groove dug by predecessors. "For instance," she writes, "there may be a witty satire, yet such a composition in so far as it is satirical is satire and in so far as it is witty is wit." Probably true, but the problem it answers is not one about which most readers have fretted. A hundred pages later she tells us that "even comedy itself may be divided into different species, such as the farce, the sketch, the comedy of manners, the romantic, the realistic, or the heroic comedy; or again it may be divided into what is called high or low comedy, according to whether the mood of the play attains penetrating depths or whether it is merely crass and trivial."[5]

The familiar ring in these passages is surely the echo of distinctions made three centuries ago, "tragedy, comedy, history, pastoral, pastoral-comic, historical-pastoral, tragical-historical, tragical-comical-historical-pastoral," as Polonius forgot the "scene individable" in his passion for ever-finer distinction. Nor do I recall any considerable clamor for further divisions in even so magisterial a work as Northrop Frye's *Anatomy of Criticism*, where literature is carefully assigned limited plots of ground like the boundaries set up by a subdivider creating suburban gardens, and comedy is sliced up into six adjoining lots or phases. This for our wisest, as Arnold said on a similar occasion; the example of these two critics only indicates how contagious is the passion for chopping. In lesser writers the substitution of subdivision for thought is prevalent; once comedy is hacked into sufficiently tiny plots, the critic is saved any real consideration of it.

For our purposes, however, it seems sufficient to indicate something of what separates comedy from some other literary modes, and so to see a little of what distinguishes it as a whole, rather than as a loose collection of discrete types scarcely on speaking terms with one another. Let us only be certain that the boundaries are set up for the examination of what is included, rather than as a rigid immigration control to exclude undesirable aliens.

Traditionally comedy has most often been defined by opposition, with tragedy as the polar mode. The truth is that the two are more like than unlike, as Plato saw. It was he who perpetrated the amusing fraud at the end of the *Symposium* when Socrates' argument "that the true artist in tragedy was an artist in comedy also" was lost forever because all the participants had taken too much wine. It is impossible to know precisely what Socrates meant (if his tolerance for alcohol was such that he meant anything at all); what seems probable is that we shall find their community in large attitudes rather than narrow forms. So thin is the dividing line between comedy and tragedy that Northrop Frye has suggested that "tragedy is really implicit or incompleted comedy," and that "tragedy is an episode in that larger scheme of redemption and resurrection to which Dante gave the name of *commedia*."[6]

In "Discoveries" Ben Jonson approached the problem timidly. "The parts of a Comedie," he wrote, "are the same with a *Tragedie*, and the end is partly the same. For, they both delight, and teach: the *Comicks* are call'd διδασκαλοι, of the *Greekes; no* lesse than the *Tragicks.*" Then, having come close to the central fact of the matter, he became frightened at the implications of the relationship between comedy and tragedy, and turned tail, scurrying into a breathless condemnation of laughter. Probably here he meant by "teach" little more than the Aristotelian concept of art as moral instruction, even though he is pushing toward metaphor the classical idea of the writers of comedy and tragedy as teachers; unfortunately, if he had more in mind, he was too hesitant to express it. What one would like to think he intended is the assertion that comedy, like tragedy (like all great art, for that matter), teaches by freeing the fetters of the mind and illuminating the meaning of experience by symbolically setting it forth.

But this may seem too general, even too mealy-mouthed, to be of any use. To come closer to comedy and tragedy, we may notice that they share another characteristic, one not common to all art: that generic quality embracing sympathy, tolerance, acceptance, even celebration of the human condition, imperfect as it is. The attitude directly opposed to this, comprising antipathy, disillusionment, perhaps disgust, is that which informs satire. Since laughter is frequently the result of both, satire is usually treated as a branch of comedy, and comedy set up as the logical opposite of tragedy. A more valid distinction would be between comedy and tragedy on one hand, and satire on the other. Satire is the mode of rejection, while comedy and tragedy are both modes of acceptance. To their affirmation satire opposes negation. "The comic writer need not spare anything in nature, but he must not fall out with Nature herself."[7] To do so is to switch to satire. (Whatever any moralists beating the drum for affirmation may say, the attitude taken by satire does not make it "lower" than comedy or tragedy. Any mode used by Swift, Voltaire, and Mark Twain, to name three at random, is hardly to be discounted.)

Comedy, tragedy, and satire, then, are not forms of literature or genres, but formulations of modes of thought, attitudes toward the world, ways of coming to terms with the meaning of its triumphs and vicissitudes. Walpole is credited with writing that this world is a comedy to those who think, a tragedy to those who feel; the statement does not get us far in understanding the two modes, but it does indicate how dependent they are upon attitude for their existence. Form and subject matter may serve more than one point of view. The same tune may function for both "Onward, Christian Soldiers" and "Lloyd George Knew My Father," and the love of animals may receive such unlike treatments as *Black Beauty* and Faulkner's *The Hamlet.* Just as in life, modes may be combined, as *Antony and Cleopatra* has comic elements as an integral part of the tragedy and *A Handful of Dust* contains satiric elements although the novel is primarily comic; the use of unalloyed mode is certainly unusual, and it is probably undesirable, as Dr. Johnson suggested of Shakespeare's works, appealing from the critics to life.

The stubborn fact remains, however, that there are works that we think of as tragic and works that impress us as comic; and we may get a better idea of comedy by contrasting it to tragedy, not because the two are totally dissimilar, in which case there would be little reason to point out the contrast, but because their family likeness makes differences more telling.

Most dictionaries wisely skirt the problem of stating the nature of comedy by suggesting that it is distinguished by a happy ending and by amusement during the course of the action. Fair enough, so far as it goes. To take up the matter of plot first: we have already noticed that the same themes may occupy more than one mode, and we may say that the typical plots of both comedy and tragedy, if stated baldly, sound remarkably alike. One or more characters stumbles, falls, then is either rehabilitated or regenerated. Catherine Morland mistakes literary conventions for life, learns their limitations, and accepts a more realistic view of the world. Lear mistakes position for nobility, painfully learns its limitations, and embraces a transcendent view of the world. "Painfully" must be added, and "transcendent" replaces "realistic"; all the same, the pattern is nearly repetitive. Error is corrected in comedy, transmuted in tragedy.

Less is at stake for Catherine than for Lear, and both the anguish and the rewards are slighter because she has gambled less. She is rapped over the knuckles, sent home unhappy from Northanger Abbey, then rewarded with Henry. "To begin perfect happiness at the respective ages of twenty-six and eighteen is to do pretty well." In comedy, even when the hazard is greater, the reward is usually conventional; it is not out of keeping with the feeling of the mode that Angelo, Mariana, and the others down to Lucio and his whore should all but dance offstage holding hands at the end of *Measure for Measure*. Like the ending of all fairy tales, its ending is contrived—not inappropriate, but artificial in the best sense of that word. Tragedy frequently gives one the sense that the original mistake of the main character brings into being a whole chain of inexorable actions resulting in punishment far exceeding the guilt of the initial mistake. In comedy the punishment exacted for a mistake or a fault of character is usually less than strict retribution might demand. And, just as the worst punishments are suspended, the rewards are of this world, since the ethos of comedy is human and not divine. In *Amphytrion 38* or the novels of John Erskine, the loves of the gods are the stuff of comedy since they are but mirror reflections of our own. Were they not, they would probably not be comic, as animals are not comic in themselves but only as they resemble humans and appear to have human characteristics.

As the characters, the rewards, and punishments of comedy must be essentially human, so must the standards and norms by which character and action are judged. One accepts that human limitations exist in comedy; in tragedy one recognizes their existence but refuses to accept them. Tragedy deals with the dreams and aspirations of man attempting to transcend the human and immediate but constantly being forced down by the limitations of the world. Prudence then becomes irrelevant because man's essential existence is not led in a prudential world. But in comedy characters typically want to succeed in a prudential world; in the incongruity between their aspirations and their true abilities lies the comedy. It is evidence of the fact that the comic viewpoint is not necessarily one of unpleasant superiority, that we find Uncle Toby's unworldliness at least as funny as Malvolio's worldliness. In comedy one tests the limits of a prudential world, while in tragedy one tests the limits of a moral universe.

It is in part because of the "happy ending" and the limitation to the human sphere that the characteristic sense of safety is implicit in comedy. There is, to be sure, a modicum of safety postulated in almost any work of fiction by our knowledge that what is to come is the record of what has never literally happened, or that, if the fiction is an account of a "true" event, the event is chosen for its shapeliness and meaning; in other words, works of any profundity must have meaning, and therefore art is less risky than life itself because a pattern is guaranteed to be implicit in it or to have been imposed upon it. In this sense of the word even the world of *Crime and Punishment* is a safer one than the one we inhabit.

But there is another meaning of safety more to the point in comedy, and that is the sense that the action will never result in total destruction and chaos. This is not quite the same thing as a happy ending; rather, it assumes that ideas may be pursued with impunity, may be investigated in the knowledge that whatever is discovered will not cause ruin.

Of the many ways that this sense of safety may be established within a fiction, one of the simplest is that employed by Shakespeare in *Measure for Measure,* the use of a control or God-figure. The Duke announces that he is to test Angelo, and since there is no reason to distrust him, we assume that the artificiality of the environment he is creating will preserve from gross harm not only Angelo but Claudio, Isabella, and the other "seemers." The conspiracy of Don Alfonso and Despina in *Cosi fan tutte* is a guarantee that the note of sadness and desertion in the opera will never overwhelm Fiordiligi, let alone Dorabella.

In prose fiction the compact of safety between author and reader may be made directly as in *Vanity Fair,* where the authorial preface is Thackeray's assurance that the Wicked Nobleman will not prevail, that the Becky Puppet will continue her liveliness, that nothing untoward will happen to the Amelia Doll and the Dobbin Figure. Even the presence of a narrator within a novel may be a concealed acknowledgement of the presence of the author, and, by increasing our awareness that what we are reading is a fiction, contribute to our sense of safety. Obviously, in all these cases the assurance springs from patent artifice and artificiality and is related to the psychic distance that is so much more apparent in comedy than in other modes. Style alone may be used in a subtler and more characteristic way of imbuing a comic work with a sense of impunity. Surely few readers have ever been in doubt about the outcome of a novel beginning, "It is a truth universally acknowledged, that a single man in possession of a good fortune must be in want of a wife." Similarly, not many members of the audience can worry that Viola is in serious danger in the second scene of *Twelfth Night* on that Illyrian seacoast, after the gently burlesqued melancholy of the Duke and his fantastical punning on the hunting of the hart. After the establishment by language of that tone of deliberate artificiality, catastrophe cannot really threaten either Elizabeth Bennet or Viola.

Opening sentences are clearly not the only guides to what is to follow, but surprisingly often they set the tone of an entire book. "I wish either my father or my mother, or indeed both of them, as they were in duty both equally bound to it, had minded what they were about when they begat me." Or, more than a century and a half later: "Stately, plump Buck Mulligan came from the stairhead, bearing a bowl of lather on which a mirror and a razor lay crossed." The comic mode announces itself at the outset of *Tristram Shandy* and *Ulysses*. "The refined moon which served Blandings Castle and district was nearly at its full, and the ancestral home of Clarence, ninth Earl of Emsworth, had for some hours now been flooded by its silver rays." One need never have heard of P. G. Wodehouse before to know from its opening words that the events of *Full Moon* will never carry out a threat to the inhabitants of Blandings.

At the beginning of the Prelude to *The Egoist*, Meredith flatfootedly states his intention: "Comedy is a game played to throw reflections upon social life, and it deals with human nature in the drawing-room of civilized men and women, where we have no dust of the struggling outer world, no mire, no violent crashes, to make the correctness of the representation convincing." It is a return to Thackeray's manner, and a modern reader's blood temperature is apt to lower considerably at the sight of Meredith's finger wagging admonishingly. The beginning of the first chapter, however, moves away from the author's intentions to the fictional world that he is creating, and we are again with Jane Austen or Wodehouse or Sterne or Joyce or Shakespeare: "There was an ominously anxious watch of eyes visible and invisible over the infancy of Willoughby, fifth in descent from Simon Patterne, of Patterne Hall, premier of this family, a lawyer, a man of solid acquirements and stout ambition, who well understood the foundation-work of a House, and was endowed with the power of saying No to those first agents of destruction, besieging relatives."

What is shared by these examples is an ironical tendency toward comic overstatement, and the clue is in the tone and diction. "High fantastical," "a truth universally acknowledged," "they were in duty both equally bound to it," "stately, plump Buck Mulligan," "the refined moon," "those first agents of destruction, besieging relatives"— all state a point of view that is outrageously invalid, and our recognition of the overstatement, by the deliberate falsity of the diction, establishes a world of artificiality, of comic safety. The interplay between statement and tone is like that in much comic opera; the effect of such interplay in these prose examples can be paralleled by the discrepancy between the elaborate punctilio of Verdi's Dame Quickly curtseying to Falstaff, and the delightful overstatement in the orchestra accompanying her repeated "Reverenza." Surely, no one was ever taken in by either her gesture or her address.

Overstatement, however, may operate as more than mere pattern of speech, for its rhetorical artificiality frequently acts as mirror to one of the most typical forms of characterization in comic works, that of the "humor" character (or mechanical, in Bergson's more modern term), whose responses are not only predictable but greater than is demanded by the stimulus. Mrs. Elton is the very pattern of the ill-bred snob, Don Quixote the definition of the romantic, Micawber outrageously beyond the bounds of probability, and so on through many of the vivid figures that give life to the pages of comedy. Not one of them is conceivable in life as we know it, however magnificently alive they are within the covers of the novels they inhabit. They are all examples of overstatement and exaggeration in character, developments of merely rhetorical exaggeration. Yet such is the safety felt in comic writing that each of them may be investigated and extended to the furthest possible limit of his humor without his incurring the punishment for deformity of character that would be exacted of him in tragedy. Defects of character may at last be gently corrected by the comic spirit, as Meredith suggested, as they are in Emma or Don Quixote, but they may equally well be noticed and left unchanged, as they are in Mrs. Elton and Sancho Panza. Even the Malvolios and Sir Willoughbys, although they are worsted at the end of the plot, are not disastrously punished for their failings (although they may believe themselves to have been).

As rhetorical overstatement may be related to comic characterization, so other rhetorical devices may underlie basic kinds of comic thought. " 'Tis better to have loved and lost," Overton assures us in *The Way of All Flesh*, "than never to have lost at all." To explain painfully the point of a fairly simple joke, it seems to me that when we recover from the surprise of the statement, we recognize that Butler is comically reversing the meaning of the Tennysonian line, and in so doing is commenting slyly upon its validity. At a fairly elementary level we can see that there is a real congruity between the verbal technique of the line and Butler's whole pattern of thought in the novel, which is a reversal of Victorian truisms in almost every field of human existence: the church proves to be devilish; the law perpetuates injustice; evolution becomes regression; and so on. Although most of us would not be disposed to accept the emendation as a true statement about life in general, we are forced to agree that within the context of the novel, loss is preferable to love. We have set out upon the familiar path of a quotation, slipped, nearly fallen, and upon recovering ourselves, found that we were going in a direction for the moment preferable to that along which we thought we were going.

Only a man with a heart of stone, Oscar Wilde once said, could fail to laugh at the death of Little Nell. Although not using a quotation on which to ring changes, Wilde is here employing the same general technique as that of Butler—using well-worn counters to lure us into unthinking acquiescence, then abruptly tricking us into attention by the startling substitution of word, and finally leaving us with a sense that the amended statement really makes more sense than the expected one.

Expectation, frustration of expectation, fulfillment that is dependent upon both the expectation and its frustration. It is surely part of a fundamental rhythm that is basic to much of man's thinking and perception, and it may be stated in other terms. "Thesis, antithesis, synthesis" will do for one set. Nor should we assert that the rhythm is uniquely the property of comedy, since it clearly underlies most conclusive thought. What we must notice about the whole proposition is that comedy is part of the mainstream of thought, not a mere tributary, and that not only in subject but in manner it may be allied to all other serious forms of speculation.

It has frequently been noted that tragedy occurs when there is a necessary choice to be made between two or more equally desirable alternatives, none of which is despicable. And the ending is "unhappy" because there is never a resolution of true alternatives; it is necessary to transfer one of them into another plane, by translating it into new terms, before they can be resolved, and then they have ceased to be true alternatives. Lear is most "truly" king when he is stripped of earthly position; but one must redefine kingship in spiritual terms to make that statement true. When one has done that, the conflict between position and nobility has actually ceased to exist, and the conclusion of the tragedy is more a restatement of what has erroneously appeared to be a dilemma than a resolution of that dilemma.

In comic writing the resolution most characteristically occurs not after redefinition of terms in order to avoid a dilemma, but when it is recognized that the dilemma never truly existed and that the perception of one has been based upon a mistake. Although Elizabeth Bennet has grown in maturity, so that she can redefine the relationship of man and woman, it is less that redefinition that fits her to marry Darcy than it is her learning that her initial idea of him was mistaken. *First Impressions* was Jane Austen's title for the original version of *Pride and Prejudice,* and it might serve as generic title for much of comedy.

What has this to do with the aphorisms of Butler and Wilde? Simply that the verbal pattern of their statements is a pattern that is repeated in large in the structure of comedy, and that the same pattern informs both language and action. Language and action both begin in the expectation of a particular movement, are diverted because the expectation is thwarted, and find a resolution that is unlike one's original expectations.

In language one may notice the same pattern or rhythm in other figures of speech, such as the epigram, and particularly in that figure most commonly associated with comedy, the pun. At bottom the function of a pun is like that of rhyme in poetry: to link by virtue of sound two words or phrases that would otherwise be totally discrete. In poetry, as in punning, the linkage may remain at the simple level of sound-likeness, or it may rise to bringing forth a new relationship, one that would not be discovered without the likeness of sound. Or, to put it another way, simple puns and rhymes are almost fortuitous, but at a more complex level they may be a way of thought. Both kinds are abundantly exemplified in Nabokov's novels. Shakespeare's interminable puns on the points of swords and the points of hose might serve as egregious examples of the fortuitous pun. A good pun may be as uncomplicated as Joyce's "Alfred Lawn Tennyson" or more involved, like the malapropism (which is only a form of unconscious punning) made by an acquaintance of mine with an inadequate knowledge of French, who referred to a married couple and the wife's lover as a *"dommage à trois."* In both cases we are jerked up short when expecting a hackneyed repetition; the unexpected resulting phrase gives new meaning to the old.

What I am suggesting then is that comedy is frequently built upon the paradox, or at least upon that aspect of paradox defined in the *Concise Oxford Dictionary* as a "seemingly absurd though perhaps well-founded statement." Schopenhauer proposed long ago that paradox was a fundamental part of comedy, but I should like to extend the meaning of the rhetorical figure to include the whole paradoxical turn of mind so often found in comedy, reflecting itself in the rhythm of language, structure, action, and character.

Laughter, as we have noted, is closely allied to comedy although not an indispensable part of it. Bergson is certainly correct in asserting that we laugh at rigid, mechanical, repetitive action, but what he does not go on to say is that we laugh even more when we are expecting continued repetition from a character but are disappointed in our expectation. Because the character has been inhuman in part, we are led to think that he is totally inhuman, and then humanity in the form of inconsistency reasserts itself. Repetition is comic; an unexpected break in that repetition is more so; and best of all is recognition of a pattern that comprehends them both. The theory of incongruity goes far toward explaining comedy but stops short of the best sort, in which the incongruous is finally seen to be congruent to a larger pattern than that which was originally perceived.

One of the examples of laughter that has often perplexed writers is that of the child who laughs when his rattle is brought out from behind our back where it has been hidden. It is true that the baby has no intellectual grasp of comedy, but this laughter is a precocious response to that fundamental rhythm that I have called paradoxical. Approach the child and give him a toy, and he may gurgle with pleasure, but there will probably be no sudden burst of laughter. However, if one holds it in both hands until he has noticed it, then thrusts it into a rear pocket, holds up both empty hands, finally holds the toy up again and gives it to him, his reaction will be quite different. His laughter will be a response to a pattern that has been momentarily obscured and that now takes into account both the apparently incomprehensible disappearance of the toy and its subsequent revelation. His response is a fundamental kind of pleasure in the rhythm of paradox, like ours in seeing the apparently inhuman made human. What has happened is not comedy, but it is closely allied to it, stemming from the same deep-seated rhythm; it is what Sydney Smith called "the sensation of wit."

This same rhythm may extend far beyond the restricted area of individual actions or even of language, to inform a particular scene or shape an entire work. In Shakespeare one of the most extended comic scenes is that of the account of the "men in buckram" in *Henry IV, Part I*. So conditioned have we been by Falstaff's habitual selfishness and mendacity that we share Poins's expectation of the "incomprehensible lies" that he will tell for his own profit and pleasure. During Falstaff's account of the robbery we shift almost imperceptibly from laughing at him to laughing with him as we discover that he has somehow realized that the Prince was one of those who took the money from him. We probably do not know at what point the realization took place, any more than the baby knows how the toy was made to disappear, but our mystification is swallowed up by seeing what we should have known all the time: that Falstaff is quicker than the Prince and that he takes as much pleasure from being the object of amusement as he does from tricking others. The kind of safety that underlies the comic situation is fairly complex. The sort that is apparently guaranteed to us initially is that promised by the complicity of the Prince in the robbery (which is not unlike the sense of safety provided by Don Alfonso and Despina in *Cosi fan tutte*); that sort proves illusory, Falstaff emerges as the real master and guarantor of the situation, and the completion of the action is not in terms that we have been led to expect, although the resolution has constantly been implicit in the action.

Like *Henry IV, Part I,* Elizabeth Bowen's *The Heat of the Day* contains superbly comic scenes in a whole that is not finally so. In both novel and play the illumination of the plot is the gradual revelation of the significance of the two men on either side of the central character, and in both works death is the worm in the bud. Early in the novel Stella attends the funeral of a cousin by marriage; although they had never met him while he was alive, two of the most reliable patients from the mental home in which Cousin Francis died on a visit are brought to the funeral to add to the scanty number of mourners. "The two were told nothing more than that this was the funeral of a gentleman who had died: they enjoyed themselves quietly and asked no questions." The best of the comedy is not that there is a surprising and perhaps incongruous attitude exhibited (the expected sadness of the funeral shown to be a source of enjoyment), but that this is, finally, the proper expression of a group of persons who are not really mourning Cousin Francis. The structure of the scene and the development of Harrison's character within it echo the rhythm of the witty language in a series of apparent advances countered by cool withdrawals, working toward funny and determinedly unsentimental resolutions. Ironically, in a book so concerned with death, the funeral becomes one of the few happy scenes in the novel. Perhaps only in retrospect do we recognize that the tone of the chapter has been set at its beginning by the hilariously muddled view of the rest of the party that Harrison is at the wrong funeral, "performing a pious duty" under a mistaken impression. It is a novel much occupied with the unmasking of wrong assumptions, and the comedy of the funeral scene parallels the main concerns of the book, in language, character, and structure, all operating with the rhythm of paradox.

The same sort of rhythm informs the wonderful bedroom scene at Lady Booby's house, which moves even that habitually grave lady to laughter and threatens danger to the person and morality of saintly Parson Adams before Fielding restores order and we realize that all along Adams's innocence has been so constant as to baffle the threat of evil and insure the ultimate restoration of that order. In *Emma* the plot clicks into place when the thought darts through Emma "with the speed of an arrow, that Mr. Knightley must marry no one but herself!" All her manipulations of Harriet, her flirting with Frank Churchill, and her trifling with Mr. Knightley are suddenly resolved as she belatedly recognizes the unacknowledged premises upon which her actions have been reared.

These examples all take an initial exaggeration or overstatement of idea or situation or character, investigate it with impunity and without arousing undue apprehension in the spectator or reader, and complete it with a resolution essentially paradoxical in feeling. All are dependent upon the sense of safety we have previously noticed. Without that, the departure from the expected (whether in language, action, or character) would not provide us with the delighted sense of rightness in the completed paradox. Adams's innocence, the misapprehensions of the funeral party, the basic good sense of Emma: all have provided us with a sense of security. In short, action, character, and structure have all been operating as paradox, which is initially a function of language. What they have in common is a fundamental rhythm that makes their community more important than their differences. And equally, from the point of view of comedy, the likenesses between, say, *Cosi fan tutte, Henry IV, Part I, Don Juan,* and *Emma* are at least as important as the fact that they come from the disparate forms of opera, drama, poetry, and fiction. Since the eighteenth century the characteristic vehicle of English comedy has been the novel, but the novel is inseparable from comic practice in general.

In its concern with a reconciliation of two seemingly opposed movements, the comic novel that operates paradoxically is like other symbolic writing in that it indicates the structure of a harmonious world by showing the nature of correspondence between apparently disparate aspects of existence. One speaks in "plain" language when advancing an argument of which one is unsure; only with certainty can one chance the associations of imagery or symbolism. In the same way, it is not safe to laugh at ideas until they are securely based. It seems to me that comedy is more than the province of intellect that Walpole suggested; it is the exclusive domain of the mature intellect.

In his *Letters on Aesthetic Education* Schiller wrote: "Man sports only when he is man in the full signification of the word: and then only is he complete man when he sports." The syntax is perhaps gnomic, the significance transparent.

NOTES

1. London: Routledge & Kegan Paul, 1953, p. 26.
2. *Entwurf einer neuen Aesthetik der Tonkunst,* here quoted from Susanne K. Langer, *Philosophy in a New Key* (Cambridge, Mass.: Harvard University Press, 1957), p. 223.
3. " 'Psychical Distance' as a Factor in Art and as an Aesthetic Principle," *British Journal of Psychology,* V, 1912, part 2, pp. 87-118. It should be noticed, however, that Bullough believes that comedy has little psychical distance (p. 111).
4. *Philosophy in a New Key,* p. 223.
5. Marie Collins Swabey, *Comic Laughter: A Philosophical Essay* (New Haven and London: Yale University Press, 1961), pp. 30 and 128.
6. "The Argument of Comedy," in *English Institute Essays,* 1948, ed. D. A. Robertson, Jr., Columbia University Press, New York, 1949, pp. 65 and 66. See also *Anatomy of Criticism* (Princeton: Princeton University Press, 1957), p. 215, where the earlier statement is modified.
7. L. J. Potts, *Comedy* (London: Hutchinson, 1949), p. 154.

THE AESTHETICS OF THE SUPRA-NOVEL

IRVING H. BUCHEN

The novel remains still, under the right persuasion, the most independent, most elastic, most prodigious of literary forms.

HENRY JAMES

Theory seems to me to be the very anathema of the novel.

BRIAN GLANVILLE

Henry Miller cherished chaos because he wished to preside over a condition of primeval plenitude that would minister to the presumptuous demands of his vision:

> We have evolved a new cosmogony of literature, Boris and I. It is to be a new Bible—*The Last Book.* All those who have anything to say will say it here—*anonymously.* We will exhaust the age. After us not another book—not for another generation, at least. . . . We shall put into it enough to give the writers of tomorrow their plots, their dramas, their poems, their myths, their sciences. The world will be able to feed on it for a thousand years to come. It is colossal in its pretentiousness. The thought of it almost shatters us.[1]

Miller can claim that *Tropic of Cancer* is to be the last book only because, theoretically at least, there exists a first book which contains in miniature all the seminal impulses of the original form; pretty much as Miller's final work would house all the essential sources of the first book's content. Such a supra-novel, like Miller's new Bible, also has an eternal or near eternal run; for although it waits patiently at the edge of time for its substance in this world, its possibilities are never fully exhausted by any single sensibility in history or by the history of sensibility. However, unlike Miller's last book, the supra-novel withholds as much as it gives; for it reminds the novelist that the bounty of possibilities from which he made his original selection does not automatically confer bounty upon the particular novel he has made. In other words, the supra-novel reserves its final fullness so as to compel the search for fecundity in the finite. If the original choice fails to stir fully or to contain meaningfully the fleshing of form, the supra-novel is eternally available for negotiation, although under stiffer terms. The immediate insight thus made available to theory of the novel is that the form is not only paradoxically both accommodating and demanding, but also more demanding the more accommodating.[2] Moreover, such interaction is never a removed or theoretical consideration for novelists but appears regularly and intimately in the tasking contention between an author's vision and his acts of embodying that vision.[3]

Although the infinite lure of the supra-novel is tempting, the fact remains that from the point of view of the mortal novel, eternal time is no time and eternal space is no space. Indeed, although each novel has what the other desires, no direct exchange is possible; the infinite can no more survive in this world than the finite can exceed the bounds of time and space. The permanent parameters that thus determine the tension between supra-novel and mortal novel are those of immortality and death—of eternal beginnings and mortal endings. Nevertheless, within that arena, a high and a low, adjusted compromise is possible. The immortal promise of the novel appears in the prospect that finite time and space will be accepted and affirmed as necessary evils in an ambitious journey to all time (eternal time) and to all space (eternal space). The mutable peril appears in the prospect that finite time and space will be resented and regarded as more evil than necessary in a narrowing journey to a tyrannical reduction of time (timely time) and space (current space).

Now what I wish to extract from this rapid discussion as an enormous illusion or a minimum claim is that the novel form, apart from whatever a novelist brings to it or whatever a critic makes of it, has a distinct and separate identity of its own. In other words, every act of artistic or critical containment is not solely an act of the artist or the critic but a contribution of the form itself. To postulate otherwise is to assume that the genre has no specific identity or laws governing its nature other than those novelists or critics impart to it. Novelists generally are saved from such presumption in that the demands they make on the form invite counter demands by the form. In other words, the initial relationship with the *Ur*-novel is not a terminal one but reappears in the secular, aesthetic relationship the novelist sustains with his yet-to-be-created world. Whatever control the choice from a plenitude of possibilities confers on the novelist, he inevitably is surrounded and perhaps submerged by a bountiful world of man and matter. To be sure, control can be maintained or regained by rooting it in a central character who tyrannically contains all that happens and thus stems the tide. But the pressure of the supreme form reminds him that he has made a choice—a narrowing, finite choice—and he either has to surrender the whole or fight for the wholeness of a single point of view. Or the novelist may disappear into history or myth and allow the story organically to tell itself. But he, too, has made a choice—a larger, finite one—but he may have to give up the uniqueness of individuality or fight for the archetypes of individuality. But whatever strategy the author employs, unless and until he recognizes that his personal artistic struggle is of a piece with the contention between the supra-novel and the mortal novel, he neither will involve his novel in a journey to all time or space nor share with the novel the joint authorship of an enduring mutable world. An initial choice thus haunts a novel to its end, and unless that mortal end bends and returns to its immortal origins, form does not unify or strain with strength.[4] What determines the significance of a novel is not any particular formalistic doctrine which separates the aesthetic identity of the author from the aesthetic identity of the form.[5] What determines it is the intensity of the relationship between the individuality of any single novel and the collective nature of the supra-novel; for the most enduring singular novels are finally as collective in nature as the *Ur*-novel is individually accommodating in form.

For the theoretician, another value of assuming a supra-novel is to urge a repositioning of theory. If theory primarily inhabits the lofty, eternal realm reserved for the *Ur*-novel, then it either may disdain good middle novels which have no Olympian pretensions or risk articulating and defining essences which exceed its capacity for formulation. If theory is essentially earthbound and in chameleon fashion shapes itself only to finite, relativistic versions of eternal possibilities, then it may either cut itself off from being responsive to presumptuous works or settle exclusively for specifics that preclude comprehensiveness. But if theory situates itself midway so that it is subject to the same cross-currents of immortality and death that beset the novelist, then theoreticians cannot only develop a theory informed by the aesthetic collisions and collusions of the form, but also measure the achievement of novelists in a range that runs from mortals to demigods. Equally as important, such a straddling of heaven and earth grants theory the historical perspective to survey the capacity of the novel to create new possibilities, revive old forms, and even tolerate last books or anti-novels[6] which seek its silence or destruction; for the aesthetic fullness of the form is inconceivable apart from its historical plenitude. Unfortunately, the present theory of the novel, which often reads like a technology of the novel,[7] assumes that the novel is either so spent or devoid of any aesthetic integrity that it can be processed or defined with finality. Equally as unfortunate, such assumptions often are supported by a view of literary history which has either denied or impoverished the aesthetic identity and protean nature of the novel and created further obstacles to a study of both.

I

History is the temporality of the eternal.

J. V. LANGMEAD CASSERLEY

Perfection is possible only in the short story, not in the novel. The short story is like a room to be furnished; the novel is like a warehouse.

I. B. SINGER

The standard historical way of containing the novel is to put it in its place—to subdue it to narrative, as Robert Scholes and Robert Kellogg have done,[8] or to dub it a form of fiction, as Northrop Frye has argued.[9] Frye is worth pursuing on this point. Frye objects to the "novel-centered view of fiction" because he believes fiction should not be limited to the novel and because writers like Swift and Carlyle should not be denied their birthright as fictionists. In place of the novel-centered view, Frye offers what is by now his justifiably famous classification of fiction into four forms. But there are a number of problems, not the least of which is the complete disappearance of the term "novel" as a comprehensive form and the substitution for it of "fiction" which is not so much defined as subdivided. The strategy is clear: hurry Swift and Carlyle past the entry gate and house them in the separate mansions of anatomy and confession. But clearly even the most illuminating definitions of sub-genres are no substitution for the definition of the genre itself, whatever its designations. In addition, no question is ever raised as to why the novel or fiction sorted itself into these particular four estates; what common denominators, if any, bind them together; and whether Frye's categories, which have an air of finality about them, preclude that there will be a fifth or sixth. However, if instead of rapidly shifting forms or overleaping a troublesome point of origination, Frye had maintained that the novel or fiction is not so much a definable form but an entrée to a gracious *Mansfield Park* or a cluttered *Bleak House,* he would properly have described the novel as a process, not a product. Surely, it is not a little to say that the novel is more a way of traveling than a point of arrival; more an invitation to wander than a secure niche; and more akin to the way a man enters and meanders through this world than to an assured resting place in the afterlife. To be sure, the novel is grossly democratic, and through such an enormous gate the inept may crowd through along with the talented. But to overleap its indiscriminate democratic openness for a rapid journey to aristocratic preserves not only severs the pilgrim from his paradise, but also totally obscures the entire issue of why the talented survive the journey and the inept do not.

Does this mean that every act of historical definition must prostrate itself helplessly before the amorphous nature of the novel or settle for definitions which are so blurred that no real clarity is possible? Not by any means. The key problem, as it was for theory, is one of bridging, except here the positioning is historical rather than metaphysical. The claims and counter-claims of a novel-centered view of fiction or a fiction-centered view of the novel, as long as they remain opposites rather than versions of each other, merely involve the substitution of one literary ideology and time scheme for another. What is needed is an historically centered view of the novel which is governed by a novel-centered view of history. Frye's characteristic way of proceeding is to root himself in bondage to the Classical period and thereby tip the chronological scale in favor of fiction as the more dominant form. Equally distortive would be a modern approach, which uses the dominance of the novel to work backwards and belittle versions at the older end of the historical line. But if the novel-centered view of the novel has any one clear contribution to make, it is the idea that the novel as a protean form moves back and forth in time and space and is as progressive, regressive, and recurrent as history is. Let me further test this trafficking between past and present with a sub-genre that gives Frye some difficulty.

One of Frye's objections to the novel-centered view of fiction is that such short shrift is given to prose romance. Merely because prose romance is older than the novel, Frye complains, it mistakenly has "developed the historical illusion that it is something to be outgrown, a juvenile and undeveloped form."[10] But who has created the problem or nourished the illusion? Novelists or literary historians? By rigidly fixing prose romance in a given set of historical factors on the one hand, and by failing to recognize the protean nature of the form to be responsive again and again to earlier forms on the other, Frye has made his view of history as static as his view of the literary form. The fact is that the evolution of culture is seldom neat, obedient, or absolutely original, and prose romances have appeared after their historical prime—Frye's fixation notwithstanding. Certainly, a novel-centered view of protean history would have avoided the silly pique of F. R. Leavis, who dubbed *Wuthering Heights* a sport and sought to export it merely because Emily Brontë had the audacity to write a prose romance when, according to the great tradition, she was not supposed to; and the equally silly exchange negotiated by Richard Chase, who sought to import the novel because it buttressed American romance.

As for Swift and Carlyle, Frye sidesteps the issue: what really determines whether Swift or Carlyle are to be given their due is not the justification of their work as anatomies or confessions but the determination of whether their anatomies or confessions, which originally drew upon the bounty of the novel, were also subject to the counter-thrusts of that form. In other words, there are fictionalized anatomies and confessions and there are anatomical and confessional novels; and they are not the same. If essentially Swift had it all his own way and failed to yield to the novel's demands to create an enduring world held together by the tension of opposition, then for all his complex cleverness what he essentially created was a fictionalized political and social tract which was so basically set from the outset that it would brook no interference. Similarly, if for all the competing points of view Carlyle created a work whose oppositional nature was always safely manageable and never overwhelming, then he essentially wrote a fictionalized confession but not a confessional novel. Novels are neither rusty bits of machinery which require lubricating footnotes to make them free-wheeling again nor a series of slack philosophical sermons which require some new breath of life. In significant novels such vitality emanates from the aesthetic contention of the form and is enriched, not sustained, by extra-literary efforts. Finally, we cannot, on the one hand, marvel at the capacity of the protean novel to function throughout history (and especially now) as the supreme time-space machine, and on the other, saddle it with a literary history that impoverishes the form as much as it does history and treats the evolution of culture as a one-way production line.

II

I am a man and alive. For this reason I am a novelist. And, being a novelist, I consider myself superior to the saint, the scientist, the philosopher, and the poet, who are all great masters of different bits of man alive, but never get the whole hog. . . . Only in the novel are all things given full play.

D. H. LAWRENCE

Theory as it now stands is more a theory of novelistic criticism than that of the novel and has achieved more coherence within itself than in terms of the form it seeks to comprehend. The reason is clear: the novel has no fixed identity and never will. Nor can its protean elusiveness ever be approximated until the perception of the form is in turn informed by the contribution of the form to that pereception. That aesthetic exchange imparts to the novel its negotiating center, for as the novelist moves his content toward meaning he encounters the novel seeking its form. What Nietzsche valued in man can be applied to the novel: "What is great in man is that he is a bridge not a goal; what can be loved in man is that he is a *going-across* and a *down-going*."[11] To be sure, under the pressure of an age and its literary traditions, it is possible to define a trend of the novel with reasonable precision, but that is at best a temporary or temporal cultural absolute. To go any further is to divest both history and the novel of their chronological infidelity or their artistic mischief. What legitimately can be defined in theoretical terms is that the novel expands and contracts within the parameters of immortality and death. What significantly can be examined in both theoretical and historical terms are the special alliances the novel forms in order to honor the amplifying and constricting demands of those parameters.

The basic and constant impulses of the novel always have been toward the panoramic or the intimate or a combination of both. The panoramic inevitably has an affinity with chronicle and, through history, naturally or presumptuously, to the collective extension of epic and myth. The intimate is invariably drawn to introspection and through psychology, humbly or desperately, to the mythic centrality of singular sensibility. The panoramic and the intimate are not accidental or occasional allies subdued to novelistic purposes. Rather their quests for collective or singular definition have about them the character of a novel. The reason history is a natural ally of the novel is that both are unfinished. All the evidence is not in and probably never will be. They thus not only mutually sustain each other, but also in significant hands are inevitably reciprocal: the novel records the form of history and the history of form. The reason psychology is a natural ally of the novel is that both are endlessly entangled in the convergence of mind and matter. And the result here, too, is reciprocal: the novel records the form of mind and matter, and the mind and matter of form. To be sure, novelists earlier and later were aware that such panoramic or psychological richness jeopardizes control—hence the attempt to arrest the proliferating multiplicity of history by reaching for the antidote of myth and the compromise of classical recurrency. And earlier and later novelists sought to still the endlessly busy and inexhaustible minutiae of the interior life by reaching finally for individualized types that promised archetypal durability. But such resistance to unbridled fecundity is not an achievement of theory or criticism but an aesthetic response to the aesthetic demands originally made by the form itself. Critics may need novels to be critics but novels do not need critics to be novels. Indeed, when the issue of the novel's pandering promiscuity is viewed not from without but from within the aesthetic identity of the form, what becomes clear is that, far from the facility of the novel being at the mercy of the novelist's manipulation, the facile novelist is clearly at the mercy of the novel's ardor. Almost all novelistic failures, especially significant ones, are the result of crushing richness. Plenitude swelled to bursting Fielding's *Tom Jones*, deluged Conrad's *Nostromo*, over-refined Proust's sensibility, and transformed Joyce in *Finnegan's Wake* into a self-parodist.

The key to the artistry of the novel is managing fecundity. The reason some novelists write themselves out in their first work is not that they have said everything but that they have not been sufficiently plagued by all the ways to say it. Whatever choice a novelist originally makes from the infinite store of possibilities available to him, all that he has excluded accompanies and tempts him along the way. The road not taken is always there to be taken or again deferred. When literary historians or critics surround a particular novel with others that resemble it, they are essentially duplicating the spectrum of choices made available to each member of the group. When a novelist has chosen wisely, then the alternatives that accompany his work situate themselves as non-competing satellites affirming the rightness of his original choice. When he has chosen foolishly, then the alternatives become part of the neglected counter-thrust of the form and enter into direct competition with the main stream of the novel and imperil its coherence and unity. The ending of *Billy Budd* provides an unusually clear example of singularity managing and sustaining multiplicity.

Melville's multiple endings display for artistic and ironic reasons a series of rejected alternative ways of telling the story of Billy Budd. Because it is possible that these alternatives did not just occur to Melville after he had finished his work but were copresent and perhaps tempting shortcuts throughout its composition, Melville essentially has defined the creative process as not solely an act of expression but an act of resistance; and his multiple endings enable him to honor both acts. His positive statement is that only art—Melville's special brand of romance and realism—can fully tell the story of Billy Budd; his negative statement is that the non-art of special pleading or of romance divorced from realism can only distort the true story of Billy Budd. The paradoxical admixture of self-expression and self-inhibition, of undisguised pride in his own craft and transparent subservience to art, not only accurately reflects the novel's aesthetic process as a negotiation between control and surrender but also suggests that, far from excluding or precluding classification on the part of theoreticians or critics, the novel actually guides such categorizing from without by virtue of the constrictions that take place from within. Nowhere is the amplifying and constricting interplay between creator and creation and between control and surrender better exemplified than in the way novels, paradoxically, begin and end.

III

Really, universally, relations stop nowhere.

HENRY JAMES

The absence of any pressure of finality, or more positively the promise of immortality, invites both a beginning without limit and an ending without end. Indeed, by virtue of its being a world continuous with and extended by the larger world, the novel is not supposed to end. And in many ways it does not. Sequels are easily posited and often actually written; John Updike just published *Rabbit Redux*. Moreover, it is standard critical practice to make all a novelist's works one or continuous with each other by examining their recurrent characters, situations, themes, and structures. Finally, it is surely not accidental that the novel thrived so long on serialization, which trained generations of authors to manage, among other things, endings that constantly were convertible into transitional beginnings. But clearly a distinction has to be made between the way a novel begins and the way it ends.

The prospect of plenitude that the novel offers, no matter how treacherously, is an accurate mirror of the possibilities of entering and meandering through this world. But the prospect of infinity that the novel offers, no matter how attractively, by rejecting conclusions, is at variance with this world. The ending of the novel is the most perilous point because that is precisely where the aesthetic beast in the jungle resides—that is the source of the novel's counter-thrusts. Underneath the beneficent face of fecundity lurks the grisly image of termination. The moment the novelist creates a beginning, he unknowingly releases an invisible ending; the life-giving act of creation subjects that life to death. Within the parameters of immortality and death, fecundity is the face of content, and termination is the agent of form. The only way the novelist can survive the embrace with death is to convert his enemy into his ally—to extract, as Jacob did in wrestling with the angel, a promise before the dawn. The promise is to transform the act of cutting off, which he cannot forestall, into an act of rounding out. The novelist survives not by overreaching for personal immortality or by collapsing helplessly before its final blur, but by extracting from it a form which sustains and even increases the life of his novel. He may, as Melville did, create an aesthetic drama which keeps permanently alive the dilemma of choosing between forms that sustain or kill. He may compel, as Joyce did, death to inhabit ancient myths and then go on to create a novel which constantly incarnated myth until death was dispossessed and myth appeared alive and expansive in Dublin. He may overwhelm death, as Sterne did, by forcing it to gorge itself like Cerberus on eternal proliferation until it burst and was forced to give back to existence its inexhaustible fecundity, which exceeds death. He may, even as Hesse did, greedily rush toward death so as to kill once and for all the stultifying notion that man is a singular identity rather than a constellation of selves that demand to live out in one lifetime the kind of diversity of lives reserved outside of life through reincarnation. He may, as Kafka did in *The Penal Colony*, build into his very work the machine of form that coincides the meaning of life with its termination and serves as the supreme summation of the aesthetic clinch of the novel. Or he finally may embrace, as Thomas Mann has Felix Krull do, the transcendence of the transitory as a legitimate escape in its own right and also as an ingenious solution to the artificiality of terminating a picaresque novel:

> The fact of life's being only an episode predisposed me in its favor. Transitoriness did not destroy value, far from it; it was exactly what lent all existence its worth, dignity, and charm. Only the episodic, only what possessed a beginning and an end, was interesting and worthy of sympathy because transitoriness had given it a soul. But that was true of everything—the whole of cosmic Being had given it a soul. Being had been given a soul by transitoriness, and the only thing that was eternal, soulless, and therefore unworthy of sympathy, was that Nothingness out of which it had been called forth to labour and to rejoice.[12]

If there is one common notion that binds together the essential attributes of the protean novel it is that of paradox; and if there is one aspect of the protean novel that I have totally neglected it is the su-

preme paradox posed by the experimental novel. I should like to conclude by summarizing the central paradoxes of the novel and add a
postscript which deals with the protean capacity of the experimental
novel to create the most ingenious solutions to the problems of form
and death.

IV

*When I reflect that the task which the artist implicitly sets himself is to
overthrow existing values, to make of the chaos about him an order which
is his own, to sow strife and ferment so that by the emotional release those
who are dead may be restored to life, then it is that I run with joy to the
great and imperfect ones, their confusion nourishes me, their stuttering
is like divine music to my ears.*

HENRY MILLER

*What an overwhelming lesson [God provides] to all artists! Be not afraid
of absurdity; do not shrink from the fantastic. Within a dilemma, choose
the most unheard-of, the most dangerous solution. Be brave, be brave.*

ISAK DINESEN

The novel is not a defined but a discovered form. Its length, direction, content, etc., are not prescribed. There is no subject too sacred
or gross for it to treat. Because it promises everything, it can be anything. If God had to create, without precedent, a world *ex nihilo*, the
novelist faces a no less exhilarating extreme: at the beginning he is
everyone, everywhere, and everything. But the way a novel begins is
not the way it unfolds. A hidden aesthetic resistance begins to impede the author's progress and challenge his omnipotence, and sooner
or later the secret sharer of fecundity turns out to be death, just as
the ironic partner of facility turns out to be overwhelming richness.
Offered generously an infinite series of initial choices, the novelist
chooses the one he believes will both sustain his created world and
grant it enduring form; for the central concern of every novel is the
survival of its world. But lest the promise of immortality be over-
whelmed or discarded by the perils of mortality and lest the necessity for finite incarnation be obscured or minimized by the lure of the
infinite, the novelist is forced to create a third world which ideally in-
corporates the essence of both. Specifically, he seeks a convergence of
time and space which reaches for the typicality of historical time and

space; he seeks an adjustment of the universal and the unique in the fullness of his representative fragment. To speak about the omniscient author or of technique as a mode of discovery apart from such permanent aesthetic negotiations is to obscure the extent to which all critical and theoretical notions are essentially borrowed descriptions of aesthetic experiences. Far from being an exclusive discovery of critics or theoreticians, the notion of technique, for example, can be applied not so much to the manner in which an author discovers or communicates his way but rather to the way the aesthetic identity of the novel communicates discovery to an author. Or to put both creators together, when the artist aligns his aesthetic identity with that of the novel so that he is as refined into his form as the form is absorbed into his novelistic world, then the way he says what he says makes form and meaning one. Even the most invisible author paradoxically remains finally a character: technique is his character, style his ego. The more impersonal he becomes, the more his world is buoyed rather than buried by matter, the more his form extracts from death the shape of completion, the closer his novel resembles the infinite extent of the supra-novel and the presumptuous daring of the experimental novel.

There are at least two kinds of experimental novels. Both build upon the basic paradoxes of the form, but whereas one finally settles for maximum paradox, the other seeks to transcend paradox completely. The essential pressure for experimentation comes from the novelist's conviction that the demands of his vision are so new and urgent and the forms available so inadequate or tired that a new form or hybrid must be created. The attendant risk is not obscurity (the experimenting novelist may cherish that possibility) but tyrannical limitation. Specifically, his experiment may be so limited to the specifics of his work that at best it may be a temporary solution to a permanent problem or a singular variation on a multiple dilemma. The inability to predict with certainty how the experiment will turn out and to what extent it may be peculiar or typical is merely the external worry of an internal uncertainty seeking a new arrangement between control and surrender. For experimentation is really controlled surprise and appears only when an author is backed up against a wall and nothing will work but his own self-astonishing way out. Afterwards, when he becomes convinced that the paradoxical game he cornered may be bigger than he himself had realized, he may crow like Dickens and ask to be called the "Inimitable." If his innovation is consolidated and extended by other hands, he may enjoy being certified as an influence. If what was new becomes, in the hands of slavish imitators, jaded, he may be designated a pernicious influence. However, the experimental novelist who seeks a transcendent solution desires to become a seminal influence.

All experimentation involves violation. Sequence is disordered, endings are given at beginnings, syntax is scrambled, transitions are eliminated, punctuation is bypassed, language is turned against itself—in short, all the linguistic binders and extenders of conventional order which insure either clarity or progression are turned generally awry. The aim is to create a condition of stasis, a moratorium in which history is halted, time is stilled and space is poised; and all await a new direction of movement which will emerge as the essential yield of the experiment. At the same time, that silent center often is preceded and followed by a dizzying or noisy swiftness. The various linguistic, stylistic, and structural violations seek not so much to destroy as to free modes of communication from the slavery of predictability or familiarity. The now more anarchistic disarray invites speedier, more spirited reconstructions or shortcuts which redeem themselves aesthetically by saying more by saying less. To be sure, the startling economy of getting someplace faster by overleaping intermediate stages risks complaints from mortals, for as Nietzsche warned, "When I ascend I often jump over steps, and no step forgives me that."[13] Above all, there is about all experimentation a certain smugness which is enormously self-possessed in its formalistic mischief. It is almost as if all experimental novels seek to reverse the function and direction of crossing the river Lethe and to compel a journey of return to, rather than a departure from, origins. The stress is always on beginnings not ends, on the fundamental assumptions of mind, man, and matter rather than on their obedient or familiar extensions which represent Lethean forgetfulness of familiarity. In other words, the center of stasis functions as a rite of passage between the insanity released by the violations and the new controlled insanity that the experiment will finally impart. Such a ritual of reorientation may be obviously advertised, as Hesse does when he forewarns his readers in *Steppenwolf* that his magic theater is "For Madmen Only," or it may be the secret method behind the madness that characterizes all the experimental novels that run from Sterne's *Tristram Shandy* to Kosinski's *Steps* to the new anti-novels. But what all experimentation has in common is the absolute determination to keep the novel moving toward its beginning rather than toward its ending; for the experimental novel is in pursuit of immortality and its various violations are not meant merely to question or to salvage the modes that sustain the reality of order but to return the order of reality to its initial and primal state of chaos. Such experimentation clearly overleaps the characteristic reciprocating negotiation of the novel form and rejects adjusted mortal endings for eternal beginnings so as to counter the infinite losses of finite incarnation. The aim is nothing less than to plumb and exhaust, fully and finally, the essence of a particular novelistic form so as to render it useless for anyone else subsequently to use. What is thus involved is not just the familiar historical aim of creating a lasting novel but the radical aesthetic aim of creating an embodied essence of the novel equal in finality and plenitude to that contained in unembodied form in the supra-novel. Such a journey back in time and space to origins is thus inevitably metaphysical, for the experimental novel seeks to achieve intimate proximity at the edge of history with the supra-novel and to affirm the protean nature of the supra-novel by becoming its most perfectly realized version and partner. Like Henry Miller, every experimental novelist believes he has written *The Last Book*.

Perhaps that is a necessary illusion, but the novel as a protean genre has the last word or is the first book, and both are yet to be finally uttered or written. Clearly, too, my own presentation here, preoccupied as it has been by clearing the field of obstacles, is neither the last word nor even the first chapter of a book on the theory of the novel. Nevertheless, I am convinced that a return to origins is the place to start. Specifically, what is needed is a theory of the supra-novel, because such a theory at least points to the existence of a definite and rigorous aesthetic identity for the novel, preserves the unfinished character of the form and its alliance with history and psychology, stresses the central parameters of immortality and death within which the novel achieves its adjusted fullness, and finally suggests that novelistic achievement can find its comprehensive standards displayed in a range that runs from immortals to demi-gods to mortals.

With such aesthetic substance, theoreticians and critics of the novel need not fret about its illegitimate origins, ape the theory of poetry, or worship the false gods of technology.

NOTES

1. *Tropic of Cancer* (1934; New York, 1961), pp. 23-24.
2. Seldom if ever is the demanding aspect of the novel discussed in theory; on the contrary the emphasis is almost always on its facility. Not surprisingly, then, theoreticians seem determined to provide the novel with the same kind of academic armor that has enabled poetry to survive the onslaughts of popularity and amateurism. That increasingly the model for novelistic theory is poetic theory is partly reflected in William J. Handy's new *Modern Fiction: A Formalist Approach* (Carbondale, Ill., 1971) which applies the methods of poetic theory to modern fiction. That the novel form does cater indiscriminately to the "democratic dregs" cannot be denied, as Margaret Kennedy noted in *The Outlaws on Parnassus* (New York, 1960): "People will often remark that they could write a marvellous novel upon their own experiences, if only they had the time; they would readily allow that more than time is required for the production of a marvelous picture, a marvelous symphony, or a marvelous sonnet. . . . So little has ever been said about the equipment necessary for a novelist that a man of wit and intellect may be pardoned for supposing that none is needed" (pp. 7, 9). The academic version of the situation was sounded earlier and more starkly by René Wellek and Austin Warren: "Literary theory and criticism concerned with the novel is much inferior in both quantity and quality to theory and criticism of poetry" (*Theory of Literature* [New York, 1942], p. 219).
3. Many theoreticians and critics are so absorbed in theory and criticism that they expect novelists to share their concerns and not be so exclusively involved with aesthetic matters and influence. The problem, I suspect, is historical. Most early theoreticians of the novel were novelists; most modern theoreticians of the novel are critics. Indeed, the steady departure of novelists from the fold of theory has led Philip Rahv to claim that unlike poets, whose critical forays have helped to shape a substantial body of theory for poetry, modern novelists have been flagrantly uncooperative:

> You can go through all the essays of Thomas Mann, for instance, without finding anything of really clinching interest for students of the novel as form; and Mann is surely an exceptionally intellectual and selfconscious artist. Nor will you find, in this respect, any truly close insights in Joyce or Proust. Both *A Portrait of the Artist as a Young Man* and *Ulysses* contain some discussions of aesthetic structure on a fairly abstract level, and these are of no help to us if we are on the lookout for the differentia distinguishing the prose narrative from the other verbal arts. . . . As for American novelists of our time such as Fitzgerald, Wolfe, Faulkner, and Hemingway, they have influenced fictional modes solely through their practice, steering clear of theoretical divagations ("Fiction and the Critics of Fiction," *Kenyon Review*, XVIII [1956], p. 279).

As far as influence is concerned, I regard as more serious the prospect that current novelistic theory seems to have had almost no real influence either on established novelists or new experimenting ones. Mailer, Grass, Borges, Barth, Donleavy, Singer, Bellow, etc., quietly have gone about their business of honoring their basic compulsions; and when their prestige provides them with a podium, they ignore theoreticians and critics and worry out loud about the nature of reality, politics, and culture or the new alliances between literature and politics and culture. Many of the new anti-novelists, who resemble enigmatic aliens from another planet, seem to regard current theoretical refinements as anachronistically earthbound. I am not suggesting that the sole or even the primary function of theory is to influence older or newer novelists; however, I do maintain that when their traditional hostility has been converted into separatist indifference, and when the gulfs between theory and novel seemed to have widened to the point where they are unbridgeable, then a one-sided victory or one won by default does not argue well for the vitality of theory or for its championing any cause except perhaps its own.

4. Edith Wharton went even further by claiming that "no conclusion can be right which is not latent on the first page" (*The Writing of Fiction,* [New York, 1925], p. 108).

5. Robert Murray Davis, in *The Novel: Modern Essays in Criticism* (Englewood Cliffs, N.J., 1969), errs in this direction, I believe, when he notes that recent critical trends happily have emphasized "the importance of the author, restoring him to a central position as shaper and craftsman that formalists would deny him on the grounds that the completed work is primary in importance and that the mimetic school tends to subordinate to the reality represented" (xi). The impression Davis creates is that the centrality of the novelist is determined solely by the critics and his visibility or invisibility by the formalistic doctrine employed. Nothing is mentioned about the author's vision or, more to the point here, the pressure that the form exerts on the author's centrality.

6. It is perhaps significant that Philip Stevick, who assembled one of the most comprehensive compilations of novelistic criticism, *The Theory of the Novel* (New York, 1967), went on to produce the first substantial compilation of anti-fictionists and in the process to exclude from that collection any criticism of theory of the novel (*Anti-Story: An Anthology of Experimental Fiction* (New York, 1971). That a serious and perhaps even unbridgeable gulf exists between theory and the form it seeks to comprehend is apparent in Malcolm Cowley's attack on Stevick's new anthology ("Storytelling's Tarnished Image," *Saturday Review* [September 25, 1971], pp. 25-27, 54). Desperately quoting from the opening lines of *Genesis,* Cowley, suffering from future shock, pleads for a return to time-saturated narrative as a way of dulling an historical irony: precisely at the point when theory has perfected its categories as a result of comprehending time in the novel, new experimental fictionists committed to space or, more unforgivingly, to space devouring time, have made those categories appear superfluous or precious.

7. This is a serious issue which I can only touch upon here. Largely in response to Wellek and Warren, a substantial body of theory, often aping poetic theory, has developed during the last thirty years. Books, articles, anthologies, handbooks, special journals devoted to the form have rapidly appeared. Even the reissue of novels has followed a new format: not allowed to stand on their own, reprinted novels have been propped up by historical antecedents and

shored up by selected current criticism. Courses on the theory and writing of the novel, often combined to create a standard of correspondence unmatched in literary history, began to produce new novelists who, like the reissue of older novelists, seemed to be buttressed both in front and in back. Finally, virtually every facet of the novel has been subjected to structural, stylistic, formalistic, epistemological processing. Aside from some outstanding seminal pieces, what is instructive about the entire theoretical enterprise is that it has created a Frankenstein.

It is one thing to observe zealous explicators overworking a novel to unearth its symbolic and mythic treasures; it is quite another to find that the same yields are being dredged up from dreadful novels that seem to have been put together on the assembly line of novelistic theory. As any critic who has proceeded with some care through the bibliography of novelistic theory and the apparently endless handbooks based on that theory is painfully aware, a pandering partnership seems to be taking place between theorists and theoretically inspired novelists. For all the cries and raised eyes to heaven about living in an increasingly mechanistic world, theoreticians have assembled all the systems and hardware to convert the craft of fiction into the technology of the novel. Older, more "humanistic" novelists find the technology dehumanizing, younger, more experimental novelists unsophisticated. The only direct beneficiaries are the academic novices who have been nurtured by courses in creative symbolizing and who are able to produce works replete with all the critical apparatus necessary to insure the right kind of popularity—the reverse snobbery of critical acceptance and analysis. Indeed, I am convinced that if we extracted all the "technology" we have theorized about or discovered in Joyce, for example, and if a new, budding Joyce were instructed as to what he had to do in theoretical terms, he would never be able to do it. T. S. Eliot provided the key warning. When Prufrock, in order to rationalize his castrating indecision, complains that he is not Hamlet or Lazarus, what Prufrock forgets is that Hamlet did not know he would become "Hamlet" and Lazarus did not know he would become "Lazarus." The novel is not a given form; it is given to be formed. To parade its complexities mechanistically or to limit its possibilities to the past is to create a theoretical standard which invites works produced by Prufrocks rather than T. S. Eliots.

8. *The Nature of Narrative* (New York, 1966).

9. "Specific Continuous Forms (Prose Fiction)," in *Anatomy of Criticism* (Princeton, 1957).

10. *Ibid.*, p. 306.

11. *Thus Spoke Zarathustra*, trans. R. J. Hollingdale (Baltimore, 1961), p. 44.

12. *Confessions of Felix Krull, Confidence Man* (New York, 1954), p. 229.

13. *Op. cit.*, p. 69.

THE GENRE
OF "ULYSSES"

A. WALTON LITZ

Standing at the confluence of so many literary traditions and genres, Joyce's *Ulysses* has become the supreme challenge for the theoretical critic of fiction. At one time or another *Ulysses* has been presented as a stark naturalistic drama, a symbolist poem, a comic epic in prose, even a conventional novel of character and situation. The problem I shall consider in this essay is easily stated: what are the rewards, and dangers, of reading *Ulysses* with a particular view of the novel *as a form* constantly in mind? If we go beyond the convenient shorthand of calling *Ulysses* a novel because it is a large and various prose work which rests heavily in the hand, and try to process it into a general theory of the novel—does this approach really yield a more delicate understanding of *Ulysses,* or does it, like so many critical strategies, produce more mischief than clarification?

We might remind ourselves at the outset that Joyce put little store in the traditional classifications of literature by type and genre. His early aesthetic, in so far as we can reconstruct it from the notebooks and *Stephen Hero,* was aggressively psychological and affective, concerned with the work's relationship to its maker and its audience. Joyce abandoned the conventional definitions of kinds derived from structure and subject matter. Instead, he defined the major "conditions" of art in terms of the artist's relationship to his creation, as in this passage from the Paris notebook:

> There are three conditions of art: the lyrical, the epical and the dramatic. That art is lyrical whereby the artist sets forth the image in

immediate relation to himself; that art is epical whereby the artist sets forth the image in immediate relation to himself and to others; that art is dramatic whereby the artist sets forth the image in immediate relation to others. . . . (6 March 1903)

Over against these broad categories, which apply to every kind of art, Joyce set the qualities of the beautiful work, borrowing his tags from Aquinas and defining "the beautiful" in relation to the act of apprehension: wholeness, harmony, and radiance are primarily phases in the mind of the audience. Similarly, tragedy and comedy are defined not in terms of structure or action, but in terms of the reader's psychology. "Stasis" is Joyce's *fin de siècle* modification of the Aristotelian catharsis, applying as in Aristotle to both tragedy and comedy; but unlike Aristotle, Joyce has nothing to say about the particular forms of comedy or tragedy, nor about the various species of literature. His early critical system is essentially a psychology of the artist and the artistic experience. The kinds of art are determined by the relationship between the artist and the image; beauty is defined through analysis of the act of apprehension. In the void between lies the work of art itself, with all its formal qualities. Like so many aesthetic theories, Joyce's is weakest where it touches the practical problems of formal criticism.

Joyce's subsequent reading of Croce (c. 1911) would have confirmed his early disregard for generic criticism, and it should not be surprising that he finally abandoned the word "novel" as a descriptive term for *Ulysses*. He seldom if ever referred to *Ulysses* as a "novel" after mid-1918, a point in time which coincides almost exactly with that moment in the process of composition when *Ulysses* ceased to resemble a conventional novel of internal-external reality and Joyce began to pour his creative energy into the various expressive techniques of his *schema*. As Joyce gradually realized his full-scale plan of symbolic resemblances and correspondences, often reworking the earlier episodes to harmonize them with the total design, he abandoned the term "novel" and began to describe his work-in-progress as a museum of different literary kinds. A letter to Carlo Linati of September 1920, which accompanied a first version of the *schema*, is typical of this new attitude:

> It [*Ulysses*] is an epic of two races (Israelite-Irish) and at the same time the cycle of the human body as well as a little story of a day

(life). . . . It is also a sort of encyclopaedia. My intention is to transpose the myth *sub specie temporis nostri.*

If Joyce felt that he had left any definite conception of the "novel" far behind by the time he finished *Ulysses,* so did the most perceptive of the early readers and reviewers. Ezra Pound saw *Ulysses,* like Flaubert's *Bouvard et Pécuchet,* as a work which "does not continue the tradition of the novel or the short story." In fact, Pound assigned *Ulysses* to the sonata form and the paternity theme, thereby taking it out of the parochial tradition of the English novel and aligning it with a whole series of continental archetypes. And T. S. Eliot, in a seldom-quoted part of his much-quoted review, "*Ulysses,* Order, and Myth," described *Ulysses* as a departure from the novel-form, not a continuation of it.

I am not begging the question in calling *Ulysses* a "novel"; and if you call it an epic it will not matter. If it is not a novel, that is simply because the novel is a form which will no longer serve; it is because the novel, instead of being a form, was simply the expression of an age which had not sufficiently lost all form to feel the need of something stricter. Mr. Joyce has written one novel—the *Portrait;* Mr. Wyndham Lewis has written one novel—*Tarr.* I do not suppose that either of them will ever write another "novel." The novel ended with Flaubert and with James. It is, I think, because Mr. Joyce and Mr. Lewis, being "in advance" of their time, felt a conscious or probably unconscious dissatisfaction with the form, that their novels are more formless than those of a dozen clever writers who are unaware of its obsolescence.

So neither Joyce, nor the most acute of his early readers, were much concerned with defining the genre of *Ulysses.* To them the significance of the work lay in its disintegration and reorganization of traditional forms, and Eliot's review has more to say about the "individual talent," about Joyce's innovations, than it has to say about "tradition." This same willingness to accept *Ulysses* as a more or less unique form, although belonging to a large family of traditional forms, marked most of the important criticism from the 1920's to the 1950's, and although *Ulysses* was constantly referred to as a "novel" there was little effort to place the work in a theoretical view of the history of fiction, or to make real critical use of generic distinctions. However, since the publication of Northrop Frye's *Anatomy of Criticism*

in 1957, *Ulysses* has become a crucial testing-ground for new theories
of fiction and new methods of generic criticism. This essay will review some of these attempts to define the genre of *Ulysses*, with an
eye toward discovering how much—and in what ways—they enhance
our understanding of Joyce's masterpiece.

Let us begin with two terms loosely adapted from E. D. Hirsch's
recent study, *Validity in Interpretation* (1967). An *extrinsic* genre is
some *a priori* notion, such as the notion of what a "novel" should be,
that one brings to the work of art as a fixed frame-of-reference; an *intrinsic* genre is our sense of the work's total form, which emerges
from a process of re-reading and re-adjustment. Clearly, most of the
recent attempts to read *Ulysses* as a "novel" have made use of some
extrinsic notion of what the form should be, the most obvious and
valuable example being S. L. Goldberg's *The Classical Temper*
(1961). Approaching *Ulysses* with a restrictive—and typically English—model of the "novel" as a dramatic and realistic form, Goldberg
seeks to reconstruct the novel which was botched or obscured by
Joyce's persistent intellectualism and his willful parade of symbolic
correspondences. Goldberg is absolutely explicit about the "model"
which governs his reading of *Ulysses*.

> *Ulysses* is [not] a case requiring special methods of interpretation or
> special assumptions about Symbols or Myths or Art in general. What
> meaning is truly realized in it, what value it has, lies in its *dramatic*
> presentation and ordering of human experience, and nowhere else. In
> short, it is not "Romance," not a joke, not a spiritual guide, not even an
> encyclopaedia of social disintegration or a re-creation of Myth or a
> symbolist poem; it is a novel, and what is of permanent interest about it
> is what always interests us with the novel: its imaginative illumination
> of the moral—and ultimately, spiritual—experience of representative
> human beings. And though it is an unusual novel, and complicated
> with extraordinary elements, its importance is founded, in the last
> analysis, on that fact (p. 30).
> . . . .
> The common assumption that *Ulysses* is a complex, symbolic poem,
> to which the ordinary interests and techniques of the novel are irrele-
> vant, is justifiable only so long as we do not forget that it is also—and
> rather more obviously—a representational novel, and much, if not most,
> of its meaning is expressed in and through its representational mode.
> It contains "probable" and significant characters, in a "probable" and
> significant setting, doing and saying "probable" and significant things,
> so that it inevitably calls into play those expectations and assumptions

we bring to the novel (as to each literary form) and which control the way we seek its meaning (p. 107).

When reading *The Classical Temper* I am always reminded of Henry James's amusing and highly illuminating attempt to disengage a Jamesian novel from Browning's *The Ring and the Book*. In his 1912 lecture honoring the centenary of Browning's birth, James confessed that he had always longed to turn *The Ring and the Book* into a novel of the "historic type."

> From far back, from my first reading of these volumes, which took place at the time of their disclosure to the world, when I was a fairly young person, the sense, almost the pang, of the novel they might have constituted sprang sharply from them; so that I was to go on through the years almost irreverently, all but quite profanely if you will, thinking of the great loose and uncontrolled composition, the great heavyhanging cluster of related but unreconciled parts, as a fiction of the so-called historic type, that is as a suggested study of the manners and conditions from which our own have more or less traceably issued, just tragically spoiled—or as a work of art, in other words, smothered in the producing ("The Novel in *The Ring and the Book*").

Just as James brought to Browning's poem a fixed notion of what "historic fiction" should be, so Goldberg brought to *Ulysses* a narrowly conceived view of the novel as a genre, but with one important difference: James is heuristic and almost playful, whereas Goldberg has the missionary purpose of saving Joyce from himself and the modern world. I find Goldberg's book one of the most useful critical studies of *Ulysses,* since it brings to the foreground several neglected aspects of the work and serves as a healthy counteragent to the more extravagant symbolic readings of the 1950's; but the "novel" Goldberg delivers is a sad diminution of Joyce's achievement. The real problem in Goldberg's critical approach is his exclusively "English" view of the novel's properties, one which slights the diversity and elasticity of the form: it is a narrowly conceived view which demands that the novel attain some kind of realism through probable dramatic action. I do not think it accidental that Goldberg's study was received with much greater enthusiasm in England than in America or on the Continent. The persistent strains of Romance and fantasy in American and Continental fiction have always made Joyce's reception easier outside of England. In the English reviews of *The Classical Temper* there was a clear feeling that Joyce had been saved for the English novel and at the same time put firmly in his place.

The Classical Temper exhibits all the virtues of a sharply defined, *extrinsic* critical approach: it is a method which extracts and clarifies the representational dimensions of *Ulysses*. But at the same time it leaves out most of the structures and harmonies that give the work a special form and special impact. Goldberg quotes approvingly as his epigraph the remark by D. H. Lawrence that "most books that live, live in spite of the author's laying it on thick." But the life of *Ulysses* resides in the thickness of the narrative, and it seems clear that midway in the writing of the book Joyce's fictional ideals ceased to have any vital relationship to those of Professor Goldberg. To insist that *Ulysses* is a traditional English novel is to corrupt it back into its origins, and to allow Joyce no significant development beyond the world of the *Portrait*. It is one thing to *evaluate* the course of Joyce's later artistic development, and I share many of Professor Goldberg's doubts and reservations. But it is quite another thing to adopt a generic frame which will allow for no sympathetic understanding of Joyce's mature art. As Arnold Goldman pointed out in a review of *The Classical Temper,* Stephen Dedalus may have chosen the "classical temper," but Joyce himself—in his 1902 essay on James Clarence Mangan—called both the romantic and classical tempers "constant states of mind." The young Joyce saw the "unrest" between classicism and romanticism as "the condition of all achievement": and the quick of *Ulysses* lies precisely in a creative "unrest" between classical representation and romantic correspondences.

At the opposite extreme from Goldberg's tendentious and at times moralistic use of generic definitions stand the works of those theorists who would construct an archetype for the novel out of the actual diversity of prose fiction. Because of the extraordinary diversity in the origins and evolution of narrative fiction, generic criticism is always falling toward one of two extremes: either a single strain—Romance, the picaresque, epic, "myth"—is selected as the norm (this would be Goldberg's method in his choice of the English realistic novel as model); or a category is invented which is so comprehensive that it can encompass all the diverse strains. Typical of the latter method would be Northrop Frye's division of fiction, the genre of the written word, into four dominant modes: Novel, Confession, Anatomy, and

Romance. In Frye's system, *Ulysses* becomes the archetypal work of fiction, the "complete prose epic with all four forms employed in it, all of practically equal importance, and all essential to one another, so that the book is a unity and not an aggregate." Frye's description of *Ulysses* is much more satisfactory than Goldberg's, since it reaches out to embrace all the diverse aspects of the work; it is, like most of the *Anatomy*, elegant, comprehensive, and of limited value to the practical critic. Frye's system is infinitely stimulating because it is a work of imagination in itself, and because it brings *Ulysses* into startling alignment with many other works of literature. In effect, Frye's method breaks through the restrictions of conventional notions about literary "influence" and enables us to see *Ulysses* in relation to works which are apparently quite dissimilar. But when it comes to dealing with the local effects and internal symmetries of *Ulysses*, Frye's theories have little to offer. It would seem that we are confronted with a stubborn paradox: the more limited extrinsic concepts of genre, such as Goldberg's model of the representational novel, can be highly effective tools for practical criticism, with sharp cutting edges; while the comprehensive extrinsic genres, such as Frye's anatomy of fiction, are almost useless to the practical critic even though they may provide convincing theoretical models. The trouble with Goldberg's method is that it willfully disregards some of the most obvious achievements in *Ulysses*; the trouble with Frye's method is its purity, which cannot accommodate the shifting mixtures of forms and kinds that we encounter in the actual process of reading. *Ulysses* is a book which talks constantly about itself, and one of the things it talks about is the diversity of prose fiction. No extrinsic notion of what the novel or fiction should be can be taken as an ideal model, and we must allow the work to establish its own *intrinsic* genre as we read it.

It would be equally foolish to approach *Ulysses* without any preconceptions about its genre (always an impossibility anyway) and to approach it with a fixed generic concept in mind. The ideal reading of the work should correspond to the ideal scanning of a picture described by E. H. Gombrich in *Art and Illusion*. We bring to *Ulysses* all the schemata available to us, both from Joyce's earlier works and from the literary tradition, since we know that without such schemata we cannot begin to see or understand; but we should also be prepared to modify and rearrange our preconceptions as we go along. Since

Ulysses demands that we understand it both spatially and temporally
—by which I mean that we should have, as we read it, a simultaneous
sense of the book as a timeless image, like the city it imitates, and of
the book developing through time—the intrinsic genre of *Ulysses* is
our total image of the work, which is recreated and modified each
time we re-read it.

Whatever *stemma* or family tree one postulates for prose narrative
(that presented by Robert Scholes and Robert Kellogg in *The Nature of Narrative* will serve very well), *Ulysses* can be viewed as a
synthesis of the myriad forms which went into the making of modern fiction. It was Joyce's intention to disintegrate the well-made
"novel" into its origins, and then to perform a prodigious act of re-
integration. Most of our difficulties with the genre of *Ulysses* fall
away when we cease to fret about a single "model" for the work and
concentrate upon the experience of reading, which involves the constant use of familiar genres and types. At the outset of *Ulysses,* the
title, the opening lines, and even the physical shape of the book raise
certain expectations about narrative, mythic, and epic forms. The
opening chapters, in their renderings of inner and outer reality, depend upon conventions and generic distinctions already familiar to
the accomplished reader of the *Portrait* or the modern novel in general. But beginning roughly with "Aeolus" and "Lestrygonians" (episodes 7 and 8), the conventional models of a "novel" begin to show
their inadequacies, and in the second half of *Ulysses* ("Wandering
Rocks" onward) we are constantly shifting our schemes of expectation as Joyce rings his changes on a number of genres and conventions, conducting us through the rich repertoire of epic, satiric, and
dramatic forms. *Ulysses* may be viewed as a two-part performance in
which the modern novel is built up and then disintegrated into its
original components. By the time we reach "Ithaca" the two extremes of historical fact and mythical fiction have been so separated
that they begin to resemble each other, fact taking on a mythic dimension through Joyce's sheer encyclopedism: in effect, the school-
room catechism of "Ithaca" provides us with the raw materials for a
novelistic ending, while the actual narrative tails away into the
farthest reaches of factual catalogue and mythopoetic allegory.

So *Ulysses* raises in acute form the central problem of generic
criticism. As E. D. Hirsch has pointed out, the generic critic is always

plagued by "a version of the hermeneutic circle, which in its classical formulation has been described as the interdependence of part and whole: the whole can be understood only through its parts, but the parts can be understood only through the whole." We are faced with a vexing question:

Is there really a stable generic concept, constitutive of meaning, which lies somewhere between the vague, heuristic genre idea with which an interpreter always starts and the individual, determinate meaning with which he ends? At first glance the answer seems to be no, since apparently the interpreter's idea of the whole becomes continuously more explicit until the genre idea at last fades imperceptibly into a particularized and individual meaning. If this is so, and if the intrinsic genre is defined as a conception shared by the speaker and the interpreter, it would seem that what I have called the "intrinsic genre" is neither more nor less than the meaning of the utterance as a whole. Obviously, it is a useless tautology to assert that the interpreter must understand the speaker's meaning in order to understand the speaker's meaning. That is a circularity no more helpful than the paradox of the hermeneutic circle as promulgated by Heidegger. If we cannot preserve a distinction between the particular *type* of meaning expressed and the particular meaning itself, then the intrinsic genre becomes simply the meaning as a whole. Nothing but confusion is achieved by calling a particular meaning a "genre" (Hirsch, p. 81).

We begin *Ulysses* with a scheme of expectations, differing from reader to reader, based on our experience of Joyce's earlier work and of literature as a whole. We respond to various signals, refining and enlarging our sense of the work as Joyce plays upon our various generic expectations. But finally, when we have read *Ulysses* several times and have settled into some sense of its total meaning, does the work remain representative of a type or kind of fiction; or has its intrinsic genre gradually become identical with its unique meaning? The prime value of some generic frame lies in the temporal nature of language. As Hirsch comments:

One basis for the distinction between genres and particular meanings can be sought in a consideration that necessitated the genre concept in the first place—the temporal character of speaking and understanding. Because words follow one another sequentially, and because the words that will come later are not present to consciousness along with the words experienced here and now, the speaker or listener must have an anticipated sense of the whole by virtue of which the presently experienced words are understood in their capacity as parts functioning in a whole (p. 82).

But is this conventional argument relevant in a work such as *Ulysses,* one of the aims of which is to surmount or circumvent the "temporality" of language? If *Ulysses* cannot be read, only re-read, as Joseph Frank argued years ago, then ultimately we have our total, spatial understanding of the work to use in place of any preconceived generic expectations, and we re-read the book against our previous experience of it as well as against our models of prose fiction.

What I am saying is that *Ulysses,* at its deepest reaches, denies the validity of genres and seeks to be wholly itself. One could argue that all successful works of literature ultimately undergo such a transformation, but I do not believe that to be true; the phenomenon strikes me as distinctly modern, and peculiar to Joyce's aims. The title and opening lines of *Paradise Lost,* to adapt an example from Hirsch, announce a subject and generic expectations that are never fundamentally altered, no matter how profound our experience of the poem becomes. To understand the opening of *Paradise Lost,* and indeed the whole poem, the sensitive reader must know the genre, and if he does not then no amount of reading and re-reading will completely reveal the poem. On the other hand, a well-trained reader who knew the genre could tell you a great deal about *Paradise Lost* without reading beyond the first pages.

The case with *Ulysses* is much more compromised. The generic signals are all there, in greater profusion perhaps than in any other work of English literature, but the ultimate schema is something every reader must construct for himself. Inevitably, therefore, readings of *Ulysses* will be more various and more indeterminate than those of *Paradise Lost.* To try to reduce this indeterminacy and "openness," as Professor Goldberg does, is to go against the nature of *Ulysses,* since the collapse of the genres is one of its subjects. One important aspect of *Ulysses* is its self-conscious commentary on literary theory, most obvious in the course of the Library episode where Stephen's view of Shakespeare's plays—like the aesthetic of the young James Joyce—is uncompromisingly anti-generic. Joyce wished to re-create the ideals of Classical art under the conditions of modern life and his own personality; but he believed that it is the "classical temper," not Classicism with its trappings of types and kinds, that leads to "the sane and joyful spirit."

Recent attempts to incorporate *Ulysses* into various theories of the novel have simply reinforced my respect for Joyce's earliest readers, and my appreciation for his youthful aesthetic. Just as the best Shakespearean criticism often begins with a generic model—revenge tragedy, Romance, historical allegory—but then goes beyond this model to talk of the total experience of the plays, so the best criticism of *Ulysses* must be a statement of the total and unique experience which the work delivers to a sensitive reader. This is the final norm against which we test, with each re-reading, the consistency of the different parts. In fact, the three stages of artistic apprehension as described in Joyce's early notebooks and fictions make a fair model for our gradual apprehension of *Ulysses*. The sequence—*integritas, consonantia, claritas*—is a movement from cognition to recognition to satisfaction. First we must understand the integrity and symmetry of the work, which involves seeing it in relation to other works and tracing the relationship of part to part: it is here that our knowledge and experience of the various traditional genres comes into play. But finally, when our experience of the different parts and their relationship is fused into a single image, the unique meaning of the work stands forth in individual clarity. Joyce's methods and intentions would seem to demand a Crocean aesthetic, where "the particular throbs with the life of the whole intuition, and the whole exists in the life of the particular. Every pure artistic image is at one and the same time itself and the universe, the universe in this individual form and this individual form equivalent to the universe" (*New Essays on Aesthetic*).

So we are led to a process of understanding *Ulysses* very like Gombrich's notion of "perceptual trial and error." As Gombrich discovered from his own experience and the experiments of modern psychologists, we cannot begin to perceive without a framework of illusions, of provisional hypotheses, and in the case of *Ulysses* these hypotheses are provided by our experience of the genres. They shape our expectations, but unless we are willing to modify them we place the work in a strait-jacket. Joyce demands a lot of the reader: like Gombrich's ideal viewer of an Impressionist painting, Joyce's ideal reader must read across the brushstrokes as well as with them, supplying provisional forms to support the artist's impressions. This process of perceptual trial and error may seem obvious, but it is worth belaboring because the present trend toward theoretical criticism of fiction contains a potential threat to a work such as *Ulysses,* which lends itself easily to categories and classifications that give so little in return. Indeed, the current trends in generic criticism may pose a threat to the whole pluralistic world in which the masterpieces of modern art developed, smoothing away the irregular achievements of Joyce's generation. One of the essential characteristics of *Ulysses* is that it resembles many other works of literature, but other works do not resemble it: the balance-of-trade is mainly one way, not reciprocal as in a world of genres and decorum. We have a double sense of *Ulysses:* a sense of how we came to understand it, through a series of perceptual adjustments; and a sense of the whole work as a timeless image. *Ulysses* lives in our minds as both process and product, always evolving and yet always the same, and any theory which threatens this double sense, whether it be put forward in the cause of the "novel" or some other genre, is ultimately self-defeating. The term "heuristic," which was invented by the nineteenth century to describe its new awareness of indeterminacy and openness, should be the motto for any sympathetic reading of *Ulysses.*

THE MODERN
MULTIVALENT
NOVEL
FORM AND FUNCTION

ALAN WARREN FRIEDMAN

Even in the field of the terminal values of form, a work of art is multivalent.

GEORGE BOAS

The admission of relativity and mutivalence does not make value illusory or judgment futile.

H. J. MULLER

The great men of letters have never created more than a single work, or rather have never done more than refract through various mediums an identical beauty which they bring into the world.

MARCEL PROUST

One of the notable phenomena of twentieth-century fiction is the extent to which it has become extended. Forster gave the term "novel" one meaning when he defined it as a prose work in fiction of a certain extent. But many novels have moved beyond "certain" to become "indefinite." For since the novel has become psychological and open, the novelist who would terminate the stream of his fiction finds that it has no necessary ending, that it goes on multiplying perspectives and possibilities—often into several or many volumes.

This is not to say that twentieth-century novels are simply longer than their predecessors—for certainly Samuel Richardson, Fielding, and Trollope, for instance, had no qualms about excessive verbiage. The later novelists, in fact, tend to write shorter novels, but once

having written them they frequently find the job less than complete
—and so write them again from a somewhat different angle or vision,
and sometimes again and again. The result is the modern multivalent
novel.

In a sense, the very extension of a novel into several volumes is an
ineffaceable act of self-consciousness (and therefore an assertion of
multiple perspectives)—far more than the perhaps largely accidental
or passive initial creative action. Just as no artist attains full expression through a single achievement—no matter how singular or sublime—so too no single work fully expresses itself by itself. More
likely it will attain the status of an historical oddity, a chance happening—like Henry Roth's brilliant but largely neglected novel,
Call It Sleep. Every artistic expression—a Michaelangelo statue, a
Shakespearean play, a Beethoven symphony, a Picasso painting—
asserts the fullest sense of itself by defining a place and role for itself
within an entire corpus. And the multivolume novel—almost invariably self-conscious and pluralistic because simultaneously both a
series of discrete parts and a unity—necessarily creates and defines a
context, a pattern, for itself. The separate volumes must stand on
their own, and yet their interrelated existences require of us a com-
parativist's eye and judgment. The whole becomes the sum not only
of the parts but also of something more: the interconnectedness between and through the parts that sweeps us back as well as forward
as we move through the several volumes. For the temporally linear
act of reading, like Proust's madeleine cake, creates responses that
ripple outward both with and against the conventional current of
time—and never more so than in the multivolume novel with its
self-contained dramas that are yet acts within a larger play. On the
grandest scale one might, with Balzac, call that play the human comedy and write a hundred of its countless acts.

The term "multivalence" derives from chemistry, where it denomi-
nates those atoms capable of combining with other atoms in multiple
combinations. Univalent atoms possess a single combining characteristic; and the word "ambivalent" has the same etymological root.
Univalence in fiction is essentially what we mean when we speak of
authorial intrusiveness, or any other device by which a single, unam-
bivalent narrative stance dominates, and thus embodies the values of

the book. Narrative ambivalence occurs when several perspectives merge, creating moral confusion. The multiple perspectives on moral reality offered by multivalent art transcend both the sanctity accorded univalence and the frenzied ambivalence of such writers as William Burroughs.

In their simplest form, multivolume novels offer linear sequels in the episodic fashion of the picaresque or the chronicle form of the *roman fleuve*. They may differ in setting and mood, but structurally and morally they are often identical. In C. P. Snow's eleven-volume novel, *Strangers and Brothers*, we participate in a sequence of events in much the same way as we do in *Robinson Crusoe* or de Sade's *Justine* and *Juliette* or Scott's Waverley novels: a series of adventures or misadventures confronts the protagonist (the passive is the proper mood, for the protagonist, though energetic *within* the actions, is generally passive between them: they befall him). Each episode contains rising action, climax, dénouement, and perhaps moral, but little of significance is sufficiently well learned to insure that the same or similar incidents will not recur to be confronted again as if for the first time. Thus, de Sade's *Justine* endures an almost endless series of similar experiences in no significant order; *Juliette* repeats the process in mirror image. Snow's *Strangers and Brothers* is technically anachronistic because "closed" (i.e., moving chronologically from early life to marriage or death, the terminal conditions that reverse the expanding action of most pre-twentieth-century novels), although stretched to great length.[1] With such fiction as *Strangers and Brothers*, multivalence means little more than multivolume: Lewis Eliot differs from novel to novel not because he is perceived differently but only because he is older.

"Multivalence" is a double-edged term: it applies equally to multiple ways of viewing and to multiple ways of being seen. A narrator like Snow's Lewis Eliot partakes of multivalence because, though a traditionally continuous character, he views his world with unique perspective at each of the eleven stages of his life Snow has him depict. Dickens' Pip and Conrad's Marlow look back on earlier versions of themselves—and contrast themselves as they had thought they were, themselves as they now think they "really" were, and (implicitly) themselves as *we* now find them to be. Ford's Dowell and Durrell's Darley, having been forced to re-experience themselves through others' eyes, now proceed to revivify and contradict what had previously seemed fixed and immutably past in their lives—and in the process they inevitably reveal more aspects of themselves than they know. Self-dramatized voices like James's narrator in *The Aspern Papers*, Cary's monologists, many of Nabokov's (in *The Real Life of Sebastian Knight, Lolita, Pale Fire*) are not actually seeking truth (as they claim), but rather want to impose their own limited visions upon the recalcitrant world about them. They too display conflicting realities about themselves, for we are aware of the distance between what they say and what they do, how they act and how they think they are acting.

Thus, many single-volume novels and single-volume parts of larger works may be dynamically multivalent. In various ways, they depict conflicting voices of significant scope and self-assuredness. A novel like *The Sound and the Fury* or *Absalom, Absalom!* or *As I Lay Dying*, for example, offers a series of partial views of events; and each view is both compelling and undercut to a large extent. In *Tristram Shandy* and *The Good Soldier*, the narrative voice—a self-conscious subjective protagonist—is divided against his ostensible narrative purpose; in such works the monologue form is multivalent because of the strongly felt presence of an implied author who is at a distance from his narrator. A similar effect results from a form I call third-person subjective; in such works as *The Beast in the Jungle*, *The Secret Agent, Portrait of the Artist*, an anonymous and undramatized though intensely personal narrator is ironically at odds with his narrated material. Most unclassifiable (because broader than any possible categorization) are novels, like *Moby-Dick* and *Ulysses*, employing a full spectrum of narrative perspectives and techniques—from the highly subjective ("Call me Ishmael," the "Proteus" chapter of *Ulysses*) to the objectification of the playlet in *Moby-Dick* and "Ithaca" in *Ulysses*.

Though employing different narrative techniques, multivalent works like Cary's trilogies, Faulkner's *Sound and the Fury, Absalom, Absalom!*, and *As I Lay Dying*, and Woolf's *To the Lighthouse* and *Mrs. Dalloway* all offer a multiplicity of unique perspectives. Each perspective is self-conscious and inadequate, but a still possible way of envisaging a reality that remains in flux even while one seeks to perceive and define it. Such works as these, then, for all their internalizing, emphasize the seen as much as the seer—and it is only a remarkable world (remarkable in its reality) that can sustain such a variety of conflicting approaches. The technically least interesting modern novels are either multivalent only in the simplest of ways (like *Strangers and Brothers*) or else only apparently multivalent (Greene's *The End of the Affair*[2]). To a great extent, the morally and aesthetically richest are, as I discuss below, multivalent in both senses of the term.

Interestingly, certain generalizations seem possible even about the lengths of multivolume novels. Most double-volume novels offer one of two kinds of re-experiencing perspectives: a self-contained series of adventures befalls a protagonist, followed by (1) a subsequent and consequent self-contained series or (2) a second and structurally equal protagonist experiencing an analogous series. The first form generally employs protagonist narration—as in Butler's *Erewhon*, Braine's *Room at the Top* and *Life at the Top*, Durrell's *Aut Tunc Aut Nunquam*—although Cervantes employs a dramatized narrator of constantly shifting dimensions and Carroll's *Alice* books use third-person subjective. The second variety varies from the dual protagonist narration of de Sade's *Justine* and *Juliette*, to the third-person subjective of Bunyan's *Pilgrim's Progress* (within the dream frame), to Twain's shift from the one type of narration to the other in *Tom Sawyer* and *Huckleberry Finn*.

The triple-volume novel also occurs in two main forms: (1) the triple perspective, as in Beckett's and Cary's multiplistically narrated trilogies (and such single-volume analogs as Stein's *Three Lives* and Dos Passos' *Three Soldiers*), predicated upon a prismatic, pluralistic conception of reality; and (2) the *Bildungsroman*—Dreiser's Frank Cowperwood series, Farrell's *Studs Lonigan* and *Bernard Carr*, Henry Miller's trilogies, Hartley's *Eustace and Hilda*, Waugh's *Sword of Honour*—tauter forms of the *roman fleuve* that more extended works generally become.

The tetralogy or quartet generally focuses on a complexly evolving central consciousness—whether it employs protagonist narration as in Durrell's *Alexandria Quartet* (and Swift's *Gulliver's Travels*), third-person subjective as in Ford's *Parade's End*, or some combination of the two as in Conrad's Marlovian narratives. Regardless of technique, all of these counterpoint the central consciousness with contrasting perspectives: with the various spokesmen for alien cultures encountered in *Gulliver's Travels;* with the frame narrators and the ostensible central characters in Conrad; with the multiple internal monologues in the last book of *Parade's End;* with Balthazar the character and *Mountolive* the book in *The Alexandria Quartet.*

Beyond four, the *roman fleuve* and *Bildungsroman* predominate, and their endlessly extendable structure imposes no necessary limit, makes little formal distinction among five-volume sequences (Scott's Waverley novels, Cooper's Leatherstocking tales), six-volume (Trollope's Barsetshire and Palliser novels, Farrell's Danny O'Neill series), the dozen or so volumes in Galsworthy's Forsyte chronicles, Powell's *Music of Time,* Sinclair's Lanny Budd series, Snow's *Strangers and Brothers,* the fifteen volumes of Henry Williamson's *A Chronicle of Ancient Sunlight,* the twenty-seven volumes of Jules Romains' *Men of Good Will,* or even the nearly one hundred volumes of Balzac's *Human Comedy.* The only significant distinction concerns that between one running story (Farrell, Galsworthy) and many stories connected under a looser rubric (Scott, Balzac). Only a few multivolume novels seem capable of this sort of length without assuming the form of the *roman fleuve:* Proust's seven-volume *A la recherche du temps perdu,* Faulkner's fourteen-volume Yoknapatawpha cycle, Salinger's still-emerging Glass family saga. These last cited are all complexly dynamic in their unfoldings, highly wrought and richly imaginative fictional constructs, for Proust, Faulkner, and Salinger brilliantly create the rich patterning of a highly wrought short story where the very lengths of their works would seem to demand the easy temporality of the *roman fleuve.*

That there are multiple ways of viewing the multivalent novel does not, of course, invalidate any one of them. To focus on one while affirming the validity of others is not only to acknowledge multivalence but to practice it as well. Games of this sort are, after all, fun to play, and perhaps also potentially meaningful—provided of course one doesn't lose a sense of perspective and assume that categorization alone represents some ultimate purpose. By themselves, such groupings can make no moral or aesthetic distinctions. Besides, categorization according to narrative mode necessarily ignores all sorts of matters of at least equal significance—tone, for example, and method of character revelation, and style. What I am after, then, are not rules but tools, an apparatus for doing a specific job in one of the many possible ways that it might be done. My concern with multivalence derives to a large extent from the fact that Wayne C. Booth's discussion of ambivalence in *The Rhetoric of Fiction* leads him into a classical contradiction. Through brilliant practical criticism, he sweeps away the significance of all such critical distinctions as between, say, "telling" and "showing" by demonstrating that successful novels transcend all abstract criteria. But he then goes on to proclaim his own: that novels fail to the extent that they are morally ambivalent.[3] As my namesake puts it:

> One wonders whether in fact Booth is—as he supposes—raising fundamental issues about judgment, clarity, and responsibility in the novel, or whether he is not looking for the old judgment, clarity, and responsibility in the newer form, worriedly searching in the newer pattern of the novel for the specific ethical process embodied in the older pattern. The antinomies of ambiguous and even rationally contradictory ethics in modern fiction are themselves, strictly speaking, a "judgment"—a judgment that implicitly asserts that it alone can help man be fully man.[4]

Antinomies imply multivalence; not an amoral relativism but a *multimoral*, pluralistic flux in which disparate and irreconcilable voices all claim (with some legitimacy) to speak with the rights and perquisites of authorial privilege.

At least at first, the result is uneasiness for the unsuspecting reader. Writing of *Don Quixote*, the archetypal modern multivolume novel, Dorothy Van Ghent says:

> . . . it would seem that "great books" . . . have a very special ambiguity distinguishing them from lesser works. In the case of Cervantes' great novel, this quality seems to lie in the constant reversibility of perspective between deeply distant extremes. . . . What the reader's attention is directed to is not one aspect (moral or practical) of an action, but the action itself, the adventure itself, as an event with many aspects. It is rather difficult for the rationalizing, moralizing intellect to think in this fashion. We feel the need of singling out some aspect as predominant and as definitive of worth-while values.[5]

Booth, a "rationalizing, moralizing intellect" if ever there was one, would seem to require Cervantes to affirm his hero's moral stance while on his quest and deny it when he is on his deathbed—or vice versa. But surely Van Ghent is right to suggest that it is a mark of Cervantes' achievement, not his failing, that we feel a double pull: that the good Don's moral posture is simultaneously compelling *and* inadequate at *both* stages of his life. To a large extent, the brilliance of the achievement lies in our being made to recognize that this is one of those frequent times when opposing moral appeals are equally valid and therefore both irreconcilable and viable. Booth would seem to ask more of Cervantes than we are capable of ourselves, in our lives; but then Booth, unlike Cervantes and most great artists, is not only dogmatic but comfortably so.

By itself, the term "multivalent" confers no special distinction. To apply it to a novel is to say little, if anything, of that novel's aesthetic or moral quality or significance. It is always a serious mistake, as Scholes and Kellogg indicate, to treat descriptive terms (novel, epic, tragedy) as if they were evaluative.[6] And just as technique is unavoidable in any mode of expression, it is, as Booth reminds us, nothing by itself. There are bad multivalent novels as well as good. For example, Graham Greene's *The End of the Affair,* unlike such religious novels as Joyce Cary's *Except the Lord* and *The Captive and the Free,* is essentially a religious statement disguised as a novel. Another way of saying this is that multivalence is reduced to a trick in this novel: the several apparently conflicting perspectives lead to univocality, not only a *deus ex machina* but God Himself. Where Cary offers contradictory but equally possible human interpretations of reality, Greene's central incident (like the falling door which may or may not have killed his protagonist, Maurice Bendrix) hinges on an extraterrestrial appeal that points us back to the pre-novel didacticism of Bunyan's *Pilgrim's Progress.* According to Bendrix, the door blown in by the exploding rocket caught and held just above him (though, oddly, he is bruised as if the door *had* actually landed on him). According to Sarah Miles, his mistress, the door did fall and kill him—and his being alive must be a miracle. She renounces her love for him because, on seeing him dead, she had promised God she would do so if Bendrix were restored to life. The rest of the novel demonstrates that her interpretation is correct, alas—for it not only destroys the characters, it destroys them *as* characters. Greene's problem here is that he fails to make dogma dramatic; Sarah and Maurice die for us just when his thesis demands that they begin to live. *The*

End of the Affair returns us to the world of Browning's *The Ring and the Book,* a world in which infallible spokesmen pronounce divine Truth—but without the poem's sustaining dramatic power. The term "multivalence" has value, then, within a sharply defined conceptual framework, and only to the extent that it provides us with critical handles on an important modern literary phenomenon. Of course it is the fiction and not the categories that matter, just as critical analyses employing them must, if they can, stand on their own merit. In Scholes's important distinction, they should enable us not to "know" but to "know about." Scholes adds: "All interpretive criticism amounts to this. That is the limitation of such criticism. . . . It clarifies, at the expense of reducing the experience of fiction, through which we 'know' a work, to a discussion through which we 'know about' it. Thus its only use is to prepare us to encounter or re-encounter the primary material, the work itself."[7] The terms and categories applied to the multivalent novel are not fixed and immutable, but part of the ongoing process of our continuing response to the demands such works make upon us.

Morality is, as Booth maintains, the sticking point in modern fiction, but only novelists unself-conscious enough to be anachronistic seek in their writings an ethic equivalent to pre-Darwinian anthropology, pre-Einsteinian physics, pre-Freudian psychology. In its own way, the multivalent novel also seeks to determine where truth lies, but it also knows that that is exactly what truth often does. It thus derives much of its dynamic tension from an anti-absolutist ethical commitment, one too self-confronting to permit any denial of the inductive immediacy of the human moment.

In fiction, morality of purpose and action is inextricably linked with manner of revelation. Conrad's complex narrative structure in *Lord Jim* aims at one crucial effect: sympathetic involvement with Jim's plight before we learn the morally damning fact of the *Patna's* failure to sink. Had we come to know Jim in a more straightforward manner, we would likely dismiss him as beneath contempt. Conrad's narrative structure does not negate the moral reality, but it creates a context denying us the luxury of a single-faceted response towards Jim: we condemn *and* sympathize, loathe and admire, reject and identify with. The union of morality and structure is also Frank Kermode's concern when he defends the presentation of horror and depravity in Golding's *Pincher Martin.* "What makes all this bearable and Golding a major novelist is the total technical control: nightmare, hysteria, every kind of beastliness and depravity are given the virtue of form." Kermode adds that "Golding's novels are simple in so far as they deal in the primordial patterns of human experience and in so far as they have skeletons of parable. On these simple bones the flesh of narrative can take extremely complex forms. This makes for difficulty, but of the most acceptable kind, the difficulty that attends the expression of what is profoundly simple."[8] This may serve as something of a rationale for what I am trying to do in this essay. For defining and codifying basic patterns of narrative revelation should facilitate our apprehending the moral center of multivalent fiction—and the way in which the two interact.

In general, the modernity of multivalent fiction results from a double self-consciousness: that of an engaging and multiply viewed narrator or implied author, and that of the novel itself seemingly obsessed with its own identity as a work of art and its relationship to those who experience it. In "modern" fiction, this awareness is often embodied in the form of a self-dramatized narrator whose focus is the telling as much as the tale: Sterne's Tristram Shandy, *Moby-Dick's* Ishmael, Pip in *Great Expectations,* Conrad's Marlow, Dowell in *The Good Soldier,* Ratliff in Faulkner's Snopes trilogy, Cary's and Beckett's cubistic narrators, Darley in Durrell's *Alexandria Quartet.* Each of these is an impressionistic explorer/creator of the physical and moral realm he seeks to define, express, and judge. "Modern" in this sense is conceived not as a temporal designation but as a quality that has been called psychological, open, indeterminate, and that often manifests itself through self-consciousness in narration. Such an approach conceives of an artistic creation as process, still in motion even when complete, a finished edifice with all the scaffolding of its construction not only still in place but permanently so. Thus, the planned formlessness of a work like *Tristram Shandy,* which not only develops forward in time but opens outward and backwards as well, embodies a modernity that reduces the socially constricted worlds of novelists like Braine and Alan Sillitoe to the merely contemporary, for their novels function in aesthetically narrow ways: as urban versions of the simple picaresque, lacking the moral and structural reverberations of the complex picaresque (like *Don Quixote* and *Huckleberry Finn*).

My approach makes certain other assumptions. It maintains, for instance, the essential interrelatedness, the unity, of (arguably) conceptually disparate works: Salinger's Glass stories, Faulkner's Yoknapatawpha County works, Conrad's Marlovian tales, all of Wolfe's novels, Joyce's *Portrait* and *Ulysses,* Huxley's *Brave New World* sequence. The very placing of these works into categories borders on critical arrogance, an implicit and unwarranted (though useful) assumption that they can be defined and circumscribed. Further, it often represents debatable literary judgment—for example, to classify Salinger's Glass stories as protagonist narration is to assert that they are all narrated by Buddy Glass and that he is their protagonist. This seems to me both defensible and responsible, but it is by no means universally accepted. To see Durrell's *Quartet* as employing participant narration plus third-person subjective is to argue that *Mountolive* is narrated not objectively (the common assumption) but from the perspective of its title character.[9] Similarly, to say that *Portrait* and *Ulysses* together comprise a single multivalent novel is to imply that *Ulysses* concerns itself with affording another way of viewing Stephen Dedalus. It does so, of course, although other things—for example, an extraordinarily vital, multiple depiction of its title character—are more central.

Such an approach, then, necessarily imposes something of itself upon these works, but it also opens up additional perspectives on them. The categories may be said to distort only if one views them as Platonic universals; what they can provide is one of many possible ways of looking at a blackbird. It should not be assumed that they are intended to do more, or that they could. In fact, even within these terms, the implicit hard-and-fast distinctions represent a further distortion: in actuality, the categories fade into each other like adjacent colors in a rainbow, each of them only subtly different from the next.

With such reservations very much in mind, then, I am suggesting that the modern multivalent novel (whether multi- or single-volume) may usefully be categorized according to three main narrative modes: (1) multifarious narration; (2) participant narration; and (3) third-person subjective. There are, in addition, variations on each of these, as well as hybrids resulting from combinations of any two or all three of these basic forms.

"Multifarious narration" is a term conceived to replace the imprecision of "omniscience." In the early days of novel criticism, the universe must still have seemed a permanent and harmoniously ordered
continuum in which God was the Artist of Nature and man strove
to emulate Him in the available media. How else account for the use
of "omniscient" to designate the most common mode of narrative
revelation? One may well believe, further, that arrogance breeds absurdity—witness the subsequent appearance of the oxymoron "limited omniscience." The need for refinement is great, but meaningful
discrimination lies, rather, in such a direction as Booth's delineating
of narrators in terms of such factors as distance, irony, degree of
dramatization, reliability, and so on.[10] It lies, too, in the utter abandonment of "omniscience" as a defining term. Scholes and Kellogg
acknowledge the irrelevant world view implicit in the term: " 'omniscience' itself is . . . a definition based on the presumed analogy
between the novelist as creator and the Creator of the cosmos, an
omniscient God. . . . But a narrator in fiction is imbedded in a
time-bound artifact. He does not 'know' simultaneously but consec-
utively." (There are exceptions—*Tom Jones* has already happened
for Fielding's narrator, thus he *knows* spatially though he must *speak*
temporally—but they are rarer than is commonly assumed.) And they
offer us "multifarious narrator" in its stead, a term properly implying
that even the most objective and removed commentator "is not everywhere at once but now here, now there, now looking into this mind
or that, now moving on to other vantage points. He is time-bound
and space-bound as God is not."[11]

The multifarious narrator, by definition limited in significant ways,
is most at home in certain novelistic modes: in the chronicle rather
than the picaresque, in the wide-ranging panoramic rather than the
intensely personal, in the realistic and naturalistic rather than the
impressionistic. This is not to say that the multifarious narrator
embodies an aesthetically or morally inferior mode, but rather that
the effects aimed at and the conventions employed are strikingly
different from those aimed at by other types of narrators. The multifarious narrator is often not terribly profound, but he must be skillfully various, light on his metaphorical (because only partially dramatized) feet. He is called upon, like an adroit and active puppet-master,
to display and manipulate a variety of figures in succession, often

several at a time—with something of a stage role for himself often included along with the rest. And when this approach affords us multiple views of events and people, then multifariousness becomes multivalence. Earlier multivolume novels rely mainly on multifarious narration. The narrative voices employed by Scott, Thackeray and Trollope (like those of Fielding and Jane Austen) are all physically distant from the action they narrate—and often intellectually and morally as well. They make little pretense of an independent reality for the characters and actions they unfold. Thus they can claim kinship with story-tellers in the oral tradition—for whom interaction with an actual audience plays an important part in the telling—and also with the modern self-conscious narrator, for whom the process of interacting with a created and creative consciousness constitutes part of the aesthetic product. Multifarious narration in the hands of implied authors like those of Cervantes, Fielding, and Thackeray is, in fact, a progenitor of self-consciousness in the modern novel.

Protagonist narration runs an aesthetic gamut from Proust's *Remembrance of Things Past* to Snow's *Strangers and Brothers*. In one sense, such works are full-scale expansions on the hints of dramatized narrators contained in multifarious narration. Proust's focus is not the chronological aging of the protagonist-narrator, but the complex and circuitous interacting of such a figure with time and memory. The process is more circular than linear, as the taste of madeleine cake summons up remembrances of things past and the narrator journeys backward and downward rather than temporally forward. Yet the linear is never lost; we are carried into the future as well because we follow not only the actions of the past but also the mind of the protagonist-narrator as it seeks to recapture and depict, and therefore create, the past in the image of the present.

In contrast, Snow's *Strangers and Brothers* is relatively non-introspective. In the process of aging, Lewis Eliot undergoes a variety of experiences; he tries not only to live them but to make sense of them—and by the end his broad, humane outlook implies, for all its chaotic disparateness, a life well and fully lived, an overall, self-validating pattern. We are not in the realm of Proustian reverberations, where the single momentary sense impression can expand to encompass a world, but in one in which such impressions are continually subsumed by the continuum of temporal events. Yet fundamental similarities do exist between the two. As Ian Donaldson notes in discussing Sterne and Samuel Richardson, life constantly intrudes on "present-tense narration."[12] The past ceases to be object and becomes process, fully alive to the exigencies of later (narrative present, reader present) thoughts and needs. In this conception of time nothing has ever purely and simply *happened,* for the past remains *happening,* never finished or behind us (thus Pursewarden, a minor character and a suicide in the first book of Durrell's *Quartet,* becomes increasingly dominant, articulate, and vital throughout the rest of it). The past lives in and through Marcel and Lewis Eliot in the continuing present as surely as they emerge from it to speak to us. One immediate consequence is that protagonist-narrators—Tristram Shandy, Ford's Dowell, Beckett's and Cary's monologists, Durrell's Darley—are often types of the self-conscious speaker who, as Booth puts it, "intrudes into his novel to comment on himself as writer, and on his book, not simply as a series of events with moral implications, but as a created literary product."[13]

Dorothy Richardson's *Pilgrimage* bears marked resemblance to Proust's extended protagonist narration, for it too is an impressionistic portrayal of an evolving interpreting consciousness grappling simultaneously with external and internal realities. But Richardson's intensely intimate narrative—like that of multivolume novels by Romain Rolland, Farrell, and Hartley, as well as James's *Ambassadors,* Joyce's *Portrait* and much of *Ulysses,* Robbe-Grillet's *Jealousy*—is cast in the form of third-person rather than first, a perspective that James calls "the indirect vision," and that I call "third-person subjective." Far from being omniscient, such a narrator as Richardson's anonymous and disembodied voice is myopic: "he" sees and feels with the eyes and senses of a single character, confining "himself" (with more or less consistency) to an individual perspective. In comparison to the multifarious narrator, the third-person subjective voice has a more narrowly defined but more penetrating role to play. He never dramatizes himself (and thus can be spoken of as "he" only for the sake of convenience) but, rather, articulates the "internalizations" of one or more central characters. The technique is inherently dualistic in outlook, for it places us simultaneously within and without the protagonist. And the dualism can be doubled (Uwe Johnson's *Two*

Views, David Lodge's *The British Museum Is Falling Down*), tripled (Stein's *Three Lives*), multiplied without theoretical limit (Woolf's *Mrs. Dalloway,* Ford's *Parade's End*).

The convention behind this narrative mode is that voice and order have been given not to the protagonist but to his thoughts and feelings, and that we can experience them directly and coherently, without such intermediary devices as participant narration employs: Pamela's and Clarissa's letters, Tristram Shandy's circuitous and frenzied writings, Gulley Jimson's "honorary secretary," Humbert Humbert's imagined jury, and the like—and without the apparent narrative chaos of such confused self-confessors as Ford's Dowell and Durrell's Darley.[14] Further, no immediacy or intensity need be lost —we are as close to Joyce's Stephen, Dorothy Richardson's Miriam, Bellow's protagonists as we could or should be. Thus, despite the formal dissimilarity, Richardson's narrative voice is far closer to Proust's than to, say, Thackeray's arbitrarily shifting narrative perspective. For third-person subjective has the force though not the form of protagonist narration, and both are equally congenial to impressionistic and stream-of-consciousness fictions.

Third-person subjective is extremely flexible and effective in the novel of personal saga—the *Bildungsroman,* the picaresque—and it has long been widely employed. From the novel's early days, writers as aesthetically and morally different as Cervantes and Bunyan have found advantage in being able to present their protagonists personally but unobtrusively (they often *intrude* as implied authors, but that is a matter of authorial predeliction rather than narrative necessity). Structurally, then, third-person subjective represents something of a mean between the relatively wide-ranging multifarious narrator who, remaining limited in depth-knowledge, shifts perspective, tone, and distance as it suits his purposes, and the intense univocality inherent in protagonist narration.

The personal modes—participant narration and third-person subjective—are often compounded in a "multiples" form that opposes the concept of time as meaningful change, and instead emphasizes the "frozen reality" of contrasting perspectives. Cary's trilogies, Faulkner's *Sound and the Fury, Absalom, Absalom!, As I Lay Dying,* Beckett's trilogy, all counterpoint multiple participant narrators to create an essentially atemporal focusing on individual uniqueness.

Similarly, novels like Woolf's *To the Lighthouse,* Forster's *Passage to India,* Lowry's *Under the Volcano,* though they all employ multifarious narration as their outermost frame of reference, gain their power from a third-person subjective dramatizing of several intensely visualized consciousnesses.

Finally, there are what might be called hybrids occurring in a wide variety of permutations and combinations: multifarious plus participant narration (Mottram's *Spanish Farm Trilogy,* Huxley's *Brave New World* sequence, Duhamel's *Pasquier Chronicles*); participant narration plus third-person subjective (*The Alexandria Quartet*); multifarious narration plus third-person subjective (Lawrence's *Rainbow* and *Women in Love,* Wolfe's novels, Waugh's *Sword of Honour*); and even all three together, multifarious plus participant narration plus third-person subjective (Joyce's *Portrait* and *Ulysses,* Conrad's Marlovian works, Faulkner's Yoknapatawpha cycle).

Of the earlier analogues of the twentieth-century extended novel, only the single-volume ones are "modern." With rare exception, the multivolume novels are morally and structurally univocal, and thus raise quite different questions about form and voice. Such works commonly assume one of two main forms: (1) chronicle or *roman fleuve* (Scott, Cooper, Thackeray, Trollope, Disraeli), or (2) counterpointed: variations on a theme or subject—the "further adventures of . . ." or ". . . revisited" (Cervantes, Bunyan, Defoe, Carroll, Twain, Butler). Both types persist in the twentieth century—(1) Galsworthy, Powell, Snow; (2) Braine, Huxley—though more complexly multivalent forms have come to characterize the modern multivolume novel. In one sense, the very extendedness of these works (regardless of intention) often *does* impart a kind of multivalence. In Braine's *Room at the Top,* for example, the moral worthlessness of Joe Lampton's ambition is clear enough, but he is still portrayed sympathetically. Only in the sequel, *Life at the Top,* do we see Lampton, having attained everything and nothing, reveal his utter hollowness. (This is not to argue that we *need* the sequel, or that it is a good book; on the contrary, it lacks its predecessor's driving energy—because it depicts Lampton as static, no longer in motion—and tells us little we could not have inferred from *Room.*) The two taken together, then, do comprise a multivalent novel because the sequel offers a differently distanced (in this case, less sympathetic) perspective on Braine's protagonist. Thus, while Braine has not shifted his moral perspective between the two books, he has done something potentially more interesting: he has *seeemed* to do so. Unfortunately, Braine's stylistic infelicities vitiate the significance of the shift—which, though undeniably present, may well be largely unintended anyway.

To varying degrees, then, every multivalent novel partakes of two determining characteristics: (1) a self-conscious awareness of itself as artifact, as product, and (2) a counterpointing of conflicting ethical stances, a process in which one or more protagonists participates or serves as object. The gamut of possibilities for both types is virtually as extensive as the art of fiction. Self-conscious structuring ranges from Tristram Shandy's mock powerlessness as imposer of aesthetic order ("Ask my pen,—it governs me, I govern not it"), to the ironic distancing of Conrad's narrator in *The Secret Agent,* from Dos Passos's intricately wrought "objective" devices like the "camera eye" and newsreel and biography in *U.S.A.* and *Midcentury,* to the mutually revelatory but similarly partial views of self and others revealed by the several narrators in Cary's trilogies and Durrell's *Quartet.* We are conscious of structure as process in such works because one or more narrators or narrative voices seem self-consciously determined that we should be.

Opposing moral perspectives may be dramatized through a fairly simple reversal of aesthetic and human norms (Wilde's *Picture of Dorian Gray*), through a re-experiencing of a still-alive past (*Great Expectations, The Good Soldier,* Proust's *Remembrance,* Durrell's *Quartet*), through morally diverse and spatially overlapping perspectives (de Sade's *Justine* and *Juliette, To the Lighthouse,* much of Faulkner, Cary's trilogies, Joyce's *Portrait* and *Ulysses*), or through the unfolding antics of a single protagonist divided against himself (Henry Miller's Henry Miller, Farrell's Studs Lonigan, Nabokov's Humbert Humbert). And of course many multivalent novels—among them the best and most interesting—employ multiple multivalent techniques.

As a further structural refinement, such novels contain one or more protagonists who function as subject of an ethical quest and are minimally distanced from the implied author (Defoe's Robinson

Crusoe, Galsworthy's Forsytes, Tolkien's ring fellows, Snow's Lewis Eliot, Powell's Nicholas Jenkins, Kemelman's Rabbi); or who function as object in novels emphasizing their indeterminate quality (Melville's Confidence Man, Houghton's Jonathan Scrivener, Lowry's Consul, Beckett's Watt); or, most often, who function as a self-conscious and multiply perceived combination of the two (Swift's Gulliver, Ford's Dowell and Tietjens, Joyce's Stephen and Leopold Bloom, the six monologists in Cary's trilogies). In some of the most complex and interesting multivalent fictions, an ostentible subject—sometimes without knowing it, sometimes discovering it only in the process of portraying himself—becomes object as well (Conrad's Marlow, Faulkner's Gavin Stevens, Salinger's Buddy Glass). Nicholas Urfe, the protagonist-narrator of John Fowles's *The Magus*, is designated "the searcher" early in the book, but he then becomes the *object* (he uses the word "victim") of perhaps the most elaborately staged questing in all of modern fiction. The results here are oddly negative, for all the trappings strip away Urfe's own masks and defenses, allowing in the end far less confidence about his actual identity—for him and for us—than at the beginning. Since so much of the emphasis is on the protagonist as self-conscious and inadequate narrator, all such characters appear in what might be called psycho-aesthetic novels—fictions whose paradigm is the modern artist gamely struggling with the intractable materials bequeathed him: himself and the world about him.

The genre is further complicated by the multiple possibilities for resolving the moral conflicts that arise. The simplest (and least "modern") is to appoint a definitive moral spokesman, like the older and wiser Pip in *Great Expectations* or the Pope in Browning's *Ring and the Book*. More problematical approaches deploy participant narrators—Ishmael in *Moby-Dick*, Dilsey in *The Sound and the Fury*, Shreve and Quentin in *Absalom, Absalom!*—offering their only partially acceptable attempts at resolutions, or ironic commentators like those in *The Secret Agent* or *Passage to India* or *Under the Volcano* offering theirs. Or else a confused protagonist-narrator will wind up mired deeper in confusion than ever (Gulliver, Tristram Shandy, Ford's Dowell, Humbert Humbert), or actually attain something resembling a moral resolution (like Henry Miller's Henry Miller, Durrell's Darley, Braine's Joe Lampton)—though only a temporary and partial one because it remains in flux. Or such works may reflect a stripping away, a negating of the central perspective, and an affirming (if at all) only by implication (*The Beast in the Jungle, The Aspern Papers, The Picture of Dorian Gray, Lolita*), or their partially self-validating resolutions may remain counterpoised against each other, none of them ever simply acceptable or rejectable (*Parade's End, To the Lighthouse,* Cary's trilogies, Durrell's *Quartet*), though various characters may express full satisfaction with what has been attained: "I have had my vision," says Lily Briscoe in *To the Lighthouse,* thus terminating the novel (though not necessarily the story).

What all multivalent fiction requires is readers willing themselves to participate in the creative and ethical processes involved in the rendering, willing to hold aesthetic and moral prejudices in abeyance long enough to experience opposing appeals and to confront their irreconcilability honestly and directly. Thus despite Booth's dismissing the showing vs. telling dichotomy as irrelevant to the rhetoric of fiction, the multivalent novel nonetheless demands of us the willing suspension of disbelief (and belief as well) that we associate with the drama. Albert Guerard rightly tells us that *Lord Jim* is a different book from first reading to second (as we are different readers),[15] but this phenomenon is far from unique. For multivalent novels typically shift their focus and apparent purposes (and thus their "facts") even as they reveal themselves to us. The ceaseless becoming of such works determines the marvelously varied continuum of challenges we are made to experience through them.

I would add only that the novel is, of course, the most malleable of art forms. And nowhere is it more endlessly various than in the broad scope of extended multivalent fictions. As a genre, the multivolume novel is a sprawling mode of artistic expression that, especially in its modern manifestations, has lent itself to a fascinating and seemingly endless variety of narrative types and forms. Despite the novel's doomwatchers, this form deserves treatment in its own right and terms not only as the powerful and exciting means of artistic and moral expression that it has been for twentieth-century writers and readers, but also because it may well be the best humanistic device we have for spanning the worlds before and beyond: the premodern locus in linear time and an already emerging future predicated upon the oxymoron of post-McLuhan literateness.

NOTES

1. For a discussion of closed and open novels, see Alan Friedman, *The Turn of the Novel* (New York, 1966), pp. 15-37, 179-88.
2. See p. 128 for a discussion of this novel's central problem.
3. ". . . [A]n author has an obligation to be as clear about his moral position as he possibly can be" (*The Rhetoric of Fiction* [Chicago and London, 1961], p. 389). This idea, which lies behind Booth's critical discussions throughout the book (see especially pp. 346-74, 378-96), seems innocuous and unassailable. But by "clear" Booth implies both "simple" and "good," and thus confuses aesthetic criteria with philosophical and ethical ones. Both extremes of narration are equally anomalous: for those who proclaim showing at the cost of telling, the *reductio ad absurdum* novel is the play, but for Booth—who effectively scores points off such proclaimers—it is, equally absurdly, the sermon.
4. Friedman, *Turn*, p. 185.
5. *The English Novel: Form and Function* (New York, 1953), pp. 18-19.
6. Robert Scholes and Robert Kellogg, *The Nature of Narrative* (New York, 1966), p. 8.
7. *The Fabulators* (New York, 1967), p. 141.
8. "William Golding," in *On Contemporary Literature*, ed. Richard Kostelanetz (New York, 1969), pp. 378, 381.
9. This is the argument that I do in fact make in my *Lawrence Durrell and "The Alexandria Quartet": Art for Love's Sake* (Norman, Okla., 1970), pp. 126-32.
10. Pp. 150-65. See also Norman Friedman, "Point of View in Fiction: The Development of a Critical Concept," *PMLA*, LXX (December 1955), 1160-84.
11. *Nature of Narrative*, pp. 272-73.
12. "The Clockwork Novel: Three Notes on an Eighteenth Century Analogy," *Review of English Studies*, XXI, 81 (February 1970), 14-22.
13. See Booth, pp. 205-18.
14. I say "*apparent* narrative chaos" because authorial control is structuring it. See Van Ghent's discussion of Sterne's false "authorial distress" (p. 88).
15. *Conrad the Novelist* (New York, 1967), pp. 153-55 ff.

CHARACTERS
(CONTRA CHARACTERIZATION)
IN THE
CONTEMPORARY NOVEL

MAX F. SCHULZ

I

Much recent fiction has shown a singular disregard for characterization that develops in self-awareness or in moral perception. Neither Benny Profane nor Herbert Stencil (in Thomas Pynchon's *V.*), nor Eliot or Fred Rosewater (in Kurt Vonnegut's *God Bless You, Mr. Rosewater*), nor F. or Larry (in Leonard Cohen's *Beautiful Losers*) is an Eugène Rastignac, a Pip, or a Raskolnikov. Great novels of the nineteenth century, contrariwise, like Victorian man, were characterized by place, time, and value system. Their fictional protagonists were defined by an ordered society and a fixed moral code. Such historical categories provided novelists with the fictive limits of self-knowledge. Man began innocent and unformed, and grew to awareness (and organized understanding) of his relationship to others and of his place in the world. It is not accidental that the nineteenth century, heir to Romantic concepts of organicism, of growth and change, gave rise to the systems of Darwinism, Marxism, and Freudianism, with their temporal suppositions. The German thinker Wilhelm Dilthey epitomized the dominant frame of reference of the age when he remarked, "We are able to know what the human spirit is only through history . . . this historical self-consciousness allows us to formulate a systematic theory of man."[1] Man was conceived as evolving socially and morally in time, and thus fiction mirrored man.

The twentieth century has shown progressive disenchantment with circumscribed and uncritical explanatory systems. The latest extremity of our skepticism (whose scientific vanguard Blake combatted with such angry epigrams as

> Reason says "Miracle": Newton says "Doubt."
> Aye! that's the way to make all Nature out.
> "Doubt, Doubt, & don't believe without experiment")[2]

dismisses the stability of the physical universe, a grim position memorably apotheosized in Vonnegut's *Cat's Cradle,* the ice-nine which destroys the world in that novel furnishing an eloquent, if devastating, rebuttal to the starry cosmos so grandly and simplistically eulogized by Newton. As monuments to the human mind's urge for order, western civilization's time-honored moral and epistemological formulations have fallen under a cloud of suspicion, and are treated as no more valid, and even less satisfactory, than fictive models honestly owned and avowed by their authors. This rejection of historical perspective, with its chronological unfolding of events, has forced novelists to make of the resultant world labyrinth—an exitless funhouse, hall of mirrors, or box-within-box (to name several of the images currently used as descriptive of the universe)—both the substance and the form of their novels. The covertly organic has been discarded in favor of the frankly artificial.

Yet, the artifice of contemporary novels, the word-play as Tony Tanner in a recent book characterizes it, has identifiable philosophical antecedents, if not direct origins, which are no less historical than the discarded conventional ways of organizing experience. Thinkers as divergent as George Lukács and Claude Lévi-Strauss agree essentially on the modalities of the literary world. It is not

> a mere "subjective" semblance or illusion, for it describes . . . an existent objective realm shared by the artist with other men, and ultimately with mankind as a whole, whence our ability to understand our predecessors. Art as the "identical subject-object" of the aesthetic process articulates the self-consciousness of the human species. Hence the artistic imagination is productive without therefore necessarily being capricious. What it brings forth is not a private world, but an ordered whole ultimately rooted in mankind's collective experience. In this sense art "reflects" a reality, but this reality is not one of "facts"; neither is it one of mere "feelings." Art is the mirror-image of an "objective" realm of values, or in different language, it states the truth about the world.[3]

Clearly, as George Lichtheim notes, the ultimate significance of artistic creation for Lukács is ontological, with art disclosing "the true nature of man as a species being."[4] Interestingly, Lukács's social determinism, as summarized here, is not incompatible with the grounds of Lévi-Strauss's social anthropology. Within the tradition of historicism that runs from Vico to Merleau-Ponty, Lévi-Strauss contends that even more basic to man's notions of himself than time and place have been the cultural patterns constructed out of his responses to natural objects and to civilized artifacts. And these configurations, found embedded in pre-linguistic myths, represent habits of mind that continue to inform man's predilection for story-telling, that is, for rendering natural mysteries into cultural coherencies. And it is not unreasonable to suspect that such structures of thought may dominate literature at those times when explicit explanatory systems lose credence.

While the fiction of the last twenty-five years is still responsive to conventional tools of criticism, it clearly calls for the development of analytical techniques derived from the same version of reality that may have contributed to its structure. In the remainder of this essay, I wish to test the effectiveness of one of these categorical imperatives of the mind as a critical instrument for coming to terms with certain kinds of contemporary fiction.

Both Lévi-Strauss and Roman Jakobson describe the mind—whether functioning culturally or linguistically—as an instrument employing binary codes to generate the raw data of sensation into meaningful structures of language. In his series of studies on the myths of the Indians of the Amazon, *Mythologiques*,[5] Lévi-Strauss analyzes a variety of mythic equations, which he contends correspond to the logic of human thought. I wish to extract from the complex taxonomic information of his marathon study of "pre-logical" myths the single dialectic of natural/artificial. Lévi-Strauss has formulated a set of equations, for example, which adhere to this fundamental dichotomy thus:[6]

	FOOD		SOCIETY		RELIGION		SOUND
NATURAL/	: :	fresh→putrid/	: :	nature/	: :	sacred/	: :	noise/
ARTIFICIAL		raw→cooked		culture		profane		silence

If his hypothesis even approximates the process that connects man-as-sensor with the world-as-sensate, such fictional structures as the novel may be assumed to reflect the same kind of configurations, especially those contemporary novels in which the author has abjured accepted systems of history with assumptions of organic and causal continuity, in favor of drawing directly on deeper irrational strata of the human brain in which presumably are still embedded pre-linguistic systems of thought. The fiction which most exactly fits the above description, offering fruitful possibilities for this type of analysis, is that which is vaguely alluded to as Black Humor. And the equation I wish to apply to this literature, under the rubric of natural/artificial, is as follows:

	CHARACTERIZATION		NARRATIVE PROGRESSION
NATURAL/ : :	embryological (organic development)/	: :	chronological/
ARTIFICIAL	doppelgänger (hero with a thousand faces)		regressus in infinitum

I realize, of course, that the Victorian world picture and the Victorian novel are intrinsically and extrinsically cultural constructs, and hence the contrary of the natural as used by Lévi-Strauss. If one restricts the focus, though, to the Victorian preoccupation with time and natural evolution, memorialized in the hypotheses of Darwin and the historical imperatives of Marx, one can recognize the intrinsic naturalism of Victorian definitions of experience. This concern with growth and duration, especially as reflected in the novel, is even more marked when contrasted to the atemporality of so much contemporary fiction.

II

Much contemporary fiction has eschewed the world of reality as defined by the logical abstractions of the past, the moral patterns of reason/feeling and duty/desire, which informed the narrative development and characterization of the great nineteenth-century novels from Charlotte Brontë to Henry James. We are not asked to identify with the developing moral awareness and self-discovery of the protagonist. A writer like Nabokov selects unsavory types to prevent reader identification. Students' bewilderment at their ambivalent reaction to Humbert Humbert, whom they recognize as the sympathetic protagonist but whom their moral training tells them is repulsive, is a recurrent situation in college classes where *Lolita* is taught. Nabokov refuses to satisfy our expectations about what a novel should be. He does not observe the conventions of realism of the nineteenth century nor the conventions of psychology and point of view of this century. He dismisses mimesis and identification with the hero disdainfully as mythology. He has said that "life is the least realistic of fictions"; hence, "reality" should always be written in quotation marks, since there is no single absolute state of reality, as our daily round of existence assumes.[7] For Nabokov the raw data of experience is not reality, is indeed at the farthest remove from reality. Hence the realistic novel which attempts verisimilitude is unreal paradoxically in direct ratio to its approximation to raw data. In actuality, as Nabokov knows, but which we conveniently forget, the realistic novel can never be anything other than a parody of the external world, no matter how hard it tries to imitate it, since the image of that world can never be equivalent to the object. Reality for Nabokov is rather the pattern which the imagination can discern in or create out of the raw data. Reality then is basically the product of a creative or imaginative act—an artistic act. And the more complex is the pattern the more "real," that is, the more comprehensive and inclusive, the "reality." Raw data in and of itself is of no importance or concern to Nabokov. Only when it is organized—the materials of life transformed into the artifacts of art—can it mean anything. And since, if all novels are parodies of something else—either the raw data of experience, dreams, reconstructed memories, or concepts of the mind—then the truest and most interesting novels will be those that frankly parody and ingenuously admit their artifice (in the same way as Cézanne and the Cubist painters rejected perspective in favor of admitting that a picture consists of paint on a canvas surface).

Nabokov, however, is a master chess player, manipulating reader reaction with cunning approximations of his fictional structure to the conventional novel. Thus, concepts of tone and point of view, for example, still serve one well as critical tools in an analysis of *Lolita*. By presenting the tale as a detective story, which forces the reader to go the route from ignorance to full possession of the facts, Nabokov realizes the effect of growth in moral awareness. Furthermore, Humbert's seeming increase in self-knowledge is strengthened by the discrete emphasis of his nympholepsy in the first half of his memoir and by the expressions of remorse for his destruction of Lolita in the second half. In keeping with this alteration of attitude, the jaunty hollow tone of the French *boulevardier* pervert similarly gives way to the guilt-ridden regret of the rejected suitor. Ostensibly, the novel pursues the linear development of the great continental novels of the nineteenth century. Actually, Humbert (I) the debonair seducer remains unchanged from start to finish of the narrative of his years with Lolita; while Humbert (II) the penitent comes into being after the killing of Quilty and during the writing of his memoir. There are two Humberts, each with his identifying tone—one is the actor in the memoir, the other is the writer of the memoir; but we are not shown one growing out of the other, only the alternation of the two by way of the upwelling of Humbert II's remorse into the antic gaiety of the story of Humbert I. In short, we have less progression than juxtaposition, less a study in the growth of awareness of one character than the presentation of two distinct characters—hence, less developing characterization than doppelgänger on the way to being ironically the hero with a thousand faces; for Humbert's obsession with nymphets, which enthralls him in bestiality, has its paradigm in the fairy tale of *Beauty and the Beast*. And just as love breaks the spell cast upon Beast, transforming him back into Prince, so Humbert's love for Lolita helps him shed his nympholepsy and allow the redeemed human to emerge, linking Humbert with the thousand and one mythic versions of man's emergence from primordial animality.

Nor are novels like *Lolita* fictional sports. The same strategy informs much contemporary fiction, leapfrogs over national generic distinctions, and ignores generational gulfs. Tactically, the two Oskars of Günter Grass's *The Tin Drum* are closer kissing cousins of the two Humberts than of the two Wilhelm Meisters, apprentice and journeyman, of Goethe's novels, whose *Bildungsroman* tradition Grass parodically professes allegiance to. And the doppelgängers mentioned in the second sentence of this essay share uncanny commonality despite Vonnegut's seniority in age over Pynchon and Cohen.

The concept of illusion versus reality—a favorite topic of critical orthodoxy of the past thirty years—offers us a useful perspective for scanning the recurrent asymmetrical doubles who people these stories. In this frame of reference Humbert I inhabits an illusory idealized world, and Humbert II the factual retributive world of society. Similarly, there are the Zemblan and American guises of Kinbote in *Pale Fire*, and the idyllic (Ardis, in Demonia) and temporal (Terra) abodes of Van in *Ada*. This antithesis unquestionably helps us to describe the contents and sort the priorities of Nabokov's novels; but its categorical imperatives fall into ambiguity when we introduce the added dimension of Nabokov's intrusive authorial control. The novels are, in other words, more inclusive and self-conscious constructs than the sum of their narrative statements. In each of the novels mentioned, the protagonist leaves us with a memoir, which is ostensibly equivalent to the narrative we read, but over which palpably looms the larger manipulative presence of Nabokov, whose editorial omniscience calls our attention ironically to the restricted and faulty versions of reality of the protagonists. It is by means of the combination of these points of view that Nabokov fits the raw data of experience into the transcendent perfection of art, containing both the faulty vision and the consciousness of it. The ultimate pattern then, one might say, as well as the only reality for Nabokov's novels, which subsumes all other constructs (such as illusory-factual) presents the growth cycles of the natural transformed, deployed, and fixed in relationships of artifice.

Thus have we arrived approximately at the generalization that Lévi-Strauss extrapolates from the binary equations (given above) into which he has reduced the ancient myths. To what extent the mid-twentieth-century writer sophisticatedly reflects the influence of contemporary anthropology and to what extent he confirms the universal habits of thought projected by that anthropology remains, of course, a moot question. Like Lévi-Strauss, one can only continue to marshall the weight of evidence.

III

John Barth's handling of the developmental-doppelgänger equation is less calculated than Nabokov's, because Barth, less certain of answers, is using his fiction to explore psychologically and historically the acts of being a man and of being an artist.

Barth's substitution of doppelgänger characters for embryogenic characterizations, and circular *regressus* for chronological narrative—in brief, his development from a writer of traditional stories to a mythicist, parodist, artificer, and Black Humorist—is a fascinating authorial odyssey. In his first two novels, *The Floating Opera* (1956) and *The End of the Road* (1958), he exhibited little inclination to depart from the conventionality of acceptable genre and philosophy. Both books define reality in terms of a literary naturalism that firmly delineates person and place, Chesapeake clams, convivial beer busts, love, sex, and unfiltered dialogue—what Gerhard Joseph has aptly called "Maryland based verisimilitude";[8] and both accept existentialism for their definition of the human situation. The combination proved to be inimicable to extending his understanding even of the human psyche's impulse at times to act and at other times to lapse into paralysis, let alone of its need to know itself. Existentialism, with its program of willed act, provided a descriptive method but no analytical guide. The same limitations characterized Barth's reliance on conventional space-time realism. In *The Sot-Weed Factor* (1960) he broke free of these limitations in his parody of the eighteenth-century novel and the picaresque hero. The increasing artifice of his fabling is also indicated by his conception, in Ebenezer Cooke and Henry Burlingame, of not one protagonist but two who are in many respects each other's double. (The double is already foreshadowed in *The End of the Road* in the pairing of Jacob Horner and Joe Morgan). Following the writing of *The Sot-Weed Factor*, Barth discovered Lord Raglan and Borges.[9] *Giles Goat-Boy* (1966) represents his effort to distil the definable dimensions of the hero with a thousand faces into one protagonist whose destiny encompasses the mythic story of man from primordial emergence to computerized immolation. This fictional exercise in ontological typology was audacious but intrinsically schizophrenic. It did not lead Barth to the essential "I." George Goat-Boy resists literary alchemical transformation of his parts into an ineluctable sense of what it is to be human. He remains simply a farrago of the old categories, contradictions, and appearances, an empirical assemblage of the flotsam and jetsam of civilization. Discarding the notion of the hero who is the sum of his parts, Barth in his *Lost in the Funhouse* (1968) and in *Chimera* (1972) has followed the lead of Borges and sought by way of the fascinating paradox of *regressus in infinitum* to combine the narrative devices of growth and doppelgänger with the phenomenological identification of creator and creation (including the inherent blurring of the line between fact and fancy) so as to wind himself back to the core of self on which a sense of ontological security hinges.

In "Seven Additional Author's Notes" appended to the first American edition's prefatory "Author's Notes," Barth alludes to "the serial nature of the fourteen pieces"[10] in *Lost in the Funhouse*. The stories act out a pattern of development, which dramatizes the life of the protagonist-narrator. Who am I as person? And who am I as author? These two questions are the systole-diastole of all fourteen stories, as they progress temporally from conception ("Night-Sea Journey"), to birth and naming—the initial gesture of identification ("Ambrose His Mark"), to consciousness as entity separate from one's parents ("Autobiography"), to boyhood prefigurement of adulthood ("Water-Message"), to adolescence with its emergent cognizance of moral and artistic categories ("Petition" and "Lost in the Funhouse"), to adult, husband and artist, wracked with the question of personal and cultural identity ("Echo," "The Meditations," "Title," "Glossolalia," and "Life-Story").

Simultaneously with the dramatization of the life cycle of one man, the stories chronicle the life cycle of the artist in a "sub-plot" that moves backward in time to the origins of man as an artistic and self-conscious entity. Two additional metamorphoses accompany this regression of the tales. Slowly, inexorably, the author-narrator merges in identity (1) with his protagonist-narrator, who is portrayed as a writer struggling to find a personality, and (2) with the archetypal bard, who has compulsively sung the story of his life since man invented words. The opening situations depicting the growth of Ambrose from child to man conform in their telling to the style of Barth's Maryland-based verisimilitude. But the realistic surface of the incidents subsequently concerned with Ambrose as adult is increasingly disrupted by multiple points of view, by self-parody and parody of other literary styles, and by disappearance of the author into the immediate and ultimately the mythic dimensions of his tale. The disintegration of the personality of Ambrose when lost in the funhouse coincides with the disillusionment of the author-narrator with the conventional subject matter and modes of fiction. In the stories that follow "Lost in the Funhouse" (which occupies a central position in the collection), the seeming breakdown in control of narration, as the narrator self-consciously struggles with plot and theme, progresses until in "Life-Story" he is reduced to telling "a story about a writer writing a story" (p. 114). Unlike such great nineteenth-century novels as *David Copperfield, Henry Esmond,* and *Great Expectations,* in which self-knowledge accompanies the protagonist's catching up to the narrator, these stories fuse protagonist-narrator with author-narrator in a *regressus in infinitum* barren of self-discovery. Protagonist and narrator become merely unending echoes of each other's creative blocks. It is not surprising then that in the story "Echo," which follows "Lost in The Funhouse," Barth probes the myth of Echo and Narcissus for an answer to the question of his authorial identity—nor is it surprising, given the properties of the myth, that the negative results are similar. Only with the last two stories—"Menelaiad" and "Anonymiad"—does Barth break out of this vortex. By the identification of his fictional and authorial selves with the anonymous *mythos* of sexual generation and artistic creation, the author-narrator finally gets an answer to the question of identity he has been stubbornly asking in each story. In Menelaus's obsessive retelling of his love for Helen and in the anonymous bard's invention of his life, the Barthian narrator recognizes his doppelgänger. The saga of his progress as human being and as artist—delineated in the stories of *Lost in the Funhouse*—is seen to be but the latest swirl in a regress having its mythic origin in the first anonymous bard who sang self-consciously of what he was about to sing. Considered as a novel (rather than collection of short stories), *Lost in the Funhouse* has a sequence that dissolves into circularity. The actual structure of the book is emphasized at the outset (although we understand the significance only after reading to the end) by the "Frame-Tale," which consists of the endless sentence: "Once upon a time there was a story that began 'Once upon a time there was a story that began "Once upon . . ."' ."

Barth's dual handling of time (horological present and mythic past) and of human consciousness (individual and archetypal) accords with Lévi-Strauss's description of the "two-fold continuum" on which myth operates: "One part of it is external and is composed . . . of historical, or supposedly historical, events forming a theoretical infinite series from which each society extracts a limited number of relevant incidents with which to create its myths. . . . The second aspect of the continuum is internal and is situated in the psycho-physiological time" of each individual.[11] *Lost in the Funhouse* develops simultaneously a chronological narrative and a recurrent mythos. By this means the author-narrator sees himself both in the serialized growth of his protagonist into a writer and in the archetypal dimensions of the eternal artist. The life cycle of the protagonist-narrator Ambrose spirals in a *regressus in infinitum* to intersect the equivalent orbit of the anonymous bard circling endlessly and historically forward to the present.

Barth seeks in such binary acrobatics more than literary or cultural continuity. He is reaching out to the boundaries of consciousness in an effort to give palpable form to human identity. Although the literary strategies of *Lost in the Funhouse* might be defined superficially as romantic, they actually diverge from those of romanticism based on a conception of the universe in which man by means of his imagination knows himself as an organic part of a larger whole. The relation of Ambrose-Barth, the protagonist-author, to the artificer archetype is not so much that of one partaking of the other (and in this participation contributing to its continuation and completion) as of one being the latest of many equivalents to the other. Borges makes the same point in his story "The Maker" when he defines himself in Homeric terms as another instance of the blind poet. Each man remains ontologically inviolate, while yet the many poets are *sui generis* the same artist. Shelley's poet merges with the west wind in its seasonal cycle and with the cloud in its meteorological cycle; Barth's protagonist-author and Borges's maker remain themselves in their enactment of the eternal role of artist. Impatient with the split between perceiving artist and object perceived (unlike Nabokov, who is content with the neo-subjectivism of the turn of the century), Barth seeks a totality that is less organic than archetypal and environmental, a conceptual totalization that includes the mystique of personality with the empiricism of psychology. In *Lost in the Funhouse* (as to a less extent in *The Sot-Weed Factor* and *Giles Goat-Boy*), he has fashioned structures of artifice that also render for us the shock of recognition of the felt life.

IV

I do not mean to imply that traditional modes of criticism should be discarded in favor of the structural principles of Jakobson and Lévi-Strauss, particularly their theory about the binary organization of human perception; but I do wish to suggest that our understanding of some recent fiction which abjures the aims of conventional realism is enriched by this methodology.

The use of doppelgängers, of course, is not new. The ambience of stopped or eternalized time, of the jettison of causality, and of the annihilation of historicity surrounding the appearance of double figures in the fiction of Borges, Nabokov, Barth, and Vonnegut, however, is new. The fiction of the late nineteenth and early twentieth centuries was equally fascinated with disguises and doppelgängers. Always, though, the frame of reference is posited on the succession of time, underscored by the impetus of the narrative. In Conrad's *Nostromo*, for example, Charles Gould is introduced to us as a man committed to an ideal of family honor and Gian' Battista as one committed to a code of personal honor. As opportunities for self-aggrandizement, power, and wealth develop, however, each compromises his ideal of manhood and his sense of honor in his captivity to a thing: Gould's to the San Tomé mine and Battista's to the barge load of silver. Each man succumbs to the matrix of his world, enmeshed in the temporality of events, of evolution, and of evolving geopolitics. At the same time each is a mirror image of the other. Yet one cannot say that our grasp of either man's fate depends on our awareness of the other's. Each one's story is complete and meaningful in itself, offering up no more than an ironical commentary on its counterpart. Nabokov's doppelgängers in *Lolita* and Barth's in *Lost in the Funhouse*, contrariwise, are bound in a dialectical relationship whose symbolic structure realizes a totality—as well as an escape from history, from the degeneration of time—that transcends the organic integrity of each. They do not evolve so much as persist, like insects suspended in amber, completed by their artful positioning in relation to each other. Humbert and Ambrose, like pre-linguistic man, re-enact in each moment their perpetual renascence, which we measure by the parodic juxtaposition of their temporal selves to their timeless archetypes, at once Pygmalions and self-created Galateas. In

"Night-Sea Journey" Barth calculatedly calls our attention in the conception of Ambrose to the return in every such conception to the primordial self—the *anakulosis*, Plato's Eternal Return, the reticulation of temporality in the infinite cyclicity of time.[12] And his organization of the collection of stories, so that they proceed from those in time to those outside of history, culminating in the mythopoeic "Menelaid" and "Anonymiad," structures this *regressus in infinitum*, this repetition of the primordial archetype, into the ostensibly linear development of the narrative.[13]

The thrust of Borges's stories—and of Nabokov's, Barth's, and to a less artistic extent Vonnegut's—is away from natural sequence and toward artificial rearrangement, away from embryological development, temporal transformations, and growth cycles, and toward ontological definitions "uncontaminated by time and becoming."[14] Was Judas Jesus, or Jesus Judas ("Three Versions of Judas"), Borges conjectures in a variation on Zeno's paradox that reduces identity to conundrum. A fascination of this fiction is watching the ostensibly organic shaped into artifice. The anomaly about such art is that the more complex its organization the more inclusive seemingly its purchase on reality.

NOTES

1. Quoted by George Lichtheim in his study of *George Lukács* (New York: The Viking Press, 1970), p. 24.
2. From Blake's M.S. Note-Book 1808-11, *The Complete Writings of William Blake*, ed. Geoffrey Keynes (London: The Nonesuch Press, 1957), p. 536.
3. Thus, George Lichtheim summarizes Lukács' underlying theoretical concepts in *George Lukács*, pp. 136-37.
4. *Ibid.*, p. 77.
5. Claude Lévi-Strauss, *Le Crû et le cuit* (Paris: Plon, 1964) and *Miel et cendres* (Paris: Plon, 1966).
6. A convenient, as well as stimulating, summary of Lévi-Strauss's main intellectual positions is given by Edmund Leach, who can by no means be construed as a convert, in *Claude Lévi-Strauss* (New York: The Viking Press, 1970). For a discussion of this set of equations see pp. 87-99.
7. Reported by Ross Wetzsteon, "Nabokov as Teacher," *Nabokov Criticism, Reminiscences, Translations and Tributes*, ed. Alfred Appel, Jr. and Charles Newman (Evanston: Northwestern University Press, 1970), p. 242. Cf. also in the same volume, Alfred Appel, Jr., on "Backgrounds of *Lolita*," p. 33, 36, 39; Barbara Heldt Monter on " 'Spring in Fialta': The Choice That Mimics Chance," pp. 128-35; and Jeffrey Leonard on "In Place of Lost Time: *Ada*," pp. 136-46. For additional Nabokovian remarks on "reality," see Herbert Gold,

"Vladimir Nabokov," *Paris Review*, No. 41 (1967), 95-96; and Kinbote's note to line 130 of "Pale Fire": " 'reality' is neither the subject nor the object of true art which creates its own special reality having nothing to do with the average 'reality' perceived by the communal eye," *Pale Fire* (New York: G. P. Putnam's Sons, 1962), p. 130.

8. Gerhard Joseph, *John Barth* (Minneapolis: University of Minnesota Press, 1970), University of Minnesota Pamphlets on American Writers, 91, p. 39.

9. John J. Enck, "John Barth: An Interview," *Contemporary Literature*, VI (1965), 12. Cf. also Barth's article on Borges, "Literature of Exhaustion," *The Atlantic*, CCXX (1967), 29-34.

10. All quotations are from the Bantam Book edition of 1969.

11. Claude Lévi-Strauss, *The Raw and the Cooked,* trans. John and Doreen Weightman (New York: Harper and Row, 1969). The quotation is taken from the Harper Torchbook edition (1970), p. 16.

12. Mircea Eliade, *The Myth of the Eternal Return* (New York: Pantheon Books, 1954), Bollingen Series, Vol. 46, p. 89n.

13. Barth derives an additional advantage from structuring his book as a collection of short stories. Arresting the narrative development by freezing it into segmental short stories works to reduce the sense of natural growth so characteristic of the nineteenth-century novel. With this artificer's feint, Barth further de-emphasizes the organic.

14. Eliade, p. 89.

NOVEL
AND
NARRATIVE

FRANK KERMODE

I

We could save ourselves much trouble by agreeing that a novel is a fictional prose narrative of a certain length, which allows for a great deal of variation between novels. But it is obvious that people want to expand it; they plump it out in various ways, and this enables them to make such observations as "This is not really a novel," or "Where have all the novelists gone?" They can specify a novel with much more accuracy than my simple formula allows; the trouble is that in doing so they represent accident as essence. This is one reason why the death of the novel is so often announced. Provisional and local characteristics are mistaken for universal requirements. The difficulty is made worse by the desire of those who understand this to dissociate themselves vigorously from the old novels that exhibit such restrictions; not only do they wish, understandably, to write novels which are free of those local and provincial restrictions so long mistaken for essential elements of the kind; not only do they sensibly want to enquire into what sort of a thing a novel really is, what goes on in the mind that reads it; they also, and less happily, assert that the newness of what they are doing distinguishes it decisively from anything that has been done before. So both sides may agree that the old novel is dead, one rejoicing and the other lamenting. The New Novel is parricide and usurper, and the Oedipal parallel is strengthened, some might say, by the self-inflicted blindness of the son.

If we have the patience to look at the difficulty more closely, we may find that a family resemblance persists, as between Laius and Oedipus, who were both lame, both deceived by oracles, and both married to the same woman. Novels new and old may have congenital defects, may take oracles too literally, and have an intimate relationship with the reader. Differences of course exist, though commentary and advertisement exaggerate them. Certain old habits have been discontinued; for example the old assumption that a novel must be concerned with the authentic representation of character and milieu, and with social and ethical systems that transcend it—what may be called the kerygmatic assumption—is strongly questioned. The consequence is a recognizable estrangement from what used to be known as reality; and a further consequence, which can equally be defended as having beneficent possibilities, is that the use of fiction as an instrument of research into the nature of fiction, though certainly not new, is much more widely recognized. But if we admit novelty to this extent, we must at once add that none of these new things was outside the scope of the long narrative of the past; what we are *learning* about narrative may be, in a sense, new, but narrative was always potentially what we have now learned to think it, in so far as our thinking is right; though perhaps for good reasons the aspects that interest us seemed less important, and were the subject of fewer or even no enquiries.

It seems doubtful, then, whether we need to speak of some great divide—a strict historical *coupure*—between the old and new. There are differences of emphasis, certainly, as to what it is to read; and there are, within the narratives themselves, rearrangements of emphasis and interest. Perhaps, as metacritics often allege, these are to be attributed to a major shift in our structures of thought; but although this may be an efficient cause of the mutation of interests it does not appear that the object of those interests—narrative—imitates the shift.

II

Compare an older historical problem. W. P. Ker tells us in his *Epic and Romance* that the yielding of the first of these kinds to the second was an epochal event: "The change of temper and fashion represented by the appearance and vogue of the medieval French romances is a change involving the whole world, and going far beyond the compass of literature and literary history."[1] He is talking about what later came to be called the Renaissance of the Twelfth Century, of which the change from a "stronger kind of poetry"[2] to another, more eclectic, less heroic, more ambiguous, was but a part. Within the larger changes in society he detects not only changes in poetry and rhetoric, but also new kinds of story-telling, which "imply the failure of the older manner of thought, the older fashion of imagination."[3] "Failure" here is too strong, surely: "change" would serve. It must be said that the re-examination of the nature and design of an instrument, in this case fiction, might well be related to other kinds of cultural change, as Ker suggests. But within the history of narrative this is interesting mainly as an example of how, from time to time, it becomes possible and de-sirable to think about the nature of narrative not as if it were given and self-evident, but as if it were susceptible of widely different de-velopments. "No later change in the forms of fiction," says Ker, "is more important than the twelfth century revolution. . . . It . . . finally put an end to the old local and provincial restrictions upon narrative."[4]

This is perhaps extravagant; "finally" is also too strong. But we can add to Ker's authority that of Eugène Vinaver, who speaks of related matters in his remarkable book *The Rise of Romance*. Look first at the kinds of difficulty encountered in the *Chanson de Roland*: its dis-crete, discontinuous scenes, its lack of "temporal and rational links and transitions."[5] It seems impossible to speak of its possessing an overall structure, or a narrative syntax, for that would imply se-quence, connection, subordination—not this parataxis. The same event may dominate successive strophes: Roland dies three times, al-ways with a difference, almost as if in a novel by M. Robbe-Grillet. Vinaver insists that if we try to lay out these strophes as temporally successive we shall distort the work, which appears not to be as inter-ested as we have come to be in the registration of an even flow of time and causality. Romance, on the other hand, does have continuous nar-rative of a sort, but the problems it sets us are equally difficult. So much is not explained. The writers seem consciously to require their readers to work on their texts (*gloser la lettre*) and supply meanings to them (*de lor sen le sorplus mettre*).[6] The reader's job is like the writer's own, the progressive discovery of non-linear significances, the reading, in narrative, of clues to what is not narrative. Creative inferences of this kind are necessary in all competent reading; here the fact is recognized and exploited in what seems a peculiar way. The coherence of a narrative may be of such a kind as to frustrate certain cultural expectations.

The complexities of Chrétien de Troyes are such that he may still, in up-to-date books, be accused of "lapses of coherence."[7] His Grail story is particularly vexatious, and scholars have solved it by inventing a Quest sequence: Miraculous Weapon, Dolorous Stroke, Waste Land, Healing. But this sequence, and *a fortiori* its mythic archetype as we discover it in the work of Jessie L. Weston, occurs neither in Chrétien nor in any early text. (Such is our rage for order that when Eliot dissolved this myth in *The Waste Land* his critics crystallized it out again.) Chrétien was not aiming at this kind of coherence, and to provide it is to violate his text—to import irrelevant constraints into the interpretation of the narrative. What he sought to produce was what Vinaver—adapting a famous formula of Cleanth Brooks's—calls "a pattern of *un*resolved stresses."[8] He did not assume that all good fiction must be of the kind of which it can be predicated that everything "fits in."[9] This position may be hard to hold; in the thirteenth century what Vinaver calls "the restraints of design"[10]—the requirements of sequence and closure—grew strong again.

Certain qualities which we may, on a narrow view, associate with well-formed narratives, are absent from that of Chrétien: closure, character, authenticated reference to settled notions of reality. The modern rejection of these qualities is, in part, a rediscovery of properties of narrative known in the twelfth century: the qualities Vinaver calls *entrelacement*, and polyphony, of resistance to closure, and to certain other expectations bred by narratives of a different emphasis.

What we discover, then, from listening to Ker and Vinaver on the *Chanson* and Chrétien is that discoveries about the nature and possibilities of narrative may, perhaps must, take place at times when there are in progress revaluations of much larger cultural scope, but that the discoveries themselves are about narrative, and are not necessarily of a character that connects them in an obvious way with the changes that accompany them. Nor do they constitute an irreversible evolution; that is why in both works there are what we think of as anticipations of the fire-new research of our contemporaries. We note also the recurrent desire to reimpose local and provincial restrictions. Narrative is prior to all such, and we need to understand how it works without identifying it with its local and transient manifestations.

III

I want now, for a moment, to talk about a single novel; for reasons which I shall try to make clear it is a detective story. This kind of narrative began to develop in the nineteenth century and reached a very remarkable degree of specialization in the twentieth. It is therefore a good example of the overdevelopment of one element of narrative at the expense of others: it is possible to tell a story in such a way that the principal object of the reader is to discover, by an interpretation of clues, the answer to a problem posed at the outset. All other considerations may be subordinated to this interpretative, or, as I shall call it, hermeneutic activity. Clearly this emphasis requires, to a degree much greater than in most stories (though all have hermeneutic aspects) the disposition, in a consecutive narrative, of information which requires us to ask both how it "fits in," and also how it will all "come out"; and this information bears upon an event, usually a murder, that precedes the narrative which bears the clues. Clearly there is a peculiar distortion of more usual narrative conventions (though readers rapidly acquire the competence to meet the new demands). I have chosen a recognized classic of the genre, *Trent's Last Case*. There is not much detailed study of such books, partly because they are by some thought unworthy of it, but also because there is a taboo on telling what happens in the end. This taboo, which, observed, frustrates comment, is relevant to my enquiry, because one of the most powerful of the local and provincial restrictions is that a novel must *end*, or pretend to; or score a point, by disappointing the expectation that it will do so. There must be *closure* or at least an allusion to it. The taboo sacralizes closure; it suggests that to give away the solution that comes at the end is to give away all, so intense is the hermeneutic specialization. But in the present context profanity is necessary and also good.

The detective story is much more concerned than narratives normally are with the elucidation of a series of events which closed either before or only shortly after its own starting point. The narrative is ideally required to provide, by variously enigmatic clues, all the evidence concerning the true character of those earlier events that the investigator and the reader require to reconstruct them. Clues are of many kinds. Some information is simply conveyed; other information looks simple but isn't. Still more appears to have a bearing on the problem but does not, or does have a bearing while seeming not to. Of course another kind of information must also be provided and processed, the kind that moves the narrative along, establishes a milieu, or characterizes the detective—as a priest, a don, an aborigine, or a peculiar old lady—or explains why so many people disliked the deceased, and so on. This information may or may not be irrelevant to the hermeneutic enterprise on which the reader is embarked; also it can conceal clues or introduce false ones. It will certainly, in so far as it takes his attention, distract the reader from his hermeneutic task. And the interplay between narrative and hermeneutic processes is so complex that information which has no bearing on the pre-narrative events may be processed by an attentive reader in senses which alter the whole bearing of the book. Ideally, however, we are always sorting out the hermeneutically relevant from all the other information, and doing so much more persistently than we have to in other kinds of novel. For although all have hermeneutic content, only the detective story makes it pre-eminent.

In *Trent's Last Case* the title itself is enigmatic: we don't find out why it's his *last* case until the final paragraph. The first sentence of the book is: "Between what matters and what seems to matter, how should the world we know judge wisely?" This has the characteristic ambiguity. The narrator explains it thus: very rich financiers, such as Manderson, the victim in this book, are extremely important in the international money markets, though they have no effect at all on the world in which wealth is really produced. (Notice also the false complicity of "the world we know," which suggests that our reading is always going to be the one prescribed by the narrator.) Of course the words refer equally to the difficulty by distinguishing what, hermeneutically, matters and does not matter in the pages that follow. It it worth adding that it does not matter whether this ambiguity was intended or not. An important and neglected rule about reading narratives is that once a certain kind of attention has been aroused we read according to the values appropriate to that kind of attention whether or no there is a series of definite gestures to prompt us; of course we may also decide not to be docile, and evade these local and provincial restrictions.

The millionaire Manderson is found dead in the grounds of his house.[11] He has been shot through the eye. No weapon is found, and there are scratches on his wrists. He is oddly dressed in a mixture of day and evening clothes; his false teeth are missing; his watch is not in the pocket designed for it; his shoelaces are badly tied. Yet he was known to be a neat dresser; he had clearly put on some of his clothes with his usual leisurely care; and he had parted his hair. Trent finds among Manderson's otherwise perfect shoes a pair slightly damaged, as if by the insertion of too large a foot. This enables him, though reluctantly, to suspect Manderson's English secretary Marlowe. He duly finds Marlowe's pistol to have been used in the killing, and he finds the right fingerprints on Manderson's tooth glass and elsewhere. However, Marlowe has a perfect alibi: he had driven through the night to Southampton on business of Manderson's. Trent correctly concludes that death must have occurred much earlier than had been supposed—the ambiguity of evidence on this point has been scrupulously indicated—and that Marlowe, on the previous evening, had dumped the body where it was found, entered the house wearing Manderson's shoes, conducted a daring imitation of his employer—even conversing with the butler and Mrs. Manderson—and then, having planted the clues which suggested that his employer died the following morning, departed for Southampton. Trent writes all this out and takes the document to the young widow, whom he likes but suspects of an attachment to Marlowe, and perhaps even of complicity. He leaves her to decide whether the facts ought to be revealed.

This is the famous "false bottom" of the book. Almost every clue, including some I haven't alluded to, has been caught up into a satisfactory pattern. Nothing happens for some time, until Trent meets Mrs. Manderson again, is assured of the mistake he has made concerning her relations with Marlowe, and proposes marriage. He confronts Marlowe, who is able to give a satisfactory explanation of his conduct on the night of the murder; he was the victim of Manderson's fiendish plot (well motivated by much talk of the millionaire's ingenuity and jealousy) to achieve revenge on his wife's supposed lover by sending him on a journey with a large quantity of money and diamonds belonging to his employer. Manderson would shoot himself; Marlowe would be found to have shot his master and absconded with the loot. Luckily Marlowe was a skilled chess player as well as a clever actor; he saw through Manderson's plot in the nick of time, correctly interpreting certain anomalies in his behavior, and, turning the car round, found Manderson dead near the spot where they had parted. Believing in the impossibility of establishing his innocence otherwise, he behaved then exactly as Trent had deduced, driving the body back, replacing his pistol in his room, and executing the charade in the house before leaving for Southampton.

The position now is that while the police still accept the explanation—good enough for them, it's implied—that Manderson was murdered by the emissaries of an American union he had antagonized, Trent believes that he committed suicide as part of his crazy scheme for revenge. But this is still another false bottom, and gentle old Mr. Cupples, scholarly confident of Trent and uncle of Mrs. Manderson, now reveals that he happened to be nearby when Manderson pointed the pistol at himself. Darting forward and seizing the weapon, he accidentally shot the financier. This incident is not, by the way, unclued; it is prepared for by concealed clues in the opening pages. Trent did not notice them, nor did we. He will not inform the police, but he does despair of human reason, which is why he calls this his last case.

If Trent had attended as closely to Cupples as to Marlowe he might not have missed these clues. The reason why he overlooked them is simple: Cupples is honest, English, and upper-middle-class. Trent prides himself on knowing the intrinsic value of people, but they rarely win his esteem unless they conform closely to that description. They must not be policemen, servants, or Americans. The characters who, as he senses it, are incapable of evil are Mrs. Manderson, Marlowe, and Cupples. Manderson, on the other hand, is too rich, too puritanical, too ruthless, and not English. In a way the police are right; the killer is an American, as it happens Manderson himself rather than American labor desperadoes.

Tricking us about the clues is of course the writer's business here; but it is important that in order to do so he may be obliged to provide information which he cannot stop us from processing in a quite different fashion. Thus it is important that Manderson is jealous, a plotter, an exploiter of the poor, and that this reflects on his nation. Mr. Cupples himself remarks that in these unprecedentedly bad times the "disproportion between the material and the moral constituents of society" is especially marked in the U.S.A. In trying to throw suspicion on American labor the book willy-nilly invites the reader to make inferences on an entirely new system. We gather that money-lust, godless and narrow morality, social unease, insane plotting, napoleonism, eventually madness, are typical of Americans. Not content with merely nationalist snobbery, Marlowe ventures a racial explanation. He has looked into Manderson's genealogy and found early Mandersons mating with Indian women. "There is a very great deal of aboriginal blood," he says, "in the genealogical makeup of the people of America." He is, wrongly, under the impression that this discovery of the Indian taint was what set his employer against him. But the charge remains true, even if he wasn't ashamed of his aboriginal blood, since Cupples can speak of his "apparently hereditary temper of suspicious jealousy." Mrs. Manderson is much better off married to Trent.

Bentley dedicated his book to Chesterton, who was capable of believing that Jewish financiers started the Boer War to induce youths to slaughter one another. As a reading of history this might be thought to fall short of competence, but taken together with what is known of the Edwardian Englishman's attitude to colonials it helps to explain a certain chauvinism in the tale, though Bentley presumably meant it to remain inexplicit. Yet the processing of clues leads us inevitably to the conclusion that this novel has a cultural significance which, if we had to attempt a formal description of the text, we might subsume under some such heading as "early twentieth-century myth of America." The processing of hermeneutic material has entailed the provision of other matter from which we may infer an ideological system: American is to English as the first to the second term in each member of this series: rich-not rich, uneducated-educated, cruel-gentle, exploiter-paternalist, insensitive-sensitive, and so on, down to colored-white. So the hermeneutic spawns the cultural.

It also spawns the symbolic. For example: Trent solves the riddle only in part (the whole solution requires the aid of the old Cupples—a goodish name for Tiresias); he supplants a man who, since he is old enough to be his wife's father, is also old enough to be Trent's. There's a good deal of displacement, of course, but the myth is Oedipal. So we see that Bentley's novel, though primarily a hermeneutic game, inevitably provides information which, if we are not docile, we may process independently of the intention or instruction of the author, who is therefore neither the source of a message nor an authority on reading. All narratives are like this, whether they belong to the nursery, the analyst's casebook, or the library shelf. Bentley's genre is evidently one in which hermeneutic information predominates; but to provide it in a narrative is to activate other systems of reading or interpretation. Trusting the tale can have unforeseen consequences, as all readers of *Studies in Classic American Literature* ought to know. The multiple, perhaps unfathomable possibilities which inhere in a narrative "of a certain magnitude" declare themselves under this kind of examination, even though the text is generically so limited, so resistant to plurisignificance.

IV

It happens—to continue with this example of highly developed hermeneutic interest—that in rejecting the old novel some self-conscious makers of the new have taken a special interest in detective stories. Their reasons for doing so are that they mistrust "depth"; they regard orthodox narrative, with its carefully developed illusions of sequentiality and its formal characterization, as a kind of life. Thus they admire the detective story, in which the hermeneutic preoccupation is dominant at the expense of "depth," in which "character" is unimportant, and in which there are necessarily present in the narrative sequence enigmas which, because they relate to a quite different and earlier series of events, check and make turbulent its temporal flow. The presence of ambiguous clues is also of great interest, especially if you give up the notion—and here is a major change—that they ought to lock together with great exactness, and abandon the attempt at full hermeneutic closure (all loose ends tied up).

As early as 1942, in a comment on his own *Pierrot mon amour,* Raymond Queneau was talking about " 'an ideal detective story' in which not only does the criminal remain unknown but one has no clear idea whether there has even been a crime or who the detective is."

Eleven years later Alain Robbe-Grillet published the first of the new
wave of new novels, *Les Gommes*, which is an approach to that ideal.
His detective goes much more seriously wrong than Trent, and it
turns out, if that is not too strong an expression, that the murder he
is investigating has not yet been committed, and that when it is the
murderer is the detective Wallas, and the victim his own father, perhaps. Since Wallas appears to be physically attracted by someone
who appears to be his stepmother, is repeatedly asked riddles about
what animal is thus and thus in the morning, at noon, etc., and
searches devotedly for an eraser of which the brand name may be
Oedipe, he has inherited Trent's Oedipal qualities; but he lives in a
very different kind of narrative, in which events and characters are
doubled; in which objects—including a famous tomato—are described
in hallucinated detail but have at best very obscure hermeneutic relevance; and which is in itself as it were false, not just false-bottomed.
Trent lives without trouble in a book which has a double flow of time,
but Wallas gets hopelessly swamped in it. Trent masters most of the
clues; the clues master Wallas. And the erasers are always at work,
rubbing out the novel. The closure is, in Barthes' expression, *à la fois
posé et déçu.* Novels, it seems, may erase themselves instead of establishing a permanent fixed reality. There are many internal relations
and echoes which have no significance outside the text, point to no
external meaning. The book seems to be trying to seal itself off from
everything outside it.

 The fashion prevailed: Michel Butor's *L'Emploi du temps,* written
a few years later, is also, in its curious and complicated and unclosed
way, a detective story. A young Frenchman, passing a year in the
bleak English northern city of Bleston, finds himself at war with it;
after seven months of passivity he rouses himself to defeat the city in
the remaining five by recapturing the lost time, writing an account
of those lost months. The double flow of time becomes extremely
turbulent. In May Revel is recounting, straightforwardly, the events
of October; in June the events of June mingle with those of November; and so on, with increasing complexity, until in September the
events of September, July, March, August, and February are all boil-
ing up together, as he not only recalls the past but frantically re-reads
his manuscript. The young writer concerns himself incessantly with
maps of the city—they have a magical relation to its labyrinths. Among

his stories the most interesting is *Le Meurtre de Bleston* (*The Bleston Murder,* but also *The Murder of Bleston*), a work of great topographical accuracy. Revel meets its author, and reveals his identity, an indiscretion which perhaps causes an attempt on the author's life. *The Bleston Murder* is, by all accounts, an elaborately clued story. And in *L'Emploi du temps* there are hundreds of clues of many kinds; but they do not work traditionally. We can see how Revel forms them into hermeneutic sequences, and we even try to do it ourselves; but they do not work out. They lie in the past of the manuscript: the Cain window in the Old Cathedral, suggesting not only fratricide but the first city and also Bleston, is incomplete, like the novel itself and other works of art in it; it is related—but how?—to all the other cities that are mentioned—Petra, Baalbek, Rome in flames, and the labyrinth at Cnossos. In the same way the mythical Ariadne underlies, but not with a perfect fit, the girl Rose; and Theseus (a mythical twin of Oedipus) underlies, with imperfect fit, the author. The book becomes arbitrarily encyclopaedic: the Old Cathedral offers one systematic world-view, the New Cathedral, with its careful carvings of plants and animals in proper modern botanical and zoological orders, a world-view appropriate to the nineteenth century; the detective-story murder took place there, and was finally avenged in the red light from the Cain window in the Old Cathedral. But all these and many other hints about the hermeneutic fit are false; all remains unclosed, incomplete, and we watch Revel fail in his attempt to hammer it all into a unity, to make the clues work like clues in a detective story.

J. C. Hamilton, author of *The Bleston Murder,* lectures intermittently on the genre. It must, he says, have two murders; the murderer is the victim of the second, which is committed by the detective, his weapon an "explosion of truth." The detective is, as so often in the tradition, at odds with the police (for Butor an allegory of the best possible relationship between himself and the reader) because he is concerned, not with the preservation of an old order, but with the institution of a new; so he cheats the police (as Trent did). The climax of his existence is the moment when his accurate vision transforms and purifies reality. Furthermore, he is a true Oedipus, "not only because he solves a riddle, but also because he kills the man to whom he owes his title and because this murder was foretold him from the day of his birth."[12] Hamilton argues further that "in the best of such works the novel acquires, as it were, a new dimension," giving among his reasons for saying this the view that such novels have narrative which "is not merely the projection on a flat surface of a series of events" but which, in addition, "rebuilds these as it were spatially."[13] Revel adds that in exploring events anterior to its opening, such a novel has a truth missing from other kinds, for we muse on our disasters after they have happened, and live our lives in these cross-currents of past and present. It was for this reason that he felt obliged to abandon the simplicities of May, when he set down what happened in October, in favor of the detective-story writer's complex movements in the labyrinth of time and memory.

But the attempt fails; the clues don't fit, or close; all the receding series of objects, works of art, mythical equivalents, are askew. No blinding explosion of truth will destroy Bleston. And these myriad disymmetries, displacing the symmetries, force us to peer, each from his own angle, into the text, make our own adjustments, institute within the text a new order of reality, our own invention. Butor himself speaks of "spatial polyphony." Barthes, examining such phenomena, will speak of "stereographic space"; in terms of the relations established within it we produce our own reading, so changing our view and, ideally, ourselves, altering our opinion as to what matters and what does not. For ordinarily we go on living in a state of truce with the world, supposing an identity between it and the arbitrary notion we happen to hold of it. The novel can be a criticism of common consciousness. It can show that our normal "fitting" is bogus; it attacks the way in which we "legitimate" our beliefs. Without forgetting that it could always do these things—it would not sound strange to say that George Eliot's novels are criticisms of common consciousness—we can allow that we are forced to produce, rather than merely assent to, an order, and that the order must be new.

Thus are the hermeneutic specializations of the detective story transformed in the interests of *truth,* in the cause of enabling us to live in the world as it is, as it simply *is,* lacking all meaning but that signified in our texts. Every novel, on this view, should be an affront to the simple hermeneutic expectation that it will *work out,* because it can only work out if we accept the false implication that the world itself is simply coded, full of discoverable relations and offering closure. Since, as sociologists assure us, "conceptual machineries of

universe-maintenance are themselves products of social activity, as
are all forms of legitimation,"[14] we need not be surprised that in
adapting the detective novel to their purposes these French writers
change it with revolutionary intent; they are usually willing to see in
what they are doing a model of larger changes in politics, or more
generally in the institution of a modern *Weltanschaüung*. For them
the Oedipal detective, no longer concerned with puzzles guaranteed
soluble and limited, becomes a herald of the new order. The problem
of reading, and not less of re-reading, because it requires us to remake
ourselves, to move about in worlds not conventionally realized, becomes the central problem. The novel is "deconstructed"; mysteries
like those of Chrétien once more challenge the reader. He must forget
how he used to read, deluded by local and provincial restrictions; he
must cease to invent structural myths, and instead develop the creative activity which narrative always demands in some measure, but
which may be deadened by over-familiarity and by trained expectations too readily satisfied.

This is, I think, to allow the new its full quantum of novelty. It
amounts to a lively awareness of, and a new way of stating, what has
always been at least intuitively known: the "openness" and the
"intransitivity," and the essential "literarity" of texts. This new
awareness is such that it ought to change conventional attitudes to
all, and not merely new, texts; but there is, of course, a difficulty here,
namely the restrictiveness of the criticism to which the new critics
aggressively oppose themselves.

v

How are we to give up the kind of reading which reinforces and
complies with "local and provincial restrictions"? We began to do so
long ago; occasionally one regrets the bad communications with Paris,
for we, who have had Professor Empson and the New Criticism with
us for forty years, hardly need to be told that texts can be polysemous,
and will hardly believe that all professors deny this. But such differences will not excuse our neglect of what is being said; nor will our
mistrust for the politics, philosophy, and polemics of the new French
criticism. They have something to teach practical critics about method
—and not only in their operations on new texts. Roland Barthes, an
early champion of Robbe-Grillet, was carried away by the theoretical

possibilities of the early *nouveau roman;* he proclaimed, before its authors were able to, that the desired "anéantissement de l'anecdote"[15] had finally been achieved. Later, with other structuralist critics, he grew interested in the attempt of the Russian Formalists of forty years earlier to find methods of describing a story or novel as a linguist describes a sentence—without regard, that is, to the meaning it may communicate, only to its structure. This suited his view that literature must struggle against the temptations of meaning[16]—that the "science of literature," as he called this new enterprise, should, like linguistics, operate within systems not of *pleins* but of *vides.* He devised the expression *écrivance* to distinguish an older literature of reference from the true *écriture.* The neo-Formalist or structuralist enterprise was in full swing about six years ago, and much machinery was devised for the scientific description of texts.[17] But Barthes grew discontented with it; it was unequal to the really important task of describing a text in its individuality and difference. In *S/Z* (1970) he developed new procedures, and tested them on Balzac's story *Sarrasine.*

A text, he argues, is not to be referred to a structural model, but understood as a series of invitations to the reader to *structurate* it. It is a network of significations, of *signifiants* lacking transcendant *signifiés,* and a reader can enter it anywhere. He must produce, not consume it; he must as it were *write* it; and in so far as it avoids external reference it may be called *scriptible.* Classic texts he calls *lisible;* they lack the plurality of the *scriptible,* possessing meaning which can only be ideological, and in some respects, such as story, possessing also a directionality that must be avoided by the *scriptible.* In other words, the *lisible* has local and provincial restrictions, the *scriptible* (of which no example is available) has not.

Barthes' analysis is conducted in terms of five codes, which are to account for what we do in the process of reading a text, to one or more of which each *lexie,* or unit of discourse, is assigned. These codes, though as yet unsatisfactory, are rather promising. Two have to do with what we think of as narrative, distinguished as the proairetic and hermeneutic codes: that is, the sequence of actions (dependent on choices), and the proposing of enigmas which are eventually, after delay, concealment, deception, and so on, solved. The other codes relate to information not processed sequentially: semantic, cultural, and symbolic, they stand as it were on the vertical rather than the horizontal axis of the work, and remain rather vague, especially in view of the prohibition against organizing some of them on a thematic basis. To study these codes is not to study meanings, but only to describe the plurality of the work as apprehended by (presumably competent) readings. In *lisible* writing (Balzac's, for instance) this plurality is limited. In a *scriptible* text it would not be so. The *lisible* adheres to an obsolete *épistème*, a kerygmatic civilization of meaning and truth. But even in the *lisible* there is movement from code to code: the same signifier may operate in both symbolic and hermeneutic codes (the castration of Zambinella in Balzac's story, or the false clues about American violence in *Trent's Last Case*). Despite the constraints of limited plurality—the commitment to closure—symbolic, hermeneutic, and proairetic may, in the *lisible,* stand in an and/or relation. We now see clearly what the authors of the *lisible* were prevented from seeing. Above all we understand that there is no *message* that is passed from writer to reader: *dans le texte, seul parle le lecteur.*[18]

If we ignore his ideological bias—itself a local and provincial restriction—we may find the codes of Barthes a very promising way of approaching the task of describing what happens when we read a narrative. On the question of the hermeneutic operations of the reader he seems, in S/Z, very limited, partly no doubt because of the character of the text examined. But there seems little doubt that he has got behind the arbitrary constraints that have been mistaken for rules; the kind of reading he describes will perhaps enable us to cleanse our perceptions in the matter of narrative. One instance might be that we should alter our notions of acceptable closure, so exploited by the specialized hermeneutic of the detective story. The questioning of this by Queneau and Robbe-Grillet was a prelude to a new understanding that hermeneutic and other forms of closure are contingent not necessary aspects of narrative. This, rather than a purely modern dissociation of narrative from kerygma, is the lesson of the new novel and also of the codes.

For it seems wrong to argue that all this establishes a sharp distinction between something called the novel, with all those qualities and conditions that seemed essential but turn out to be period trappings, and some leaner narrative that has cast them off. We have seen how even the classic detective novel, with its not always perfectly fitting clues and its uncontrollable play between hermeneutic and symbolic codes, prefigures "stereoscopy." New insights into the nature of modern fiction are equally insights into the novel—for all novels verge on the stereographic in so far as they satisfy the reader (a crude criterion, admittedly, but defensible).

Because *Sarrasine* is interesting in this way, though it was published in 1830, Barthes calls it a *texte-limite*; although it is an instance of what he calls, sardonically, *Pleine Littérature*, it stresses, by its very subject, namely castration, and in many of the ciphers which reflect it, an interest in want, in emptiness; it exploits the collision of castration with sex, of emptiness with plenitude, of Z with S. So that although it is on the wrong side of that firm line which, for Barthes, cuts off the modern from the classic, *Sarrasine* happens to be a book that not only illustrates the limited plurality of the classic, but adumbrates the *Littérature Vide* which, in the present *épistème*, succeeds it just as sign is held to have succeeded symbol.

The inference appears to be that all the novels of the past in which we find much to admire partake of the modern precisely in so far as they are not patient of interpretation that assumes limited meaning. Barthes, under the influence of a domestic French quarrel, always talks as if establishment critics deny that position. Outside France this is, of course, untrue. In a sense he is saying, in a new way, something we have long known about the plurality of good texts.

Yet some critics do continue to feel some *horreur du vide*. The invention of myths to explain Chrétien's allusions to the Grail stories is a handy example of a continuing critical passion for closure, the more interesting in that there are fictions more or less contemporary with these mythical inventions that are expressly designed to frustrate closure. James provides classic instances, notably in *The Sacred Fount*. It does seem to be taking us a long time to understand the implication of these experiments in enforced plurality and imperfect closure. Yet the success of our interpretative enterprises on the novels of, say, Dickens, is evidence that in our unmethodical way we have made good guesses about such implications, and noticed that there seems no easily ascertainable limit to the number of *structurations* they will bear: what we reject we reject intuitively. More simply still, the very length of anything we call a novel should warn us that it will contain much information of which the critic, no matter how committed to the single full interpretation, makes no use. He explains it away or ignores it; sometimes behaving as if he thought there are things necessary for novels to do—because they are novels and need to seem "true"—that are nevertheless hardly his business ("pour faire vrai il faut à la fois être précis et insignifiant," as Barthes[19] remarks). At best he is dealing with a remarkably small proportion of the information provided in the text, information which may, as we all know, be processed in so many ways that a plurality of readings is ensured.

As I've noted, novelists themselves long ago exploited this knowledge that their medium was inherently pluralistic; to the name of James one need add only that of Conrad, who invented the hermeneutic gap long before Robbe-Grillet expanded it to engulf the whole text. These writers saw ways of using the fact that the senses of a narrative are always, in some measure, *en jeu;* they exploited this discovery and wrote to show how crucial it was despite the obscurity in which it had remained. So Barthes has found a possibly useful way of talking about something which the researchers of novelists had already brought to light.

To take a simple example: in *Under Western Eyes* Rasumov leaves Russia to serve as an *agent provocateur.* We are not told until later how he contrived to do so: his cover was provided by an oculist. The novel has a great many allusions, few of which could be regarded as important to the narrative, to eyes and seeing. Some of these relate to the difference between Russians and others, to the difference between Russia and Switzerland; and others are concentrated in the representation of Miss Haldin. All this could be schematized in terms of Barthes' codes as proairetic, hermeneutic (he provides for delay in the solving of an enigma), semantic, cultural, and symbolic; and the fluent interplay between the codes is evident. It is indeed very complex, much more so than in Balzac; and it is from writing of this kind that the need to invent formal means to describe the pluralities grows, rather than from wish to develop an instrument capable of analyzing any narrative (though Barthes might deny this). A copious interplay of plural significances was the invention of novelists examining the potential of narrative; our competence to read them is dependent upon the existence of texts requiring such competence.

It is, by the way, perfectly correct to say, as Barthes would, that the question as to whether Conrad intended the visit to the oculist to signify in all these ways is beside the point. It is simply in the nature of the case. This is the sense in which it is true that *dans le texte seul parle le lecteur.* And having learned from certain texts how to speak, the reader will do it in others, including the classic, the *lisible;* that is why we can always find new things to say about a classic text; we can structurate it anew. There has been a change in our reading, not in the texts; we know that a novel does not simply encode a message from an author, and this knowledge became explicit when we had to deal with novels like *Under Western Eyes,* which asserts the fallibility of all that it seems to assert right down to its last page, which offers not closure but a hermeneutic booby-trap.[20] Its views on Russia, whatever they may be said to be, are not Conrad's; his were not Western eyes. Here is a difference in points of view that produces an authentic stereography. And that expression "points of view" will serve to remind us that there have been earlier attempts, in the Anglo-American tradition, to come to terms with the problems that engage Barthes. They are inherent in narrative; he did not discover them, nor has he shown that they came into being with the great cultural changes of the modern era.

VI

The French theorists want a novel without transcendental reference as they want a world without God. They want it to be impossible for anybody to "recuperate" the local and provincial which is inherent in the *lisible.* And in the course of their research they have made discoveries. They have noticed, as D. H. Lawrence did, that the novel may be a way of demonstrating that it is possible to live, because it is possible to read, without accepting official versions of reality. The excitement of the discovery has led them to believe that there may be a kind of novel in better faith than any before it by virtue of its abandoning the old assumptions and cultivating the text of pure sign, without external reference, without symbolism, without structure, receptive of all structures the reader produces. But this exaggerates— perhaps for ideological purposes—the novelty of some aspects of narrative, which, though now given much attention, are a selection from the set of permanent possibilities. As we saw at the outset, it was as possible for Roland to die three times as it is for a Robbe-Grillet personage; and Chrétien understood something of the now-fashionable "emptiness." Nor would it be difficult to multiply historical instances; after all, when we speak of a classic what we mean is a text that has evaded local and provincial restrictions.

There has, in short, been a renewal of attention to aspects of narrative which did not cease to exist because they were not attended to. When we remake our great novels—as we must, and as we have, of recent years, remade the nineteenth-century English classics—we shall find that they all have certain qualities of *Sarrasine,* as Barthes defines them, and also certain qualities of twelfth-century romance, as Marie de France defines them. They will always invite us to plural glosses on the letter, to ingenious manipulation of the codes; it is their nature to demand that we produce rather than consume them, and that we liberate them from local and provincial restrictions, including, so far as that is possible, our own. As to Barthes, it may seem odd to suggest that he has outlined a method for the formal description of a classic; but I believe that is what he has done, and the keenness and brilliance of his insights into *Sarrasine* tells us the same story. If you continue to speak well of narrative it follows that you will speak well of the novel.

NOTES

1. 1896; ed. of 1931, p. 6.
2. P. 49.
3. P. 322.
4. P. 349.
5. 1971, p. 5.
6. Marie de France, quoted by Vinaver, p. 16.
7. R. S. Loomis, *Arthurian Tradition and Chrétien de Troyes* (1949), p. 6; quoted in Vinaver, p. 40.
8. P. 47n.
9. P. 51.
10. P. 52.
11. It is only fair to say that this banal summary does no justice to a very entertaining puzzle.
12. *Passing Time,* translated by Jean Stewart, ed. of 1965, p. 143.
13. P. 158.
14. P. L. Berger and T. Luckmann, *The Social Construction of Reality,* (1966) ed. of 1967, p. 108.
15. *Essais critiques* (1964), p. 65.
16. *Essais critiques,* p. 267.
17. See *Communications* 8 (1966), and T. Todorov, ed., *Théorie de la littérature* (1965).
18. *S/Z,* p. 157.
19. *S/Z,* p. 75.
20. For a fuller discussion of the example, see "The Structures of Fiction," *Modern Language Notes* 84 (1969), 891-915.

THE
GENRE
TODAY
REVISITED

FICTION AND
CINEMATOGRAPHY

NOVEL
AND
CAMERA

LEON EDEL

Novelists have sought almost from the first to become a camera. And not a static instrument but one possessing the movement through space and time which the motion-picture camera has achieved in our century. We follow Balzac, moving into his subject, from the city into the street, from the street into the house, and we tread hard on his heels as he takes us from room to room. We feel as if that massive "realist" had a prevision of cinema. A movie camera would "shoot" this same business in a montage of a few seconds. What we lose in the process is the power of the Word. We are confronted instead with the power of the Picture.

Wherever we turn in the nineteenth century we can see novelists cultivating the camera-eye and the camera movement—Tolstoy not least in those brilliant racing sequences, near the opening of *Anna Karenin*, with a superb sense of montage. The country-fair scene of *Madame Bovary* is well known. Flaubert's "cinema" was prophetic— he panned, he closed up, crowds, individuals, glimpses, and used not only sight but sound—for Emma and Rodolphe on their balcony listen to the windy oratory of the prize presentations, and the clichés mingle with the clichés of Rodolphe's love-making. They even serve as editorial, as when the word *merde* crashes into a particularly banal *mot d'amour*. Under the guise of his "picture" and "scene" Henry James was also a camera-eye. What else is "point of view"? Maria Gostrey scans Strether's countenance, and Strether scans Maria's.

The reader becomes Maria; then Strether. And then he is allowed to move a short distance away so that he may see the two together, face to face. A great anomaly in the history of painting and fiction is that the painters tried very hard to get away from the camera, where the novelists sought by every possible means to embrace it. And yet to say this is to simplify and exaggerate a matter requiring considerable refinement. What we know is that, with Balzac, "realism" came to the novel, and novels were discussed increasingly—and still are—as if they were "real" (never more so than by psychoanalysts who talk of Emma as if they had her on the couch, or of Anna as if she had been under observation for years as a manic depressive). So great was the "reality" of these nineteenth-century fictional personages that we often forget that they never lived: that they are poetized archetypal figures, figments of imagination. The real and the imaginary-real have become confused. *Ulysses* is cinematic—Nighttown especially, with its phantasmagoric "dissolves," its perpetual montage, and its faithful adherence to Dublin real rather than Dublin imaginary. Did not Joyce write to an aunt or sister to count the number of steps of a given stoop so that his word-picture would be photographic? Where James invented Woollett to avoid the need for specification, Joyce gloried in recording Dublin signposts, real names, real people. *Ulysses* is all camera and sound track. And this confusion of reality with the imagined real is being further compounded in our time by Mr. Mailer's flirtation with the cinema; and Susan Sontag, after her flirtation with fiction, now attempts visual fiction. Before them Robbe-Grillet tried to turn his novel into a series of camera shots and cultivated the banishing of affect from his language (as if this were possible). He also gave us his scenario-film *L'Année dernière à Marienbad.*

The camera was invented so soon after the invention of the novel that the two have come down to us like a pair of siblings, each intent on asserting itself and capturing the attention of the world. Richard Stang in his book on nineteenth-century fictional theory quotes a paragraph from the *Westminster Review* of 1841—very early indeed —a comparison of camera and fiction:

There is an instinct in every unwarped mind which prefers truth to extravagance, and a photographic picture, if it be only of a kitten or a hay-stack, is a pleasanter subject in the eyes of most people (were they brave enough to admit it) than many a piece of mythology.

The early critics of realism often invoked the camera, understandably; but we also know that the votaries of realism in fiction thought of themselves as far more richly endowed than the limited little black box, which had to be manipulated and called for so much tranquil posing before any picture could be obtained. The camera was a presence, and for some a threat; certainly for the painters, since it was a question of one kind of visuality versus another. Yet even the impressionists, who went in search of light and air and sought out their subjects directly—leaving the studio for the rivers and fields—in a certain way also emulated the camera. What else is Claude Monet being when he paints the façade of Rouen cathedral at different hours of the day? It is as if he were putting on canvas a series of snapshots—in color. Here too, recognizing this, we must refine our problem. It is more complex than a mere competition between two recording media.

Without tracing the novel's comparatively short history, we know that it achieved its greatest heights of "realism" in the nineteenth century with Flaubert on the side of art and Tolstoy on the side of "reality"—the difference being that of "shaped" and unshaped reality. The Russians, slower in evolving a formal literature, brought great perfection to the novel-form and made it life-like and gave it extraordinary emotional power. The French moved in what seems a logical evolution from Balzacian realism to the extended documentary realism of the naturalists—and then to the counter-revolt of the symbolists, comparable to the revolt of impressionism in painting. In England, the novel began with exuberant and often jocular pictures of life, and much caricature and wit; it sought social and moral substance, with a characteristic disregard for "technique." The English novelists cultivated largely the mode of happy amateurs telling good stories. It was left to an American, who in his youth had disassembled novels as other children treat trains or carriages or automobiles, to try to establish "ground rules" or modes for the art, and to possess the "know-how." This was perhaps the most American side of Henry James. He disassembled the novel and then rose brilliantly above it, into a freedom of his own. With a detached and yet passionate Olympianism he wrote "the art of the novel" as Bach wrote, late in life, "the art of the fugue." When an art reaches this point in its history—

the point of codification—we may assume that it is nearing its end. Where has it to go? It may take other shapes, but it has run its course, it has tested most of the permutations and combinations. The symbolist novel brought us Joyce's two idiosyncratic and labyrinthine performances which indeed stand outside the evolution of fiction, being strange Rabelaisian (though without the *joie de vivre* of Rabelais) or Swiftian books, called novels only because they were written in prose (*Ulysses*) and a mixture of prose and poetry (*Finnegans Wake*). In technique the novel has not moved far beyond the "stream-of-consciousness" of our time, save for certain ventures into the discontinuities of surrealism or chance effects. Virginia Woolf and William Faulkner were the last authentic practitioners of subjective narrative, thus bringing the novel in English around to where Goethe had said it should have started—without influencing very much the development of the novel in his own country. Goethe had recognized from the first that in the novel "reflection and incidents should be featured; in drama, character and action." The novel, he further said, had to proceed slowly, and "the thought-processes of the principal figure must, by one device or another, hold up the development of the whole." Mann would, with his strong Germanic intellect, achieve this: but it was Proust who would create the greatest novel of sensibility that at the same time would embody a picture of an entire society.

The changes in our time have been in the direction of simplification of the novel-form or of its thematic content—absurdity, alienation, dissociation. This is reflected in the novel of discontinuity or, at the other extreme, intense inner-directed personalism. It has yielded works as different as *The Stranger,* or the tropisms of Nathalie Sarraute, Ralph Ellison's *Invisible Man* or the Mailerian strut which emulates the strut of Hemingway, but which now moves fiction into the realm of that other reality, *reportage;* as Truman Capote, achieving the greatest incongruity of all, has attempted to report truth and call it fiction. We have ended with simplifications, imitations, or film. Novelists are now at the point the painters reached long ago.

The painters had their *crise* of the camera early; it wasn't perhaps a conscious or specific crisis, but the camera was one of the determinants of the course painting took in our time. Since the art of the brush is visual, it had to contend with the direct objective visuality of the camera: and it found its solution by warning the painter that he could never be a camera.

James, ever the theorist, used the terminology of painting: "principle of composition" and "picture" became critical terms for the discussion of the novel, and "foreshortening" was derived directly from the lexicon of the painter. "The most fundamental and general sign of the novel, from one desperate experiment to another, is its being everywhere an effort at *representation*," wrote James, adding that this was "the beginning and the end of it." And again, "it is the art of the brush, I know, as opposed to the art of the slate-pencil; but to the art of the brush the novel must return." He would probably have to amend this today. He would substitute "camera" for "slate-pencil" and would perhaps argue that the novelist had to turn back to the art of the word. James believed in the future of the novel because he felt that it was the most elastic of the literary forms, and that among the baubles of art which man has a way of using up and then discarding, the novel could least be discarded, since it embraces man's fundamental need to go on telling stories. The stories, however, were to be stories in words; and one remembers how jealous James was of illustration, how he held an illustrated story to be an affront to the artistic imagination. We also remember his short story "The Real Thing," a veritable parable for the art—in which the illustrator, confronted with models who are *real*, cannot paint them; there is nothing left for the imagination. But models emulating the real could be rendered with a bold and free use of the impressionism and symbolism of art.

Henry James was writing at the threshold of the cinema. He went to see the primitive bioscopic inventions, yet it never occurred to him that they might involve any threat to the verbal art—so safe did the Edwardians feel in their citadel of words, so authoritative, so ensconced for the future. James did recognize the appeal of cinema technique; he described one such image in his late tale "Crapy Cornelia," where at a given moment the character White-Mason looks at a woman's head "crowned with a little sparsely feathered black hat," and it "grew and grew, came nearer and nearer while it met his eyes, after the manner of images in the cinematograph." Joyce would not only describe this kind of camera technique; he would imitate it. He wanted to found a movie-house in Dublin; and *Ulysses*, as we have noted, in its adherence to angles of vision and its constructed scenes, is almost wholly cinema. So Dorothy Richardson, working at the same time as Joyce, learned to move toward or away from a camera, while keeping us within the intense subjectivity of her heroine. One recalls how, in her pioneering way, she carefully pictured London buildings moving toward the riders on the top of a bus; or our glimpse of her heroine after boarding the German train, seeing the platform flow away from her—as we have seen in countless movies. Miss Richardson acknowledged in her novel, without naming it, her indebtedness to the method of *The Ambassadors*, but presently she became herself a film critic, and moved from the early "cinema," devised in fiction, to the actual experience of photographic vision. Soon enough there would be the "camera-eye" of the surrealists and Dos Passos.

In the years since we have moved from camera devices, anticipated or imitated, to the camera itself, to the direct exploitation by novelists of the camera-visual. A novelist addicted to his word-world might wonder how the two can be integrated—novel and camera—beyond the ways in which they have used one another. With the talking pictures—that is, the use simultaneously of sight and sound—and with the third dimensionality to come, the verbal forms cannot compete. Fable-telling becomes picture-sequence, and the novel is often set aside for the picture. The novel, I believe, is in a bad way, not because we do not have fine craftsmen in our time, but because it has been shoved aside by technology, just as music—played music in salon and hall—has given way to the tape recorder and stereo, and printing is beginning to feel the effect of xerox and computer and other photo-reproducing processes.

To say all this, however, even in this general and perhaps exaggerated way, is not to have said, by any means, the last word. We must reckon, in the multiple technologies of the electronic, with the *conditioning* of our new generation. A generation nurtured on the visual is less inclined to bother with the visual of print; the photo-visual gives one a greater sense of being "in" something; it requires much more imagination to read. Camera-vision cripples the use of the mind's eye. Our newest children are losing this eye, the eye of verbal wonder. They have had camera with their pablum. I speak of segments of the young, for in so large a populace there remain the verbally cultivated, always a minority, to exercise a certain moderating influence. In all this we must give serious thought to the nature of television.

What is striking in television—that is, fictional as distinct from documentary television—is that we are confronted with a combination of absolute reality and utter fantasy—absolute reality being used to render the fictions that have been concocted for us. Literature never creates this kind of reality. Balzac may be considered to have been a camera: yet when he moves us from town to street, from street to house, from house to individual rooms, and then we come upon his personages, we do so always with a quantity, and quality, of verbal suggestion that we in turn have to translate, in the very nature of reading, into mental images. The rooms, the people, the furniture, the very wallpaper, become a part of our mind's eye. But a camera moving from town-to-street-to-house-to-rooms-to-people does so with a rapidity of movement that demands a quickness of eye, an association of images, and asks nothing of our mind's eye. It is all there for us to see, not to imagine; it is only the eye, rarely the mind's eye, that must be quick, and there is almost too much for it to take in. New generations doubtless will learn how to match greater mental grasp with ocular activity—but our imagination will be summoned for other tasks. The novel of our time has toyed with verbal montage, with immediacy and discontinuity, but in its wildest dreams of "realism" it has never been able to be as camera-real as the ambulant camera. This brings us to an important distinction between fiction told in pictures, and fiction told in words. Miss Marianne Moore long ago gave us an aphorism by which we may find guidance. Poetry, she said, consists of "imaginary gardens with real toads in them." Cinema-fiction, we can say, consists of real gardens with real toads—an absolutism of the immediate image, and an immediacy which operates quite differently from the immediacy of the word-novel. It takes place in time, like music, rather than in space, like print. We are moreover *in* the picture: we move with the people whom we see in close-up, and in ways impossible in the "realism" of daily life. Distance is there, but it is evanescent camera-distance. We can seldom achieve such closeness in the pages of a book.

Not only are we looking at the real gardens and the real toads, but this reality is, at the same time, a total fiction. By seeming to give us the entire reality, however, such realism, the realism of the camera, is essentially more fictional than book-fiction, which makes no such claims and is thus more "real," in its limited expression of "reality," than the pretentious "realism" of the camera. And this is the true schizophrenia of camera-realism. Reality is mixed with fiction in such doses that the fiction all but disappears; it is there, in the Joycean formula, like the author, behind, beyond, the fantasy made real. But in its denial of its own fictional aspects, it loses a sense of make-believe and of wonder—the effect is as if the camera opened its mouth to declare that it can give us intrinsic instead of merely extrinsic knowledge of other people. What this might do to the audience is a matter for psychology and sociology. I will only say that recent pop art and the current bizarreries of American dress may reflect a kind of total absorbtion of visual image and may also warn us of the power, the propaganda reality, of real gardens with real toads in them.

Let us return to the novel, that lost beautiful form, so free and so wide-ranging, so elastic and so filled with our imaginations combining with the imagination of the novelist. It is now in a struggle no less acute, no less *acharné,* than that of the painter who found he had to dissolve realities into new realities; for he discovered that a click of the camera could render a landscape with greater "representation" than was possible to him. Painting at once sought to escape the literalism of the camera. To be sure, there have always been artists of the camera, who on their side tried to use their lens as if they were painters. Alvin Langdon Coburn attempted such effects very early and with considerable success; yet even he became dissatisfied and later experimented with abstractions and form shapes. In our own time some photographers have gone to an opposite extreme: instead of seeking blur and chiaroscuro, they have accepted the sharpness of image possible to them, and worked for a kind of *nature morte,* the fluid moment of time made rigid, as if all life had stopped at the moment of the click of the camera. They seem to have felt that the more literal and "frozen" the picture, the truer they are to the camera-medium. In some photographs, however, one is aware of the eye at the keyhole, the eye looking through the lens seeking both shape and instantaneity and above all close-up—things the novel achieved only in a limited way and with considerable risk. Chance is often the camera's best ally in capturing the evanescence of movement and form, the conversing, active, gesturing, facially plastic man or woman. Some photographers indeed "shoot" images as if they were shuffling a deck of cards. I speak of the still camera, not the moving picture. They take a fast succession of images, with a prodigal use of film, capturing one after another, so that ultimately chance will yield them a single image filled with all the vitality and "bounce" of life, one that will suit the editor—representing the fact, caught in an essential moment. The viewer of camera art can look at life with his own eyes, and then at pictures of life-pictures—and at closer quarters than life ever allows. So many of our novels simply imitate this. I find myself resisting novels that begin in this manner:

> Alfred Amber walked across the room, unbuttoning his shirt with nervous agile fingers; a cigarette dangled from his lips; he inhaled, exhaled, and walked through clouds of his own smoke. Light pushed through narrow slits of window; and Alfred Amber's narrow slits of eyes looked at the sprawling figure on the bed, its legs spread in an upside-down V.

Who cannot guess the rest, to the last tired click of the verbal cliché? In a moment the reader will be invited to the close-up; closer than in life, a magnified gargantuan genital encounter. Alfred Amber might as well be a petroglyph, he is drawn with such primitive linear strokes, approaching the upside-down linear V. In the newest novels such mechanical figures do not know how to act because their authors endow them not with human action but simply with camera movement; being products of the age of the camera, they offer us their scenes not as pictures but as snapshots. Characters light or extinguish cigarettes in a haze of smoke. Bodies thrust themselves out of chairs. Women slink or shake themselves loose. The figure on the bed is a horizontal petroglyph, an aperture, whose legs have become single lines. Nothing is described save action, a series of actions, as in a movie. The camera can do this better than the novel. There is a logic in a camera working for a closeup; it needs by its very nature only to catch surfaces and seek constant variety. In life the human eye does not look as closely at things as a camera lens. We do not usually bend over someone else's expanse of skin to examine its goose pimples. We may observe a couple embracing or kissing on a bench in the park, but we don't walk over to these lovers and watch at six inches lips pressed against lips. What we see is the entire kiss—that is, two bodies involved in a kiss, not just lips and chins and noses. When film or novel moves into a close-up, we are involved in a kind of continual fragmentation of human action. News cameramen, when they want to be nasty, photograph individuals in the act of mastication; they aim at the open mouth and the teeth, to capture the ferocity of chewing, which we normally cannot see; in life we do not stare down masticating mouths. True, we might say that the camera thus gives us glimpses otherwise denied us. Joseph Conrad liked to describe teeth; but we never are given the bare fact of their action. To *see* them masticating is simply to be given an image we might want to call cannibalistic. In Conrad they are part of a human being and do not have the separateness of a set of teeth in wax or plaster in a dental office. Yet the novel today seeks this kind of close-up, tries to turn itself into a camera instead of escaping like the painters from the camera's tyrannies. Robbe-Grillet, who was an agronomist and accustomed to seeing plants under microscopes, has sought to use words without feeling, as a camera possesses no feeling, and captures only what the lens sees. It is the person looking at the picture who will have the feeling. The photographer may have had feelings, but they are immersed and dissolved in the high tension of his work—usually less leisurely than a painter's. And then his feelings are conveyed only in the choice of objects, the angles of the *nature morte* or area of coverage; he is snapping real gardens, real toads. The novelist or painter is engaged in using and rendering feeling in every word written, every stroke of the brush; and no matter how hard Robbe-Grillet works to find feelingless words, he cannot in reality discover them. The "new novel" in France nevertheless does illustrate an attempt to break away from camera-reality, in spite of its objectivism; and Virginia Woolf's manifesto, in which she called on novelists to get at life without a rearrangement, to capture "the moment," was in a sense recognizing the age of the camera, while at the same time groping for some escape from its absoluteness. She spoke of life as a "luminous halo, a semi-transparent envelope surrounding us from the beginning of consciousness to the end" and of the novelist's task as being to convey this kind of transparency and luminosity. She was pleading for a novel freed from the slavery of its own traditions, from its old ways of being either truth-telling, romance, character-mongering or comedian, or fantastic-satirical, or psychological or poetical, even though she knew that great novels had been written in all of these ways. The essence of her plea was for imagination, freedom, sentience. It did not occur to her that what she was really confronting was total visuality. She had been exposed early to the post-impressionists and she admired their freedom of attack on reality, their reconstituted and reorganized realities. She was all for the novel giving us "an epitome as well as an inventory." Perhaps today she would have to say an epitome rather than an endless series of monotonous stills and close-ups, of cliché-figures moving across the pages of books as they move across the screens of television sets.

Although he speaks in other terms and other historical contexts, Mr. Bellow is saying what Mrs. Woolf said when he meditates on the shallow people that inhabit our novels. Perhaps we have had too many novels. People no longer seem to need them. On the other hand, pictorial biographies—real pictures of real lives—exist in abundance, and there will be more of these in the coming years. The camera is ubiquitous.

The visuality of our time can be, of itself, a virtue. We are endowed with two magnificent organs with which to take in the world and assimilate it to all our senses. Is it not therefore understandable that novelists should want to render this visuality in words, even as the camera has recorded it with its magical substitute for the human eye, by a means that gives permanence to life's pictures? The answer is obviously in the affirmative; and all our great novelists have been exceptionally "visual" in their use of words. The camera is a part of modern civilization. Sometimes tourists are so busy taking pictures that they have no time to enjoy sensually the landscape before them. They have time merely to peek at it through one eye. And however much some of us may feel that an hour spent looking at one landscape is better than a camera record of a dozen landscapes, framed in so small an area or rendered close up, we must recognize that the sensual endowment of the individual varies, and that not everyone has the capacity to contemplate and meditate and feel a landscape— or even read a book. However, this is not the issue here. I do not urge camera-smashing, Luddite fashion. The issue is that the novel, in trying so desperately to become a camera, has ceased to be on the whole anything else, has ceased to be itself. It has stopped dead—and no longer knows that man not only acts, but thinks, that he has visions and fantasies, that he is the only reflective animal in existence, and that when a novel gives us the thinking man as well as the acting man, it makes possible an extraordinary enlargement of life. We know only our own thoughts, never the thoughts of others. Fiction, by invoking the use of the verbal imagination—that is, by making us active and imaginative readers, rather than inert picture-watchers—gives us the magical sense of being in relation with the world and with our fellow men and in ways that we can only rarely be, even though we are alone in a room with a book.

THE DEATH AND REBIRTH OF THE NOVEL

LESLIE A. FIEDLER

I

If the novel has recently had to die in order to be reborn (and if that fact still remains unperceived in some quarters), it is because for a century or more many of the chief practitioners of the genre—and an influential group of critics as well—managed to forget that at its most authentic the novel is a form of popular art. The true novel, as invented once and for all in the middle of the eighteenth century by that extraordinarily anti-elitist genius, Samuel Richardson, is in fact the first successful form of Pop Art to have entered a culture more and more dominated by such sub- or quasi- or para-literature. It must be clearly distinguished, therefore, from traditional High Literary Art (an art dependent on limited literacy) as well as from Folk Literary Art (an art dependent on mass illiteracy); since it is related, not to such forms as Epic, on the one hand, or the Folk Ballad, on the other—to nothing which precedes it, as a matter of fact, but to much which follows: the comic strip, the comic book, cinema, TV.

Like these latter, it is an artform which tends to make the classic distinction between literacy and illiteracy meaningless—or at least challenges it in ways disconcerting to traditional humanists; for it is a product both of the Industrial Revolution and of the political shifts in power which have replaced aristocratic or class-structured societies by one version or another of the mass society. In such highly developed, classless societies (which have destroyed the *myth* of class, however strongly analogous distinctions persist in fact), it seems possible and desirable to mass-produce forms of narrative not only for proper literates, but for quasi-literates as well, i.e., for those who have acquired the mechanical skills of reading without being inducted into the elite culture which was their original context. The new electronic media have gone a step further by substituting images on the screen for words on the page, thus further reinforcing the disjunction between being able to apprehend a tale and acquiring the "standards" associated exclusively with books for judging its "value." Works of this kind tend to be successful or unsuccessful rather than "good" or "bad," to be sold or scrapped rather than canonized or rejected.

The development of the novel, at any rate, was in the beginning and has remained ever since intricately connected to the development of modern technology and the modern means of mass distribution. Its fate depends on the machine and the marketplace—not solely (or perhaps even primarily) on the growth of talent and perception in some lonely producer sustained by an equally lonely sponsor. The printing press was, of course, the first mass-production device in our culture; and the novel was the first literary form invented to be reproduced by Gutenberg means—rather than one which came to be thus reproduced, after having been invented for oral transmission or recording in painfully copied manuscripts.

Its history is linked to the development of many associated technologies—not merely with that of movable type—though it has, of course, changed with the invention of linotyping, stereotyping, and other means for reproducing texts and illustrations more quickly and cheaply. A critical event in the early decades of the nineteenth century, for instance, was the discovery of new procedures for making cheap paper, which made possible the "penny novel" with its new appeals to a new mass audience—especially its exploitation of the "serial" technique, episodic and breathless. Similarly, the development of less expensive means of binding encouraged the growth in the United States just after World War II of mass-distributed paperbacks, so that gradually the airport bookstand and the supermarket book-display came to replace the public library and the classic bookstore as the source of popular literature. And at last books came to be created for such distribution, with the development of that peculiarly ephemeral form, the "paperback original," as disposable as Kleenex.

Distribution as well as production, then, has been essential to the changing shape of the novel, as it has moved tentatively but inevitably toward more and more popular forms—becoming finally the closest thing possible to a mass art within the limits of literacy. The early invention of the circulating library and its evolution into the public library represented a first step in this direction. But an even more radical departure from traditional ways of making books accessible (the shift from the private to the public library being, after all, a change in degree rather than kind) was the creation of the railway-station bookstall in England, as certain entrepreneurs realized the sense in which the railway had made possible new opportunities for reading while traveling. Obviously, stage coaches with their dark interiors and jolting motion made reading difficult if not impossible, but the train provided exactly the setting (and the airplane has perfected it with focused reading lights, etc.) for the leisurely consumption of expendable brief books intended to lighten the particular tedium of travel. Finally, the railroad station and airport bookstall has become the model for the bookshelf in the supermarket, on which novels appear as the commodities they are, ready always for the impulse-buyer —and competing in allure against soapflakes and breakfast cereals with their bright jackets and catchy slogans.

Moreover, as is well known, the marketplace is a storehouse of dreams in advanced or post-capitalist societies, and commodities are, as it were, the incarnate dreams of the masses. The machine is, in this sense, the Shaman of our culture, the Dreamer of its communal dreams; and the machine-produced commodity novel is, therefore, dream literature, mythic literature, as surely as any tale told over the tribal fire. Its success, too, depends on the degree to which it responds to the shared dreams, the myths, which move its intended audience. Form and content, in the traditional sense, are secondary, optional if not irrelevant—since it is, in the first instance, primordial images and archetypal narrative structures that the novel is called on to provide.

This means, then, that the novel (as opposed to all forms of High Art) is disconcertingly independent of its medium and, by the same token, immune to formalist criticism. Dickens' *Pickwick Papers*, for instance, originally conceived as a supporting text for certain cartoons of sporting life, became a novel almost inadvertently; and once it had succeeded, it projected its chief characters and events into the mythological Public Domain, from which they could be recaptured in the form of prints, wall-hangings, ceramic jugs, etc. Similarly, those adventures could be "continued" by other competing popular authors (truly mythic materials being as independent of copyright as of medium); so that George Reynolds, for instance, could feel free quite quickly to write an account of "Pickwick Abroad," "Pickwick Married," even a seemingly perverse account of Pickwick and Sam Weller becoming teetotalers. Some authors of truly popular novels have been disconcerted by the peculiar availability of their creations—so that Cervantes, for example, long before the birth of the bourgeois novel proper, could not understand why it was acceptable rather than scandalous that the protagonist of his Mannerist proto-novel, *Don Quixote*, be appropriated by another less gifted author. So some novelists even now are troubled by the movies' appropriation of their books—though their objections are, of course, allayed by the present practice of paying for what (being myth) is actually in the Public Domain, quite as if it were private property.

Other authors, however, have come to realize what is at stake and cheerfully collaborate in the confusing communal game. William Goldman wrote a film story called *Butch Cassidy and the Sundance Kid*, then himself later turned it into a novel for paperback sale. The reverse process is to turn over what begins as a novel (*Little Big Man*, in this case) to screenwriters, directors, and editors to make into a film. There is finally, and quite regardless of the will of the original author, a special affinity between the authentic (i.e., mythic) novel and the cinema; so that it sometimes seems as if all such novels want to metamorphose into movies, being merely the embryos of the films they finally become, a kind of chrysalis yearning to be a butterfly. And there is a rude justice in this development, since, from the start, certain popular novelists apparently yearned for, dreamed the invention of, the movies—Sir Walter Scott, for instance, creating effects (he loved to be called "the master of motion") which in their rapidity and scope need the movie camera and the broad screen to fulfill them.

The novel, along with the meta-literary forms which follow it, thus subverts traditional notions of authorship and genre; and, by the same token, it is politically subversive as well. Indeed, all Pop Art subverts —rather than sustains or confirms—the social order in which it appears, undercutting necessarily the values of the established classes (or sexes or ethnic groups), even though those classes may think they are using such art for their own ends and therefore subsidize it generously. Elitist art produced in elitist societies can be controlled by those who pay for it; for instance, Maecenas got his million dollars' worth out of Vergil, who really created in the *Aeneid* the propaganda poem in the interests of imperial Rome for which he was paid, however he may have marginally indulged his own melancholy. And even in recent times, elitist authors have continued to serve the same function—despite a deep conviction that their chief goal was to *épater la bourgeoisie*. In the end, they provided documents, beautiful and witty, obscene and terrible, for classroom analysis and library cataloguing—exploiting even the Unconscious in the interests of "Culture."

But the authors and audience of Popular Art, and the marketplace mechanism which is their nexus, are typically unconscious of the Unconscious—which is to say, they operate on levels beneath the perception and control of anyone, even of the authors themselves. The novel is subversive because it speaks from and for the most deeply buried, the most profoundly ambivalent levels of the psyche of the ruling classes: in American terms, those parts of the White, Male psyche most drastically repressed in the patriarchal, Anglo-Saxon Protestant form of bourgeois industrial society which has flourished in the United States. But to these parts of the buried mind and the impulses they nurture, our literature has traditionally given the mythic names "Woman," "Negro," "Indian"—"Female," Niggerish," "Savage."

It seems, in fact, a psycho-social law that the social and economic oppression of certain groups in any society entails always the psychological repression of certain parts of the mind in the oppressing group. Popular literature, therefore, speaks for both oppressor and oppressed, joining together all elements in the community, no matter how embattled and disjoined. In myth, the pre-conscious and the unconscious find a voice capable of reaching the audience on the level of dream and nightmare, where alone those are unified who, on the level of full consciousness (the level of theme and ideology and form appropriate to high art), are hopelessly sundered.

II

In light of the foregoing, it should be evident that the attempt, conspicuous during the second century of the life of the novel, to make

the novel High Art has been in some sense misguided. Yet beginning
with, perhaps, Flaubert, and reaching a climax in the work of Proust,
Mann, and Joyce during the period we have come to call "Modernism," fictionists of real talent and devotion have attempted precisely
that: the creation of the Art Novel, which is to say, a work of fiction
intended not for the marketplace but the library and classroom; or its
sub-variety, the Avant-Garde Novel, which foresees immediate contempt followed eventually by an even securer status in future Mu-
seums of Literary Culture. In the last decades, however, more and
more novelists, plus a growing number of critics, have come to realize
the obsolescence of the Art-Avant Garde novel, and have abandoned
the attempt to distinguish any longer between "true art" and "junk,"
"serious books" and "mere entertainment" in favor of the former. Indeed, they have come to realize that the great, the authentic line of
fiction runs through such producers of entertaining "junk," "schlock"
and "schmalz" as Dickens and George Reynolds, Balzac and Eugène
Sue and Jules Verne, James Fenimore Cooper and H. Rider Hag-
gard, Raymond Chandler and "Vernon Sullivan," Zane Grey and
San Antonio and A. E. Van Vogt.

It would be foolish, of course, to institute an opposite kind of discrimination and exclusion in the last decades of the twentieth century, since only a further impoverishment of the novel would be produced by banning and burning, however metaphorically, Art Novels,
or even by despising their faithful readers. Art novels will continue
to be read and relished by an elite audience, among whom I number
some of my best friends and most distinguished colleagues; and even
I myself will sneak off from time to time quite shamelessly to read,
say, James Joyce's Ulysses, which I have already gone through six or
seven times—with continuing profit and pleasure, as well as growing
annoyance. Nonetheless, that activity has come to seem to me more
and more irrelevant, and the continuing production of such books I
find an act of desperation, when it is not mere antiquarianism or a
bit of charming eccentricity.

To put it as bluntly as possible, it is incumbent on all who write
fiction or criticism in the disappearing twentieth century to realize
that the Art Novel or Avant-Garde Novel is in the process of being
abandoned wherever fiction remains most alive, which means that
that sub-genre of the novel is dying if not dead. And this is what, it

turns out, all those prophecies of the Death of the Novel (including my own) have meant, though we did not earlier understand this very well. To be sure, some writers even in the United States continue to write as if that death had not occurred, but so do certain men and women continue to attend church services despite the well-advertised Death of God. No wonder, however, that such posthumous services seem funereal rather than pious—quite as funereal as posthumous art novels like the latest works of Saul Bellow or John Updike, Alberto Moravia or Alain Robbe-Grillet.

It is, finally, less comprehensible and forgivable for American writers to make such an error, since the culture of the United States is more favorable to perspicacity in this regard, its writers naturally immune, as it were, to the temptations of High, i.e., European, Art. After all, the late entry of America into Western history meant that our national existence began at precisely the same moment as the novel itself, and that we have *no* prehistory (except as we attach ourselves to a larger Anglo-Saxon tradition) of Epic or Poetic Tragedy. Even our underlying national *mythos* is a Pop Myth and our Revolution consequently a Pop Revolution, as compared, for instance, with either the French or Russian Revolutions, which began with ideological disputes and the formulation of high-level manifestoes. Our own War of Independence, on the contrary, began not with abstract ideas at all (though later we composed ideological documents to justify a *fait accompli*), but with a group of quite grown-up men dressing up like Indians and dumping into Boston Harbor that supreme symbol of effete European civilization, British tea. It is an event cued by a boy's dream, only later translated into the Declaration of Independence under the auspices of Thomas Jefferson, himself a small boy in love with gadgets, though he fancied himself a displaced *philosophe*.

In any case, we have demonstrated a clearer understanding than almost any other culture (except perhaps the British by fits and starts in all the books left *out* of F. R. Leavis' "Great Tradition") of the essentially popular nature of the novel, its necessary hostility to the modes and canons of High Art as defined by Renaissance Criticism. Certainly, before there was a respectable or even demi-respectable novelist, a self-conscious literary "artist," in the United States, we had produced hosts of best-sellers (cf. the long gap in time between Susanah Rowson and Hawthorne or even Charles Brockden Brown).

Moreover, the careers of our most eminent novelists even after Brown have been dominated by the pattern of first flirting with, then rejecting the temptations of High Art. The career of James Fenimore Cooper is typical in this regard; he began by imitating Jane Austen but quickly lapsed into providing for the unsophisticated the thrills of captivity and escape in the wilderness. And more recently our most talented fictionists have begun by emulating the European *avant-garde,* only to seek refuge in the American popular press. Think of how quickly Faulkner and Hemingway moved from "little magazines" to journals catering to the mass audience, which Scott Fitzgerald never turned away from at all. It is instructive in this regard to remember what literary histories seldom record, that the greatest of all Faulkner's stories, "The Bear," first appeared in *The Saturday Evening Post* at a point when that journal appealed to the lowest and broadest level of popular taste. Moreover, the version of Faulkner's story published in those pages, and edited to suit precisely that taste, is superior to the final version expanded and blurred in the interests, no doubt, of "art" as understood by a small-town provincial.

Examples could be multiplied indefinitely of careers which, like Hemingway's for instance, begin in the pages of elitist magazines and end in a special issue of *Life.* Most exemplary of all, however, is the case of Nathanael West, who started by imitating the *surréalistes* in *The Dream Life of Balso Snell,* but in his three later books turned to boys' fiction, bleeding-hearts journalism, and the Hollywood scene in quest of a more authentic subject matter and style. *A Cool Million, Miss Lonelyhearts,* and *The Day of the Locust* are not merely about pop culture; they are in the deepest sense themselves pop culture, their structure and tone modeled after the comic strip and the burlesque show "blackout."

I suppose it is Mark Twain who set the pattern once and for all, which only Henry James among our truly talented novelists has managed to eschew by pursuing "High Art" in condescending exile. But Henry James belongs only one third to the American tradition, being also an English novelist, and even in some sense a French one who merely happened to have written in another language. Even now, in any event, we see among the laureates of the dissenting young the same movement (think of Leonard Cohen, for example, or Richard Brautigan) from the "underground" press to the Mass Market and the production of commodity-art—whether in print, on the screen, or on records.

III

To speak to the people, moreover, means to speak in the language of the people rather than in some artificial tongue invented by academicians precisely for the purpose of creating an elitist or hermetic art. And in this regard, too, Americans have a marked advantage over more homogeneous cultures like that of France. Ever since the final decades of the last century at least, ours has been an ethnically various community in which no single dialect has ever managed to maintain special authority among all the others. The American school system has in fact tried desperately—particularly in classes in "English," all the way from kindergarten to the freshman composition course in the university—to brainwash generations of more recent immigrants into accepting as their own the dialect spoken by a handful of White Anglo-Saxon Protestants in a few Eastern seaboard cities; but this attempt has conspicuously failed. No eminent American novelist, at any rate, has ever forgotten the necessity of speaking to and for, not the Ruling or Established Classes (linguistically as well as ethnically distinguishable in the United States), but to everybody, and *for* one or another of those minorities who, generation after generation, represent the emergence into daylight of hitherto repressed elements in the American psyche. And to do this he has had to borrow from the least reputable dialects of the excluded—or to contrive a dialect of his own, even more disreputable and anti-Wasp.

The American Novel—ever since Theodore Dreiser surely, perhaps ever since Mark Twain—has used this counter-language to attack the Wasp values of our earliest ruling class, which is to say the imported Humanism of New England. By the same token, it has spoken first for a later North European migration that bypassed the old urban centers of culture in Boston, Philadelphia, and New York on the way toward the Midwest (Dreiser himself is an example, as are Hemingway and Steinbeck); then for the children and grandchildren of the defeated Confederacy, the Scotch-Irish planters and peasants of the South (Faulkner plays such a role, along with Truman Capote, Katherine Anne Porter, and Carson MacCullers); and almost at the same moment for more recent immigrants to the Big Cities, old and new: the Irish, the Italians, and especially the Jews (Saul Bellow or Bernard Malamud are conspicuous examples) and the Negroes, who had not yet learned to call themselves Blacks (James Baldwin is such a spokesman, as are Richard Wright and Ralph Ellison and even Leroi Jones up to the point where he renamed himself Moslem-style).

Even more important, however, than the actual breaking through to speech of such real minorities—elected generation after generation to say what their ethnic predecessors had found too dangerous or alien to utter—has been the attempt to represent the Alien Other, along with what seems most foreign in their own souls, by members of long-established or recently successful groups in the community. Especially notable in this regard has been the effort on the part of the most gifted White American authors to project—through a kind of magical ventriloquism—the authentic voices of those two non-European groups in whose presence and on whose backs, as it were, transplanted Europeans have built American culture: the voices of Indians and Negroes, Red Men and Black. In the great popular (which in this sense must also be called "populist") books of America, these non-European voices can be heard in dialogue with the voices of certain runaway ex-Europeans, creating an interchange as vital to our culture as the conversation of Kings and Fools in the literature of the High Renaissance.

It all begins with Chingachgook in James Fenimore Cooper's *Leatherstocking Tales* (if Twain taught our writers how to talk American, Cooper long before him taught them to dream American), with the release of the voice of the expropriated Indian. And the process continues when, for the first time, the dumb Black Slave is heard crying out in rage through the Babo of Melville's "Benito Cereno," or praying in faith and humility through Harriet Beecher Stowe's Uncle Tom, or pledging an impossible and perfect love through Nigger Jim in Mark Twain's *Huckleberry Finn*. When Cooper re-imagines himself as Chingachgook speaking to Natty Bumppo, or as Mrs. Stowe pretends she is Tom addressing young Marse George, or Twain projects himself as Jim talking to Huck, it is not merely as if two kinds of Americans sundered by exploitation and hate, but also as if two halves of the long-sundered American soul had found a way to communicate. No wonder that this is the point at which our authentic literature begins, and no wonder that the dialogue continues to this very day.

IV

Yet, for a little while during the reign of "Modernism," the age of Proust, Mann, and Joyce, of T. S. Eliot and the belated cult of Henry James, the time of the New Criticism with its odd blending of fascist politics and aesthetic formalism, these basic facts of American life and art were forgotten. And during the first four or five decades of the twentieth century, many of our most talented writers took themselves off to the cafés of Paris or the universities of England in order to learn certain "Modernist" modes of High Art: first an antibourgeois and disreputable experimentalism, an elitism redeemed partly at least by the risks it entailed; then the Eliotic tradition, in which the Avant-Garde had turned wan and genteel. In both cases, however, the "alien" voices evoked tended to speak European: sometimes actual literary French or British English, sometimes Medieval Italian or Confucian Chinese; though from time to time, the inflections of Boston Irishmen or New York Jews or Alabama "darkies" emerged in a kind of counterpoint—condescended to or broadly burlesqued.

By the Sixties, however, there was everywhere in the United States a sense that the Neo-Classical critical modes stimulated by Eliot and practiced by such Southern Agrarians as John Crowe Ransome, Allen Tate, and Cleanth Brooks had exhausted their small usefulness. Their analyses, it became clear, had made possible some reforms in pedagogy, and had even illuminated a handful of neglected lyric poems, chiefly by John Donne; but they had done nothing to explain the great novels of our own tradition or to encourage any new achievement in that genre. Indeed, even in poetry, their example served to inhibit rather than to spur new developments after 1955. There occurred simultaneously, therefore, a reaction away from Eliot in verse, and from his preferred novelist, Henry James, in prose; so that, looking back at the past decade from the vantage point of 1973, we discover that the most vital and moving novels of the period fall into two anti-Jamesian categories: the Anti-art Art Novel and the neo-Pop Novel.

Two eminently successful and representative examples of the first type, which can also usefully be described as the End-of-the-Novel

Novel, are Vladimir Nabokov's *Pale Fire* and John Barth's *Giles Goat Boy*: a strange pair of books really, the former not quite American and the latter absolutely provincial American. Yet they have in common a way of using typical devices of the Modernist Art Novel, like irony, parody, travesty, exhibitionist allusion, redundant erudition, and dogged experimentalism, not to extend the possibilities of the form but to destroy it. Such novels are the literary equivalent of those auto-destruct sculptures built to blow themselves up after a certain time: infernal machines intended not to explode a barracks or factory or palace but themselves, i.e., the very notion of Art which they embody. We may begin, for instance, by thinking that *Giles Goat Boy* is a comic novel, a satire intended to mock everything which comes before it from *Oedipus the King* to the fairy tale of the Three Billy Goats Gruff. But before we are through, we realize it is itself it mocks, along with the writer capable of producing one more example of so obsolescent a form, and especially us who are foolish enough to be reading it. It is as if the Art Novel, aware that it must die, had determined to die laughing.

Even those two most resolutely elitist makers of Anti-art Art Novels have, however, not been able to resist completely the new impulse of fiction to emulate more popular modes. Each has produced in his career one book (in Barth's case, actually one and a quarter of another) which falls into the second camp, neo-Pop; and that fact is testified to by each of these books—and none of their authors' others —having been translated almost immediately into movies. It is a characteristic of neo-Pop, of Popular fiction in a post-cinematic age, that at its most authentic it constitutes, as it were, the embryonic form of a film—words on the page being, as we have already observed, often just a transitional stage on the way toward the even more broadly available narrative form of images on the screen.

In any case, Nabokov's *Lolita* and Barth's *End of the Road* are books in which, for once, the auctorial voice, academic and witty, gives way from time to time to other, more primitive and alien voices released from the psychic underground. In Nabokov, it is the voice of the young American girl which overwhelms that of her author, and in Barth, that of the Black man. The latter is unavailable to Nabokov, who after all merely passed through America on his way from Russia and France toward Switzerland. Like any good European from

Richardson to Flaubert or Tolstoy, he releases rather the voice of the largest oppressed group in Western culture, the voice of Woman; but in his case, it is an American woman who speaks, or more precisely, a highly sexed American girl: America *as* a highly sexed American girl of twelve conducting an appropriate dialogue in automobiles and motels with the aging European male, who learns at long last that he is more seduced than seducing.

John Barth, however, is totally an American, or more precisely a Southern American from Cambridge, Maryland, where only a few years ago scenes of violence between Blacks and Whites involving the revolutionary Negro leader Rap Brown made national headlines. And it is quite proper that a Black speak in the most popular of his books, a Black Medicine Man–Psychiatrist, at once guru and shrink, who releases for a little while from paralysis the typical Barthian White anti-hero. But Barth was not as fortunate in the movie made of his book as Nabokov was with his—having fallen into the hands of Terry Southern, a scriptwriter with elitist aspirations, who eked out Barth's popular fable with fashionable politics and chic visual devices. We must wait, therefore, for the filming of the closest thing to deep popular fantasy he has ever produced, hoping that its filmwriter will not betray the hilariously pornographic one-fourth of *The Sotweed Factor,* in which the voice of a Red Girl is projected: the story of that figure of romance buried deepest in our imaginations, Pocahontas. In diaries presumably written by Captain John Smith and a traveling companion—candid accounts presumably long hidden from us all—we are at last told the scandalous truth about what really went on between the frisky Indian girl and the good Captain, who concealed her sexual problems and his, as well as their astonishing solution, behind a pack of pious lies. And surely someday some shameless maker of "skin-flicks" will detach this impious account from the learned travesty which constitutes the rest of *The Sotweed Factor,* giving both Barth and Pocahontas their just reward at the box office.

V

Meanwhile we must be content, on the page and on the screen, with the fiction of other writers—all younger than Nabokov and some junior even to Barth—who have been working more consistently with the same sort of deep popular archetypes. Typically such writers, though by no means immune to pornography, have preferred sentimentality naked and unashamed to the defensive irony which Barth and Nabokov have inherited from the dying tradition of Modernism. Moreover, they have tended to abandon both the Woman and the Black Man in favor of the Indian and his traditional comrade, the marginal White in flight from the values of White civilization. It is not merely a matter of turning from the example of Twain to that of James Fenimore Cooper in search of our deepest fantasies, but also a way of responding to certain political and social realities. Movements like Black Power and Women's Liberation have claimed for Negroes and Females the right to mythicize themselves (indeed, to re-name themselves), so that the Indian has become the sole oppressed minority still dumb enough to sit upon the White Male ventriloquist's knee, i.e., to speak for the still repressed areas of his psyche.

But to re-evoke the Indian means to re-invent the Western, after all the most authentically and uniquely American of all Pop fictional forms. And certainly the Western has taken the center of the stage as the novel has been reborn in the declining years of the twentieth century. It is by no means the sole popular form to have replaced the defunct Avant-Garde Novel, its renaissance being matched by that of the Fairy Tale, the Detective Story, Science Fiction, and, of course, "Pornotopia"—the pornographic fantasy. Porn, as a matter of fact, being the oldest as well as the most disreputable and best-loved of all forms of the novel (one of Samuel Richardson's first imitators was, to be sure, John Cleland, author of the elegantly pornographic *Fanny Hill*), has flourished with especial vigor, providing for American writers too Wasp-ish or elitist to release the Black or Red voices in themselves access to the mass market—a conspicuous instance of this kind being John Updike. And Porn is genuinely subversive and mythological, since it is at its most authentic not merely "dirty," i.e., on the other side of certain vestigial taboos, but also a form of literature in which the male author imagines, and tries to render in the female voice, what it feels like to women to be sexually possessed by men.

But perhaps pornography can no longer remain pure in our world, to which such abstract, anti-mythological pornotopias as the Marquis de Sade's *One Hundred and Twenty Days of Sodom* seem finally a little tedious. It tends rather to be blended into other sub-genres of the novel which provide greater opportunities for mythic depth and narrative interest, producing such hybrids as the porno-thriller, as in the case of James Bond, the porno-detective story, as in the case of San Antonio, the porno-fairytale, as in that of Donald Barthelme, and the porno-Science Fiction story, as in the work of Philip José Farmer.

Farmer's classical novella "Riders of the Purple Wage" (whose epigraph is "The family that blows together grows together") proved once and for all that even Science Fiction, which long seemed altogether immune to sex, could be redeemed for the lubricious imagination. And he remains, perhaps, the last best hope for that sub-genre, which seems to be enduring a crisis at the moment, as its most prized practitioners, like J. G. Ballard and even Kurt Vonnegut, try to emulate such outmoded elitist techniques as symbolism and surrealism—in an effort to enter what they take to be "the mainstream" of fiction, i.e., the defunct tradition of the Art Novel. Nonetheless, such early books of Vonnegut as *The Sirens of Titan,* written for the marketplace rather than the library, out of his heart rather than his head, are read and re-read still by readers aware of the true nature and fate of the novel, as is Heinlein's even more naive attempt at emulation, *Stranger in a Strange Land.*

And in the Soviet Union (which with England and America is one of the few countries to have produced significant quantities of good Science Fiction) the work of such popular dreamers and secret rebels as the Strugatsky brothers indicates ways into the future more promising than those being explored by the Anglo-American "new wave" of science-fantasy. Similarly in France, San Antonio has provided models for making the detective story part of the neo-Pop movement, models which have found no echo or analogue in the United States, where (with the possible exception of Ross MacDonald) the form seems to have been run into the ground by second- and third-generation imitators of Dashiel Hammet—its deep archetypes turned into stereotypes forever once they had been visually fixed in John Huston's magical film (and by Humphrey Bogart's magical face), *The Maltese Falcon.*

In American fiction of the last decade, it is primarily the Western which has revived the truly popular and subversive possibilities of the novel—not the Western as narrowly redefined in an earlier revival which began with Owen Wister's *The Virginian* and reached a climax in the fifty or more novels of Zane Grey; but the Western defined broadly enough to include recent books as superficially different from each other as Ken Kesey's *One Flew Over the Cuckoo's Nest*, Truman Capote's *In Cold Blood*, and Norman Mailer's *Why Are We in Vietnam*—the John F. Kennedy Western as opposed to the Theodore Roosevelt Western. All of these, like their ultimate prototype in James Fenimore Cooper, inventor of the Andrew Jackson Western, contain at their center a dialogue between White Man and Red; but in all, it is worth noting, the Red Man is only half Red —a half-breed—caught between the two worlds of civilization and nature.

Meanwhile, the same process of hybridization has been going on from the other side as well, and here, too, in life as well as in art. The physical hybrid represented by the "breed" has deep roots in our past, and once appeared as the symbol of utter villainy and apostasy in the naively racist films of pre-World War II. But that once mythically potent figure moves us no more even at the level of the popular arts, and certainly seems of little importance in the social realm. What does concern us urgently in life and art alike are the spiritual and psychic hybrids who constitute a substantial minority of our young, appearing particularly in well-to-do, cultured White families: young males of European stock who, without a physical "cross in their blood," have chosen, following the example of Natty Bumppo, to live lives more like those of Indians than of their fathers or grandfathers. Unlike our ancestors dumping tea, they have resolved to play Indian not just temporarily for one crucial night, but full time for a substantial portion of their lives. We see them everywhere around us on streets and by the side of the road, or in images broadcast by their press and ours—wearing headbands, beards and moccasins, braiding their uncut hair, smoking the ceremonial "medecine" of the Red men, living in abandoned *hogans* or newly constructed teepees, organizing their lives tribally or sweeping out of their wilderness refuges to raid supermarkets and department stores.

Are they Red or White is the question which their life-style poses;

and further, are *we* Red or White, we who have fathered them? No wonder, then, that certain newer novels, the neo-Pop books and films we have been discussing, begin, as it were, with their basic confusion about the line between Red and White; and end by suggesting that our membership in one group or the other is a matter of choice rather than necessity, will rather than fate, psychic set rather than genetic inheritance. On the one hand, there are such historical movies (typically derived from earlier print fiction) as *A Man Called Horse,* which started as a short story by Dorothy Johnson, or *Little Big Man,* which began as a subtle and hilarious yarn by Thomas Berger—both dealing with the adventures of a protagonist, initially White, who moves back and forth between the two worlds of White and Red as defined by the nineteenth century. That Berger is a novelist with rather old-fashioned elitist ambitions (*Little Big Man* is his only Western), and Dorothy Johnson a professional writer of Westerns, thought of primarily as a source of paperbacks and of popular films like *The Hanging Tree* and *The Man Who Shot Liberty Valance,* makes little difference; both are still committed to a view not quite disentangled from a past in which Red could be basically distinguished from White, whatever the peripheral confusions.

On the other hand, there are now movies like *Midnight Cowboy* (which pre-existed as a novel by James Leo Herlihy) and *Easy Rider* (which was dreamed directly onto the screen) in which the setting is contemporary, and the ethnic confusion, therefore, so far advanced that there is no need for actual Red Men to appear at all. We are able these days to recognize mythological Indians, whatever their skin color—as we do in the young protagonists of *Easy Rider,* those self-defined Savages going down the highway on motorbikes (and why not motorcycles, which finally are no more alien to Indians than the horse to which Europeans introduced them some five hundred years ago) toward inevitable defeat at the hands of Whiter White Men than themselves—Rednecks and Hardhats carrying on still the tradition of genocidal warfare against the Savages, quite like General Custer himself.

In *Midnight Cowboy* the original cast of the *Leatherstocking Tales* is reborn, but in apparent travesty, since the latter-day Natty and Chingachgook return as palpable counterfeits. Yet they prove true counterfeits in the end. Natty may have turned into a self-deceiving, self-defeating dishwasher from Dallas who sports a cowboy outfit only for its presumed erotic appeal. But when he comes to the big City in hopes of making it with rich women and affluent old queers, he discovers himself in a real Wilderness: an urban jungle where he encounters in Ratso a true Noble Savage, a defeated Apache of the city streets, who dies finally in his arms—transforming a Greyhound bus into the contemporary equivalent of a clearing in the virgin forest. And if Ratso is not really a Redskin, he is not really quite White either—being an Italian, a Dago, a Wop, which is to say, a Mediterranean: an ethnic status considered from the Wasp point of view half-way to being colored.

And while these transformations have been portrayed on the screen, they have been going on in life as well, coming together finally as Hollywood has learned not merely to recognize but to exploit for its own purposes the ambiguity of life-style in the dissident youth communities. When the movie *Little Big Man* was being made in the heart of what is both the old and the new American West, word was sent out of Billings, Montana, to all the agricultural communes in the region that any hippies and freaks who could sit a horse could have a job. If they had long hair and no beards, they could play Indians in the reconstruction of Custer's Last Stand; and if they had beards as well, they could portray the White soldiers who were annihilated in that famous battle. But here is the final twist of what thus becomes for our time a total parable of the total confusion of value and genre and race, and finally of levels of reality.

At the moment of the rebirth of the novel, all order and distinction seem lost, as High Art and Low merge into each other, as books become films—metamorphosing as they change into truer or falser but, in any case, quite other visions. And, at last, fact and fantasy, reality and dream blur together, creating a confusion scarcely distinguishable from madness. But who any longer knows what "madness" is in that world into which the hybrid low-high novel-film transports our sons and daughters—or is it rather our daughter-sons and son-daughters. In that world, they learn to transcend race as well as sex (or is it they who teach the lesson), to be, though born White, imaginary Redskins—or rather to aspire to a state in which that distinction, too, becomes meaningless. Toward the end of *Little Big Man* (that joint creation of Thomas Berger and Arthur Penn), the aged Indian Chief,

Old Lodgeskins, pleads with the adopted son he is about to leave forever not to go crazy, whatever else may become of him. But to move from the culture and mental set of the Indian to that of the White Man, as that son will presumably do once his Indian mentor is dead, means precisely to go crazy in Indian terms: to enter a world where the chief activities of man, hunting and war, are conducted for ends that make no sense at all. And in White Man's terms, the reverse process—that of entering a world where one dreams the future at will and can choose to die at any given moment—seems equally insane.

Small wonder, then, that *Little Big Man* is narrated in fact in the psychiatric ward of a hospital, as is revealed at the beginning and end of the story-film. Its protagonist, a presumed one-hundred-and-eleven-year-old sole survivor of the Battle of the Little Big Horn, has been, that is to say, already declared "mad" by the authorities who decide such matters in our culture. And we are, therefore, deliberately left in doubt about whether his account of Custer's Last Stand is the truth about the American West finally revealed, or only the hallucinated pseudo-memories of a psychotic. But why not *both*, the novel suggests even more clearly than the film, whose tone seems often out of control; since to "go West" has always meant to die and be reborn, and to do so deliberately is, after all, nuts—a form of insanity. In the end, therefore, the truth of our history, like any other, proves to be not saner but madder than the timid half-schizophrenia, the polite official paranoia of the school History Books. Indeed, its authentic madness can be caught perhaps only in a form which to begin with has given up all pretense of providing anything but "fictions," whether in words on the page or flickering images projected in darkness like dreams themselves.

Here lies the ultimate subversive implication of all post-Death-of-the-Novel Pop fiction, especially the Western, a genre which—perhaps for that very reason—threatens to assimilate all others at the moment. Sam Peckinpah, for instance, can, as *Straw Dogs* has demonstrated, turn even a provincial English village into a mythical West, where men learn to be Men or perish. And recently that prototypical form has begun to swallow up even what seems most alien to it, the College or Academic Novel, as became clear in America's 1971 entry at the Cannes Film Festival, *Drive, He Said*. I was doubly delighted seeing that eminently moving film, since some five or six years ago I was one of the judges who gave the novel from which it was made an award, a prize I regretted a little after re-reading Jeremy Larner's not-quite-successful book in the interim. But I must have sensed in his account of life in the university the embryo Western which only a movie (on which its author collaborated with actor-director Jack Nicholson) could deliver, once the shears of the film editor had cut the umbilical cord which attached it to the obsolescent form of print.

It is not, however, until the final scenes of the movie that we are aware of how, step by step, a New England college setting has been transformed by the dream-magic of cinema into an ultimate wilderness, a true West. When one of its pair of student protagonists, a disappointed college revolutionary called Gabriel, strips off his clothes and confronts us stark naked, we know we are in the presence of the Noble Savage reborn. Betrayed by comrades and lovers, as well as the social system he does not cease to despise but learns he cannot really transform, Gabriel decides to go mad as consciously and deliberately as men once decided to go West. Properly enough, his madness leads him to strip himself of all the accoutrements of a culture grown totally alien, and to enter in his bare skin the animal house of the Zoology Department, where he releases from their cages all the experimental animals—not merely the harmless guinea pigs and white mice, but such natural horrors as tarantulas, gila monsters, and rattlesnakes. It is as if he had taken quite literally the injunctions of Walt Whitman (to whom they remained always merely metaphorical) to free himself and his world of everything symbolized by cages and clothes. And the college authorities, realizing that such confusion of metaphor and fact is true madness (i.e., can no longer be contained within the limits of a college catalogue and given "credit" as Guerilla Theatre, or whatever), dispatch two guards to capture him.

The film ends as those two guards advance, restraining-jacket in hand, toward the last Noble Savage in the throes of his final vision. But he waves off his would-be captors, assuring them that no straight-jacket is necessary, since he is saner than they or, indeed, the whole world they represent. "It is you who are mad," he cries, "I'm sane, I'm sane!" And at that point, the audience divides (certainly this was the case in the university theatre where I saw the film); the young in the house sure that he speaks the simple truth and the older spectators no longer sure of anything. For at that point we are all of us (with or without a modicum of qualifying irony) committed to the myth of the West and the boy who embodies it—inside his naked skin, as it were, and his bewildered head, hallucinating with him, as we always tend to do when a work of art most moves us at the level where young or old, naive or learned, mad or sane, we are one with each other.

But that level is not projected by structure and style, words and fade-outs, figures of speech and montage. It is evoked only by primordial images and communal dreams, sometimes anonymous and terrible, sometimes called by such homely names as Natty Bumppo or Gary Cooper or Tom Mix. In that realm, our remotest ancestors lived day and night, sleeping or waking, horizontal or vertical. We, however, once we have left our crumpled beds, tend to forget that we inhabit it still, must always inhabit it—until madness overtakes us, temporarily or forever, or we are therapeutically inducted back into it by such popular works as I have been discussing: works popular not despite the fact but precisely because they are subversive and un-sane.

LITERARY
REALISM
AND
THE FACTS
OF LIFE

ON
LITERARY
REALISM

ALICE R. KAMINSKY

Semanticists have warned us so often of the limitations of language that it has become platitudinous to talk about the ambiguity of words. Yet the gap between knowledge and action is aptly illustrated by the way in which the term *realism* is used in relation to the novel. I single out the novel because its special contribution has usually been associated with its development as the literary form that aims to describe life truthfully, or realistically. Traditionally the novelist is supposed to be most concerned with what is real. Even when he uses myth or symbolism, he employs such devices to enlarge our understanding of the world. And today the avant-garde reviewer, who presumably no longer believes that to label a work realistic is to give it the highest accolade of criticism, ends up discussing such issues as truth and meaning in the novel. Although someone occasionally derogates realism as a meaningless term or proscribes its use in literary exegesis, it continually appears in both scholarly and critical analyses. In fact, the reviewer of J. P. Stern's *On Realism* begins his criticism in the *Times Literary Supplement*[1] with the statement: "One way or another the concept of realism in literature is attracting a great deal of attention at present." Unfortunately, the word realism is often used as if every reader clearly understands it to have one single meaning, for no attempt is made to define it.[2] It is either taken for granted as being a self-explanatory expression, like motherhood or communism, or else it is condemned as a classic example of linguistic abuse.

Thus we need to make clear the sense in which literary realism can be employed in critical jargon.

Since philosophers, scientific theorists, and even laymen have been grappling with the concept of the real for centuries, it seems appropriate to examine the meaning of realism outside the context of literature. On the one hand, the root part of realism, *real,* is quite an ordinary word, used in everyday discourse, as in "This is a real monkey," or "This is real caviar," or "This is real fur." Indeed it is such a well-established word that most people would be surprised if they were asked, for example, to explain what they mean by a real stone. They would probably react as Samuel Johnson did; they would kick the stone and insist that feeling and seeing the stone would suffice to explain its reality. On the other hand, real is a special word because it does not have one single, specified, fairly constant meaning such as that signified by blue, rat, or radio. This is not to say that it is ambiguous in the sense that the word *good* is ambiguous—that it is a word which can, in the same context, have a multiplicity of meanings. But since we do speak of a real diamond, a real color, a real bargain, and a real world, it is evident that real is used in different ways. To discover how it is used in relation to the novel complicates the task of definition even more. For it is one thing to speak of reality in the phenomenal world, and still another thing to speak of reality in a world that is avowedly non-existent except as a product of the author's imagination. What sense can we make of this baffling oxymoron—"a real fiction"?

Presumably the writer who is interested in people, places, and things is imitating or at least extrapolating from what he takes to be the real world. At some point he has to ask "What is this so-called real world?" "What is human existence?" The moment he asks these questions, he is dealing with philosophical issues. What is truth? What actually exists and what is only appearance? Philosophers and writers have had to confront the same problems. And indeed one of the greatest philosophers berated the artist for failing to tell the truth. Plato was so distrustful of the poet that he practically barred him from his ideal Republic. What he wanted from the poets of his age was more than the divine frenzy of inspiration. He wanted them to describe the world in a truthful way. In his view poets merely produced third-rate imitations of a reality they did not grasp. Homer, for example, represented the gods in ridiculous situations. Only philosophers seemed capable of understanding the forms or essences, whereas most men seemed to have a very limited intimation of ultimate truth.

Platonism has also been called conceptual realism because of its insistence that the concept or universal is what is truly real, rather than the individual thing. The real is what is common to all individuals of a class, that is, the concept or universal which is beyond the world of sense. (For example, individual men come and go, but the essence, species of man, remains permanent.) Thus the concept man is more real than the individual man. Conceptual realism has had a very pervasive influence and is to this day embodied in the beliefs of those who seek in literature the universal truths that are implicit in the transitory confusions of everyday experience.

During the Middle Ages an attempt was made to dislodge the influence of Platonic realism. One of the important scholastic controversies concerned the repudiation of the Platonic doctrine by the nominalists, who maintained that universals were mere names and only individual things existed. But the nominalist position was too extreme and too prone to give rise to radical heresies. It was Aquinas who, by combining Aristotle's modified Platonism with the nominalists' emphasis on individual things, gave us the concept of realism that was to exert a dominant influence in Christian thought and religiously oriented literature. Aquinas, following Aristotle, believed that the objects we observe are indeed real, but that buried in them is another aspect of what is real, namely, the form or universal. The form makes the body what it is. Thus it is the form which makes us grow and mature from childhood to manhood. In Aquinas' adaptation of Aristotle's revision of Platonism, an original, single substance, God, who is endowed with all ethical values, is added to the list of what is real to account for existent things in the universe.

Great novelists like Dostoievski and Tolstoy have this same view of reality as consisting of individuals in whom the universal is reflected. In *The Brothers Karamazov*, Dimitri, Ivan, Aloysha, Fyodor, and Grushenka are supposed to represent flesh and blood people who love, hate, and desire. But Dostoievski is also preoccupied with another kind of truth. He obviously wants us to believe in what he has Aloysha say at the end of the novel when Kolya asks: "Karamazov

. . . can it be true what's taught us in religion, that we shall all rise again from the dead and shall live and see each other again, all, Ilusha too?" Aloysha answers: "Certainly we shall all rise again, certainly we shall see each other and shall tell each other with joy and gladness all that has happened!"³ For Dostoievski could not accept the notion that the only reality was to be sought in material phenomena on this earth. The belief in universals has provided many a novelist with the basis for predicating immortality and a superior, eternal other world. Tolstoy had no scruples about delivering his religious sermons in his own voice as well as through the characters of *War and Peace*. Tolstoy bluntly says,

Man is the creation of an Almighty, All-good and All-wise God.⁴

And the character Prince Andrey, near death, thinks:

Love is God, and dying means for me a particle of love, to go back to the universal and eternal source of love.⁵

The Platonic-Aristotelian kind of realism remained essentially unopposed for many centuries, but by the eighteenth century philosophic speculation resulted in a new view of what is purported to be real. Empiricists like Hume and objective idealists like Kant, with all their differences, did agree that objects do not have an existence independent of the perception we have of them. Reality is formed and tempered by the human mind. As a result the empirico-idealism philosophy has had a great influence in stressing the significance of mind rather than things, of subjective rather than objective phenomena. The names of Locke, Hume, Berkeley, Kant, Hegel, Schelling, and Schopenhauer represent the view prevalent after the medieval and before the modern era that reality is to be found by investigating the operations of the mind. But this view, which led to an extreme solipsism, could not long survive without undergoing great revision. A reaction set in against the adulation of the mind as the knower of and perhaps even the creator of reality. This reaction involved a rejection of subjectivism, of the view that the mind is totally responsible for the creation or the modification of the known world. From the end of the eighteenth century until the twentieth, speculation began to center more and more on the common-sense doctrine that the objects of sense perception are experienced without being affected in any significant way by the mind or consciousness of the knower. Thus G. E. Moore was able to say, "The more I look at objects round me, the more I am unable to resist the conviction that what I see does exist, as truly and as really, as my perception of it. The conviction is overwhelming."[6] This emphasis upon the externality of things, independent of but revealed to the mind, was to prove congenial to the development of science because it stressed the importance of facts. But it was also most congenial to the development of a kind of realism which we associate with the novels of Flaubert, Stendhal, Balzac, Zola, Dickens, George Eliot, Thackeray, George Moore, Hemingway, and Faulkner, to name only a few. The avowed aim of these writers was to observe and describe life truthfully.

Réalisme, in the French sense of actuality, in the sense of portraying things as they really are, in the sense of presenting objectively and concretely the observable details of actual life, is the term usually applied to the literary movement of the nineteenth century. Propelled by the example of the scientist, a novelist like Zola was led to believe that he could apply scientific method to the study of human behavior and incorporate the results of his observations in novels which contained authentic records of actual people and events. The writer, then, in Zola's view, does not invent; he studies nature like the scientist. He observes the miner, prostitute, alcoholic, or peasant and uses the profuse information he accumulates to construct a plot which will convey the truths of the existent world. That such truths often turn out to be sordid is obviously not the fault of the artist, but evidence of a defect in nature and society and in man's relation to that society. By revealing the ugly, animalistic tendencies of man, and by showing how he is the product of a relentless determinism, the naturalistic novelist hopes to increase our knowledge of reality.

The naturalistic doctrine expounded by Zola does not preclude the possibility of change, despite its insistence on determinism and on the physical rather than the spiritual nature of man. An unabashedly hopeful aim is clearly sounded at the end of Germinal and its horrific description of mining life in France.

> An overflow of sap was mixed with whispering voices, the sound of the germs expanding in a great kiss. Again and again, more and more distinctly, as though they were approaching the soil, the mates were hammering. In the fiery rays of the sun on this youthful morning the

country seemed full of that sound. Men were springing forth, a black avenging army, germinating slowly in the furrows, growing towards the harvests of the next century, and their germination would soon overturn the earth.[7]

Zola's optimistic scientism has been justly criticized for its unwarranted assumption that the novelist should imitate the scientist. Critical consensus rejects the notion that a writer must avoid inventing fictional characters and events and must rely exclusively on historicity. Furthermore, the question arises as to whether the novelist can imitate the methods employed by the scientist. C. S. Peirce has given us an excellent definition of the scientific attitude:

> Its fundamental hypothesis . . . is this: There are real things, whose characters are entirely independent of our opinions about them; whose realities affect our senses according to regular laws, and, though our sensations are as different as our relations to the objects, yet, by taking advantage of the laws of perception, we can ascertain by reasoning how things really are, and any man, if he have sufficient experience and reason enough about it, will be led to the one true conclusion.[8]

It might be noted that Peirce's extreme confidence in science was no more justified than Zola's. However, Peirce was concerned with "real things," whereas Zola dealt with fictional people who were incapable of undergoing scientific scrutiny in the manner prescribed by scientific methodology. Unquestionably, there was something rather naive about Zola's naturalism. But his attempts to simulate the conditions of scientific exploration continued to influence later writers.

When the "tough-minded" philosophic realists of the early twentieth century—G. E. Moore, R. Sellars, C. D. Broad, B. Russell, M. R. Cohen, A. N. Whitehead, and J. Dewey—reaffirmed without equivocation their belief in a real, pluralistic universe and rejected the search for universals or essences, they reinforced the commitment of many novelists to the task of recreating the objective, actually experienced world. In addition they were influenced by the ideas of Freud and other psychological theorists to examine with frank and uninhibited curiosity another dimension of experience, human sexuality, which had long been treated with dishonest obliquity. Thus "scientific" psychology provided the kind of subjective data which the novelist could use when he stressed the interiority of characterization.

This growing concern with the subjective or inner life of man led writers like Proust, Joyce and Beckett to repudiate the kind of realism which provides us with an inventory of the surfaces and lines of the phenomenal world. When Beckett described Proust's contempt for the "grotesque fallacy of a realistic art . . . for the realists and naturalists worshipping the offal of experience, prostrate before the epidermis and the swift epilepsy, and content to transcribe the surface, the façade, behind which the Idea is prisoner,"[9] he was expressing the disaffection of many modern writers with cinematographic realism. They reject the emphasis upon the façade of experience and concentrate instead upon revealing in their own special ways the truths of intersubjective experience. They use the stream of consciousness and other unconventional devices to convey reality as it seems to them to be actually experienced. Most interesting of all is their preoccupation with language, which reflects still another shift of emphasis in philosophic thought.

Currently many philosophers do not seem to be preoccupied with the traditional questions concerning what is or is not real. Instead they try to establish the logical relationships among certain expressions of language. Thus a linguistic philosopher would ask whether the sentence "There is a table in the room" is logically equivalent to the sentence "I see a table." At first glance, there does not appear to be any relationship between traditional and contemporary philosophic approaches because the former seems to be concerned with what there is, and the latter with what is expressed in language. But, as James Cornman has recently noted,[10] linguistic philosophers must think there is some relation between the two approaches because the linguistic problems studied by the contemporary philosopher involve the very words used to express the traditional questions. The jargon today is different, but the issue is still the same old one: what is reality? The only major difference is that the modern thinker has come to recognize that analyzing what is real depends not only upon mind and experience but also upon language. Thus in philosophy the study of language has become a most significant means of explicating what is true or what is false. We should, therefore, expect present-day scrutiny of the concept of literary realism to reflect that concern.

Morse Peckham's discussion of literary realism can be used as an example of the type of analysis which focuses its attention on the semantic nature of the problem. Like others before him, Peckham views language as a system of signs.[11] He therefore proceeds to distinguish between two basic kinds of signs: the immediate and the mediate. The immediate sign would be the actual object itself which is directly observed. Thus, for example, the actual tree I see is an immediate sign. A mediate sign would be the word *tree* or the picture of a tree, or any representation which is not the actual object itself. A mediate sign may call attention to an immediate sign, but it is never itself an immediate sign. All signs, mediate and immediate, elicit responses, but there is no necessary connection between sign and response. "Any sign can be culturally linked to any response." Responding to a mediate sign such as a word means seeking for the referent of that word, a referent which may itself be the immediate sign. But there is never any certainty that the referent exists, or if it does exist that it will be found. However, in scientific expression, mediating signs are very closely allied to what they signify and for this reason they are our only valid source for judgments about the world. Immediate sign-behavior involving the actual physical manipulation of the environment gives scientific inquiry its special kind of validity. But literature employs words which are mediate signs; the referents for such words may not actually exist in the physical environment, nor does the writer engage in the actual physical manipulation of the environment in the way that a scientist does. The signs used by the novelist are always a "blend of culture, personality, convention and innovation." For this reason the sentences of literary realism can never have the precision and clarity of the descriptive sentences of science. In fact, Peckham concludes, the discussion of literary realism is futile because the language of literature is of such a nature that its signs are necessarily ambiguous and therefore no distinction can be made between what is real and unreal.

Now I do not think that we have to accept the extreme position that literary realism is a pseudo-problem. Intellectual activity of any kind involves correlating words to their referents. It is certainly true that novelists do not necessarily engage in the technical analysis of words or in environmental manipulation. The scientist deals with signs which are supposed to refer to existent phenomena, while the novelist deals with signs that need only refer to imaginary constructs.

This is why it is possible for the scientist to change the environment, whereas the novelist cannot do so because his world is created by his imagination. But first, it is important to note that since scientists also use words, they are inevitably involved in the task of relating words to something outside the word, and this process often results in ambiguity. *Phlogiston* was for a time an accepted scientific term, but it was Lavoisier who showed how it was devoid of meaning and referred to nothing. Secondly, some scientists cannot manipulate their data; for example, exactly how do astronomers move the stars? Peckham seems to believe that there are certain fundamental sentences which relate directly to what is publicly observable, whereas the language of literature does not have such basic expressions. The words in a novel lack the purity of those used by the scientist because they are vitiated by subjective influence. But this, of course, assumes that science employs a basic set of indefinable terms devoid of such subjective influence. However, as Nelson Goodman has noted, there is no basic set of indefinable or primitive terms:

> It is not because a term is indefinable that it is chosen as primitive; rather, it is because a term has been chosen as primitive for a system that it is indefinable in that system. No term is absolutely indefinable. And if indefinability is taken to mean incomprehensibility, incomprehensible terms have no place at all in a system. In general, the terms adopted as primitives of a given system are readily definable in some other system. There is no absolute primitive, no one correct selection of primitives.[12]

No language system has absolute primitive signs, neither the one used by science nor the one used by the writer. Translated into Peckham's terminology, this would mean that all signs, mediate or immediate, could be made to stand for primitive terms in a particular language system and that, in effect, there are no absolute immediate signs. There are simply signs adopted as primitives of a given system.

Thus while Peckham's discussion is a step in the right direction with its emphasis upon the linguistic nature of the problem, the questionable distinction between mediate and immediate signs does not help us to obtain a clear understanding of what realism means. In his own way Peckham is searching for some absolute definition of what is real. It seems to me that an ordinary language philosopher like J. L. Austin makes more sense, when, instead of searching for absolute explanations, he analyzes the real in terms of how it actually functions in various kinds of discourse.[13] He lists four uses for the word *real*:

1. It is "substantive hungry." The word *real* requires that we must answer the question, "a real what?" "Real" must refer to something else, a real house, a real tree.

2. It is a "trouser word." The negative sense of real is most important, that is, "wears the trousers." Something is real only in the sense in which it might not be real. The function of real is to exclude possible ways of not being real, as a real fish is different from a fish because it excludes different ways of being not a real fish, such as being a picture, a dummy, or a toy.

3. It is a "dimension word." It is the most comprehensive and general term in a group of similar terms—for example, proper, genuine, live, true, natural, authentic; and in the negative sense, artificial, fake, false.

4. It is an "adjuster word" which helps to meet unforeseen and difficult demands of language, such as to describe a new animal that looks like a pig but is not a real pig.

Obviously the meaning of "real" depends upon the context in which the word appears. That it has these four main uses and signifies different things in different contexts does not make it a pseudoconcept. On the contrary, it turns out to be a very versatile and valuable term in everyday language. It should also be able to function most effectively, to use Austin's terminology, as an "adjuster word" in criticism. It can help us to meet a "difficult demand of language" which requires us to describe a character who is not a real person but who looks like a real person. It would not at all disturb the average individual to be told that fake fur looks like real fur in certain ways, for such a comparison would help him to understand the sense in which the quality of fake fur approximates the quality of real fur. But some literary theorists do seem to be disturbed by the approximative nature of the comparison between the fictional and the real character or event. Albert Camus has insisted that the writer can never be realistic in the true sense of the word because he can never duplicate all that is involved in an actual occurrence.[14] And how wonderful it would be if we could, as Thoreau observed, invent that "Realometer so that future ages might know how deep a freshet of shams and appearances had gathered from time to time. . . . Be it life or death, we crave only reality."[15]

But, unfortunately, the Realometer does not exist and the craving for reality must be satisfied by more tentative results derived from inference and hypothetical formulation. Scientists do not scrap the notion of truth in a pique because they cannot find final, definitive answers any more than literary critics should scrap the notion of realism because the novelist cannot recreate everything involved in an actual event on the written page. Einstein's theory of relativity has replaced Newton's theory, and the relativity hypothesis may give way to still another explanation; this does not prevent the scientist from working with certain kinds of data which are considered factual in the light of available knowledge. Although there is no absolute definition of *atom* (for scientific definitions are always subject to revision if new information makes such modification necessary), the scientist does not reject the use of the word *atom* in his research. Analogously, because no absolute definition of *literary realism* has been disclosed, we should not summarily reject the term.

The relativity of scientific knowledge does not imply that scientific statements have the same degree of corrigibility. Some statements, such as the following, are clearly more fundamental and less likely to undergo scientific rejection:

1. Time will never stop.
2. Motion exists.
3. Nothing can be both green and purple at the same time and in the same respect.
4. Two plus two equals four (but not necessarily two peaches plus two peaches equals four peaches).
5. If A is the father of B, then B is the child of A.

A few other non-falsifiable statements might be added to the list, such as "I know that I exist" or "I have a pain." But most scientists would regard our knowledge as being essentially probabilistic with the preponderance of the sentences we use falling into the category of being true or false in the light of the state of knowledge at a given time. Thus, if science is permitted a relativistic view of reality, surely it is permissible for the truths of the novel to be equally relativistic. The truth of the novelist, whatever it may be, is not to be condemned because it is not the whole truth, for indeed there is no whole truth.

It might well be argued at this point that what has been said thus far readily applies to natural phenomena, but that human behavior, with which literature deals, defies such analysis. It is a critical cliché these days to praise a novelist for revealing "the mystery of human life." Certainly no one would want to deny that human beings are rather complicated animals and a lot harder to understand than chimpanzees. But surely there are certain lawlike sentences which describe what we as men and women do on this earth, sentences which can be regarded as fairly well-established, though not necessarily absolute truths:

1. We are born by being ejected from the womb of the female of the species.

2. We are mortal. We die in different ways, but we all die, and we all live with death as an irrevocable eventuality.

3. *Generally* we cling to life and do not like to die, although some of us under certain conditions commit suicide and seek to fulfill a death wish.

4. We feel hunger, thirst, sexual desire, love, hate, etc., and these feelings cause us to behave in odd ways and they make us happy or sad or both happy and sad. There are many other words in the language to describe these emotional reactions.

5. For various reasons we commit violent acts; sometimes we kill each other on an individual basis or in planned group activities called wars.

6. Laws exist to protect our rights and to punish those who disobey the rules.

7. In one way or another we are all affected by the environment of the family, job, city, country, etc. The result is that we have to contend with both inherited traits and the effect of environment upon such traits.

8. We are not born equal. Some of us are smarter, some richer, some stronger, some more beautiful, etc.

9. At some time or other we wonder about the meaning of life (unless we are cretins); some of us lessen the feeling of *angst* by accepting the belief in a Supreme Being; some of us reject such a belief and seek solace in theories about a world without God. Some of us, of course, end up with *nada*.

10. We use language to communicate our ideas, unless we are physically or mentally defective.

No doubt this list would not satisfy everyone. It does not have the kind of precision which the truths of science are supposed to have, but by and large these statements have the force of general truths obtained by observation of human behavior and can be said generally to characterize some conditions of human existence. This is why there are no new plots in literature. Every age provides new variations on the same old themes, but there are no new human instincts to dramatize. As G. W. Brandt wisely observed: "There is basically only a limited number of plots; they can be seen, in different guises, recurring down the ages. The reason is in life itself. Human relationships, whilst infinitely varied in detail, reveal—stripped down to fundamentals—a number of repetitive patterns. Writers straining to invent a plot entirely fresh have known this for a long time." Goethe referred to thirty-six tragic plots, while Schiller could not even tabulate that many.[16] And in relation to the novel itself, Ortega y Gasset noted that the limited number of plots available to the novelist, which had been overworked over the years, made it practically impossible for the modern writer to find new subject matter.

> It is erroneous to think of the novel—and I refer to the modern novel in particular—as of an endless field capable of rendering ever new forms. Rather it may be compared to a vast but finite quarry. There exist a definite number of possible themes for the novel. The workman of the primal hour had no trouble finding new blocks—new characters, new themes. But present-day writers face the fact that only narrow and concealed veins are left them.[17]

However, the modern experimental novelist would not be disturbed by the "narrow" vein, for what matters most to him is the variation on the theme. The conventional novelist has used the "closed" form of fiction, his rationale being that since individual life has the order of a beginning, middle, and end, the novel should reflect such order. Thus he places the actions of characters in some sequence (plot) to reveal the resolution of a conflict or problem, and his story generally ends in a death or marriage or other specific event. But for the writer who views life as being chaotic and disordered, the open form of fiction is more relevant since it enables him to reject conventional forms and substitute his own patterns of expressions. In his "open" novel he does not conclude with definitive resolutions but instead offers his readers what are often highly ambiguous references to the continuing experience of the protagonists beyond the final pages of the novel.[18] But whatever he does, he cannot avoid using words as signs relating to observable things open to public view. Even someone like Samuel Beckett, who parodies realism in *Murphy* and *More Pricks than Kicks,* and who insists that he is dealing with nothing, cannot escape dealing with something. What else is he doing but actively involving himself in the question of what is real in *Murphy?* At the M. M. M. Sanatorium Murphy comes to loathe the complacent, textbook scientific conceptualism

> that made contact with outer reality the index of mental well-being. . . . The nature of outer reality remained obscure. The men, women and children of science would seem to have as many ways of kneeling to their facts as any other body of illuminati. The definition of outer reality, or of reality short and simple, varied according to the sensibility of the definer. But all seemed agreed that contact with it, even the layman's muzzy contact, was a rare privilege. On this basis the patients were described as "cut off" from reality. . . . The function of treatment was to bridge the gulf, translate the sufferer from his own pernicious private little dungheap to the glorious world of discrete particles, where it would be his inestimable prerogative once again to wonder, love, hate, desire, rejoice and howl in a reasonable balanced manner and comfort himself with the society of others in the same predicament.[19]

Beckett is obviously satirizing the psychologist's concept of reality in this passage. In *Watt, The Unnamable,* and other works his preoccupation with the nature of reality is a pervasive obsession and is reflected in every linguistic trick he employs. No matter how much the novelist manipulates language, no matter how often he rearranges words or letters in strange patterns, he still has to use them as signs which have some relationship to things that are usually called real. The reader has to decipher these signs, and to do this he must in some way relate the words to actions, objects, and feelings he can understand.

For those who remain dissatisfied, the path from Joyce and Beckett leads directly to the *nouveau roman* or the anti-novel. Contending that no novelist can really compete with the facts of life, with concentration camps and wars, the anti-novelists have recommended a new approach to reality. All the old attempts to imitate the real world by using plot, psychological probings of character, and social and political philosophizing they find boring and overworked. Raymond Queneau, Michel Butor, Nathalie Sarraute, Claude Simon, Robert Pinget, and Alain Robbe-Grillet belong to the French school of writers who have experimented with the kind of narration Joyce, Proust, and Kafka pioneered, involving verbal montage, shifting points of view, interior monologues, and unresolved ambiguities. Their kind of anti-novel seeks genuine innovation through the exploration of new aims. Robbe-Grillet has expressed the credo of what he calls the "new realism."

> What constitutes the novelist's strength is precisely that he invents, that he invents quite freely without a model. . . .
> [Art] is based on no truth that exists before it; and one may say that it expresses nothing but itself. It creates its own equilibrium and its own meaning. It stands all by itself, like the zebra; or else it falls. . . .
> Instead of being of a political nature, commitment is, for the writer, the full awareness of the present problems of his own language, the conviction of their extreme importance, the desire to solve them *from within*. . . .
> Does reality have a meaning? The contemporary artist cannot answer this question: he knows nothing about it. All he can say is that this reality will perhaps have a meaning after he has existed, that is, once the work is brought to its conclusion.[20]

Now what can it possibly mean to "invent quite freely without a model"? How can a novel "express nothing but itself . . . and its own meaning"? What does it mean to say that the novelist solves the problems of "his own language *from within*," reality coming into being only after the work is concluded? What Robbe-Grillet seems to be saying is that the novelist uses his imagination to construct characters and events which have no necessary relationship to anything extrinsic to the novel itself. His "own language" would then seem to be some kind of private language. The relation of words in such a work of fiction might then be compared to the relation of musical instruments in a string quartet. They relate to each other, but not to anything outside the musical setting; for example, the viola responds to the cello, the cello to the violin, the violin to the viola, and all three respond to each other. This is, however, a misleading analogy.

Musicians use notes to achieve sound; the writer uses words to achieve meaning. Perhaps the musician does not have to do more than identify the notes he plays and the order in which he plays them in relation to other notes sounded by other musicians. (Very likely this is an oversimplified description of a complicated process.) But the author who selects words cannot avoid knowing they refer to something which a reader is supposed to fathom. We ought here to remember Wittgenstein's famous demonstration that anyone who tries to construct a private language is doomed to failure because language has to be able to distinguish between true and false statements and this makes it essential to use public verification.[21] A language must have rules by virtue of which it is possible to distinguish between the correct and the incorrect use of words. In a private language we rely solely on our memory of what words mean. Since memory can play us false, no objective criterion exists for characterizing the correct or incorrect sentence. A legitimate use of words entails a commitment to verifiable objects so that what is called a *dog* on March 10 is not as a result of a lapse of memory called a *fif* on March 30.

We can now understand what Robbe-Grillet's view entails. If nothing in the novel has to be judged in terms of a model external to the work itself, then no need exists for any kind of public verification, and there is no objective criterion for distinguishing between the correct and incorrect use of words. Everything the novelist writes is incapable of being falsified and the novel becomes the prime example of the tautology.

Other critics like the *Tel Quel* group in France have argued that to create a new and more genuine kind of reality in the novel, the writer must divest language of its associations with the presuppositions of prevailing social systems, particularly with the delusions of modern bourgeois society. This is a fascinating aim, but leading philosophers like Russell, Wittgenstein, Carnap, and Quine consider it impossible to achieve such a goal. With frenetic zeal the new novelist experiments, seeking to displace what Roland Barthes calls a fabricated realism, "condemned to mere description by virtue of this dualistic dogma which ordains that there shall only ever be one optimum form to 'express' a reality as inert as an object, on which the writer can have no power except through his art of arranging the signs."[22] But the creator of the *nouveau roman* does not have any more power over "inert reality" than the creator of the old novel, and when he innovates by arranging his signs differently, he is simply substituting one kind of fabrication for another. In actuality, he ends up serving the same old wine in new bottles. What he does not seem to be able to displace is the one element common to all works which have some relationship to reality.

For a novelist works with a special kind of hypothetical question, the subjunctive conditional, "What would happen if such and such were to happen?" Note that he does not use the material conditional form of the hypothetical question, "What does happen if such and such does happen?" (Unless he is merely recording historical events, and then he is not writing fiction.) And when he deals with "If A were to occur, then B would occur," the novelist must be responsive to the possible reaction of a possible reader. Thus in a very important sense the novelist and the contemporary philosopher are concerned with the same kind of sentence, known either as the subjunctive conditional, the contrary-to-fact conditional, or more simply as the counterfactual.[23] The philosopher asks why it is intelligible, that is, verifiable or confirmable, to say, (1) "If John Smith were to jump through the window, then he would probably die," while it is not intelligible to say (2) "If John Smith were to jump through the window, then little pink elephants would appear." In both of these sentences, the antecedent, the *if clause,* is false. John Smith does not actually jump through the window and probably never will. But contemporary logic stipulates that, with minor exceptions, whenever the antecedent of an *if-then* sentence is false, the entire sentence is true! (Why this is true is demonstrated by a special kind of logical proof called the truth table analysis, available in most modern logic texts.) However, only one of the sentences concerning John Smith is intelligible to us. As the philosopher points out, in ordinary usage sentence (1) is taken to refer to a genuine possibility while sentence (2) is not taken to refer to such a possibility.

Similarly, in this sense, the novelist deals with a genuine possibility because he works with the contrary-to-fact conditional in such hypothetical situations as "If Dorothea Brooke were to marry the pedant Casaubon, she would not be happy." "If Grimm were to find Joe Christmas, he would castrate Christmas." "If Molly Bloom were to engage in an interior monologue, she would eulogize the glories of sexuality." And not only in *Middlemarch, Light in August,* and

Ulysses are we confronted with the subjunctive conditional, but also in a "new" novel like Robert Pinget's *L'Inquisitoire* we will find it formulated as the classic detective story question: "If a crime were to occur, then X would be responsible for the crime." When the intelligent reader accepts these counterfactuals, he is in effect judging them to reflect something true about human life, even though at best they are hypothetical and even though it would be difficult to explicate them in rigorous scientific or logical terminology.

It is precisely because the novelist works with the formula, "If A were to occur, then B would occur," that veracity for him has to be a flexible rather than a rigid notion. The counterfactual explains why he never has to be limited to the description of the lines and surfaces of existing objects. Joseph Conrad and Saul Bellow both write about Africa, but the judgments we ultimately make about the truth of *Heart of Darkness* or *Henderson the Rain King* are only minimally concerned with the accuracy of the physical descriptions of that continent. Also I doubt whether anyone has actually experienced either Marlow's or Henderson's adventures in quite the way that they do. Nor does it matter whether anyone has actually experienced them. To write realistic novels is to deal with imaginary events and characters and with the hypothetical formulation of possibilities, in other words with the counterfactual, for the sake of illuminating political, social, economic, psychological, or moral "truths" of an age. This kind of veracity seems to be a necessary condition for the creation of a good or a great novel, although obviously the mere use of effects which attempt to distinguish between the real and the counterfeit can no more guarantee a good novel than close observation of nature can automatically produce a scientific discovery.

Finally, since we have no way of distinguishing between the real and the non-real in any absolute sense, perhaps we should adopt the relativistic outlook, shifting and amorphous as it may seem to those who seek a theory of mimesis which will reveal the essence of reality. Accepting the view that realism means different things in different contexts, Harry Levin comments: "When Professor [Erich] Auerbach [in *Mimesis*] finds no formula for the presentation of actuality . . . in different languages at different epochs, he impressively documents our need for assuming a relativistic point of view."[24] Thus Levin argues for recognizing different kinds of literary realism, although he warns that divergencies should not make us overlook the "fundamental impetus" of art to adapt itself to changing views of reality. And indeed the divergencies of conceptual, scientific, social, Marxist, psychological realisms or naturalism, verism, or veritisim serve to underscore the indefatigable capacity of the novel to reflect the successive and fluctuating interpretations of the nature of man and his world. Fortunately, the novelist is not a pugilist and we do not have to pick a winner. We do not have to choose between George Eliot and Proust; we can choose both. A long list of characters have helped us to enlarge our understanding of what it means to be human and a long list of events remind us of what it means to have a human experience. The total accumulation of visions radiating from different angles of the mirror provides us with insight into the nature of the so-called real world. Thus while literary realism does not answer metaphysical questions about the nature of reality, it is far from being a pseudo-concept and it has a valid function to perform. It functions like that strange, straight line in mathematics, the Asymptote, which approaches but never meets the Curve, destined to remain forever tangential to infinity.

NOTES

1. February 19, 1973, p. 146.
2. See, for example, T. O'Neill, "Cassola on Realism," *Modern Language Review*, 65 (July, 1970), 552-57; Frederic Jameson, "Metacommentary," *PMLA*, 86 (January, 1971), 13, and *"La Cousine Bette* and Allegorical Realism," *PMLA*, 86 (March, 1971) 241.
   Richard Locke ends his review of John Updike's *Rabbit Redux* (*New York Times Book Review*, November 14, 1971, p. 24) with "I can think of no stronger vindication of the claims of essentially realistic fiction than this extraordinary synthesis of the disparate elements of contemporary experience."
3. Trans. Constance Garnett (New York, Random House, n.d.).
4. Leo Tolstoy, *War and Peace*, trans. Constance Garnett (New York: Random House, n.d.), p. 1134.
5. *Ibid.*, p. 925.
6. G. E. Moore, *Philosophical Studies* (London: Routledge & Kegan Paul, 1948), p. 96.
7. Trans. Havelock Ellis (London: J. M. Dent, 1948).
8. Charles S. Peirce, *Chance, Love, and Logic: Philosophical Essays* (Magnolia, Mass.: Peter Smith, 1949), p. 26.
9. Samuel Beckett, *Proust* (New York: Grove Press, 1957), pp. 57, 59.
10. James W. Cornman, *Metaphysics, Reference, and Language* (New Haven: Yale University Press, 1966), pp. xi-xxi.

11. Morse Peckham, "Is the Problem of Literary Realism a Pseudo-Problem?", *Critique: Studies in Modern Fiction,* 12 (November, 1970), 95-112. See also Harold Osborne, *Aesthetics and Criticism* (New York: Philosophical Library, 1955), pp. 70-78.

12. Nelson Goodman, *The Structure of Appearance* (New York: Bobbs-Merrill, 1966), p. 64.

13. J. L. Austin, *Sense and Sensibilia* (Oxford: Clarendon Press, 1962), pp. 68-77.

14. Albert Camus, *The Rebel,* tr. A. Bower (New York: Alfred Knopf, 1954), pp. 238 ff.

15. *The Variorum Walden,* ed. Walter Harding (New York: Twayne, 1962), p. 94.

16. George W. Brandt, "Plot," *Cassell's Encyclopedia of World Literature* (New York: Funk and Wagnalls, 1954) I, 422.

17. José Ortega y Gasset, *The Dehumanization of Art and Other Writings on Art and Culture* (Garden City, N.Y.: Doubleday, 1956), p. 54.

18. See Alan Friedman's discussion of the open and closed forms of fiction in *The Turn of the Novel* (New York: Oxford University Press, 1966), pp. 15-37.

19. Samuel Beckett, *Murphy* (New York: Grove Press, 1938), pp. 176-77.

20. Alain Robbe-Grillet, *For a New Novel: Essays on Fiction,* trans. R. Howard (New York: Grove Press, 1965), pp. 32, 45, 40, 141. See also Stephen Heath, *Nouveau Roman: A Study in the Practice of Writing* (Philadelphia: Temple University Press, 1972).

21. Ludwig Wittgenstein, *Philosophical Investigations,* trans. G. E. M. Anscomber, 3rd ed. (New York: Macmillan, 1958), pp. 92 ff.

22. Roland Barthes, *Writing Degree Zero,* trans. A. Lavers and C. Smith (New York: Hill and Wang, 1967), p. 68.

23. Roderick M. Chisholm, "The Contrary-to-Fact Conditional," *Readings in Philosophical Analysis,* ed. H. Feigl and W. Sellars (New York: Appleton-Century-Crofts, 1949), pp. 482-97; Nelson Goodman, *Fact, Fiction and Forecast* (Cambridge, Mass.: Harvard University Press, 1955).

24. Harry Levin, *Contexts of Criticism* (New York: Atheneum, 1963), pp. 69-70. On the other hand, J. P. Stern in *On Realism* (London: Routledge and Kegan Paul, 1972) attempts to resolve the dilemma by expounding a theory of family likenesses among realistic writings.

REALISM
RECONSIDERED

GEORGE LEVINE

Realism would seem now to be a tired subject, and to revive it is to
risk repetition and boredom. Unfortunately, however, the word "realism" is only tired, not dead, and whatever it refers to seems also more
or less alive; certainly the problems raised by its meaning in literary
contexts persist. In England there has been a continuous tradition of
realistic writing, most recently in self-conscious repudiation of various modes of modernism, and in a very recent book David Lodge
comes close to insisting on the almost precise overlap between realism
and the novel as a form. Since, moreover, his point is to prove that
the novel is not dead, he is also obliged to prove that realism, too,
lives.[1] In any case, "realism" seems to be a term from which there is
no escaping in discussions of fiction, even now.

It is, of course, a commonplace of criticism that "realism" is an
elusive word, that it has been recklessly and carelessly used; but despite some very serious efforts, it has been impossible, finally, either
to provide it with a consistently precise definition or to banish it.
Even to argue that it describes a kind of phantom, something that is
not and never has been, is to affirm a fairly comfortable position
which has long since lost its shock value.[2] But it is important to note
that the word has a relatively short history in English, appearing for
the first time somewhere in the middle of the nineteenth century;
and it developed, for the purposes of English fiction, on an analogy
with French fiction.[3] And the very fiction it was used to describe—

that, for instance, of Thackeray, or Mrs. Gaskell, or George Eliot—is regarded by modern artists as profoundly unrealistic in the sense that it surrendered to the happy ending and to coincidence, that it consistently omitted certain aspects of reality, that it tended to assume an intelligible universe.[4]

Part of the modern growth of self-consciously anti-realistic literature and criticism has surely been the result of a rejection of Victorian conceptions of reality, but the idea that literature should be describing reality or truth is implicitly present still. The most interesting fiction of our day frequently seems to be game-playing, to be enjoying—as in Borges, Barth, and Nabokov—the possibilities of language and pleasures of literary parody. But the games themselves, while suggesting powerfully the writers' consciousness of the way verbal structures intervene between us and reality, provide for us new possibilities of reality. Reality has become problematic in ways the Victorians could only barely imagine, yet much of the energy of modern fiction comes from sources similar to those which directed earlier realism: from a conscious rejection of the notions of reality implicit in earlier fictions and from a sense of the limits of the power of language to render reality at all. The method of Robbe-Grillet, as he himself has made clear, is an attempt to get more precise about reality as it is experienced by human consciousness.[5] With this notion of changing realities in mind, we can, moreover, make some sense of Erich Auerbach's treatment of Virginia Woolf as a great culmination of the tradition of literary realism.

Most of the confusions about the word "realism," I would argue, come from an initial confusion between an historically definable literary method and a more general (perhaps inescapable) attempt to be faithful to the real. Since reality is both inexhaustible and perpetually changing to human consciousness, the word "realism" had no chance of a stable meaning. Despite all its dangers, the word has the one virtue of forcing us to wrestle with some of the central problems of criticism and of art.

The question it poses initially is, not so simply, whether literature in any sense describes the real, extra-literary world. And that question, of course, leads to others: is it the function of literature to record reality or to illuminate, even create, new possibilities? What value can there be in a mere record of reality? Is it possible to render reality when perception can never be pure and the medium of language seems inevitably to influence its subject?[6] How can one judge literature on the basis of its fidelity to the real when the real itself is so elusive and variable? Questions like these are the province of philosophy and aesthetics, but they must enter into criticism, and they certainly underlie most of our assumptions of value. Every literary generation has to struggle with them, though I do not propose here to do so directly. Although much of what I say will remain at a high and dangerous level of abstraction, what I want to do here is help toward the development of a critical approach to fiction which will at once deal with our immediate or naive sense that fiction is somehow like life, that appropriate terms of judgment can be found in the comparison of fiction to what really happens in life, that the novel is the most mixed of literary forms and therefore the one most responsive to extra-literary pressures, and with our more literary awareness of fiction as a structure of language working out from earlier structures and profoundly limited by the medium of language itself.

I

My bias, then, is historical, and I am convinced that criticism of fiction would profit from a fuller and more precise sense both of the traditions of the novel and of the changes in sensibility and perception which have affected those traditions. In its only even relatively precise sense, realism is an historical phenomenon, a literary method (or methods) rather than a literary or metaphysical ideal. Obviously, the second notion influenced the first, and historically speaking it is fair to say that writers thought that in adopting realism as a technique they were in fact moving closer to the truth. What is interesting here is that at one point in European history writers should have become so self-conscious about truth-telling in art (which I take to imply the growth of doubt about art in society) that they were led to raise truth-telling to the level of doctrine and to imply that previous literatures had not been telling it. Surely this is an important development in intellectual and cultural history, but surely too criticism is misled which works on the assumption that realistic novels—those of George Eliot, say—represent real life more accurately than do the narratives of Milton, or Melville, or even Fielding.

So extraordinary a book as Auerbach's *Mimesis* can itself be taken as fostering the confusion by implying that Western literature has been moving constantly toward a finer and finer approximation to reality. If we read the book in that way, we can fall into the trap of assuming that there is some sort of absolute reality toward which artistic consciousness, in a kind of Hegelian dialectical movement, is progressively moving. Auerbach's great value lies not in his treatment of Virginia Woolf as the greatest "realist" because her techniques most precisely record the nature of psychological reality and the flux of experience, but in his wonderful treatment of the various styles of writers as they attempt to deal with new versions of reality, and in his implied assumption that the language of each writer creates the new reality. Perhaps the most fruitful approach to the problem is suggested by E. H. Gombrich's *Art and Illusion*,[7] a book which deals with the way in which artistic creation and audience perception are controlled by the conventions for the representation of reality within art and society. Artists have taught us to *see* differently; the way we see is culturally conditioned, so that lines suggesting depth to us may seem mere lines to those living in a different culture.[8]

Realism, like any literary method, reflects both inherited conventions and a way of looking at the world, a metaphysic, as it were. It implies certain assumptions about the nature of the real world, assumptions which need not be made explicit in any realistic text but which certainly constitute a ground of meaning. Among other things, it has, surely, implied that ordinariness is more real—at least more representative and therefore truthful—than heroism, that people are morally mixed rather than either good or bad, that the firmest realities are objects rather than ideas or imaginings. English realism, the type with which I will be most directly concerned, tended, moreover, to assume that the real is both meaningful and good, while French realism has consistently tended away from such moral assumptions to lead more directly to the notion of an indifferent universe and to that even more specialized kind of realism, naturalism.

Whatever the specific assumptions, one way to deal with the problem of realism is to locate those assumptions and to identify the conventions (including, in particular, assumptions about how literature ought to be affecting its audience). When a literary method comes to be called realistic it tends to imply several things: first, that there is a dominant and shared notion of reality in operation, upon which the writer and his audience can rely; second, that this notion is self-consciously replacing an older and currently unsatisfying one which is open to parody and rejection; third, that there is moral value (to be debated by those who continue to defend the older notion) in the representation of that reality. This obviously leads to confusions because the argument seems not to be about the nature of literary technique but about the nature of reality. Such confusion is redoubled by literary debates over whether, even if the artist's version of reality is accurate, the recording of that reality is rightfully the function of art. Much nineteenth-century criticism of realistic writers—of such different ones as George Eliot and Zola—was precisely of this kind. As Linda Nochlin suggests, such criticism assumed that writers "were doing no more than mirroring every-day reality. These statements derived from the belief that perception could be 'pure' and unconditioned by time or place."[9]

Just as realism implies certain metaphysical or quasi-metaphysical assumptions, so does criticism of it. In order to proceed with my argument, I need at this point to make clear as well as I can the assumptions upon which my analysis will—more or less ingenuously —be based. For economy's sake, I lay them out in propositional form, although they have not the rigor of philosophical argument. I do intend them as a coherent and gradually developing argument but believe it possible to accept some of the propositions without accepting all that precede or follow. I should, furthermore, preface them with two qualifying remarks: first, that the ideas apply most directly to the classical tradition of the nineteenth-century English novel (although I do believe them applicable, with some qualifications, to all fiction); and second, that like all truisms mine appear to me to be debatable or, at least, occasionally to disguise what is moot by leaving key words incompletely defined. At the risk then of either banality or obfuscation, let me begin.

1. All fiction is fiction.
2. All fiction emerges from the consciousness of the individual writer and is therefore shaped in the way that consciousness perceives.
    2a. The writer's consciousness will necessarily be deeply in-

volved in the shared assumptions of his culture and in at least some of the traditions of fictional form.[10]

2b. The writer's perceptions as well as his language will be largely controlled by these assumptions in combination with his private psychological needs.

3. The basic materials of fiction are words, and words are the means by which each consciousness constructs and orders its world and by which each private world is made shareable.

   3a. Words, as implied in 2a, are invested with the assumptions and history of the culture.

   3b. Words inevitably carry not only the burden of description (and perception) but the burden of value. A change in language implies a change both in perceptions and values— and, concomitantly, a change in the forms of fiction.

4. The fundamental form of fiction is, therefore, the working out in language of the possibilities imaginable by the writer in the direction of the most complete shareable fulfillment of his values.

   4a. Mimetic language, the language of "realistic" fiction, explores not only the possibilities of what is but the possibilities of what should be (as limited by the shareable assumptions implicit in the language, the culture, and the writer's mind).

   4b. Insofar as the descriptive and prescriptive tendencies of language and fiction are separable, the descriptive tends toward disorder, the prescriptive toward order, the one to integrity of detail, the other to coherence of design.[11]

5. The predominating energy in most fiction, however discursive, episodic, or apparently formless, is not the representation of reality but the shaping of the rendered experience. It is, in other words, formal, and manifests itself traditionally in plot, but also —as new critical analyses have suggested—in patterns of imagery, motifs, relationships.[12]

6. If romance can be stipulatively defined as a form in which pattern dominates over plausibility, in which the central figure achieves the fullest possible freedom from the limitations of a restricting context, in which ideal values are worked out and shown to be viable, romance is the underlying form of most fiction, whatever its ostensible mode.

6a. Romance is the translation of the writer's perceptions into narrative, i.e., the imposition of form on experience.

6b. The imposition of form on experience is the mode by which literary conventions are transmitted. Curiously, the most intense and personal feelings and perceptions tend to take the most formally recognizable shapes. In Frye's convincing paradoxical formulation: "It has been a regular rule that the uninhibited imagination, in the structural sense, produces highly conventional art."[13]

6c. Romance is also the mode by which the particular psychic needs of the writer are most directly placed, as imaginative projections, in narrative.

7. Although novels may aspire to create the illusion of reality and to tell the truth, the most fruitful direct approach to fiction is through a focus on romance elements, the romance being the generator of form.

8. Form in any given novel is meaning since it determines the relations of the surface elements.

9. Patterning is the distinctive quality of fiction and of language, the material of fiction; and patterning is a reflection of the translation of experience into mind and feeling.

9a. There is no such thing as raw experience, since that implies some kind of experience undisturbed and unmodified by mind or feeling.

9b. Fictional language differs from non-fictional rather in the degree to which engagement imposes meaning than in any formal way. Realism attempts to create the illusion of non-fiction as the writer struggles to come to terms with, as Frye puts it, "things as they are and not as the story-teller would like them to be for his convenience."[14]

10. All fiction is fiction.

II

Such abstract speculation on truth, reality, and perception is likely to miss out on the most obvious fact about fiction—its special power to amuse and engage us through narrative, to arouse expectations and provide satisfying resolutions.[15] And it is for this reason, among others, that I have insisted on the fictionality of fiction. Fiction is shaping, giving precedence to form over reality and even plausibility, when necessary.[16] It is the working out of imaginings and desires and needs, and its form is an expression of these. Traditionally, literature was taken as being both sweet and useful, *dulce et utile*. But the realist aesthetic tends to subsume both of these under the heading "form" as opposed to that of "truth." And a good part of the energy of English realist art was devoted to attempting to make it possible to combine the sweet and useful with the truthful.

By the end of the nineteenth century the difficulty of such an enterprise was clear. Oscar Wilde's wonderfully satiric and intelligent dialogue "The Decay of Lying" is a rich assertion of my rather more pallid propositions 4 through 4b, an attack on the conventions of realism dominating at the time and a recognition of an apparent incompatibility between form (coherence of design) and truth (integrity of detail). "What Art really reveals to us is Nature's lack of design," says Vivian.[17] The whole dialogue comes to equate imagination with lying, or, to put the better face on it, lying with imagination. It argues that what we value in art is the lying, not the mundane recording of a patternless and unattractive universe. "It is always the unreadable that occurs," Vivian says.[18] In this and the companion dialogue, "The Artist as Critic," Wilde suggests how the liar actually creates reality for us, although he would never allow himself so solemn a formulation. Wilde (or Vivian) goes on to suggest the virtues (heaven help us) of lying, and in so doing links together—beautifully for my purposes—the notion of entertainment, lying, imagination, and creativity:

> For the aim of the liar is simply to charm, to delight, to give pleasure. He is the very basis of civilized society, and without him a dinner party, even at the mansions of the great, is as dull as a lecture at the Royal Society. . . . Nor will he be welcomed by society alone. Art, breaking from the prison-house of realism, will run to greet him, and will kiss his false, beautiful lips, knowing that he alone is in possession of the great secret of all her manifestations, the secret that Truth is entirely and absolutely a matter of style; while Life—poor, probable, uninteresting human life—tired of repeating herself for the benefit of Mr Herbert Spencer, scientific historians, and the compilers of statistics in general, will follow meekly after him, and try to produce, in her own simple and untutored way, some of the marvels of which he talks.[19]

This is no joke.

The emphasis on lying should remind us of how much our admiration of great fictions depends not on their recording of life but on their creation of it through language and of how deeply all fiction is indebted to literature and its traditions: "Art," says Wilde, "finds her own perfection within, and not outside of, herself. She is not to be judged by any external standard of resemblance. She is a veil rather than a mirror."[20] This is a happier way of putting Frye's assertion that "Literary shape cannot come from life; it comes only from literary tradition."

At the very least, these ideas seem valid in arguing that fiction is not to be judged "by any external standard of resemblance." Much of the weakness of criticism of the great novels in the central tradition of nineteenth-century realistic fiction is a result of the tendency to judge by such an external standard. We can see quite clearly now that disparagement of the "spontaneous combustion" episode in *Bleak House* because such things do not happen, or of the fairy-tale quality of *Jane Eyre* because it is mere wish-fulfillment, is entirely beside the point of the special qualities of those books. To criticize in this way is to equate "realism" with "truth," and with "truth" as we happen to define it. Surely, the relation between art and truth is more complicated and interesting than that.

Of course, it will not do to dismiss entirely the mimetic element in the language of realism and simply to assimilate realism to romance. Frye is surely oversimplifying when he says that "literary shape cannot come from life," even though he means here overall structure rather than local detail. The pressures on literary form come not only from literary tradition but from the form of each writer's belief in the nature of reality. That this form is culturally influenced does not mean that it is exclusively shaped by literature —as witness, for example, the literary effects of *The Origin of Species*. The realistic method does develop out of conventions of empiricism. In her extremely interesting qualification of the views of Gombrich, Linda Nochlin, accepting our view that realism is an historically locatable technique rather than a direct expression of truth, points out that "if one takes the opposition between convention and empirical observation in art as a relative rather than an absolute criterion, one can see that in Realism the role played by observation is greater, that by convention smaller."[21] As an example, she shows how Constable, though he based his paintings of clouds partly on the work of Alexander Cozzens, an eighteenth-century engraver, nevertheless painted clouds as *he* saw them, and they are readily identifiable as to type, where Cozzens' clouds are not. I would argue, moreover, that the commitment to what was taken as observed reality significantly reshaped the larger structures and subject matters of fiction.

Yet patterning remains the distinctive quality of fiction, and it is with this patterning that novelists must, finally, come to terms, even if one of their initial motives is the telling of truth. For the truth must be the truth as they see it and in a mode whose traditions themselves entail a shape. The history of the novel in English from Defoe to the present reveals the dominance of "lying" in the convention of realism itself. Realism has been only one of the novel's modes, though a central mode, and its pressures have led the novelist to struggle—through all its transformations—to deal with "things as they are" rather than as he "would like them to be for his own convenience." But the struggle was never quite won because the obstacles realism itself created to the writers' imaginative needs led, inevitably, to its abandonment or at least radical revision. There developed a recognition, which we can see in Hardy, Conrad, Virginia Woolf, and others around the turn of the century, that things as they are are themselves a convention, and that the convention was a peculiarly painful one.

III

Wherever we look in the history of English fiction, we are unlikely to find a novel unequivocally "realistic" according to any of the definitions we have been used to working with. Realistic heroes get a bit too heroic, coincidences intrude to resolve difficulties, society fails to impinge as completely on the fate of the protagonists as would seem appropriate, elements of the exotic or violent or excessive appear. I come back to arguing that realism is a hybrid and that the definitions we work with, however useful they may be locally, correspond to ideals rather than to novels. Our definitions are derived, at their best, from a wide variety of works and apply not merely to style, but to form and subject as well. In roughly outlining here what the realistic style, form, and themes or subjects are frequently taken to be, I don't want to make any special claims for my version of realism. Rather, I want to make it clear, first, that realism, in this sense at least, is a relatively brief historical phenomenon; and second, that the different aspects of the definition are latent with self-contradiction, a self-contradiction which, I would suggest, implied the death of the tradition at its very start and helped push realism into later extreme and even anti-realistic forms like naturalism, or Virginia Woolf's stylizing of consciousness, or Joyce's brilliant psychological games.

The style of realism is plain, direct, more or less colloquial, uninhibited by the conventions of other literary genres, and thick with the details of the phenomenal world. The form of realism is free from the constraint of poetic ordering, of mythic patterning, concentrating on the individual rather than the type and creating him and his narrative in great particularity. The narrative movement follows the direction of biography or history, subject to the interests of plausibility rather than of shapeliness and coherence. The subject of realism is the ordinary, characters thoroughly mixed rather than heroic, noble, or immaculately virtuous, who live in and whose fates are determined largely by a society (itself carefully implied or described) which entails for its survival a life of compromise for all of its members.

Anybody who has read any two supposedly realistic novels knows that this won't do. Yet I am inclined to think that nothing else will, either, unless the definition becomes so simplified that almost any work can fit it. David Lodge, for example, has recently defined realism comfortably as a literary mode that "treats fictional events as if they were a kind of history, or to denote a literary aesthetic of truth telling."[22] This, of course, has a strong ring of authenticity about it, but it would lump indiscriminately together works like *Vanity Fair*, *Middlemarch*, *Wuthering Heights*, *Jane Eyre*, *Moby Dick*, *The Scarlet Letter*, *Madame Bovary*, *Crime and Punishment*, *Little Dorrit*, and *Lady Chatterley's Lover*. Very few novelists could be excluded. Once we begin to get precise about the definitions, confusions inevitably enter.

As I have suggested, these confusions are present from the very beginnings of what we take to be the realistic novel, and I want here to provide some fairly obvious examples of what I mean. William

Hazlitt once remarked that the novels of Defoe "leave an impression on the mind more like that of things than words,[23] and such testimony suggests that Defoe qualifies as a realist on the criterion of style. And yet Defoe's purported editing of *The Life and Surprizing Adventures of Robinson Crusoe, of York, Mariner* (1719) is surely the first great lie of the realistic tradition. The book was to be taken as true, and clearly many readers did so take it. The style, so thick with things, so direct and credibly that of a Mariner, so unliterary, was essential in making the story seem true. But the story does not match our notion of a realistic subject. Defoe took, rather, the extreme case and built upon it a texture of the commonplace in order to make it believeable.

The ironies are obvious. At this distance, it is difficult to imagine anyone believing the story: though the details carry some conviction, the accumulation of them surely does not. We recognize a fantasy in which man, by virtue of his intelligence and practical assiduity, conquers nature. Robinson is obviously the romantic hero in a new form, and the fact that Defoe's novel did so readily transform itself into a classic story for children and an almost perfect myth of laissez-faire capitalism and the new commercial society suggests immediately how tenuous and time-bound notions of realism are likely to be.

Though it fulfills the criterion of realistic style and that of realistic form (to a certain extent), the subject of *Robinson Crusoe* can only be taken as realistic if we read it allegorically: Robinson as the typical commercial man. The tradition of allegory is to a certain extent present in the narrative, but Robinson is quite particularly imagined. At the same time, Defoe is careful to make him seem ordinary: "mine was the middle state, or what might be called the upper station of low life," says Robinson.[24] And the book is not at all uncharacteristic of novels within the realistic tradition in giving mythical shape to bourgeois ideals or in mixing the ordinary and the extraordinary. The mixture is far more characteristic than the exclusive presence of one or the other. The domestication of the extraordinary or the recognition of the wonderful in the ordinary is as central to the whole tradition of realistic fiction as it is to the *Lyrical Ballads*.[25] And whether to call any given work a romance or a realistic novel becomes almost a matter of preference.

A passage early in *Robinson Crusoe* provides a perfect text for understanding some of the tensions that persist through the realistic tradition among style, subject, and literary form. Robinson's father urges him to recognize the happiness of his "middle state":

He bade me observe it, and I should always find that the calamities of life were shared among the upper and lower parts of mankind; but that the middle station had the fewest disasters, and was not exposed to so many vicissitudes as the higher or lower parts of mankind; nay they were not subjected to so many distempers and uneasinesses either of body or mind, as those were who, by vicious living, luxury, and extravagances on the one hand, or by hard labour, want of necessaries, and mean or insufficient diet on the other hand, bring distempers upon themselves by the natural consequences of their way of living; that the middle station of life was calculated for all kinds of virtues, and all kinds of enjoyments; that peace and plenty were the handmaids of a middle fortune; that temperance, moderation, quietness, health, society, all agreeable diversions, and all desirable pleasures, were the blessings attending the middle station of life; that this way men went silently and smoothly through the world, and comfortably out of it, not embarrassed with the labours of the hand or of the head; not sold to the life of slavery for daily bread, or harassed with perplexed circumstances, which rob the soul of peace and the body of rest; not enraged with the passion of envy, or secret burning lust of ambition for great things; but in easy circumstances sliding gently through the world, and sensibly tasting the sweets of living, without the bitter, feeling that they are happy, and learning by every day experience to know it more sensibly.[26]

This is advice that Robinson himself professes to believe, especially at those moments when he is endangered by not following it. But following such advice would have made an insufferably dull book, and Robinson is only allowed to achieve this middle station by way of purgation for disobeying his father and God, and as a good businessman should, by great industry. The novel itself fully contradicts the ideas laid out here while making the dull world available to Robinson again at the end. It is popular because it avoids the middle station while at the same time extolling it. Admiring the middle station and the energies that earn it, Defoe largely invents a form that will become central to the realistic novel: the story of the romantic youth who must learn to deal with reality. The excessive, the extraordinary, the coincidental, far from violating the structure of the book, are what give it its peculiar interest and power—and plausibility be damned.

The case is not much different with *Pamela,* that other candidate for paternity (or maternity) of the English novel. Here again, as with Defoe, the novelty is in style rather than subject. It is a style appropriately plain and direct. In addition, it is, unlike Defoe's, dramatic, creating in the serving girl's record of her adventures an immediacy and excitement quite new in fiction. To be sure, to take such a poor creature as heroine of a serious work was to attempt another fairly new thing, but neither this subject nor the style can alter the fact that *Pamela* is almost the purest of all romances. Its subject, after all, is virtue rewarded, the pauper made princess, innocence triumphant over evil, evil converted by innocence.

Fielding, in the interests of greater fidelity to the real world as he understood it, conceived a fiction which is partly a parody of the Richardsonian mode, partly a self-conscious literary extension of other, higher forms. Foregoing the disguise of truth for the dignity of authorship and the pleasures of entertainment, Fielding took as his subject Human Nature and represented it in forms transparently generalized and typical rather than with an exclusive realistic preoccupation with individuation and specialness. If Hazlitt and Thackeray thought of Fielding as *the* great realist, we can also see him as the self-conscious manipulator of plots, a friend of the God-out-of-the-machine, and as the proselytizer for the values of tolerance and moderation and authentic gentlemanliness. For the sake of this moderation, Fielding devised a story and a style which are anything but ordinary. His mode is the inverse of that of Richardson and Defoe, but it leads us to the same point: the invariable mixture of realistic elements with others.

There is no need to catalogue all the great novelists in the English tradition to make the case, but Fielding's more undisguised relation to romance suggests a later aspect of the tradition that needs to be considered here. If we think of Scott, with what he called his big "bow-wow" style, as opposed to Jane Austen, we are likely to accept an aspect of the Victorian myth of Scott as a romancer. Like Defoe, Scott chose actions not ordinary but almost epic in scope, and he sought for them far enough back in history so that they might have about them a romantic glow. Yet, as he says in his Introductory chapter to *Waverley* (1814), he wanted to describe "those passions common to man in all stages of society, and which have alike agitated the human heart, whether it throbbed under the steel corselet of the fifteenth century, the brocaded coat of the eighteenth, or the blue frock and white dimity waistcoat of the present day."[27] The central aim is Fielding's once more—the portrayal of human nature. Yet the heroes of *Waverley* or of *Old Mortality* are no Tom Joneses: they are Fergus MacIvor Vich Ian Vohr, or the pretender Charles Stuart, or Balfour of Burley, or Claverhouse. The crises of the lives of the non-historical figures—like Waverley himself—seem bound up in historical battles on which the fate of nations may turn.

Yet as most commentators on Scott have pointed out, the true heroes of the Waverley novels are passive figures who submit to history rather than create it.[28] In the long run these heroes do not triumph over circumstances but, with the help of Scott's blatant manipulations of plot, retreat from history into the comfort of obscurity. They turn out, like Edward Waverley, to be more domestic than poetic or chivalric.

Waverley, in the tradition of Robinson Crusoe, but less practical and ingenious, is the antecedent of the deluded romantic hero of Victorian novels who must learn that the real world is not responsive to his dreams and who must accept a more or less happy compromise with the larger forces of society and history. Waverley's real disposition, Scott tells us, "notwithstanding the dreams of tented fields and military honour, seemed exclusively domestic."[29] When he disentangles himself from the pretender, Charles Stuart, and the Jacobites, Waverley feels "himself entitled to say firmly, though perhaps with a sigh, that the romance of his life was ended, and that its real history had now commenced."[30] He is, moreover, the hero of a novel about which the narrator can say: "I do not invite my fair readers, whose sex and impatience give them the greatest right to complain of these circumstances, into a flying chariot drawn by hippogriffs, or moved by enchantment. Mine is an humble English post-chaise, drawn upon four wheels, and keeping his Majesty's highway."[31]

Of course, there is romance in *Waverley*: the excitement of several generations of readers was not based altogether on a misunderstanding. The romance is there, in the historical action itself, in the exotic and beautifully evoked Highlands, in the extraordinary heroism of Vich Ian Vohr, the chivalric style of Charles Stuart. The point again is that we have here that characteristic combination of attitudes and styles which, though they have the appeal of romance, lead finally to an eulogium of middle-class virtues, much like those Robinson Crusoe's father wishes for his son. They are the virtues of domestic peace and practical accommodation to reality—the central subject of realistic fiction. We can add to the confusion by recognizing that this is one of the central preoccupations of much romantic fiction. Even so extraordinary a Gothic novel as Mary Shelley's *Frankenstein* insists on these values. The book's style and subject are so clearly outside the realistic tradition that it has never been taken as central in the development of the classical realistic nineteenth-century novel. But surely, the melodrama of the language and of the action lead the reader—and Frankenstein himself—back to those unambitious domestic virtues which the monster instinctively loves and from which deviation is made to seem disaster. In one of its aspects, the realistic novel can be seen as a special form of the Frankenstein motif: the extraordinary man (and novelist) must tell his tale of extreme action and extreme suffering so as to persuade the listener to remain firmly and happily fixed in the contingent, difficult, unromantic, and unexciting reality which determines the true shape of the world. We may in fact find that the most interesting and attractive parts of the novels are those which deal with the romantic adventures of their heroes. The most sympathetic heroes are those who put ordinary reality to the stretch. But that is because both writer and reader are likely to recognize that each man contains within him something of the Promethean over-reacher. Finally, however, Captain Walton, in *Frankenstein,* must give up his expedition to the Arctic just as the wedding guest in Coleridge's *Ancient Mariner* must accept the Mariner's story without committing the Mariner's sin. Those who sin like the Mariner, whether it be Mr. Dombey in his pride, Lydgate in his Frankensteinian quest for the tissue of all tissue, Becky Sharpe in her social climbing, or Pip in his Great Expectations, must suffer and come to terms with defeat and an uncongenial world.

Thematically, then, the tradition of realism is incoherent with ambiguities and self-contradictions, forcing the novelist to deal with excess—which inevitably becomes the most exciting part of his work —in order to reject it. As the tradition progresses, the contradictions become more manifest. As novelists struggle to confine themselves to the ordinary actual, that actual increasingly looms as an obstacle to their own deepest desires and most intense energies. There is a Frankenstein in every great realistic fiction struggling to get out. Works which insist on the obstacle are driven to long and fluid—sometimes only precariously relevant—descriptions of the harsh, unaccommodating actual, and the realistic novel begins to look like the "large, loose baggy monster" of James's criticism. Moreover, in order to deal with the Frankenstein within them, realistic writers were focred to impose structures of coincidence on "things as they are." These structures, while they tended to make actions meaningful and the fates of their heroes tolerable to themselves and their audiences, were essentially antagonistic to what the structure of "things as they are" seemed to require.

The struggle to sustain meaning and pattern within the limits of realistic style, subject, structure, and theme became almost unbearable, and the novel slowly but inevitably shifted its focus inward and receded from contemplation of the social and contingent. The social and contingent seemed not worth the compromise they entailed. And thus, in the hands of such varied writers as James, Hardy, Conrad, and after them Virginia Woolf and Joyce, the novel became shapely once more, and at the same time preoccupied with its own methods. Since the artist himself, a Frankenstein in words, was the only figure who could create meaning out of experience, the artist inevitably became the new hero of fiction. But to trace this development would take me well beyond the limits of my argument here, though tracing it and learning to understand in less abstract terms precisely the connections among the various developments in fictional art seem to me the crucial work of the student of fiction. Such a study would entail consideration of at least three factors: the position of individual artists in relation to their art and their society; the literary traditions out of which realistic fiction developed; and the social transformations which increasingly isolated the writer from his society, drove him inward, and forced him to discover the only possibility of meaning and value in art itself.[32]

IV

The best and clearest example I know of the way the commitment to realism imposed intolerable burdens on the writer comes in the career of George Eliot. It will be useful here to conclude by very sketchily looking at what I take to be a point of crisis in the context of the literary traditions of realism of which I have been talking.

I have tried to argue that even the definition of "realism" artificially abstracted from novels contains within itself elements of its own destruction. Naive realism in art is both a theoretical and practical impossibility. Modern criticism, itself the expression of an altogether revised notion of reality and based on very different metaphysical assumptions, has made us aware of the way the medium interposes itself between the writer and the subject and, in particular, of the way the human imagination creates rather than simply reflects reality.[33] But even without these new perceptions, we have seen that Defoe was not a realist in our definition, but what we might call a possibilist;[34] that Richardson dressed up romance in the clothing of an eighteenth-century servant. Later, Jane Austen, ridiculing the absurdities of the sensational novels of her own day, adopted a style and a subject most appropriate to her own possibilities as an artist: what began as parody became subject and structure. By the time we reach the self-conscious realism of George Eliot, we are already on the brink of new transformations in literary method.[35]

Tracing Jane Austen's novels from *Northanger Abbey* to *Persuasion,* one can see how her realism developed partly as a parodic response to Gothic and Sentimental novels she had known. Scott talks about the difference between her kind of realism and that of Defoe and Richardson. When the novel, in their hands, made "its first appearance, the novel was the legitimate child of the romance; and though the manners and general turn of the composition were altered so as to suit modern time, the author remained fettered" to romance. And his heroes, Scott says, though they were not to be heroic in the traditional way, were expected "to go through perils by sea and land, to be steeped in poverty, to be tried by temptation, to be exposed to the alternate vicissitudes of adversity and prosperity"; the hero's life "was a troubled scene of suffering and achievement."[36] The new realism is different because "in our civilized days" there are "few instances capable of being painted in the strong dark colours which excite surprise and horror." Thus the new novel of Jane Austen practices "the art of copying from nature as she really exists in the common walks of life, and presents to the reader, instead of the splendid scenes of an imaginary world, a correct and striking representation of that which is daily taking place around him." Jane Austen's commitment to the ordinary, her rejection of extremes, her adoption of a prose brilliantly exact and satirical, are exactly appropriate to her ironic perception of both literature and life, but they were not achieved through self-conscious theorizing; and her art is without the sense of the deep and sacred responsibility of the artist to truth.

When George Eliot picks up this tradition, much of the irony and some of the roots in parody remain visible; but she adds to the tradition a deep belief in the moral responsibility of the artist to speak only the truth and to render reality in all its particularity. The aim was to reconcile her readers to their lot as ordinary and flawed human beings. Full of the sense of intellectual discovery that pervaded the avant-garde circles of her time, she was determined to make her art speak more truthfully than novelists had hitherto been able or committed to do.

The famous if self-consciously awkward seventeenth chapter of *Adam Bede* explains that her "strongest effort is to give a faithful account of men and things as they have mirrored themselves in my mind." And although she is aware of the trap of the mirror (of the fact that it is a distorting medium), she goes on to say: "The mirror is doubtless defective; the outlines will sometimes be disturbed, the reflection faint or confused; but I feel as much bound to tell you as precisely as I can what that reflection is, as if I were in the witness-box narrating my experience on oath."[37] She thus struggles to make it clear that her hero, Adam Bede, is not perfectly virtuous, but too proud and unbending, that her villain, Arthur Donnithorne, is no villain but a misguided and vain though generous and well-intentioned man, and that Mr. Irwine is both a fine man and a fine clergyman despite a certain spiritual laxness.

But in *The Mill on the Floss*, George Eliot reaches a point that might be taken, symbolically, as a crisis of realism. The narrative leads to a situation in which satisfactory resolution is unattainable in the terms her adopted realistic mode would allow. Again we have the central situation of the realistic novel, the gradual education of an excessively romantic heroine into a correct notion of the nature of reality and a correct understanding of the role of personal desire and aspiration in the real world. But Maggie Tulliver cannot accept the terms available to Catherine Morland or Emma Woodhouse—marry into society and submit to its restrictions. The resolution George Eliot finds is melodramatic and, finally, regressive. Maggie's acceptance of her own limits comes in a retreat to childhood and death in the embraces of her hitherto rather hateful brother. By the time of *Daniel Deronda,* George Eliot had in effect renounced the limits of realism by renouncing the possibility of satisfactory life within society as she understood it and by making her hero extraordinarily virtuous and sending him off to Israel to found a new nation.

Inconsistent with George Eliot's own early views as this may seem to be, the development is in fact completely consistent with other elements in the realistic tradition. We have already seen Trollope arguing that the good novelist always mixes realism with the sensational. We can see as well that the tradition of English realism was bound up with a faith in the possibilities for meaning and satisfactory fulfillment of self within the limits of the "real." But that faith is, in one aspect, simply a continuation of the literary tradition of romance, which insists on the power of the hero to overcome the limits of his constricting social context. At the risk of oversimplifying, we can say that the later developments in George Eliot's art indicate the collapse of a faith in the meaningfulness of the real world and the collapse of faith in the dominant reality of the empirically verifiable. One of the paradoxes of the history of realistic fiction is that, far from insisting on resolutions which we would now take to be truthful— that is, resolutions in death, suffering, frustration, missed opportunities, and absence of meaning—it becomes an essentially comic form. It represents a life full of meaning and resolves difficulties, however complex and dangerous, with the traditional mythic harmony of marriage. The marriage of hero or heroine to a true mate becomes a kind of reconciliation of the individual and society. Part of the paradox disappears when we see realism in the convention of romance. But we can also see that realism could only be endurable as long as it was possible to think of the world as having shape and meaning. Thus, the disappearance of the happy ending suggests the disappearance of the method of realism itself. Maggie's death in the arms of her brother suggests that the technique of realism has moved into stormy waters.

The Mill on the Floss can be seen, then, as a kind of crossroads in

George Eliot's art—forcing her to the idealization of figures like Romola and Daniel Deronda afterwards—and also in the history of English realism. Reality becomes a kind of quicksand, and we arrive quite naturally at an art which focuses on individual consciousness and the unintelligible flux of experience. Meaning can only be bestowed by the individual consciousness, and the tradition of romance manifests itself in the power of that consciousness to create meaning and patterns where most ordinary observers would see none.

I am thus forced back to my starting point. Realism was never at any stage in its curious circular history free of the central pressure to give shape and meaning to experience. Those apparently unrealistic elements in realistic fiction are not to be seen as aberrations in the writer's control over his own method but rather as crucial to the formative energy of the novel. Attention to these elements in our criticism will allow us more fully to understand and value the formal elements in each work and what Goldmann calls its "objective" meaning. "Objective" here means something much like what I was referring to as metaphysic, but it also implies those meanings which inevitably and unconsciously reflect the values and attitudes of the writer's society. In any case, we should be ready to see realism as anything but an unmediated record of reality (since it comes filtered through organizing perceptions, unconscious social pressures, and a language thick with conventions), and to remember that all fiction—even realistic fiction—is fiction.

NOTES

1. David Lodge, *The Novelist at the Crossroads* (London, 1971), p. 4.
2. See, for a discussion of the confusions surrounding the word realism, Erich Heller, "The Realistic Fallacy," *The Listener*, 53 (May 19, 1955), 188-89. Reprinted in George Becker, *Documents of Literary Realism* (Princeton, 1967). Heller suggests the emptiness of the word, as does my "Realism, or, In Praise of Lying: Some Nineteenth Century Novels," *College English*, 31 (January, 1970), 355-65.
3. The word seems to have been borrowed from the French in the 1850's. See Richard Stang, *The Theory of the Novel in England, 1850-1870* (New York, 1959), p. 145; and two essays to which Stang alludes, R. G. Davis, "The Sense of the Real in English Fiction," *Comparative Literature*, 3 (Summer, 1951), 200-17; and "Balzac and His Writings," *Westminster Review*, 60 (July, 1853), 199-214. The latter essay still seems to assume a naive realism, but its brief discussion of the term is useful in suggesting—correctly—the close connection between realism and romanticism.

4. The most obvious and popular recent example of the attitude is in John Fowles' *The French Lieutenant's Woman;* but, of course, while rejecting naive notions of realism and insisting instead on imaginative reality, Fowles exploits Victorian realistic techniques and writes a new best-seller.

5. Alain Robbe-Grillet, *Pour un nouveau roman* (Paris, 1955). At one point he says, "Tous les écrivains pensent être réalistes," and after a brief discussion he argues that "on doit conclure que tous ont raison" (p. 135).

6. See Linda Nochlin, *Realism* (Harmondsworth, Middlesex, England, 1971): "The commonplace notion that Realism is a 'styleless' or transparent style, a mere simulacrum or mirror image of visual reality, is another barrier to its understanding as an historical and stylistic phenomenon. This is a gross simplification, for Realism was no more a mere mirror of reality than any other style, and its relation *qua* style to phenomenal data—the donnée—is as complex and difficult as that of Romanticism, the Baroque or Mannerism" (p. 14).

7. Ernst Gombrich, *Art and Illusion* (London, 1960). No summary can begin to cope with the argument of this brilliant book. Some of its orientation, however, is suggested by one key sentence: "Art is born of art, not of nature" (p. 21).

8. Linda Nochlin's book (see n. 6, above) is in part an attempt to qualify Gombrich's argument by showing that although realism is conventional, it differs from other conventions in its commitment to empirical truth: "It was not until the nineteenth century that contemporary ideology came to equate belief in the facts with the total content of belief itself; it is in this the crucial difference lies between nineteenth century Realism and all its predecessors" (p. 45).

9. Nochlin, p. 14.

10. See Lucien Goldmann, *The Human Sciences and Philosophy,* trans. Hayden White and Robert Anchor (London, 1969): "Every manifestation is the work of its individual author and expresses his thought and way of feeling, but these ways of thinking and feeling are not independent entities with respect to the actions and behaviour of other men. They exist and may be understood only in terms of their inter-subjective relations which give them their whole tenor and richness" (p. 128). See also Henry James, "The Art of Fiction," collected in Leon Edel, ed., *The House of Fiction* (London, 1957): "A novel is in its broadest definition a personal, a direct impression of life." Gombrich, however, writes, "If art were only, or merely, an expression of personal vision, there could be no history of art" (p. 4).

11. On points 4a and b, Northrop Frye's essay "Myth, Fiction, and Displacement," in *Fables of Identity* (New York, 1963), is particularly helpful, and I should confess to a deep debt to its arguments, which have provoked (in both senses) much of my most recent thinking on the subject. Frye argues that "the realistic writer soon finds that the requirements of literary form and plausible content always fight against each other" (p. 36). The entire essay brilliantly explores the difference between imagination as a creative and structural power and imagination as a reproductive power, between "recognition of credibility, fidelity to experience," in fiction, and "recognition of the identity of total design." In Frye's terms, art "deals, not with the world that man contemplates, but with the world that man creates" (p. 31). When art " 'imitates' nature it assimilates nature to human forms," a point not very different from the one that I am making. But Frye makes too sharp a distinction between literature and life by making too sharp a distinction between credibility and coherence.

12. Complicated qualifications would have to be made here because recent developments in fiction have self-consciously rejected or parodied the traditions of the great realistic novels of the nineteenth century. My major concern here is with the classical novel, from Richardson to Lawrence, but I would be prepared to argue that even for fictions like those of Nabokov, Barth, Butor, or Robbe-Grillet, this assertion is applicable.

13. Frye, p. 27.

14. *Ibid.*

15. See Sheldon Sacks, *Fiction and the Shape of Belief* (Chicago, 1964). Sacks discusses the way in which genre imposes directions on narrative structure.

16. The traditional English realistic novel tended to work itself out so that the audience's aroused expectations would be satisfied by at least some rough poetic justice, usually distributed by virtue of appropriate coincidences. As an aspect of a changing vision of reality, the fiction of writers as different as Hardy and Zola tended, whether by coincidence or circumstantially realistic patterning, to make the absence of poetic justice precisely the aesthetic point of their fictions. The revised reality produced a revised aesthetic with its own kind of perversely satisfying resolutions and satisfactions. See Kenneth Graham's discussion of Zola as a romancer in *English Criticism of the Novel 1865-1900* (London, 1965), pp. 56-61.

17. "The Decay of Lying," reprinted in Richard Ellmann, ed., *The Artist as Critic: Critical Writings of Oscar Wilde* (New York, 1968), p. 290.

18. Ellmann, p. 292.

19. *Ibid.*, p. 305.

20. *Ibid.*, p. 319.

21. Nochlin, p. 18.

22. Lodge, p. 4.

23. William Hazlitt, *Lectures on the English Comic Writers* (London, 1910; originally published in 1819), Lecture VI, p. 107.

24. *Robinson Crusoe* (New York, 1961), "I Go to Sea," p. 9.

25. In his *Autobiography* Anthony Trollope, in his characteristic businesslike and sensible way, suggests the continuity of this romantic tradition in the novel: "Among English novelists of the present day, and among English novelists, a great division is made. There are sensational novels and anti-sensational, sensational novelists and anti-sensational, sensational readers and anti-sensational. The novelists who are considered to be anti-sensational are generally called realistic. . . . All this is, I think, a mistake—which mistake arises from the inability of the imperfect artist to be at the same time realistic and sensational. A good novel should be both, and both in the highest degree" (London, 1953; originally published in 1883), p. 194.

26. Robinson Crusoe, pp. 9-10.

27. Walter Scott, *Waverley, Or, 'Tis Sixty Years Since* (New York, 1964), "Introductory," p. 34.

28. See Alexander Welsh, *The Hero of the Waverley Novels* (New Haven, 1963), and Györg Lukács, *The Historical Novel*, trans. Hannah and Stanley Mitchell (London, 1962).

29. *Waverley*, ch. lii.

30. *Ibid.*, ch. lx.

31. *Ibid.*, ch. v. Cf. the second paragraph of Charlotte Brontë's *Shirley*, another realistic-romance, with a more intensely romantic tinge.

32. For a general discussion of this process from the point of view of social and cultural context, see Malcolm Bradbury, *The Social Context of English Literature* (New York, 1971).

33. The Victorians, too, could be aware of the distorting power of the medium, as in the quotation from *Adam Bede,* below. See G. H. Lewes, "Principles of Success in Literature," *Fortnightly Review,* 1 (1865).

34. See Scott's review of *Emma, Quarterly Review* (October, 1815), 189.

35. See Stang's discussion of idealism and realism, pp. 160-61.

36. Review of *Emma,* 189.

37. *Adam Bede,* ch. xvii.

REALISM
IN THE
ANGLO-AMERICAN
NOVEL

THE PASTORAL MYTH

JOHN W. LOOFBOUROW

If the "realistic" novel is taken to mean a kind of fiction that results when the artist and his audience share the same assumptions, a definition I recently proposed,[1] there will, of course, be different realisms at different times and in different contexts. Fictions as diverse as *The Vicar of Wakefield* and *The Grapes of Wrath* may be realistic, each in its proper time and context, while a work that was not realistic in its own time, say *Tom Jones,* may seem so to a later audience with different assumptions. My original purpose in proposing a series of contingent realisms was to avoid the dilemma of defining "reality," a problem that has plagued criticism from the Victorian novelists to Erich Auerbach's *Mimesis* and Harry Levin's *The Gates of Horn.* A version of one of perhaps two prevailing concepts of "realism" is offered by Georg Lukács:

> Man is *zoon politikon*, a social animal. The Aristotelian dictum is applicable to all great realistic literature. Achilles and Werther, Oedipus and Tom Jones, Antigone and Anna Karenina: their individual existence—their *Sein an sich,* in the Hegelian terminology; their "ontological being" as a more fashionable terminology has it—cannot be distinguished from their social and historical environment. Their human significance, their specific individuality cannot be separated from the context in which they were created.[2]

Since Lukács does not suggest that anyone else thinks of this sequence of characterizations as "realistic literature," it appears that his sufficient criterion is that these works seem true (or "real") to *him;* the common denominator he proposes (social, historical relevance) is defined only by Lukács' own sense of relevance or "reality" (a criterion on which, it is true, such perceptive criticism as Matthew Arnold's has sometimes been based). A second prevalent concept of "realism," typified by George Becker's critical theory,[3] attempts to achieve greater objectivity by accumulating as many descriptive elements as possible but can never be sufficiently inclusive; either some techniques, some kinds of content, which have demonstrably seemed "realistic" in a given context, are excluded, or there are, in the final analysis, no definitive principles.

If, on the other hand, as I suggest, "realism" is defined by the preconceptions of artist and audience, the question arises whether particular realisms may be so various that the concept will have no critical value. Can realisms of sufficient content and duration be identified? Are they entirely distinct, or are there meaningful relationships as well as disparities between different realisms? I am going to try here to describe the development and modification of a particular realism that is limited in scope but is still inclusive enough to be useful in critical analysis, the realistic convention as it is recognized in English and American fiction.

To begin with, I should like to consider whether, if any realisms existed in Western European literature before the eighteenth century, one would expect to find certain characteristics present from the beginning. Comedy, tragedy, epic, which were recognized from the first, can be partly defined by typical protagonists and their relationship to the world they inhabit; perhaps realism can be interrelated in the same way. Comedy and tragedy, for example, share the same fictive world, a deterministic world which cannot be changed by the actors, who must either adapt to it (comedy) or be destroyed by it (tragedy); this is why both comedy and tragedy are fatalistic, why Jaques' sentiments are as appropriate in *As You Like It* as "the readiness is all" in *Hamlet.* But comic and tragic protagonists are clearly antithetic—Everyman in comedy, ready to adapt, the Hero in tragedy, defying the conditions of his "world." The tragic protagonist, the Hero who challenges fate, finds his counterpart only in epic—but the epic "world" is a contingent world, a world of possibility that may be altered by the protagonist's actions, so that his energies are not self-destructive (as in tragedy) but are, rather, self-fulfilling.

If I want to lay out a simple, graphic relationship between these three conventions, I find that a fourth is needed to complete the cycle. Since the missing convention involves an Everyman protagonist and a contingent "world" (thus most Europeans and Americans appear to have perceived themselves), it seems not unreasonable to call this convention realism:

TRAGEDY	COMEDY
Deterministic World——————Deterministic World	
Heroic Protagonist	Everyman Protagonist
Heroic Protagonist	Everyman Protagonist
Contingent World——————Contingent World	
EPIC	REALISM

This scheme is only a hypothetical structuring of relationships among Western European literary conventions, not an argument for the early advent of realism (perhaps the ancient audience did not want its own "reality" reflected in fiction); and it is not a sufficient definition of *any* realism—probably, for example, it would not exclude *Rasselas* or *Peter Pan*. If, however, all European realisms do presuppose an Everyman protagonist in a contingent "world," it follows that the realistic resolution is apt to convey little sense of change, because the Everyman (unlike the epic Hero) will not be able to exploit the alternate possibilities of his fictive "world."

The Everyman protagonist and the contingent "world" are, I think, persistent aspects of realism in English and American novels. In the three novels I shall discuss, ranging from mid-eighteenth century to mid-twentieth, they are self-evident, as they are in all the instances I can call to mind. On the other hand, there are at least two aspects of this realism which have changed appreciably even in so short a time. Changing expectations often obscure the fundamental continuities that characterize a particular realism, so that it is important to recognize them and decide whether they are definitive or not.

One way this realism has changed is in demanding an ever-greater accumulation of particulars—a phenomenon, already noted by many critics, that probably reflects a growing conviction of the "unreality" of universals or "types." Such particularization, increasing throughout the nineteenth century, probably reached its apogee near the mid-twentieth and has tended, more recently, to diminish. The technique is, however, significant only in extended narration. Particularization in brief scenes has always been practiced; short sequences from Homer or Chaucer or Shakespeare are, in effect, as particular as Dreiser, Dos Passos, Hemingway. This raises an interesting point, which I should like to emphasize, that the "short story" can tell us little about realisms. It is only when, for example, particularization becomes the descriptive technique of a long fiction that it represents a "modern" phenomenon. Once again, the accumulation of particulars is not a sufficient criterion for any given realism, but in the realistic fiction under consideration it does, in fact, increase from the eighteenth century to the twentieth; correspondingly, there is progressive particularization in the three successive novels I shall discuss.

A second changing aspect of this realism is the elimination of the "narrator." In my first two instances (mid-eighteenth and mid-nineteenth-century novels), the narrator is integral; in the third, a recent novel, he is carefully camouflaged, though not imperceptible. This is doubtless because, when the "type" has lost its "reality," the "typified" narrator is also "unreal." Two solutions have emerged. Either overt "narration" (authorial interpolation, commentary) is eliminated in order to create the effect of an objective representation (Dos Passos, Hemingway), or the generalized "narrator" is converted into a specific individual (a "particular") as in "point of view" or first-person narration (James, Barth—the ultimate mode is autobiographical). These assumptions rest on the premise that the audience is, in fact, illuded, though Johnson long ago pointed out that, in the theatre, for example, the observer knows quite well that he is conniving at a deception.

The concept of the illuded audience brings up a curious general question about realisms—whether, indeed, the audience is likely to "identify" with them. We all may, of course, "identify" with fictions so as to lose our sense of normative "reality"—but are they often *realistic* fictions by anyone's criteria? One may, equally, "identify" with a wish-fulfilling daydream that no one would describe as realistic. It may be that the pleasure in realisms comes *not* from identification but from recognition of the artist's imitative skill, the expertise of his illusion. When the reader thinks "How real!" perhaps he is not ex-

pressing "empathy" (as he might be with a sentimental melodrama).
No doubt artist and audience have, in recent years, mutually assumed that the intrusion of the narrator is "unreal"; but one may
wonder, nevertheless, whether the response to successful realism does
not include an unconfessed awareness of the contriver's successful
artifice. A mirror is a more impersonal representation than a painting, yet the painter who contrives a "likeness" will always deprive
the mirror of an audience.

Having premised, as stable elements in the realism I am discussing, an Everyman protagonist and a contingent fictive "world,"
and, as changing factors, a progressive emphasis on particulars and
the suppression of the narrator, I should like to propose that what
gives essential continuity to English and American novelistic realism
is the persistence of the pastoral myth as its definitive convention. In
a preliminary way, I mean the myth of procreative community in a
context where man and men and men and nature are in essential
harmony, where the "natural order" is "reality" and the artificial and
the mystic are equally rejected. In most such realism, an intrusion
into the "natural order," limited or extensive, resolved or unresolved,
serves to verify, by contrast, the validity of the "truly natural." When
this myth is absent, I suggest, we are hesitant about whether to call
a fiction realistic—in Henry James, say, or Virginia Woolf—though
we are sure that D. H. Lawrence's novels are realistic despite their
obtrusive "symbolism." In Lawrence, of course, the pastoral affirmation is insistent and nearly unqualified. It is true that, in less reassuring contexts, from Dreiser to Hemingway, the *absence* of "natural
order" may be satirically stressed—but such satire, itself, implies the
pastoral premise; the transcendent, the artificial are rejected, Nature
ought to be Good, Man *ought* to be Natural. Other affirmations are
never attempted; and when a fiction presents different values its
"reality" is questioned, whether as an evasion of "life" (James,
Woolf) or as a form of fantasy (Firbank, Nabokov).

A brief consideration of pastoral, adequate at most for my purpose,
is appropriate here. Pastoral has been divided into many types but I
wish only to make a broad distinction between what I shall call "Arcadian" pastoral, as in the Virgilian *Eclogues,* and what I shall call
"Bucolic" pastoral, as in the *Georgics.* Arcadian pastoral is concerned
with the analysis of love; its rural setting is not meant to represent

the "natural order." Arcadian rusticity, whether in Sannazaro or Sidney, is a stylized simplification where the complexities of courtly or urban life are ideally eliminated so that the mystery of love can be presented at its purest and most typical. Bucolic pastoral, by contrast, its origin in agricultural precepts, is primarily concerned with man's relation to nature, with the order of "natural" processes which man can cultivate, and with the communal order which is man's own Bucolic "nature" and which enables him to achieve a reciprocity with the "natural" context in which he lives. During the Renaissance, Arcadian and Bucolic pastoral sometimes fuse in Christian parable, as in Spenser and Milton—Christ as Pastor suggesting the Bucolic mode, Christ as Lover, the Arcadian. Nevertheless, a fundamental distinction persists and can be recognized at least until the nineteenth century.

Arcadian pastoral, however, has connotations which make its "truth" suspect for the English audience after the seventeenth century. Its setting, its situations are definitively "artificial," a merit for the Renaissance, since, in the corrupt "natural" world of traditional Christianity, the transcendent "idea," Love, can only be realized "artificially." After the disintegration of the Renaissance in England, however, the immanence of ideal "types" is no longer credible; the institutional "incarnation" of the Church in Rome, the political "incarnation" of the Divine in the King, the Natural manifestation of God's order in the order of the spheres, have been subverted by the Reformation, the Commonwealth, and the New Astronomy. Consequently, an artistic convention which was valued for its artificial idealizations becomes, for the post-Renaissance, a representation of abstractions, of unrealities instead of ultimate truths—"artificial" becomes a pejorative epithet. Arcadian pastoral, preeminently "artificial," seems to the English eighteenth century vacuous, even fraudulent, and becomes an object of satirical caricature.[4]

Bucolic pastoral, on the other hand, affirms precisely the values of Shaftesbury (later, of Rousseau) that gradually create the "reality" of the Anglo-American audience. When transcendent "reality" was abandoned to the church, alternative universals were proposed—Reason by Descartes (and Locke); Nature by Shaftesbury (and Rousseau). Reason, the English eighteenth century's first alternative, proved over-vulnerable to rational attack, whether from Berkeley, Hume, or Kant; but in the latter part of the century, Nature—instinct and emotion in creatures, rhythmic process in the environment, innate reciprocity between the two—had superseded Reason. During the Renaissance, when "nature" was itself the imperfect reflection of a divine "original," Bucolic pastoral, like Arcadian, was an "image" of a transcendent (though different) "idea," not a mundane representation. For the Romantics, however, Nature became "real" and Arcadian pastoral was discredited. It was, I think, about this time that Bucolic pastoral ceased to be recognized as "pastoral" at all and became, for Englishmen and Americans, a basic existential "reality."

English novelists of the eighteenth century never fully accepted Augustan rationalism; pastoral "reality," however, was not immediately assimilated. In *Robinson Crusoe,* the part of Defoe's island that seems a "planted garden" is the site of primitive cannibalism, suggesting that brutality is not "unnatural"; in *Moll Flanders,* America, the New World of "nature," is ironically populated by the prisons of England. Fielding, often described as a benevolist, represents the human animal so sardonically as to belie the attribution and his first novel is implicity anti-pastoral; *Joseph Andrews,* after a brief prelude, satirizes the City where, indeed, the protagonist is callously cast adrift—but the callousness of the City is nothing to the brutality of the Country and it is not until Joseph travels through scenes of rustic bestiality and arrives at his country home that he is totally in the power of Lady Booby, whose predatory nature transforms the rural scene into a struggle for survival. "Enthusiasm," instinctive Grace, is caricatured by Smollett; and even Sterne, whose sentimentalism conciliated the Romantics, introduces Nature in the most ignoble manifestations and pairs his pastoral Maria (mad for love) with a goat (Sterne's habitual insinuation) rather than the traditional sheep. But such skepticism becomes increasingly rare as Nature beguiles the later eighteenth century and assumes the missing place of immanent divinity.

It is not, I think, until Goldsmith's *Vicar of Wakefield* (1766) that the English novel fully commits itself to the "reality" of Bucolic pastoral (Goldsmith may have intended peripheral irony; I think he did, his converts did not). *The Vicar's* pastoral promulgated a convention that was, I believe, to become the realism of English and

American novels. Although the term "realism" was not current when Goldsmith wrote, it seems clear that, as time passed and until well into the nineteenth century, readers increasingly felt that his premises reflected their sense of "reality" (they did not, of course, equate this "reality" with pastoral myth, but accepted, rather, the representational criteria of their time). For Burke, *The Vicar's* merit is its pathos[5]—an ethical or, perhaps, aesthetic criterion; but for Goethe, Forster writes, "the fiction became to him life's first reality . . . on the very brink of the grave, he told a friend that in the decisive moment of mental development the *Vicar of Wakefield* had formed his education."[6] Certainly, Sir Walter Scott singles out qualities that will eventually be called "realistic"—*The Vicar* offers, he says, "a fireside picture of such a perfect kind, as perhaps is nowhere else equalled. It is sketched indeed from common life, and is a strong contrast to . . . exaggerated and extraordinary characters and incidents. . . . We return to it again and again, and bless the memory of an author who contrives so well to reconcile us to human nature."[7]

Goldsmith's fidelity to "nature" is recurrently stressed in Forster's *Life* (1848), where *The Vicar's* popularity is described as "the reward of simplicity and truth, and of not overstepping the modesty of nature"; in Goldsmith's characters, Forster insists, "Nature pleases to imitate herself."[8] Finally, in 1857, G. H. Lewes' letter introducing George Eliot's earliest fiction to Blackwood compares her first story, *Amos Barton,* to Goldsmith's novel in terms that foreshadow her own claim that her only subject is "the real": "According to my judgement such humour, pathos, vivid presentation, and nice observation have not been exhibited (in this style) since the 'Vicar of Wakefield.' "[9] Since the mid-nineteenth century, the general expectation of particularized description and the distrust of self-confessed narrators have made Goldsmith's and, later, George Eliot's fiction seem less realistic; but the presence or absence of Goldsmith's "Nature" has continued, I believe, to determine whether or not a contemporary novel is recognized as realism. I should like to discuss, briefly, the characteristics that make *The Vicar of Wakefield* prototypic.

Goldsmith's protagonist, Dr. Primrose, is both profoundly pastoral ("a priest, an husbandman, and the father of a family," the author's "Advertisement" points out) and a true Everyman whose mode of life exemplifies the community of men and nature—"The year was spent in moral or rural amusements, in visiting our rich neighbours, or relieving such as were poor" [Ch. I]. Basic values are soon established. Transcendent idealisms are tacitly rejected—the ballad, "Edwin and Angelina," which begins by disparaging terrestrial pleasures ("Man wants but little here below, Nor wants that little long"), soon dismisses the visionary and affirms the "natural" by revealing, beneath a pilgrim's disguise, the hermit's true love and natural mate ("The lovely stranger stands confest A maid in all her charms" [Ch. VIII]). Artificiality is condemned (artifice is either fraud or fantasy) since it conflicts with Nature—the City, for example, a form of civil artifice, is opposed to "natural" human community. Dr. Primrose values "those natural ties that bind the rich and poor together" and praises the "middle order of mankind" which is "the true preserver of freedom, and may be called the People" [Ch. XIX]. He insists that man's benevolent, communal instinct is innate in the natural order— "It is thus that reason speaks, and untutored nature says the same thing. Savages that are directed nearly by natural law alone are very tender of the lives of each other"—and considers social injustice a product of civilization—"It is among the citizens of a refined community that penal laws, which are in the hands of the rich, are laid upon the poor" [Ch. XXVII].

The Vicar's values have, I believe, become definitive in Anglo-American realism. Often, though by no means always, such fiction also reiterates Goldsmith's fable: the "natural order" is subverted by the "artificial," a crisis of sexual violation is followed by an imprisonment that both represents and purges the "artificial," and an eventual release is succeeded by the restoration of "community" in and with "nature." The Vicar of Wakefield begins in rural innocence; affectation, incipient in the Vicar's family, is encouraged by the deceptive graces of visiting urban "ladies" (prostitutes, in fact), protégées of the sophisticate, Squire Thornhill; the corruption implicit in mercantile commerce (as opposed to "natural" agriculture) is exemplified when one of the Vicar's sons is cheated while bargaining at a neighbouring Fair; the Primroses, collectively tempted by artifice, commission an allegorical painting of their family; the Vicar's oldest daughter is seduced by Squire Thornhill at the center of the novel; the familial community is disrupted and the Vicar is imprisoned, but, even in prison, transcendent values are eschewed in the Vicar's sermon, which treats dying as a sensation rather than a transfiguration, asserting that "nature kindly covers [the pangs of death] with insensibility" [Ch. XXIX], and anticipates a very human heaven; at last, through the agency of the uncorrupted Burchell, the Vicar is released, the family is restored, and the novel ends with a pastoral, domestic feast.

In *Adam Bede* (1859)—my exemplary instance of mid-Victorian realism before the elimination of the narrator—George Eliot preserves *The Vicar's* fable with modifications. Eliot, commenting on her own narratives, wrote that "art must be either real and concrete, or ideal and eclectic. Both are good and true in their way, but my stories are of the former kind"; and Blackwood assured her that *Adam Bede* "is so true. The whole story remains in my mind like a succession of incidents in the lives of people whom I know."[10] Reminiscences of Goldsmith make me think that Eliot intended, in *Adam Bede,* a serious if equivocal allusion to *The Vicar of Wakefield* (she wrote, in a letter to Blackwood, "I don't desire better than to lie side by side with [Goldsmith] in people's memories"[11]). In *Adam Bede,* as in *The Vicar,* a local Squire returns to a rural community where he seduces a rustic maiden; Eliot's climactic scenes, like Goldsmith's, are set in prison as a consequence, diversely, of the sexual violation; in *The Vicar* the Squire's name is Thornhill, in *Adam Bede* it is Donnithorne.

This allusion, however, if intended, is partly ironic, since *Adam Bede* is conceived as a "modern" pastoral representing the new "Darwinian" nature[12] (although "determinism" is modified by human choice, as in the final marriage of Adam and Dinah, and the "contingent" world of realism is reaffirmed). Eliot dramatizes painful consequences that Goldsmith evades—the seduced girl, unlike the Vicar's daughter, bears and abandons an illegitimate child; the initial community cannot be restored, a new one must be created. Intentional reference to Goldsmith's novel is further suggested by passages in *Adam Bede* that seem almost to take issue with passages in *The Vicar of Wakefield*. In Goldsmith, for example, Dr. Primrose's sermon deplores the fact of human pain: "Why man should thus feel pain, why our wretchedness should be requisite in the formation of universal felicity. . . . These are questions that never can be explained"

[Ch. XXIX]. In Eliot, the narrator, by contrast, ascribes man's regeneration to the experience of pain: "Let us rather be thankful that our sorrow lives in us as an indestructible force, only changing its form, as forces do, and passing from pain into sympathy—the one poor word which includes all our best insight and our best love" [Ch. L]. Goldsmith, unlike later realists, drew casually on his experience in *The Vicar* and presented generalized, "typical" scenes; conversely, Gordon Haight shows that George Eliot, in preparing *Adam Bede,* laboriously collected data for that accumulation of particulars that has been a progressive aspect of our realism.[13] The difference between Eliot's method and Goldsmith's is expressed in a further pair of passages that suggests purposeful allusion on her part; both writers include digressions on the art of painting and, once again, Eliot seems almost to be arguing with her predecessor. In *The Vicar,* Dr. Primrose rejects artistic verisimilitude for the graces of inspiration: "We might as well prefer the tame correct paintings of the Flemish school to the erroneous, but sublime animations of the Roman pencil" [Ch. XV]. In *Adam Bede,* by · contrast, the narrator insists, "I delight in many Dutch paintings . . . I turn, without shrinking, from cloud-borne angels, from prophets, sibyls, and heroic warriors, to an old woman bending over her flower-pot, or eating her solitary dinner" [Ch. XVII].

If, in *Adam Bede,* George Eliot modifies the affirmations of *The Vicar of Wakefield,* it is, nonetheless, ultimately to preserve the same existential values, to evoke the same pastoral "reality" under different conditions. "Nature," in Eliot, is sterner than in Goldsmith (who did not have to cope with Evolution), but the natural process is still the fundamental "order" with which man must identify—the conclusion of *Adam Bede* suggests that man's development through pain will revitalize the "natural" human community. Neither "artificial" conventions (Hetty's Arcadia, Arthur's chivalry) nor visionary "truth" (Dinah's religious commitments) are relevant. Though Hetty's suffering cannot be retrieved and Arthur cannot be absolved, self-denial and "natural" fulfillment unite in the marriage of Dinah and Adam and a procreative new "Eden" is symbolically created in rustic Loamshire.

The Crying of Lot 49 (1966) by Thomas Pynchon, a very recent realism, is my final instance. This novel seems at first to discredit the pastoral affirmation; the final effect is a barely hopeful pessimism. Indirectly, however, Pynchon's fiction reveals the same values, the same sense of "reality" that has characterized my earlier examples. It is true that in *Lot 49* modern America is a mechanized wasteland; but, by the same token, it is as "unreal" as it would be for Goldsmith or George Eliot. It is true that nature and community seem almost unobtainable in Pynchon; but the only "reality" worth seeking, nevertheless, resides, as in *The Vicar* or *Adam Bede*, in returning to nature and achieving community.

Pynchon's satire exposes and deplores the lack of modern "community"; recurrent names—San Narciso, Oedipa (the heroine), the Paranoids, Mike Fallopian—are symptomatic. Romance (Oedipa as Rapunzel in her ego-tower [Ch. 1]) is rejected—the transcendent, as in earlier pastoral, is "unnatural," hence invidious. San Narciso, seen from above, resembles a "printed circuit" [Ch. 2]—artifice and urban life are, likewise, predictably condemned. Phrases like "the infected city" [Ch. 5] are thematic, while, conversely, a consolatory pastoral motif appears at the center of the novel in the elegiac comment on dandelion wine delivered by one of the few sympathetic characters in *Lot 49* ("You see, in spring, when the dandelions begin to bloom again, the wine goes through a fermentation. As if they remembered" [Ch. 4]). Since in Pynchon the context is satiric, the sequence of the conventional fable is disordered. The seduction, which occurs early in the novel (Oedipa has intercourse in a motel room), is perforce meaningless because there is no viable "natural order" to violate; police and prison intervene briefly near the end of the novel ("But the cops." "I'll be a fugitive" [Ch. 5]), as though the earlier convention had become compulsory, but since the community, in Pynchon, is itself a prison, this motif is equally irrelevant. Nevertheless, there is a symbolic surrogate for the missing "community" in *The Crying of Lot 49*—the possibly spurious secret society, Tristero, a covert mail service, a mode of communication or "community," which operates through repositories marked WASTE (obversely significant, presumably, in this communal wasteland); the heroine becomes committed to verifying the existence of the Tristero. As the novel begins, it is the sea, nostalgically evoked, hardly presented as the characters move nearby on the California coast, that represents the "reality" of the "natural" as contrasted with artificiality—"the unimaginable Pacific, the one to which all surfers, beach pads, sewage disposal schemes, tourist incursions, sunned homosexuality, chartered fishing are irrelevant" [Ch. 3]; near the end, it is rather "the land" that is Nature, even in America, where the heroine laments and seeks "community":

> As if there could be no barriers between herself and the rest of the land. San Narciso at that moment lost (the loss pure, instant, spherical, the sound of a stainless orchestral chime held among the stars and struck lightly), gave up its residue of uniqueness for her; became a name again, was assumed back into the American continuity of crust and mantle. . . . What was left to inherit? That America coded in Inverarity's testament, whose was that? . . . She remembered drifters she had listened to, Americans speaking their language carefully, scholarly, as if they were in exile from somewhere else invisible yet congruent with the cheered land she lived in. . . . For there was either some Tristero beyond the appearance of the legacy America, or there was just America and if there was just America then it seemed the only way she could continue, and manage to be at all relevant to it, was as an alien, unfurrowed, assumed full circle into some paranoia [Ch. 6].

The Crying of Lot 49 dispenses with the narrator of the earlier novels; particulars are poured lavishly onto the page; and Pynchon is presenting the "reality" that resulted from the existential assimilation of Bucolic pastoral in the eighteenth century. The sustained satire of *Lot 49,* while stressing the absence of "natural order" and offering little hope for man, envisages no alternative "reality"; there *should* be "natural community," and if there is *not,* there is nothing ("For there was either some Tristero beyond the appearance . . . or there was just America"). Since the present argument premises that "realism" is a collective attitude, the classification of a particular fiction as "realistic" would require a poll of readers; the selections used for exemplification here were made, of course, on the basis of a cursory sample of opinions, but the reader is at liberty to substitute his own choices. The persistence of pastoral "reality" in English and American novels is suggested by observing that when pastoral is paired with contemporary narrative techniques, realism is ascribed at once (in the 30's, Steinbeck's bucolic of polemical visions, for example; Joyce Cary, in the 40's, whose Gulley Jimson personifies Nature subverting Artificiality; Cheever; Updike; Roth); when, on the other hand, the pastoral premise is absent (Nabokov, for example, or Ivy Compton-Burnett), the same techniques will not be recognized as quite "realistic."

Three novels may not seem enough to make an adequate case; but since this discussion has been a first attempt to describe a particular realism, it is at best imperfect and would, if the principle were accepted, need revision and amplification. Further efforts to analyze such limited realisms might help to define some of those cultural assumptions that are so little questioned that they are not recognized at all. At the same time, various realisms might, eventually, reveal interrelationships that could reconfirm or redefine the larger, critically useful generalizations. And if, by developing such generalizations from the analysis of particular realisms, the theory of realistic art could be separated from the problem of reality, our future critical efforts might be less arduous and less frustrating.

NOTES

1. "Literary Realism Redefined," *Thought*, 45, 178 (Autumn, 1970).
2. Georg Lukács, *Realism in Our Time* (Harper Torchbooks, 1971; a reprint of Vol. 33 of the World Perspectives series), p. 19.
3. George Becker, "Introduction" to *Documents of Modern Literary Realism* (Princeton: Princeton University Press, 1963).
4. See my minimal discussion in *Thackeray and the Form of Fiction* (Princeton: Princeton University Press, 1964), pp. 53-54.
5. Ralph M. Wardle, *Oliver Goldsmith* (Lawrence: University of Kansas Press, 1957), p. 170.
6. John Forster, *The Life and Adventures of Oliver Goldsmith* (London: Bradbury & Evans and Chapman & Hall, 1848), pp. 368-69.
7. Ioan Williams, ed., *Sir Walter Scott on Novelists and Fiction* (London: Routledge & Kegan Paul, 1968), p. 71 ("Oliver Goldsmith").
8. Forster, *Life*, pp. 357, 361.
9. *The George Eliot Letters*, ed. Gordon S. Haight (New Haven: Yale University Press, 1954), Vol. II, p. 269.
10. Gordon S. Haight, *George Eliot* (New York and Oxford: Oxford University Press, 1968), pp. 239, 272.
11. *Letters*, ed. Haight, p. 303.
12. U. C. Knoepflmacher, *Religious Humanism and the Victorian Novel* (Princeton: Princeton University Press, 1965), p. 37 and *passim*.
13. Haight, *George Eliot*, pp. 249-50.

LOOKING FOR
KELLERMANN; OR,
FICTION AND
THE FACTS
OF LIFE

MARVIN MUDRICK

There is an early scene in *The Metamorphosis*[1] as comical and heart-breaking as any in fiction. Gregor Samsa, having awakened one morning to find himself "transformed in his bed into a gigantic insect," tries to be reasonable about the event (doubtless it's only nerves), tries to think his way through it or around it, tries to take his mind off it by recollecting his ineffectual life, but it persists ("It was no dream"); he won't of course come out of his room or let anybody in; his parents and sister are alarmed; he will be late for work; the chief clerk arrives from the office to investigate his tardiness; still he delays, trying with his altered voice to placate and reassure them (but " 'That was no human voice,' said the chief clerk"); and at last, edging his unfamiliar bulk out into the room where the others are waiting, he presents them with the shape and size of the problem:

> . . . he heard the chief clerk utter a loud "Oh!"—it sounded like a gust of wind—and now he could see the man, standing as he was nearest to the door, clapping one hand before his open mouth and slowly backing away as if driven by some invisible steady pressure. . . .

Gregor knows it's now or never:

> ". . . Where are you going, sir? To the office? Yes? Will you give a true account of all this? One can be temporarily incapacitated, but that's just the moment for remembering former services and bearing in mind that later on, when the incapacity has been got over, one will certainly work with all the more industry and concentration. I'm loyally

bound to serve the chief, you know that very well. Besides, I have to provide for my parents and my sister. I'm in great difficulties, but I'll get out of them again. . . ."

He fails, however, to make the intended impression:

". . . Sir, sir, don't go away without a word to me to show that you think me in the right at least to some extent!"

But at Gregor's very first words the chief clerk had already backed away and only stared at him with parted lips over one twitching shoulder. And while Gregor was speaking he did not stand still one moment but stole away towards the door, without taking his eyes off Gregor, yet only an inch at a time, as if obeying some secret injunction to leave the room. He was already at the hall, and the suddenness with which he took his last step out of the living room would have made one believe he had burned the sole of his foot. Once in the hall he stretched his right arm before him towards the staircase, as if some supernatural power were waiting there to deliver him.

Gregor perceived that the chief clerk must on no account be allowed to go away in this frame of mind if his position in the firm were not to be endangered to the utmost. . . .

Gregor therefore attempts a decisive movement, which temporarily galvanizes his petrified mother into upsetting the coffee pot:

The chief clerk, for the moment, had quite slipped from . . . [Gregor's] mind; instead, he could not resist snapping his jaws together at the sight of the streaming coffee. That made his mother scream again, she fled from the table and fell into the arms of his father, who hastened to catch her. But Gregor had now no time to spare for his parents; the chief clerk was already on the stairs; with his chin on the banisters he was taking one last backward look. Gregor made a spring, to be as sure as possible of overtaking him; the chief clerk must have divined his intention, for he leaped down several steps and vanished; he was still yelling "Ugh!" and it echoed through the whole staircase.

Nothing remains but for Gregor's father, "hissing and crying 'Shoo!' like a savage," to drive him back into his room and slam the door shut behind him.

Terms like "allegory," "symbol," "ambiguity" will carry a Kafka critic through the scene, but they won't give him the feel of it. "It was no dream," says Kafka, tactfully warning us to pay attention. Gregor is an unallegorical king-size bug with problems. The chief clerk is a man in a funk. Their encounter, which is funny but not profound, opposes a resistible force with a movable object, and doesn't teach us anything except how not to behave in emergencies. Besides, the chief clerk is busier than his function warrants. He does something like a vaudeville routine, straight man turned top banana, profiting by an unforeseen opportunity. The comic focus here isn't Gregor, it's the chief clerk: in the course of the scene Gregor's plight gracefully dwindles into a sufficient pretext for the chief clerk's consternation, which (stunning invention) Kafka savors and indulges. The scene might have been very different, terse, more solicitous of Gregor and the plot, without such lingering emphasis on the chief clerk's pop-eyed suspension of disbelief as, staring and staring, he backpedals with tremendous slowness to the point from which, at length, he will be capable of breaking the spell and hurling himself down the stairs to freedom. The chief clerk, if he hadn't delighted Kafka, might have been all function. How will the world, not merely Gregor's family, react to Gregor's new condition? The chief clerk could show us. In fact he does show us, so amply that what he shows becomes less noteworthy than what he is: not a meaning but a presence.

Life, springing up like mushrooms, is Kafka's subject, what he looks for whenever he isn't at the mercy of his despondency. Here are two pieces of evidence from his diaries.[2] In an entry of 1911—*The Metamorphosis* was written in 1913—he described, without yet recognizing what it was, the stony ground out of which the story would come:

> February 19. When I wanted to get out of bed this morning I simply folded up. This has a very simple cause. I am completely overworked. Not by my office but my other work. The office has an innocent share in it only to the extent that, if I did not have to go there, I could live calmly for my own work and should not have to waste these six hours a day which have tormented me to a degree that you cannot imagine, especially on Friday and Saturday, because I was full of my own things. In the final analysis, I know, that is just talk, the fault is mine and the office has a right to make the most definite and justified demands on me. But for me in particular it is a horrible double life from which there is probably no escape but insanity. . . .

In the other diary entry, the manifestation Kafka always looks for is already so nearly explicit in the congenial circumstances that he can discover and describe it at once:

November 27[, 1910]. Bernhard Kellermann read aloud. "Some unpublished things from my pen," he began. Apparently a kind person, an almost gray brush of hair, painstakingly close-shaven, a sharp nose, the flesh over his cheekbones often ebbs and flows like a wave. He is a mediocre writer with good passages (a man goes out into the corridor, coughs and looks around to see if anyone is there), also an honest man who wants to read what he promised, but the audience wouldn't let him; because of the fright caused by the first story about a hospital for mental disorders, because of the boring manner of the reading, the people, despite the story's cheap suspense, kept leaving one by one with as much zeal as if someone were reading next door. When, after the first third of the story, he drank a little mineral water, a whole crowd of people left. He was frightened. "It is almost finished," he lied outright. When he was finished everyone stood up, there was some applause that sounded as though there were one person in the midst of all the people standing up who had remained seated and was clapping by himself. But Kellermann still wanted to read on, another story, perhaps even several. But all he could do against the departing tide was to open his mouth. Finally, after he had taken counsel, he said, "I should still like very much to read a little tale that will take only fifteen minutes. I will pause for five minutes." Several still remained, whereupon he read a tale containing passages that were justification for anyone to run out from the farthest point of the hall right through the middle of and over the whole audience.

These things happen, and there is no help for them. The chief clerk, quite beside himself (nobody else to turn to, no salvation anywhere), spontaneously invents an attitude of prayer: "he stretched his right arm before him towards the staircase, as if some supernatural power were waiting there to deliver him." Kellermann, frightened and irrepressible, exercises his will against an audience that does its magical disappearing act in bursts of cold energy. These things are perfectly straightforward and clear. The chief clerk and Kellermann are as real as mushrooms, they cannot be said to "stand for" anything else since they never cease to be only themselves, they are too dense to dissipate themselves.[3] At the instant when Kafka notices them, circumstances have braced them into self-definition, toward the accomplishing of which the circumstances (the story, the plot, the situation, the moral, the theme) are merely necessary machinery.

The chief clerk and Kellermann are expansive and pure instances of life in print. Life isn't always easy to recognize in print, it may be diffused over many pages of incident and contingency, it may go by in a phrase or a barely perceptible turn of events while the reader's attention wanders, it may too quickly get lost or mangled in the machinery; but the reader of fiction has no alternative to looking for it, since everything else is already laid out in Northrop Frye's elegant Linnaean categories, or Wayne Booth's conventional morality disguised as an inventory of handy devices, or Ian Watt's sociology, or Albert Guerard's Jungian recipes, or R. S. Crane's infatuation with thoroughly lubricated plots, or F. R. Leavis's rack-and-thumbscrew culture-obsession. Looking for Kellermann, the reader isn't employing a critical procedure, rather he's disclosing a human quality—companionableness, perhaps. Nor is this quality biased in favor of so idiosyncratic a writer as Kafka (who anyhow is far more often praised for his private machinery of mystification and self-pity, out of which he was only occasionally able to dislodge such Mozartian farce as the early pages of *The Metamorphosis*). Indeed, the quality is probably more often prompted and gratified by the novels of Trollope.

Critics have had a hard time with Trollope. He won't sit still for a portrait (sometimes he looks like minor-league Austen, sometimes like an unflashy and tough-minded Thackeray, sometimes like a cigars-and-whiskey George Eliot); he is obviously an intelligent and talented writer who merits examination; having published more than fifty books, he must have written well in some and ill in others, and —worse luck—even critics have to read a fair number of them before venturing to make distinctions.

Yet Trollope is an astonishingly consistent writer, who gave the Victorian lending-library subscribers exactly their money's worth with almost every installment. According to Trollope his secret, which he revealed (posthumously!) in his *Autobiography,* was that he had succeeded in his deliberate aim of turning novel-writing into an honest and well-paid craft of this many hours and that many words per day:

> Every word of . . . [*Lady Anna*] was written at sea, during the two months required for our voyage, and was done day by day—with the intermission of one day's illness—for eight weeks, at the rate of 66 pages of manuscript in each week, every page of manuscript containing 250 words. Every word was counted. I have seen work come back to an author from the press with terrible deficiencies as to the amount supplied. Thirty-two pages have perhaps been wanted for a number, and the printers with all their art could not stretch the matter to more than

twenty-eight or -nine! The work of filling up must be very dreadful. I have sometimes been ridiculed for the methodical details of my business. But by these contrivances I have been preserved from many troubles; and I have saved others with whom I have worked—editors, publishers, and printers—from much trouble also.[4]

(*Lady Anna,* by the way, is a solid and convincing novel.) Actually, Trollope had found out how to do most efficiently what he would likely have done if penury had obliged him to scribble day and night in an attic on a diet of bread and water. He was by temperament and talent a journeyman novelist (the term doesn't mean "bad novelist"), and his novels are models of immediate unmeretricious attractiveness, credible intrigue, momentum, suspense, breadth of knowledge about social and personal relations, satisfying disentanglement and resolution. He hasn't much gift for long or climactic scenes; he would rather ruminate and sum up than dramatize; he doesn't do low or rural characters well, and he often does them at immoderate length; he tends, especially when he grows anxious about the reader's memory of previous installments, to be prolix and repetitive (and even for so unprecedented a manufacturer of words "the work of filling up" two or three triple-decker novels per year may now and then have been, if not "very dreadful," at least troublesome). But his shortcomings are as evident in the novel Trollopians consider his masterpiece, *The Way We Live Now,* as in any they consider weak and mediocre, in which moreover most of Trollope's skills are as evident as they are in *The Way We Live Now.*

The brilliant anomaly among Trollope's novels is *Barchester Towers.* It's the only Victorian comedy of manners that can be mentioned with *Pride and Prejudice* or *Emma.* For once, Trollope allows his characters the scope of unsuperintended talk and activity with which they can begin to assert their full claim on us and on one another (by comparison, *The Way We Live Now* is watchful and mature); the most audacious claim, the Signora Neroni's to be all at the same time mysteriously and perhaps hideously crippled, beautiful and clever, irresistible and immune, a comic and slightly sinister apparition of uninhibited will as she rides like the wind into Mrs. Proudie's reception:

> At last a carriage dashed up to the hall steps with a very different manner of approach from that of any other vehicle that had been there that

evening. A perfect commotion took place. The doctor, who heard it as he was standing in the drawing-room, knew that his daughter was coming, and retired into the furthest corner, where he might not see her entrance. Mrs. Proudie perked herself up, feeling that some important piece of business was in hand. . . .[5]

The Signora having arrived, "Mr. Slope hurried into the hall to give his assistance":

He was, however, nearly knocked down and trampled on by the cortège that he encountered on the hall steps. He got himself picked up as well as he could, and followed the cortège up stairs. The signora was carried head foremost, her head being the care of her brother and an Italian man-servant who was accustomed to the work; her feet were in the care of the lady's maid and the lady's Italian page; and Charlotte Stanhope followed to see that all was done with due grace and decorum. In this manner they climbed easily into the drawing-room, and a broad way through the crowd having been opened, the signora rested safely on her couch. She had sent a servant beforehand to learn whether it was a right or a left hand sofa, for it required that she should dress accordingly, particularly as regarded her bracelets.

Thereupon Trollópe settles down next to the lady and for a full paragraph admires her:

And very becoming her dress was. It was white velvet, without any other garniture than rich white lace worked with pearls across her bosom, and the same round the armlets of her dress. Across her brow she wore a band of red velvet, on the centre of which shone a magnificent Cupid in mosaic, the tints of whose wings were of the most lovely azure, and the colour of his chubby cheeks the clearest pink. On the one arm which her position required her to expose she wore three magnificent bracelets, each of different stones. Beneath her on the sofa, and over the cushion and head of it, was spread a crimson silk mantle or shawl, which went under her whole body and concealed her feet. Dressed as she was and looking as she did, so beautiful and yet so motionless, with the pure brilliancy of her white dress brought out and strengthened by the colour beneath it, with that lovely head, and those large bold bright staring eyes, it was impossible that either man or woman should do other than look at her.

Projectile, serpent (lamia), *femme fatale,* splendid in the "grace and decorum" with which she and her attendants "climb easily" over any intermediate bodies, an unaccommodated presence coming into focus in electric repose as Venus among the barbarians, she is more than a match for that Gorgon of the diocese, Mrs. Proudie, who can't re-

frain—denouncing the susceptible Mr. Slope—from invoking demon-
ology to explain the Signora's magnetism:

> ". . . Do you think I have not heard of your kneelings at that crea-
> ture's feet—that is if she has any feet—and of your constant slobbering
> over her hand? . . ."

Trollope never does so well with anybody else, not even elsewhere
in *Barchester Towers* (though Bertie Stanhope, the Signora's brother,
is almost as overpowering in his casual indiscretions to the Bishop at
the same reception), not even elsewhere with the Signora herself,
with whom in a provincial Victorian setting he can do little, after all,
except find a sentimental function for her in the plot.

Customarily, Trollope is too prudent to be tempted by phenomena
that threaten to exceed the requirements of his plots. If he weren't
also a passionate man, there wouldn't be much else to say about the
mass of his work. He prides himself on being a craftsman, what he
aims at is fitness, but he is a passionate man: his job as he sees it is
to keep things under control, but he starts with the handicap of
having a great deal to control. Some of the fun of reading him is in
looking for moods that don't fit, feelings that get rather out of hand,
surprises. For instance, he is the only Victorian novelist who gives
the impression that men and women sometimes touch each other for
purposes neither celestial nor infernal but simply because they like
to. To be a Victorian novelist, however, is not to be in a position to
take exuberant advantage of this insight, which makes itself felt as
more than an ultrasonic vibration only in the guise of Trollope's
knowledgeable gallantry toward his female characters, or, more ec-
centrically, in his fixed conviction about the way in which women
fall in love.

Trollope believes that a woman falls in love just once, perhaps on
the most accidental provocation with the most trivial man, but that,
once she has given her heart (Trollope's locution), she is helpless to
change; no other man on earth has a chance, lovable and excellent
though he may be, to rouse her (and Trollope has a very specific
sense of what *that* means). The conviction tinges with oddness many
otherwise impeccably serviceable plots (including the plot of *The
Way We Live Now*), but in one instance drives Trollope into putting together a plot that might without absurdity be called Sopho-

clean in its arterial connections with the feelings of the characters. *The Vicar of Bullhampton* opens as an idyll about the likable and happily married young vicar and his wife, who with the best and most auspicious intentions try to arrange a marriage between his best friend, the squire, and her best friend, who happens to be visiting them. But, as the vicar and his wife don't know, the wife's friend has already "given her heart" elsewhere. The consequences, in the gradually darkening landscape of the novel, are immitigable misery for the squire, a breaking of old ties between all of them, and something like an awakening out of Eden for the vicar and his wife. Trollope's own strong nature, which ordinarily he represses for the sake of his constructions, takes its revenge on the pastoral circumstances of the novel: Trollope's fixation is the plot; passion is the plot.

Of course the novel everybody praises for its plot is *Tom Jones.* "Upon my word," exclaimed Coleridge, confounding English music-boxes with Greek violins, "I think the Oedipus Tyrannus, The Alchemist, and Tom Jones, the three most perfect plots ever planned." In "The Concept of Plot and the Plot of *Tom Jones,*" R. S. Crane cites Coleridge as well as other enthusiasts, and attempts with a few neo-Aristotelian flourishes to rationalize what everybody sees in all that whizzing and whirring machinery. Crane's (and Fielding's) euphemism for the machinery, whenever its motions more than usually deny the likelihood of will and reason in human events, is "Fortune"; but just once Fielding manages a shocking and authoritative intervention into a character's most intimate concerns by Fortune herself. It occurs in the scene in which Captain Blifil, at the summit of his influence, swelling with mischief, scheming and scheming, plainly the capital villain with a voluptuous career ahead of him in the remaining nine-tenths of the novel, suffers a brusque and unanticipated reverse:

> But while the captain was one day busied in deep contemplations of this kind . . . just at the very instant when his heart was exulting in meditations on the happiness which would accrue to him by Mr. Allworthy's death, he himself—died of an apoplexy.[6]

A novelist who can afford to cut off the villain in his prime is being altogether serious about the terrible chanciness of life. For a moment in the novel, Fortune isn't a label or an excuse but the goddess incarnate.

Aside from this apotheosis, however, the plot of *Tom Jones* is machinery, and the characters are the ignoble functions that the plot deserves. One critic Crane fails to cite is Dr. Johnson, who, comparing Fielding's characters with Richardson's, remarked, "Characters of manners are very entertaining; but they are to be understood by a more superficial observer than characters of nature, where a man must dive into the recesses of the human heart"; and Johnson "used to quote with approbation a saying of Richardson's, 'that the virtues of Fielding's heroes were the vices of a truly good man.'" Fanciers of carefree and undiscriminating coitus rise in a body to defend Fielding and Tom himself against this last, presumably puritanical indictment; but the indictment is elastic enough to comprehend, besides the censure of Tom's philandering, a more general censure of the characters of the novel. "Good" and "bad" alike, not only do they lack principle, they aren't—in spite of accepted critical opinion—typically subject to impulse, sexual or other; on the contrary, they are as unimpulsive and opportunistic as the plot.[7] Henry Fielding, justice of the peace for the district of Westminster, tends to regard the human heart as typically a cloaca of mean calculations which, if they didn't for the most part cancel one another out, would make the world as uninterruptedly disagreeable as it must often seem during the proceedings of a petty law-court:

> Mrs. Honour had scarce sooner parted from her young lady, than something (for I would not, like the old woman in Quevedo, injure the devil by any false accusation, and possibly he might have no hand in it) —but something, I say, suggested itself to her, that by sacrificing Sophia and all her secrets to Mr. Western, she might probably make her fortune. Many considerations urged this discovery. The fair prospect of a handsome reward for so great and acceptable a service to the squire tempted her avarice; and again, the danger of the enterprise she had undertaken; the uncertainty of its success; night, cold, robbers, ravishers, all alarmed her fears. So forcibly did all these operate upon her, that she was almost determined to go directly to the squire, and to lay open the whole affair. She was, however, too upright a judge to decree on one side before she had heard the other. And here, first, a journey to London appeared very strongly in support of Sophia. She eagerly longed to see a place in which she fancied charms short only of those which a raptured saint imagines in heaven. In the next place, as she knew Sophia to have much more generosity than her master, so her fidelity promised her a greater reward than she could gain by treach-

ery. She then cross-examined all the articles which had raised her fears on the other side, and found, on fairly sifting the matter, that there was very little in them. . . .[8]

Page after page is expended on such arithmetic, the incantatory recitation of which Fielding's admirers are pleased to consider a comic, because fearlessly realistic, exposure of motives. As for the motive of common decency, the author of *Tom Jones*—benevolent and spacious survey of mankind—seems in his researches to have missed it entirely, or to have confused it (as in Allworthy) with complacent brainlessness. In this world of moral defectives, the only cure for Mrs. Honour's calculation is Tom's "impulse" to commit carefree and undiscriminating coitus. Or as Crane says, finding mankind as little to his taste as Fielding does, Tom is "a young man whose lack of security and imprudence more than offset his natural goodness, living in a world in which the majority of people are ill-natured and selfish." How glum, and what a squinty perch of condescension from which to take the measure of the rest of us.

But most of us don't appear at our best in a courtroom. Kafka's Kellermann is feeble, crafty, dauntless, as full of incommunicable truths as any incompetent writer or living soul; but, observed from the conscious height at which Fielding exerts his vested authority, he would only resemble every other prisoner at the bar. Fielding himself is Tolstoy's judge Ivan Ilych, or "the celebrated doctor" to whom the judge is compelled, in his mortal extremity as a poor forked animal, to bring his appeal:

It was not a question of Ivan Ilych's life or death, but one between a floating kidney and appendicitis. And that question the doctor solved brilliantly, as it seemed to Ivan Ilych, in favour of the appendix, with the reservation that should an examination of the urine give fresh indications the matter would be reconsidered. All this was just what Ivan Ilych had himself brilliantly accomplished a thousand times in dealing with men on trial. The doctor summed up just as brilliantly, looking over his spectacles triumphantly and even gaily at the accused. From the doctor's summing up Ivan Ilych concluded that things were bad, but that for the doctor, and perhaps for everybody else, it was a matter of indifference, though for him it was bad. And this conclusion struck him painfully, arousing in him a great feeling of pity for himself and of bitterness towards the doctor's indifference to a matter of such importance.[9]

Tolstoy shows here how Fielding, confronted by Fielding, might be metamorphosed into Kellermann; he even shows how such an unimaginable Fielding might become attuned to a voice of conscience that begins to sound, hair-raisingly, like the voice of God:

> The pain again grew more acute, but he did not stir and did not call. He said to himself: "Go on! Strike me! But what is it for? What have I done to Thee? What is it for?"
>
> Then he grew quiet and not only ceased weeping but even held his breath and became all attention. It was as though he were listening not to an audible voice but to the voice of his soul, to the current of thoughts arising within him.
>
> "What is it you want?" was the first clear conception capable of expression in words, that he heard. . . .

The only novelist writing in English who has a comparable didactic boldness is D. H. Lawrence. In the 'thirties it was fashionable to dismiss Lawrence for this preoccupation with matters of life and death; in the 'seventies it's becoming feasible to explain why, "a tubercular plebeian cuckold married to a healthy aristocrat," he went as wrong as he did.[10] But the case of Lawrence the valetudinarian lowbrow needn't detain us because, all by himself, Lawrence the journeyman novelist is a maker of moments and episodes that pass the Kellermann test and that oughtn't to offend the healthiest aristocrat.

An instance is Chapter XIV ("Water-Party") of *Women in Love*. It has very little polemic, it's mostly action: feelings, meetings, transformations. The four principal characters converge into it with their powerfully conflicting demands, and arrive at the end of it committed to the current of mingled purposes that will carry them together all the way into one sort of exile or another, one sort of consummation or another. The symmetry of the chapter has the look of Fate, but Fate as choice—not what is done to them (by a despotic author or by Captain Blifil's Fortune) but what they freely and grandly do to themselves; thus they can just as freely, before they choose, pause in a timeless place to take their pleasure:

> The sisters found a little place where a tiny stream flowed into the lake, with reeds and flowery marsh of pink willow herb, and a gravelly bank to the side. Here they ran delicately ashore, with their frail boat, the two girls took off their shoes and stockings and went through the water's edge to the grass. The tiny ripples of the lake were warm and clear, they lifted their boat on to the bank, and looked round with

joy. They were quite alone in a forsaken little stream-mouth, and on the knoll just behind was the clump of trees.

"We will bathe just for a moment," said Ursula, "and then we'll have tea."

So they bathe, and "when they had run and danced themselves dry, the girls . . . sat down to the . . . tea," which

. . . was hot and aromatic, there were delicious little sandwiches of cucumber and of caviare, and winy cakes.

"Are you happy, Prune?" cried Ursula in delight, looking at her sister.

"Ursula, I'm perfectly happy," replied Gudrun gravely, looking at the westering sun.

When Gerald "rescues" Gudrun from the wild cattle, she is brought back with a bump to time and love and other daily threats:

"You think I'm afraid of you and your cattle, don't you?" she asked. His eyes narrowed dangerously. There was a faint domineering smile on his face. "Why should I think that?" he said.

She was watching him all the time with her dark, dilated, inchoate eyes. She leaned forward and swung round her arm, catching him a light blow on the face with the back of her hand.

"That's why," she said, mocking.

And she felt in her soul an unconquerable desire for deep violence against him. She shut off the fear and dismay that filled her conscious mind. She wanted to do as she did, she was not going to be afraid.

He recoiled from the slight blow on his face. He became deadly pale, and a dangerous flame darkened his eyes. For some seconds he could not speak, his lungs were so suffused with blood, his heart stretched almost to bursting with a great gush of ungovernable emotion. It was as if some reservoir of black emotion had burst within him, and swamped him.

"You have struck the first blow," he said at last, forcing the words from his lungs, in a voice so soft and low, it sounded like a dream within her, not spoken in the outer air.

"And I shall strike the last," she retorted involuntarily, with confident assurance. He was silent, he did not contradict her.

Gudrun determines their fate and then prophesies it: transitory words as she speaks them turn to stone; prophecy is like symbolism, it sacrifices the fact to the meaning. Gudrun has already forgotten what she discovered with Ursula by their little stream away from the hubbub of the festival—that the living make no sacrifices, that they give up nothing, have their cake and eat it too. But timeless dallying by a stream is easier on the nerves than the mere daily facts of life. Gudrun, uncomfortable with mere facts, stares them to stone: for Gudrun and Gerald, the festival that ends in death by water must be portentous and symbolic (whereas for the other pair of lovers, readier to take facts as they come, it's an eventful party that ends very badly).

What Gudrun discovers once and forgets quickly in *Women in Love*, Walter Morel in *Sons and Lovers* exemplifies unthinkingly every morning of his life. Lawrence, lapsing for a moment from the parricidal vindictiveness with which elsewhere in his autobiographical novel he pursues his father's ghost, shows us in a single passage not what the elder Morel is *like* (wretched husband and father, clod, boor, drunken brute) but what to himself, out of the world's eye, he always and adequately *is:*

> He always made his own breakfast. Being a man who rose early and had plenty of time he did not, as some miners do, drag his wife out of bed at six o'clock. At five, sometimes earlier, he woke, got straight out of bed, and went downstairs. When she could not sleep, his wife lay waiting for this time, as for a period of peace. The only real rest seemed to be when he was out of the house.
>
> He went downstairs in his shirt and then struggled into his pit-trousers, which were left on the hearth to warm all night. There was always a fire, because Mrs. Morel raked. And the first sound in the house was the bang, bang of the poker against the raker, as Morel smashed the remainder of the coal to make the kettle, which was filled and left on the hob, finally boil. His cup and knife and fork, all he wanted except just the food, was laid ready on the table on a newspaper. Then he got his breakfast, made the tea, packed the bottom of the doors with rugs to shut out the draught, piled a big fire, and sat down to an hour of joy. He toasted his bacon on a fork and caught the drops of fat on his bread; then he put the rasher on his thick slice of bread, and cut off chunks with a clasp-knife, poured his tea into his saucer, and was happy. . . .[11]

Life is the pleasure of one's company, the pleasure of routine and need. Symbols, whatever they point to and stand for, suggest that life is breaking down and coming apart. Life undivided is the density of particulars, of things and persons:

> . . . he went upstairs to his wife with a cup of tea because she was ill, and because it occurred to him.
> "I've brought thee a cup o' tea, lass," he said.

"Well, you needn't, for you know I don't like it," she replied.
"Drink it up; it'll pop thee off to sleep again."
She accepted the tea. It pleased him to see her take it and sip it.
"I'll back my life there's no sugar in," she said.
"Yi—there's one big 'un," he replied, injured.
"It's a wonder," she said, sipping again.
She had a winsome face when her hair was loose. He loved her to grumble at him in this manner. He looked at her again, and went, without any sort of leave-taking. He never took more than two slices of bread and butter to eat in the pit, so an apple or an orange was a treat to him. He always liked it when she put one out for him. He tied a scarf round his neck, put on his great, heavy boots, his coat, with the big pocket, that carried his snap-bag and his bottle of tea, and went forth into the fresh morning air, closing, without locking, the door behind him. He loved the early morning, and the walk across the fields. So he appeared at the pit-top, often with a stalk from the hedge between his teeth, which he chewed all day to keep his mouth moist, down the mine, feeling quite as happy as when he was in the field.

In *War and Peace*, the prisoners who are about to be shot "could not believe it because they alone knew what their life meant to them, and so they neither understood nor believed that it could be taken from them."[12] Mortal and incommunicable flesh and blood, "they alone knew": but Tolstoy knows, and makes us know too. Gudrun alone knows, refusing to be known, what it is to tear herself from Gudrun loving to Gudrun hateful; Morel alone knows on his pulse the blessedness of the morning; Captain Blifil alone knows, an instant before he is struck down, the inextinguishable satisfactions of villainy. And the omniscient author (not at all in the sense of a handy device for expert novelists) knows, though it's just as well that the character doesn't know that the author knows: imagine poor Kellermann seeing Kafka in the audience and knowing—through some diabolical dispensation—what it is to be Franz Kafka sitting out there observing Bernhard Kellermann in the very act of making an immortal ass of himself. Thank God for privacy, or the delusion of it.

Life, private or not, is always excessive and singular (but a machine is an allegory, functional and full of resonances), life is Trollope's obsession about women in love, or Chaucer's fascination with the excessive and singular phenomenon of flesh and blood in a prodigious sweat:

> His hakeney, that was al pomely grys,
> So swatte that it wonder was to see;
> It semed as he had priked miles three.
> The hors eek that his yeman rood upon
> So swatte that unnethe myght it gon.
> About the peytrel stood the foom ful hye;
> He was of foom al flekked as a pye. . . .
> He hadde ay priked lik as he were wood.
> A clote-leef he hadde under his hood
> For swoot, and for to keep his head from heete.
> But it was joye for to seen hym swete!
> His forheed dropped as a stillatorie. . . .[13]

(This is the Canon suddenly arriving among the Canterbury pilgrims.) "But it was joye for to seen hym swete!": life delighting in life, God delighting in Creation. Chaucer sees things this way all the time.

The least allegorical, and therefore the most novelistic, of long works of fiction is Chaucer's *Troilus and Criseyde*. It is continuously intense, energetic, familiar, clear, and joyous, rather like Walter Morel's morning extended temporally, spatially, and socially in all directions with perfect inclusiveness and every momentary adjustment of scale, from feelings as vividly private as Morel's through the exchanges of passionate love to the public grandeurs of the Trojan War. But all feelings are private and personal, the war is for Helen, Pandarus wouldn't do his thankless job if he didn't love both Troilus and Criseyde, love is the universal agent. Chaucer's irony—which doesn't undermine and set at odds, but binds and reconciles—is the sign of life that invites us into this world of light.

It's an irony free of guile, it doesn't give with one hand what it takes back with the other. When at the very beginning Criseyde, abandoned in Troy by her turncoat father and "wel neigh out of hir wit for sorwe and fere," comes to Hector pleading for mercy,

> Now was this Ector pitous of nature,
> And saugh that she was sorwfully bigon,
> And that she was so fair a creature;
> Of his goodnesse he gladede hire anon,
> And seyde, "Lat your fadres tresoun gon
> Forth with meschaunce, and ye yourself in joie
> Dwelleth with us, whil yow good list, in Troie. . . ."[14]

There are three distinct reasons, in descending order of importance, for Hector's response: (1) he is naturally merciful; (2) he sees that she is badly frightened; and (3) he sees that she is beautiful. The first reason is enough to ensure the substance of his response; the second ensures its gentleness; the third suffuses it with the superfluous and delightful warmth that any good man feels doing a disinterested good deed for a beautiful woman. Think of Fielding's "irony"—the leers and monkey tricks—let loose on a similar situation.

When Pandarus complicates his life by taking on the role of Troilus's envoy, advocate, mouthpiece, surrogate with Criseyde, he also complicates an old game, a domestic affection, a subliminal love affair of his own. Pandarus and Criseyde love each other as the amusing man-of-the-world uncle and the beautiful, unattached (she's a widow) courtly-lady niece; they enjoy the pleasure of each other's company; they gossip and joke and are comfortably familiar; they share the intimacy which confidently approaches and stops just this side of unexplorable possibilities. Pandarus will win for Troilus only if he avoids losing his own game. His advantages are his quick-wittedness, his ability to keep talking through the frostiest embarrassments, his assured sense—since he loves both Troilus and Criseyde —of the propriety of his mediation between them. His disadvantage is that, as all three of them know, in this sort of mediation even love isn't a good enough motive; that an uncle, however motivated, oughtn't to be promoting an affair which involves his niece. And Criseyde is a stubborn opponent, she is all alert resistance: Pandarus must prove every point and in effect prove it over again, as if it had never been proved, when he comes to the next one; in the game as Criseyde enforces the rules, Pandarus's sole alternative to another Sisyphean labor is a stroke of genius. So when, Pandarus, having apparently cleared the way earlier, brings Criseyde her first letter from Troilus, she instantly reacts with fear and anger, reproachfully, in unfeigned opposition:

> Ful dredfully tho gan she stonden stylle,
> And took it naught, but al hire humble chere
> Gan for to chaunge, and seyde, "Scrit ne bille,
> For love of God, that toucheth swich matere,
> Ne brynge me noon; and also, uncle deere,
> To myn estat have more reward, I preye,
> Than to his lust! . . ."[15]

Whereupon Pandarus, having fulminated for a stanza or two against the incomprehensible finickiness of women, delivers his stroke of genius:

> "But thus ye faren, wel neigh alle and some,
> That he that most desireth yow to serve,
> Of hym ye recche leest wher he bycome,
> And whethir that he lyve or elles sterve.
> But for al that that ever I may deserve,
> Refuse it naught," quod he, and hente hire faste,
> And in hire bosom the lettre down he thraste,
>
> And seyde hire, "Now cast it awey anon,
> That folk may seen and gauren on us tweye."
> Quod she, "I kan abyde til they be gon";
> And gan to smyle, and seyde him, "Em, I preye,
> Swich answere as yow list youreself purveye,
> For trewely I nyl no lettre write."
> "No? than wol I," quod he, "so ye endite."
>
> Therwith she lough, and seyde, "Go we dyne."
> And he gan at hymself to jape faste,
> And seyde, "Nece, I have so gret a pyne
> For love, that everich other day I faste—"
> And gan his beste japes forth to caste,
> And made hire so to laughe at his folye,
> That she for laughter wende for to dye.[16]

Pandarus has made Point One over again, he makes Point Two via special-delivery, and he and Criseyde stroll off together laughing toward the not yet formulated Point Three, with the somewhat agitated hearts of lovers and friends who know that the unfinishable game is worthy of them both.

Chaucer's irony doesn't demand scapegoats, it isn't a judgment of the stupidity or self-deception or wickedness of others. It's a road map, rather, of the twists and turns and abrupt halts by which everybody hopes to come out sooner or later straight (as when Criseyde freezes till Pandarus finds the right way of posting the letter); or it may be a bit of *double entendre* to emphasize that life is complex even when in the heat of emotion somebody considers it simple (Troilus, lamenting Criseyde's absence, apostrophizes her palace: "O thow lanterne of which queynt is the light"[17]—"queynt" meaning "quenched," but also to the ear the vulgar word for the female genitals); or it may be a reminder of personal claims that, attentive only to love, lovers can at some peril to their humanity neglect and ignore. Chaucer's best instance of such a reminder is so quiet and brief, and so subordinated in the text to the excitement of what is about to happen, that arriving at it readers usually don't, though they should, stop short.

The instance occurs at the center of the poem, toward the center of Book III, just before the lovers are brought to bed together. Criseyde, still refractory to anything more drastic than fine speeches, has been invited by Pandarus to spend the evening in his house, at a time for which the astrological signs, as Pandarus interprets them, promise heavy rain. The storm will justify his persuading Criseyde to stay, and its racket will cover other sounds and talk in the night. Criseyde comes (she doesn't know, but may well surmise, that Troilus is already on the premises, concealed and trembling somewhere), it pours and thunders, and Criseyde agrees to spend the night. Pandarus does everything but draw diagrams as he explains the arrangements that will put Criseyde off in a room by herself: in the next room, the only one directly accessible to hers, beyond an open door will be her attendant ladies; in the room on the other side of theirs, Pandarus (this is a medieval house, without corridors). It appears, then, that Criseyde is effectively isolated for the night; and, though Chaucer doesn't record Criseyde's reactions, he may intend us to assume that at the start of the evening she is full of expectation and prepared to continue holding out, later puzzled and perhaps disappointed, finally resigned to the prospect of an untroubled sleep.

In the middle of the night Pandarus goes to fetch Troilus, drags this "wrecched mouses herte" through a trap-door into Criseyde's room, softly closes the door on the sleeping women in the next room,

> And as he com ayeynward pryvely,
> His nece awook, and axed, "Who goth there?"
> "My dere nece," quod he, "it am I.
> Ne wondreth nought, ne have of it no fere."
> And ner he com, and seyde hire in hire ere,
> "No word, for love of God, I yow biseche!
> Lat no wight risen and heren of oure speche."
>
> "What! which wey be ye comen, *benedicite*?"
> Quod she, "and how thus unwist of hem alle?"

"Here at this secre trappe-dore," quod he.
Quod tho Criseyde, "Lat me som wight calle!"
"I! God forbede that it sholde falle,"
Quod Pandarus, "that ye swich folye wroughte!
They myghte demen thyng they nevere er thoughte.

"It is nought good a slepyng hound to wake,
Ne yeve a wight a cause to devyne.
Youre wommen slepen alle, I undertake,
So that, for hem, the hous men myghte myne,
And slepen wollen til the sonne shyne.
And whan my tale brought is to an ende,
Unwist, right as I com, so wol I wende. . . ."[18]

And Pandarus goes on to tell his slapdash story about Troilus (who all this time has been cowering, undiscovered by Criseyde, in a corner of the room), a lie that proves to be the last link in Pandarus's great chain of persuasion. Meanwhile the three preliminary stanzas quoted above are liable to slip past unexamined as the reader and the lovers sweep toward the long deferred event.

Nothing slips past Chaucer, however; least of all, anybody's claim and right to be noticed. Loved and admired and (more or less) heeded as he is from the beginning by both Troilus and Criseyde, Pandarus at once becomes the necessary instrument—compliant and sensitive no doubt, but instrument nevertheless—of their conjunction. All this time he has subordinated himself utterly to what they are bound to do, and now that they are about to do it he is programmed to shut himself off like a good little machine. One move is left for him, his transcendently lonely and most dangerous risk. Troilus for the present is an emotional basket-case ready for nothing but love, and Criseyde is radiantly ready to give him anything but love. Pandarus concludes that only a really spectacular invention—say, a faked crisis, an astounding lie in the middle of the night, with Troilus available for immediate transfer into her bed—will have a chance of overwhelming and defeating her. But what can Pandarus say at the moment when Criseyde awakens, in the dark, to find her uncle apparently alone with her in the room he has so elaborately arranged for her to be undisturbed in? "Who's there?" she says. "My dear niece," he replies, identifying himself and using the reassuring word of affection, "it's me. Don't wonder or be afraid." And he comes nearer and whispers in her ear, "Not a word, for the love of God, I

beseech you! Don't let anyone get up and hear what we're saying."
Criseyde, by now completely alert and uneasy but not yet certain
whether she should be alarmed, asks, "How did you get in without
their knowing?" "Here, at this secret trap-door." "Let me call somebody," says Criseyde.

She has virtually decided to be alarmed. If she calls to her women,
of course not only Pandarus's plan but Pandarus himself will be
ruined. She must now, it seems, decide that her uncle, who has always been loving and useful, is turning out to be more loving than
she had thought; that, pretending to be speaking for Troilus (John
Alden for the tongue-tied soldier Captain Standish), he has in fact
been speaking for himself (he too is human, as it's a shock to recall,
he too has desires, he isn't a machine, people expect to be paid for
their labor and their love, maybe he hasn't tacitly accepted the limit
beyond which nothing); and, if her suspicions are well grounded,
then even an awful scandal—what will the women think as they rush
into the room where in the dead of night Pandarus stands by Criseyde's bed?—is preferable to the alternative. "God forbid," says Pandarus, "that you should commit such a folly! They might think what
they never thought before." Providentially, Criseyde isn't a flighty or
hysterical woman, and Pandarus keeps talking calmly and sensibly:
"It isn't good to wake a sleeping dog [Pandarus's lust? the women's
malice?], nor to give anybody cause to speculate. Your women are all
asleep, I can guarantee, so that, as far as they're concerned, the house
might be about to fall down and they'll sleep till the sun shines. And
when my tale is brought to an end, without anyone's knowing, just
as I came, so will I leave." The danger is past, the cock-and-bull story
about Troilus's "jealousy" redirects Criseyde's attention back to her
will-I-won't-I dilemma, Pandarus can be forgotten again by readers
and lovers except as instrument, and the momentarily immobilized—
as if during the blink of an eye—narrative resumes its not quite imper-
turbable journey.

For a moment, though, Chaucer raises Pandarus's personal claim
(as Kafka raised Kellermann's). Pandarus is possibility, the path not
followed, what might have happened if the world were as crazy as it
is (the audience would leap up as one woman with torrential applause
and shout, "It's only you we love, Bernhard Kellermann! So give us
another six or eight of those unpublished things from your pen!"),

what mostly it's better not to muse over because people ought to know their place and stay there (out of the picture). Kellermann and Pandarus are both sublime because each inconveniently exists, in defiance of other people's tastes and impulses. The difference between them is that Kellermann doesn't know his place and Pandarus does: Kellermann is the comic sublime; Pandarus in the course of the poem is many things besides, but at this moment he is the tragic sublime. The way to dispose of such figures is to say that they are "larger than life" —which is an inadvertent way of saying that, in the world as well as in fiction, Kellermann is larger than all the life-size and circumambient machinery.

NOTES

1. All quotations are from Franz Kafka, *The Penal Colony,* trans. Willa and Edwin Muir (New York: Schocken Books, 1948).
2. Quotations are from Franz Kafka, *Diaries 1910-1913,* ed. Max Brod, trans. Joseph Kresh (New York: Schocken Books, 1948).
3. Like those enigmas of astronomy, "the 'black holes' predicted by the general theory of relativity: objects so compact that even light cannot escape their gravitational pull." Melvin A. Ruderman, "Solid Stars," *Scientific American,* 224, No. 2 (Feb. 1971), 24.
4. Anthony Trollope, *An Autobiography* (New York: Doubleday, n.d.), pp. 259-60.
5. This passage and the ones following are from Chapter X of *Barchester Towers.*
6. Book II, Chapter VIII.
7. *Joseph Andrews* is a better novel because (1) in it Fielding, having undertaken the obligations of parody, is content to work on a smaller scale, toward comic effects that are relatively unforced and good-humored; and (2) the fact that the target of the parody is *Pamela* requires Fielding to keep his hero chaste no matter what, and so provides a (parasitic and burlesque) internal tension which is Fielding's most plausible approximation of a moral order.
8. Book VII, Chapter VIII.
9. This passage and the one following are quoted from the translation by Aylmer Maude, included in Leo Tolstoy, *The Death of Ivan Ilych and Other Stories* (New York: New American Library, 1960).
10. The reason, we now learn, was his morbid attitude toward women. As "Briefly Noted" (the anonymous reviewer) of *The New Yorker* noted briefly in a review of Kate Millett's *Sexual Politics* (September 19, 1970, p. 137): "Miss Millett proves men's wickedness mainly from the work of several writers who are contemptuous of or hostile toward women. She is an acute literary analyst. Unfortunately for her argument, though, the authors she has chosen are in such psychological trouble themselves that it is hard to agree that they express typical attitudes toward women. Ruskin, for example, was impotent. D. H. Lawrence, a tubercular plebeian cuckold married to a healthy aristo-

crat, evidently had to assert his dominance in fantasies on paper, but few men have been so overmatched in marriage. *Et ainsi de suite.* Most of Miss Millett's masculine theorists writing about women are the sexual equivalent of Hitler writing on government: striking, unsound, and out of the main line of cultural evolution." On the evidence of this review, "Briefly Noted" is a ninety-proof mainlining swinger of either sex, rather like Tom Jones of the novel or the movie or the TV show. *Und so weiter.*

11. This passage and the one following are quoted from Part I, Chapter II.

12. Book XII, Chapter XI.

13. "His dapple-gray horse was in such a sweat it was something to look at; he seemed to have been running it for three miles. His yeoman's horse too was in such a sweat it could scarcely move. About its breastband the foam stood high; it was all flecked with foam, looking like a magpie. . . . He had been spurring his horse like a madman. He had a burdock-leaf under his hood to take the sweat and protect his head from the sun. But it was sheer joy to see him sweat! His forehead dripped like a still. . . ." (From *The Canterbury Tales,* The Canon's Yeoman's Prologue, ll. 559-80.)

14. "Now Hector was merciful by nature, and saw that she was in great distress, and that she was so fair a creature; out of his goodness he comforted her at once, and said, 'Let your father's treason go to the devil, and you yourself in joy dwell with us, as long as you please, in Troy. . . .'" (*Troilus and Criseyde,* I, 113-19.)

15. "Full of apprehension she stood motionless, and did not take it, but her easy manner changed, and she said, 'Bring me no letter or petition about such a matter, for the love of God; and also, dear uncle, have more regard for my honor, I beg you, than for his desire! . . .'" (*Ibid.,* II, 1128-34.)

16. "'But so you carry on, nearly the whole lot of you, that the one who most desires to serve you, what becomes of him matters least to you, and whether he lives or dies. But for all I may ever have coming to me, don't refuse it,' he said, and held her fast, and thrust the letter down into her bosom, and said to her, 'Now throw it away at once, so that people can see and gape at both of us.' Said she, 'I can wait till they're gone'; and smiled, and said to him, 'Uncle, I beg you, such answer as you would like provide by yourself, for truly I will write no letter.' 'No? then I will,' said he, 'so long as you dictate.' At that she laughed, and said, 'Let's go to dinner.' And he kept making jokes at his own expense, and said, 'Niece, I have such great torment for love that every other day I fast—' and brought out his best jokes, and made her laugh so hard at his foolishness that she thought she would die laughing." (*Ibid.,* II, 1149-69.) Scholars who have heard that Chaucer's source for *Troilus and Criseyde* is Boccaccio's *Il Filostrato,* but haven't read it, will be relieved to learn that here —and in the other passages cited in this essay—Chaucer is either inventing out of thin air or, as in this case, converting a platitude into a stroke of genius. Boccaccio's platitude: "Somewhat troubled by this, Pandarus said: '. . . I have spoken to thee so much of this, thou shouldst not now be over-nice with me. I pray thee, do not deny me now.' Criseida smiled as she heard him, and took the letter and put it in her bosom. Then she said to him: 'When I find time I shall read it as best I can. . . .'"

17. *Ibid.,* V, 543.

18. *Ibid.,* III, 750-70.

TONE, INTENTION, AND POINT OF VIEW

TONE
IN
FICTION

WALTER F. WRIGHT

"Give me the right word and the right accent," wrote Joseph Conrad in his "Familiar Preface," "and I will move the world." The word and accent were inseparable, for, beyond conveying a literal meaning, the word must have the proper ring. Every phrase must contribute to the author's pronouncement on the world he was creating, and that pronouncement was not merely a description of phenomena or a statement of some idea. It was something quite beyond these. It was a manifestation of his feeling for events and situations—that is, a matter of tone.

After browsing in several novels of "sexual sentimentality," Arnold Bennett protested in his *Journal* that they lacked "nobility," that they did not "arouse a single really fine emotion." In his candid manner he admonished himself, "That is what there has got to be in *The Old Wives' Tale*—a lofty nobility. I got it now and then in *Whom God Hath Joined,* but in the next book I must immensely increase the dose." No poet himself, Bennett sometimes read poetry and sometimes listened to music to refresh his sense of nobility when it had begun to wane.

In a note written after his novel-writing career was ended, Thomas Hardy obliquely summed up his aim both as poet and as novelist. Generally agreeing with an article that praised Ibsen and that quoted Shaw in support, Hardy nevertheless concluded, "But neither writer dwells sufficiently on the fact that Ibsen's defect is a lack of the essentiality of beauty to art."

All three authors were in their somewhat different ways preoccupied with the same thing. Not, of course, that they would minimize all that goes into the craftsmanship of story-telling; but that they were dealing with the informing principle of great art. They recognized, to be sure, that a novel must have thematic unity, that it must have an Aristotelian beginning, middle, and end, with variety, suspense, augmentation, and a reversal; that the characters must be convincing for the parts they performed; and that the scenes must be concretely realized. They were aware that the mingling of exposition, narration, and dramatic rendering all involve a painstaking concern for technique, and that a novelist must be both master architect and expert stonemason, designer of windows and fitter of bits of stained glass. But what of the edifice when all the craftsmanship was completed and the last slate and every carved figure were in place? What would distinguish the masterwork from the highly competent?

In his essay "Books" Conrad laid down the first principle of fiction: "In truth every novelist must begin by creating for himself a world, great or little, in which he can honestly believe." The creative act begins anterior to any application of architectonics or craftsmanship, and the author's feeling for the kind of world he wants to create must inform their use. The novelist starts with an awareness of reality. Life exists and the universe exists, but the novelist is well aware that neither his senses nor his imagination can give him more than a limited impression of their nature. He starts, in short, with a painful recognition of finiteness and incompleteness. Mortality itself makes of human consciousness a fragmentary series of glimpses, to be discontinued abruptly by hazard. The imperfection of mental grasp and of memory means that the welter of our sensations is never brought to order or coherence. What has seemed precious is pushed aside as new things are born in our consciousness and in turn take their fugitive lodging places in our memories.

Some of the experiences are for the moment exciting, suggesting that life is a great romance of adventure. Some are hilariously incongruous, as if life were made for laughter. Some bring only a sense of anguish, perhaps even of terror or horror. They all come tumbling into the range of our awareness in no inevitable sequence and their stay is of uncertain duration. Yet the mind craves order and a semblance of permanence. Finding chance and frustration everywhere apparent, it seeks to transcend them, to fit impressions into patterns and to identify relationships. It makes use of logic; if two premises exist, then a conclusion seems demonstrable. Or it may analyze and classify; if labels can be invented to epitomize kinds of theoretical experience, then all experiences can be sorted and situated in their proper territories, with the boundaries more or less precisely defined. The ultimate achievement of such logical analysis and compartmentalization, however, is arbitrary and fragmentary. It pretends that the infinite can be made finite, that the unending concatenation of atomically small and multifarious happenings and sensations can be stopped, examined as in a still picture, and described with assurance and completeness. What it ends with is, of course, an abstraction.

This may be pleasing to contemplate, and in science it is obviously a necessity. But in the realm of literature an abstraction is an unreality. The pretense that one examines human nature scientifically and by methodical induction arrives at generalizations which he then gives embodiment in fiction is an illusion. What Zola and others who have followed his method have arrived at has only the verisimilitude of an inductive process.

Still, the artistic mind is no less obsessed than the scientific with arriving at a belief in design and continuity, and it sets up its own patterns. Having experienced a variety of sensations, ranging somewhere between ecstasy and abject despair, the artist finds himself searching for their essence. Since, however, they are fragmentary and elusive, he has to go outside them to find some way of identifying them and of saving them from the annihilation which in actuality the succeeding hour, or even moment, may bring.

A scientist may chart a series of separate measurements and draw what he believes is an authentic line joining them. The artist subjectively senses the peaks and abysses of human experience and finds himself imaginatively playing with the variety of lines that may unite valley with valley or peak with peak or symbolize their alternation and duration. What he arrives at is Conrad's created world, a world that is not verifiable through any process of scientific method, but is simply a manifestation of belief.

If an author is not quite honest, or if he is lacking in courage, his creation will be one of willful belief, and the reader who has already done his share of trying unsuccessfully to achieve a pleasing belief will reject it as insufficient. He may even say that it is untrue. What he means is that it does not accord with his own imaginative apprehension of himself and of the universe.

If one does accept an author's created world, what is it that makes for his sense of affinity with its creator? It is not that the evidence is overpowering. He knows full well that, however realistic the work of fiction may seem, the proportions and emphasis are entirely the author's own, that the incidents and the characters are feigned. Nor is it a process of deduction that leads to conviction. He may have no quarrel with what seem to be either the premises or the conclusions, and yet find himself outside the fictional work and uninterested in entering it. On the other hand, although the beliefs implicit in the work may strike him as mere superstitions, he may tolerate them without hesitation.

What is it that inherently matters, that makes one as he reads a novel feel more at home with his own sensation of existence and helps him to a finer awareness? It is essentially the tone. If the reader finds himself captivated by it, all significant issues are resolved.

It is not true that life is a breathless series of adventures rising to a climax and subsiding into happy contentment. Nor is it true that life adheres to a formula by which suffering brings calmness of mind, with "all passion spent." Nor does mere understanding of a given cause-and-effect sequence make for philosophic acceptance of actuality. In short, life is not what fiction gives. Fiction does not discover truth through its imitation of life. Nor would it serve any useful purpose if it did. What great fiction does is to suggest an attitude toward the multiform and varicolored incidents and phenomena of which we are or can become aware. Its validity in reference to truth is not in the truth it presents, but in the perspective it suggests. And that perspective is really ultimately concerned with the adventures of the imagination. Were one to imagine an existence made up of wonderful, exhilarating adventures, what might be its features? If human sadness were not to be left as a jagged series of incomplete emotions, what kind of orderly progression might it take, and might the very pain end in a melancholy at once poignant and precious? The great work of fiction addresses itself to these kinds of subjects. It proves nothing, but it does ask the reader to see through the author's eyes and, above all, to feel.

Conrad remarked that the function of his works was "before all to make you see." He was speaking very literally, for it was first of all the visual image that the reader was to share. What the reader was to see was, of course, those things which conveyed Conrad's own feeling for the world he had created. It is significant that Wordsworth in his preface considers the substance of a poem to consist ultimately of the poet's feeling. And in his preface to *The Princess Casamassima* Henry James stresses the same essence in fiction. The prerequisite for his characters who serve as "registers" is that they must "feel their respective situations." Feeling as understood by Wordsworth and James presupposes what James called "awareness," but it is a thing beyond mere intellectual perception, and it depends on the quality of the mind that perceives. Since a character's manifestation of that quality—essentially sensibility—is the measure of the author as creator, it is one—by no means the only—embodiment of the author's own feeling. It is neither abstract nor finite, but concrete and, in its suggestiveness, unlimited.

Since the feeling is shared by author and reader, it is in the largest sense social. In so far as it is concerned with the relations of two or more human beings it involves morality. If the substance be pathos, the morality resides in the compassion, which itself springs from a sense of affinity—what Conrad called the solidarity of mankind. This is something which the author does not try to defend by argument; rather he only strives to convey his own appreciation of it. If he is successful, the very idiom and rhythm of his language reveal his own feeling of the situation which he has imagined.

To illustrate from Conrad's *Lord Jim*—it is not merely that honor is a valuable quality, perhaps even a necessity if man is to be other than a miserable wretch. It is that a battered French ship's officer can, almost in the same breath, treat his own heroic action as a rather casual matter, tolerantly condone the cowardice of others, and suddenly break forth in an impassioned invocation of honor, after which he subsides into a seemingly unimaginative stolidity. The impression left by the French lieutenant's sometimes broken sentences is that life can be terrible, it can be endurable, it can be an ecstatic romance of adventure. As he speaks of man's inherent cowardliness his pauses become longer, and when his pensive monologue lapses into silence, he sits brooding apparently about his own failures. Then, as if in a sudden rebirth, he glimpses his ideal of conduct—"But the honour—the honour, monsieur! . . . The honour . . . that is real—that is!" (*sic.*) Some things he has defined with precision; but his images, his cadences, the sudden shift from dejection to exaltation, while his voice remains quiet and almost casual—these are the oblique expression of his feeling for things. They express an awareness that cannot be fully articulated. In short, whatever revelation Conrad has given as to the nature of man's soul and of his plight is finally a matter of tone.

As for Bennett—he worked in a much more subdued manner than Conrad. But at his best in *The Old Wives' Tale* and the *Clayhanger* novels he kept before him the concern for nobility. In what did it consist? Many of the incidents in Bennett's pages are deliberately ultraordinary. And yet even these, Bennett maintains, make life worthwhile, for they do reveal a glimpse of romance and they attest to inherent human dignity. All this Bennett tells us, not in so many words, but by the pensive, usually melancholy, atmosphere with which he surrounds his characters and their gentle, patient acceptance of their fates. Without sentimentalizing, he has asked us to share with him the realization that events are as they are felt to be. Once again, beyond the facts themselves and the ideas is the tone.

And when we turn to Hardy, we are dealing with a poet who wrote novels. The plots of *Tess of the D'Urbervilles*, *The Woodlanders*, and *Jude the Obscure* are as improbable and melodramatic as those of *The Hand of Ethelberta* and *The Laodicean*. Some of the characters are no less wooden, and the range of experience is probably narrower. But the spirit of beauty is seldom present in the latter two, and it seems to hover over the other three. It is her childlike trust that has permitted Tess to recover repeatedly from the blows of fate. In the Harpers version of her cry of anguish to Angel—"Only—only—don't 'ee make it more than I can bear"—the "stopt-diapason note" of her voice and her naive lapse into the dialect of her childhood go beyond the literal substance of her words to convey Hardy's feeling both for her tragedy and for the winsomeness of her spirit. And without worrying about the contrivances that finally leave Marty South alone by the grave of Giles Winterborne, we catch the very rhythm of her eulogy: "But no, no, my love. I never can forget 'ee; for you was a good man, and did good things!" In the cry of Tess and the "chorus" of Marty, Hardy has echoed immemorial sorrow and shown that it can be beautiful. And as Jude lies dying we find comfort in the recognition that the universal lament from Job—"Let the day perish wherein I was born"—gives to an obscure life an heroic magnitude. The words are bitter, and yet they connote an acceptance of the inevitability of fate, and the reader closes the book with a better understanding and a better *feeling* of the nature of tragic catharsis. There is a final symmetry that permits one to echo the chorus from *Samson Agonistes,* in which Milton first speaks of what one has learned from Samson's story and then dismisses his audience as at last "calm of mind, all passion spent."

For Hardy nature itself was almost a sentient being, with its own range of tone. In the "bleached and desolate upland" which Tess must traverse there is a "new kind of beauty, a negative beauty of tragical blankness" or, in the alternative version, an identical beauty of "tragic tone." Not even the philosophic apparatus which Hardy later constructed in *The Dynasts* can justify such a view of the cosmos. Yet, as the offspring of imagination and feeling it transcends reason.

How do all these novels differ from Zola's *L'Assomoir?* Not in the authors' philosophies, for both Zola and Hardy were inclined toward determinism. Not in their truthful realism, for each could be painstaking in his concern for verisimilitude. It is that, at his best, Hardy was a poet, whether in verse or fiction, and indeed often the better in prose.

When we turn to Henry James, an author who chose usually to write in a reflective manner, we find only a variation of our theme. At times James did compose phrases that might almost fit in a poem, as when, in "The Middle Years," he let his novelist hero sum up the artist's ideal: "We work in the dark. We do what we can. We give what we have. Our doubt is our passion and our passion is our task. The rest is the madness of art!" or when, at the end of *The Wings of the Dove,* to indicate the poignancy of the tragedy which their evil machinations have wrought, he let Kate half-wailingly reply to her one-time lover, "We shall never be again as we were." More typically James carefully elaborated the tone of his characters' feelings about the events that befell them. Thus, in *The Ambassadors,* which is replete with incidents that might turn a less idealistic mind to cynical revulsion, James depicts Strether's persistence in seeing experience as he has found it represented in a Lambinet painting of quiet pastoral life. In the novel James repeatedly demonstrates that the social world in which Strether moves may equally well be viewed as an ugly, egoistic, hypocritical jungle. But he also asks the reader to venture with him in seeing it, not through silly, sentimental eyes, but through the rare imagination of a noble and compassionate mind, which, not by means of reason, but through spiritual alchemy, transmutes it into the substance of mature romance.

One could multiply examples, but a single striking illustration may suffice. In *The Waves* Virginia Woolf dispensed with most traditional features of story-telling; instead, she presented a sequence of moods, symbolized by the light on the waves as the day progressed and given concreteness through the thoughts and words of her characters as the scenes shifted from childhood to age. In a lyric manner she imagined life as a series of pictures, each having its own peculiar tone, and each contributing to a symphonic form.

As one recalls *The Ambassadors or Tess* he remembers their protagonists and many of the separate incidents. In contrast, some weeks after reading *The Waves* one may recall the characters and scenes only as if at a distance and through a haze. Yet no more than with Mrs. Woolf's characters is it really the precise features of Strether or of Tess that matter; it is one's feeling that through their special response to a set of purely imaginary phenomena he has refined or even transformed his own apprehension of his mortal being in an immortal universe, and that he has been led to an appreciation of the human predicament that is comforting, aesthetically satisfying—perhaps unqualifiedly beautiful—and, in so far as truth is attainable in a limitless and elusive world of spirit, essentially true.

All this, if a novel has been fully successful, is what it has communicated from author to reader. If it has not done this, its coherence of plot, its psychological consistency, its arguments, explicit or implied, and its craftsmanlike competence are inconsequential. If it has done so, then it has achieved a lesser or greater miracle. For through complete submission to the tone which the novelist has created the reader experiences an imaginative refreshment, perhaps even a rebirth. When he turns from the novel back to his sole self, the circumstances that surround him are no more orderly than before. But he is inclined to feel them in a new way. It is this which, in the Jamesian sense, represents the madness—and the miracle—of art.

TWO-TONE
FICTION
NINETEENTH-CENTURY TYPES
AND EIGHTEENTH-CENTURY PROBLEMS

ROBERT B. HEILMAN

I

By "two-tone fiction" I mean novels in whose impact we sense some inconsistency or discrepancy or variation or departure from the expectation established by the apparently controlling devices employed by the novelist. I avoid the term *ambiguity* because it has been excessively called upon and because, if used precisely, it means an unresolved semantic doubleness, which is not my subject here. Hence, also, I do not use *doubleness;* besides, it inevitably reminds a reader of "the double vision," that is, a quality of creative consciousness which also is not what I am talking about. I have thought of *duplicity,* which might do in literal terms, but which would seize attention in the wrong way by pointlessly setting up moral vibrations and then ignoring them. *Duality* could be the key term, but it has a faint aroma of criticism-factory jargon. Thus, by process of elimination, "two-tone." At the risk of oversimplification I use "two" rather than "three" or "poly" because in my experience the split or discord (if it comes to that) is characteristically between two tonal qualities rather than more. (It might be theoretically argued that a work of multiple tonal currents is an impossibility because the consciousness out of which it would have to come would lack the degree of integration needed for the labor of composition. But that is another issue.)

Two other notes to chart the drift of this essay. "Two-tone" does not allude to traditional combinations of different generic effects denoted by such terms as "tragicomedy" and "romantic tragedy." With these two-genre or mixed-genre works we live easily, and if we do not immediately grasp a central coherence, we take it to be there and we feel obligated to search for it. "Two-tone" implies rather a problem or difficulty, not necessarily an irreconcilable disunity, but at least a divergence that excites inquiry. Second, "two-tone" is not the same as "two-meaning." This is of course a ticklish issue, and I don't imply that "tone" and "meaning" are easily separable. Talk about "tone" has to do with the "feeling" of a work, and this may be related to meaning in several ways: because we "feel" in such-and-such a way about a work, we may attribute such-and-such a meaning to it; or, conversely, we may be detecting a certain meaning, which automatically elicits one feeling rather than another. It may be that we "feel" differently about *The Turn of the Screw* if from the beginning we believe either that the governess is destroying good children or that she is failing to save bad ones. But need we? In either case the tone is one of horror and of the sinister, and no reader mistranslates this into, say, the romantic or the comic. If there is ambiguity of sense in *The Turn,* there is no evasiveness or oscillation of tone. But when both uncertainties are present, I want to deal with the tonal problem, be it one of wavering, of alternation, or of persistent doubleness. This is a slightly different enterprise from the more frequent critical labor, the exegesis of non-explicit meaning. If I do not talk about "what the author is saying," it is that it seems irrelevant to, or else implied by, the discussion of tone.

If there is a question of tone, one may just describe it, or one may speculate about the reason for it. The issue may arise from a not wholly lucid or consistent communication of the narrative substance, possibly the case in Pynchon's *V.* It may arise because the author has, so to speak, different "intentions" that are in control at different times, or because he is overtaken, half unawares, by a subtle change in attitude. It may arise because he has unstable responses to a character or situation, or, at a deeper level, has emotional contradictions that express themselves in fictional elements of not wholly congruous impact. It may be that he is operating within conventions that we do not understand and that can accommodate tonal results in which only we of another era or culture see disparities. Lady Murasaki's *Tale of Genji,* for instance, appears (as it comes through in Arthur Waley's translation) to alternate between a fairy-tale manner (wonder at the glory and magnificence of characters and occasions and trappings, always hyperbolically described) and a social realism wholly conversant with the emotional and psychic traumas of insecure amatory and courtly life (such as appears in a lesser fictionist like Aphra Behn or a greater one like Proust). Murasaki can even reach a plane of fine moral realism. On one occasion the hero, Prince Genji, laments his illicit passion for Fujitsubo, the consort of the Old Emperor (his father). He cries out against "foeman fate" and the "bonds" that "would hold him back from Paradise." Fujitsubo quietly replies, "If to all time this bond debars you from felicity, not hostile fate but your own heart you should with bitterness condemn" (Part II, Ch. 1). But after such plunges into the heart of the matter Murasaki easily reverts to the alternate practice of letting Genji glow with the fused talents of Don Juan, Frank Merriwell, and John Kennedy. We do not know whether this two-tone effect emerges from an inherent disjunction in the tale, or whether an eleventh-century Japanese, spontaneously applying the conventions of his day, would have felt a congruence which I believe is not available to a modern Western reader.

There may be various sources, then, for two-tone fiction. Though cause-hunting is too uncertain a business to be the central occupation here, I will try some speculations about the origins of certain shifts. If such hypotheses make sense, they may shed a little light on novelists or their processes or products.

II

The novels which I think deserve the fullest treatment are *Moll Flanders* and *Pamela*. The problems which they present, however, will be most meaningful if we can see them in a context of what happens in a number of other novels; besides, even a brief account of these will develop the theoretical framework a little further.

The two-tone effect may be incidental, cardinal, or pervasive. Several examples of each will be enough to make the distinctions clear.

In Scott's *Rob Roy* the effect is incidental but recurrent; though it is not characteristic of the novel as a whole, it appears in a number of episodes. Morris the government agent characteristically sets Scott off in different directions. We first see Morris as so fearful a traveler toward Scotland that he is totally ludicrous, a "humor" in the old sense; he creates the tone of farce. But then we are told that he is carrying both money to pay the troops in the North and "despatches of great consequence" (Ch. 7)—an assignment inconceivable for such a character as Scott has created. Our responsiveness to him is balked by colliding pieces of fictional evidence. Then we are given the wrong kind of shock when Morris, a prisoner, is brutally drowned by the order of Helen MacGregor (Ch. 31): a tale cannot jump from hilarity to horror unless such gross reversals are its main burden. Bailie Nicol Jarvie, also a prisoner of Helen's, "could not so suppress his horror, but that the words escaped him in a low and broken whisper,—'I take up my protest against this deed, as a bloody and cruel murder—it is a cursed deed, and God will avenge it in his due way and time'" (Ch. 32). Thus Scott commits Jarvie to unqualified moral outrage. Fifteen lines later, when Helen asks Jarvie what he would say about the drowning if she were to free him, Jarvie replies, "Uh! uh!—hem! hem! . . . I suld study to say as little on that score as might be—least said is sunest mended." While Scott accurately perceives the inconsistency that flows from self-interest, he puts this in such gross, pell-mell fashion that we have another kind of farce —that of coarse automatic action—and hence a violent leap from horror back to hilarity (so blatant that on the next page Scott even makes a mild effort to mitigate it). One other case, partly comparable: in order to reward his hero Frank with Osbaldistone Hall, Scott has to kill off Frank's five male cousins, all young men presumably in good health; so on a page or so he rips off five fatal accidents (Ch. 37). Here again is the farce of automatism—the row of routine knock-downs, here irreversible, but still pratfalls in spirit. Yet we are then to take seriously the shattered state of the surviving father, and to applaud the justice of Frank's becoming lord of the manor.

Repeatedly Scott is unable to forgo farce, though it clashes with some other effect that he does not regard as trivial. He will play for horse laughs at any time, without concern for tonal congruence. He is an entertainer, a Dickens who can clown or cry at will in a series of readings. A rather fancy theoretical approach would be to attribute to Scott's work a "unity of entertainment": entertainment always means change, novelty, diversity, so that a sequence of tonally disparate passages might seem to embody the Platonic idea of entertainment. But this would confuse the art of the novel with the art of the vaudeville program. Still, it puts a brake on facile charges of inconsistency.

It is a temptation to think that a novel with the "unity of entertainment" reveals as much about the audience as about the author. But it is too easy to condescend to audiences which for a century, most of it post-dating Coleridge's provision of a more rigorous concept of unity, included readers of literary sophistication and critical acumen. Better, perhaps, to assume in the humanity of the nineteenth century a wide spontaneous responsiveness to the Scott fare—and then to postpone the question of why this has been considerably narrowed down in our day, which can hardly be thought to have a greater proportion of knowledgeable and skeptical readers.

The two-tone effect is "cardinal" when we can see a hinge at which the novel apparently swings from one kind of effect to another. This may happen rather late in the game: witness the arguments over whether the main substance of Lawrence's *The Rainbow* sustains the buoyant ending. There are significant, more central instances of the cardinal two-tone effect in Thackeray's *Vanity Fair* and Meredith's *The Ordeal of Richard Feverel,* and here we can hardly help speculating about what led the authors into these striking swings.

Becky Sharp lives by her wits, untroubled by conscience or consequences; she puts things over on others, schemes, calculates, gets ahead, advances opportunistically from one game to another. We rejoice in her successes and are sorry when she doesn't pull it off; that is, the rogue is heroine, and the tone is picaresque. But this is true for only half the novel or a little more. The tone changes when Becky makes victims of the innocent, whom we are compelled to respond to as victims and who therefore compel us to yield to them the sympathy which once flowed naturally to Becky. When Becky deceives her husband, ignores her son, and fleeces the landlord Raggles and the servant Miss Briggs, she is no longer the amiable rogue profiting from the follies of others or beating them at their own game but a merciless cheater of nice guys. Thackeray did not have to do it this way: he might have kept Rawdon and the boy Rawdie out of sight or made them into a rascal and a brat whom we couldn't like. But he either rejected this way of keeping to the picaresque, or didn't think of it. Instead, he turned on Becky.

When Becky changes from charming gameswoman to gravely dishonest operator, the picaresque gives way to a sharply satirical tone (this is really a change in genre, too). Maybe Thackeray was not altogether comfortable with the picaresque; maybe the homilist or moralist in him nudged him toward a judgment-making form; maybe the cultural atmosphere in which he wrote (if it is safe to make any assumptions at all about it) or his sense of readers' expectations pulled him away from the amoral picaresque mode.

We can make two critical judgments of this tonal swing, but neither is wholly satisfactory. If we call it a failure, we risk the pedantry of going by rule in a somewhat Rymeresque way, and of ignoring a considerable history of imaginative responses that seem to have had no difficulty with the tone (any more than they have had with lack of unity or decorum in Shakespeare). One needs to be aware of this danger. Still he may regret the loss of the picaresque, with its particular delights, and feel that Thackeray turned unnecessarily against Becky and thus used her to support the moral judgments to which he was inclined. The other approach is to justify the tonal swing by arguing that Thackeray grasped the inevitable implications of the picaresque and carried the mode into the depths into which it has to lead if the writer does not arbitrarily stop short. In this view, the non-moral has at its heart the immoral, the rogue is only the smile upon the villain's face, and responsible art must go all the way to the bottom of things. Though this theory is not implausible, unhappily it would commit every work to a kind of metaphysical relentlessness that would eliminate not only the diversity of appeal inherent in a diversity of modes but also the specific satisfaction proper to each mode, which can exist as a mode only by accepting conventional boundaries instead of essaying a universal inclusiveness or ultimateness. Picaresque, we may assume, pleases by making possible a vicarious exercise (or catharsis, perhaps?) of everyman's rascality (taste for slick profits, sleight of hand, the opportunism of wits, effrontery, etc.), of his need for interludes of non-morality. Traditional picaresque art, of course, ritually acknowledges the insufficiency of the picaresque way of life by having the hero end up in jail. It seems a pity that, with Becky, Thackeray should have transubstantiated the ritual acknowledgment into a flesh-and-blood demonstration of moral culpability.

The cardinal alteration in tone is very evident in *The Ordeal of Richard Feverel,* in which Meredith regrettably drifts away from his *métier,* comedy, and into satirical melodrama. In comedy the protagonist is perceived ironically in his inconsistency, his self-deception, or his folly, and potentially he has the grace to understand them; in satire his failings persist and may assume the tinge of vice; in melodrama we see his ill-doings and his victims. These modes may of course be combined, but Meredith does not commit the *Ordeal* to a combination. Instead he creates a superb comic tone which we expect to hold throughout, and then loses his grip on it: we see his detachment yielding to a sharp animus. This first appears when Mrs. Doria Forey, rebounding from Richard's marriage, forces her daughter Clare, whom she had trained to fall in love with Richard, into a substitute marriage with a man twice her age. This totally incredible marriage kills or helps kill Clare, and Meredith hangs on to the pathos by post-mortem readings from Clare's diary. Up to this disaster the novel views Mrs. Doria with gentle irony as a marrying mother with "a System" of her own (Ch. 38), an amusingly straightforward practical contrast to Sir Austin's elaborate theoretical scheme for educating Richard. Now she becomes a monster. Meredith simply loses his grip on his point of view. We may theorize that he got angry at Mrs. Doria and felt the need to denigrate her by making her guilty of involuntary manslaughter. (A little later, in a second burst of sentimental haste, he puts her through a second conversion, this time into a remorseful and suddenly wise woman.)

It is difficult to avoid the conclusion that Meredith lets himself get angry several times and hence falls into the change of tone that puts us off. First, two small protective steps. I am not coming up with the mawkish cliché that an author must "love" his characters; his obligation is rather detachment and thoroughness, which are undermined by anger (as by "indignation" and "compassion," those other social virtues which are often mistaken for literary virtues, though they are appropriate only to the narrow mode of satire). Second, it has been argued that Meredith prepared for a "tragic" ending by some early verbal, imagistic, and symbolic hints; but these in no way counterbalance or even modify the comic tone which is masterfully established by language and event in the first half of the book and which make a comic conclusion seem obligatory. Meredith is truly brilliant in spotting the nexus between love and egotism, between benevolence and love of power; the paternal love that animates Sir Austin's "system" is fused with an *amour propre* that takes over when his love-and-power seems rejected. The loving dictation of another's welfare contains the love of dictation; the subtle but persistent images of deity define the role into which Sir Austin instinctively falls; and the balked father becomes the offended divinity "trying" (Ch. 39), i.e. in this case punishing, the child who follows another love and thus comes under another power. This development is psychologically and morally right. The problem is whether the situation which he has created compels Meredith to keep Sir Austin so rigid in feeling offended and in probing for a surrogate power that disaster is inevitable. I am sure not. Meredith shows the comic way out of the impasse when Sir Austin is trying to dissuade Richard from an excessive response to his adultery and to the man who had engineered it: "Sir Austin detained him, expostulated, contradicted himself, made nonsense of all his theories." He is even "seized with unwonted suspicion of his own wisdom; troubled, much to be pitied . . ." (Ch. 48). This is the true comic solution, and Sir Austin might have been brought to it before it was too late, before his love of power had minimized the power of his love to deflect Richard from melodramatic follies. Meredith has also endowed Richard with a faculty for occasional ironic self-criticism that might have checked his romantic extremism, deep as this is in him. But Richard is a victim, not only of his and his father's folly, but of Meredith's apparently growing need to do Sir Austin in. After having potentially rescued Sir Austin from humorless rigidity, Meredith again turns on him aggressively and in the final chapter belts him around unmercifully. Either through anger or through a misinterpretation of his own role he has surrendered the almost magical comic tone which he might have maintained triumphantly to the end.

III

I hope that all this does not sound picky, for my intention is not to find fault but to give some accounting of certain felt dissonances in fiction. The discussion of the two-tone situation that is "pervasive," the final topic, is less likely to sound captious, for here one cannot point to specific incidents or great divides that encourage the sketching of alternatives. When bitonality is pervasive, it is a given, and one can only identify it and seek just ways of coming to terms with it. First, several preliminaries to set up the immediate context, and then the main subjects, *Moll Flanders* and *Pamela*.

One quick example: the two-tone effect moves toward pervasiveness in Parts I and II of *Gulliver's Travels,* in which Lilliput and to a greater extent Brobdingnag figure principally as parodies of Europe but also as Utopian constructs. The effect is truly pervasive in Part IV, in which initial and persisting sympathy with Gulliver must increasingly compete with the sense of him as disturbed and unreliable. Yet here we should probably refer the basic problem less to duality of tone than to ambiguity of sense.

Representative cases of pervasive two-tone effect without the intellectual equivocalness that begets continual counter-exegeses (as with Gulliver and the Houyhnhnms) occurs in three of Hardy's major novels—*The Mayor of Casterbridge, Tess of the D'Urbervilles,* and *Jude the Obscure.* Here we have clearcut tales of failure and disaster; we know who gets it in the neck (or wins by a neck); there are no *sotto voce* intimations of victory-in-defeat, or other paradoxes or reversals, to render the fictional thought susceptible of opposite interpretations. The bitonality reflects, then, a duality in Hardy's feeling about the sources of misfortune; one kind of feeling leads him into a formal theory, the other rests on his artistic intuition. On the one hand he nags, on the other he perceives and records; on the one hand he blames cosmos and society, on the other he apprehends character as fate. Repeatedly he speaks of the Mayor's off-and-on wife Susan and of his daughter Elizabeth-Jane as miserable victims, even while they are surviving difficulties and in time successfully achieving heart's desires; Hardy is inclined to blame Angel Clare and exonerate Tess, even while imaginatively relating their actions to representative complexities in their natures; and he almost regularly treats Jude and Sue as undeserving victims while giving them emotional and psychic constitutions out of which happier lives could hardly have come. Hardy, then, is both an involved protester (with the advantage of knowing that not much can be done about the imperfections complained of) and a detached artist. He wavers between his grudges and his grasp of things. The former leads through plaint and polemic to a tone of despair; the latter through understood actuality to a tragic tone. Here, however, I want to say just enough to introduce the general issue of pervasive doubleness of tone, and so I only skim over points that I have elaborated elsewhere.[1]

One way of dealing with pervasive bitonality is to assume, in the novelist, some falling short of unity of consciousness (an inevitable human state that in the non-creative appears in day-to-day inconsistencies, "changes of mind," etc.). By "falling short" I do not mean a disastrous shortcoming, because I cannot think of a work that "fails" conspicuously because of an internal incoherence of such origin. On the contrary, the non-achievement of consistency may even help save a writer from himself: if Hardy, for instance, had been able to force his portrayal of life into conformity with his doctrine of hostile forces, he would surely have written lesser novels. Many years ago Kenneth Burke speculated about a division of impulses in the writer, about the co-presence of one belief or commitment which would dictate a formal direction and course, and of another which might give especial vitality to parts of the work at variance with the formal commitment. This can happen when a writer assents, wholeheartedly as far as he knows, to prevailing habits of thought or feeling but also entertains, perhaps unknowingly, sympathies or passions outside the main currents of his time (a pattern often seen in Dickens); or when he registers equally the impulses of a given sensibility or way of life that are actually contradictory or at least seem so as they are sharpened up in the work of art (e.g., mariolatry and *amour courtois* in some romances); when unfettered energies lead to accents that we do not reconcile easily with the apparent overall emphases of the work (such as the snobberies, self-defensiveness, and condescensions that get into Charlotte Brontë heroines); or when doctrinal fixity begets one order of assertions, while imaginative flexibility opens the door to fuller and less simplistic fictional statements (as in Hardy). These are possible ways of accounting for the bitonality that appears in *Moll Flanders* and *Pamela*.

IV

Though the coexistence of two tones may a priori seem unlikely in an eighteenth-century work, the problem is attested to by the quarreling over *Moll Flanders* and the fluctuations of attitude to *Pamela*. In *Moll* the division is between the story of spiritual regeneration (Moll as repentant sinner, and her tale as cautionary guide to error and evil), and the story of worldly success (Moll as pound-and-pence thinker, and finally as rich woman). Interpreters get into trouble when they discover an underlying oneness: at one extreme Moll is said to have convinced us of her goodness, and at the other she is read as a satirized embodiment of bourgeois materialism. Ian Watt has pretty well disposed of such rewritings of the book and has offered a very satisfactory reading: that what appear as inconsistencies to us were not so to the kind of Puritan mind that saw no contradiction between spiritual salvation and material security. My approach differs from his in that I find two tones present in the book and attribute them to Defoe's mixture of talents and convictions (without trying either to derive these from, or to declare them independent of, the historical context).

The two tones have different manifestations. They assume a principal form as early as the fourth and fifth paragraphs of the novel. The fourth ends with Moll's saying that she was "brought into a course of life which was not only scandalous in itself, but which in its ordinary courses tended to the swift destruction both of soul and body." The fifth begins: "But the case was otherwise here. My mother was convicted of felony for a certain petty theft scarce worth mentioning, viz. having an opportunity of borrowing three pieces of fine holland from a certain draper in Cheapside." The tone in the first is moral earnestness; in the second it is amoral flipness. The tone of moral earnestness recurs throughout the novel—in self-criticism (often with verbal self-abuse: "whore," and so on), in reproof of others, in much talk about the "reproaches of my own conscience," in expressions of remorse and assertions of repentance, in allegations of moral improvement (the book ends with Moll's promise that she and her husband will "spend the remainder of our years in sincere penitence for the wicked lives we have lived"). But another tone is created by the more numerous passages in which Moll records all her monetary losses and "profits"; by her treating gains from sex relationships as manna from heaven to be held on to; by the failure of her conduct to match her protestations (she erupts with verbal horror at her incestuous marriage, but for financial reasons feels compelled to keep the secret—"and thus I lived with the greatest pressure imaginable for three years more"); by her sound worldly observations (careless, imprudent mistresses "are justly cast off with contempt"); by an indifference to children (clashing with occasional violent protestations of maternal feeling); by the ease with which she becomes a thief; and particularly by occasional shrewd observations on herself which undercut her didactic pronouncements, frequent as these are ("But it is none of my talent to preach," "I am not capable of reading lectures of instruction"). In a word, there is on the one hand the naive and uncriticized rhetoric of repentance and instruction; on the other, the shrewd moral realism of a worldly old lady who doesn't kid herself ("sometimes I flattered myself that I had sincerely repented"). The result is the bitonality of the reform story and the hardboiled success story, or, in characterological terms, of the willed innocence and the periodically erupting knowingness that we often see together in the ideology-directed minds of our own day.

I believe that the situation is most successfully described in generic terms and that the basic tones in *Moll* are those of two modes that were to have a considerable play in the rest of the century—the picaresque and the sentimental novel. The former, if I am right, is basic in Defoe. The most zestful scenes, the ones in which he is most spontaneous and buoyant, are those in which Moll is skillfully putting things over on others, outside the law but roguish rather than criminal, doing serious hurt to no one, making a small or maybe large profit and then of necessity hurrying on to the next exploit—most notably in the score or so of thieving episodes that begin at midstory, lively and often gay; but also earlier when Moll helps a woman get a husband by a planned manipulation of style and rumors, on the principle that one must "deceive the deceiver"; when Moll gets herself a husband by the same tricky campaigning ("though he might say afterwards he was cheated, yet he could never say afterwards that I had cheated him")—that always has a part in her man-hunting ("it was necessary to play the hypocrite a little more with him"; "I played with this lover as an angler does with a trout"); when rumors of her own wealth lead to her marrying her "Irish" husband, her long-term spouse; when she shifts with such readiness from whore to thief and instinctively masters a new expertise. Others play like games, and we also see Moll as the victim of calculation, experiencing the bad lack that belongs equally to the picaro's diet: picaresque from two perspectives ("double fraud," she calls it in one ironic case). Moll has the complete picaresque spirit, anti-regular in acquisitive action, but wholly orthodox in prejudices and ideas: she is skeptical of Catholics, doesn't think it proper to be married in an inn at night, doesn't paint, will enter liaisons for money but not for "the vice" of it, and of course vociferously supports the conventions and moral codes of her society (a picaro is never a rebel). And it is just a certain excessiveness in this moral line that creates the tone of the sentimental novel. (In not wanting to call *Moll* picaresque, Robert Alter works from the implicit assumption that the novel has to be wholly one thing or another.)

Historically the sentimental novel is several different things. Here I refer to the Puritan version which gratifies a certain consciousness by a happy ending compounded of monetary and moral triumph—a staple of fiction from Richardson to Horatio Alger. It is not necessary to demonstrate how much of this there is in *Moll*. The contrast with *Vanity Fair* is interesting: Thackeray puts the picaresque behind him by turning the rogue's ceremonial comeuppance into substantial punishment, Defoe in the opposite way by having the ceremonial comeuppance (Moll in the jug) superseded by a substantial going up in the world. Was Defoe's climactic crowning of virtue (riches plus verbal self-chastisement for out-of-bounds sex) a penance for his undoubted joy in the picaresque? Defoe was a complex fellow, and even these two dominant tones, as I take them to be, do not altogether exhaust the tendencies one sees in *Moll*. The novel reveals that he was something of the instinctive entrepreneur, of the bookmaker with a very accurate intuition of a public's contradictory yearnings—of its desire, to pick a central case, for clean thoughts and dirty scenes: you can enjoy the illicit lustful embrace when you know that you are only gaining a painful saving knowledge of evils to be shunned. When Moll and a man sleep naked in the same bed for two years, enjoying "all the familiarities" but the ultimate one which would terminate their "innocence," and thus proving that nude loving-kindness need not be naughty, Defoe pulls off a classical piece of pre-free-speech porno. His strong documentary sense is less strip-teasing but still titillating when he gives us three detailed price-schedules for birthing a bastard, and it appears neutrally in his schematic psychology: he is at times not a bad psychologist, but in a logical and theoretical rather than an imaginative way; he has made a tenable paradigm of human responses, but he cannot flesh it out with a convincing imaginative fullness (he knows that man can become habituated to anything, but he so speeds up the process of habituation that we don't believe it).

In *Pamela* there is none of the picaresque (except insofar as there is something delightful in some of Mr. B.'s bedroom schemes) but much of the sentimental that presents virtue (pertinacious rejection of out-of-bounds sex) as the best policy, with dividends in money, marriage, and status. What the opposing tone is, we have to see. The mingled tonality partly accounts for the clashing receptions of *Pamela* over the years: from glorification to routine laudation to indifference to calumniation. "Changing taste," perhaps, but fluctuations of esteem may come less from optical changes in the beholder than from his focusing, at different times, upon different aspects of the work: *Clarissa* has come back, not because our values have changed again, but because we have learned to recognize, in the novel itself, elements that were always there and that indeed, even though not then consciously perceived, must have accounted for its original sweeping impact. The lack of a similar revival of *Pamela* is due partly, of course, to its lesser range and depth and the greater naiveté of its official "message," but more largely, I think, to the fact that its surface is easier to disparage and its non-didactic or nonsentimental substance is less likely to engage us actively than is the desperate extremism of sexual attitude in *Clarissa*. In our day sex plus evil is more appetizing than sex plus human decency. *Pamela* suffers because *Shamela* tells us the kind of thing we like to hear, and hence we trust it despite our knowing that parodies distort part-truths rather than mirror whole ones.

When someone as unpretentious and shrewd as J. B. Priestley takes a moral heroine of two centuries and declares her a "sly chit"— for us a congenial way of describing one who does not quick give it all away for free—it may seem a rather solemn academic perversity to protest that this will never do. But we cannot dismiss Pamela as a moral cheat just because her creator carelessly betrays his view that virginity is an investment. For that was not the only reading of life made by Richardson's not-so-simple eyes. If it had been, he would have lacked the qualities that enabled him to understand the adverse criticism and to make the readjustments that he did make in *Clarissa;* nor, I wager, would *Pamela* have been capable of making the impact that it did make. For, like Hardy a century and a half later, Richardson had an imagination as well as a doctrine; through it he grasped a different life than that of the profit motive, and along with the sentimental created quite a different tone—that of the mature comedy in which human beings through new understanding and alteration earn a stable relationship (rather than having it given them gratis, as in one of the plots of romantic tone). In this sense Pamela and Mr. B. are a link between Congreve's Mirabell and Millamant and Austen's Elizabeth and Darcy—a slender link, granted, because Richardson's humor and taste cannot quite be relied on, but still a dramatization of the awareness that men and women can learn, make concessions as well as demands, and thus reach satisfying *modi vivendi.*

As a matter of fact, Richardson imagined Mr. B. not only as a tedious or sinister seducer but as a bright, repeatedly witty, often charmingly ironic man who can challenge Pamela's rather heavy defensive style with amusing logical tours de force. But Mr. B. is a classical comic figure because he has an *idée fixe* which is at variance with reality: he thinks that as a woman and a servant Pamela is a pushover, and he has to learn that she is an individual. Here Richardson, long before Austen and Meredith, was practicing the best kind of woman's liberation: each woman is to be seen as a person, not as a member of a class. Mr. B.'s task is really harder than Pamela's, for what she has to do is intuit in Mr. B. a latent personality of much greater range than appears in the would-be seducer and rapist. She moves gradually in this direction, responding to a measure of charm that Richardson successfully establishes in Mr. B. (sketching the profound reading of character that he would achieve later in Lovelace). Fairly early in the story, while Pamela in her letters home is formally resolving to flee from the terrors of Mr. B.'s house, she writes more than one P. S. in which she briefly cites reasons for delaying this irrevocable act; in this rather skillful use of the P. S. Richardson suggests the presence in her of an impulse set off from the main body of conscious program, one that she herself does not fully appreciate (Letters XVI, XIX, XXIII). This impulse can be interpreted, of course, as sexiness, love of danger, the shrewd sense that Mr. B. is more of a pushover than she, or sheer snobbery. Since there are different tones in the book, I do not deny such possibilities, but it is entirely consistent with other events to see her as drawn by Mr. B.'s general male attractiveness, which has been made quite real. Richardson's gift is to create in both parties a potential charm that is overlaid by their combat stances (these, by the way, we can read, not as passé morality, but as one symbolization of the war of the sexes); the true power to charm has to be actualized in the surrender of the combat role and the risking of the generous act that has no guaranteed outcome. This is the pattern of conduct that Richardson sees as emerging when the mutual charm survives the rigidities of attack and defense: Mr. B. frees Pamela, risking the loss of her, and Pamela returns voluntarily, risking a renewal of the aggressiveness that she has struggled against. But this rapprochement, far from being imposed by the author as deus ex machina, has been prepared with extraordinary thoroughness.

This tone of the high comedy of sex obviously does not displace the sentimental tone of the didactic elements, but the latter has been so much noticed that it needs no further demonstration here. The comic sense, on the other hand, has not been appreciated, and it does need attention. One of its ingredients, it is worth noting, appeared in Molière: a partial distortion of character by hysterical tendencies. Richardson may or may not detect the hysteria as such. In Pamela there is a certain infusion of it which he seems not to identify; I refer to Pamela's intemperateness in, and even something of a clinging to, the fright and anxiety created by Mr. B.'s bedtime maneuvers, but more particularly to the incredible delays resulting from Pamela's nervousness about changing from an engaged girl to a married woman. Richardson is overly bent on establishing that when it comes to being bedded down, a decent woman shows reluctance, and avoids willingness lest it seem impatience; so he lets Pamela's reluctance drift into the neurotic. On the other hand he gives a magnificent, and wholly knowing, picture of the hysterical in Lady Davers' hostility to Pamela as her sister-in-law: Richardson sets out to demonstrate social snobbery and Pamela's conquest of it, but he virtually loses sight of this didactic project in the portrayal of Lady Davers' unchecked emotions, of their sources in her bringing up and in her past relations with her brother, and of her unwillingness to surrender the morbid pleasure of luxuriating in them. This very long episode late in Part I makes a fine contribution to the mature comic tone which always competes with the sentimental tone for the possession of Richardson's first novel. If we are not aware of it, we miss a genuine source of strength in *Pamela*.

Once more: to speak of the two-tone novel is not really to point to a type of failure. Granted, rightly or wrongly one may regret the replacement of an established tone in this novel or that. But more often one may point to a situation in which an insistent tone is challenged by another which is responsible for our sense of quality in the work: the merits of disunity, so to speak. One thinks of bitonality, then, less as a merit or a demerit than as a fact of artistic life which emerges from a fact of all human life: our characteristic nonachievement of total unity, whether in perspective or feeling or values. Unexceptioned integration occurs, in novels as in people, only at two levels: at a level of very simple organization where, from the beginning, there is no room for complexer modes of response, and, at the other, in very special individuals (persons, fictions) in which greater complexities have by extraordinary discipline or special power been brought into a felt and demonstrable unity (the saint, the demonic being; *Don Quixote, The Princess Casamassima, Doktor Faustus*). In between we may expect to find a considerable range of personalities and fictions marked by the coexistence of tones that are not ideally compatible. We may find this troubling, a sign of shortcoming; or we may find it encouraging that a lesser singleness, which might have become dominant, has been opposed by the entry of a more capacious mood, a larger feeling for the *is* and the *ought* that are the borders of reality. For each work in which bitonality appears the problem is to describe it as lucidly as possible and to assess its impact on total quality. In other words, to acknowledge the presence of bitonality is not to give up the critical problem but to redefine or relocate it. It is to give up the quest of the holy grail of organic oneness—a quest which is sometimes quite valid but which, when it is not, may lead to some torturing of the literary countryside in which the critic rides. Lest he find himself whipping dissident elements into a oneness to which they are not disposed—or recklessly gluing masses of shards into the semblance of an encompassing shapely grail—he might first test for evidence that he has a two-tone situation, if not something still more centrifugal, on his hands. He will have to look out for a tendency to resist the evidence, because admitting tonal non-unity can seem an ignominious retreat from the taxing ultimate critical problem. But if he successfully resists his resistance, he will still, as we have seen, have much to do. Reconciling a sense of quality with an aesthetic situation supposed to be adverse to quality is no small task. It will involve him in deriving merit from spontaneities not checked by a rigidity of aim or thought that is one route to uniformity, i.e. unity, or in discovering how counter-intentions can collaborate, either to bypass the more restricted effect or somehow to reproduce, in the work itself, the consciousness with unresolved tensions, which, as long as these are representative divisions rather than chaotic pressures out of which creation could not come, can create their own kind of vitality.

NOTE

1. In "Hardy's *Mayor* and the Problem of Intention," *Criticism,* 5 (Summer, 1963), 199-213, and *"Gulliver* and Hardy's *Tess:* Houyhnhnms, Yahoos, and Ambiguities," *Southern Review,* 6 N.S. (April, 1970), 277-301.

NARRATIVE DISTANCE, TONE, AND CHARACTER

WALTER ALLEN

In 1857, having some twelve months earlier finished his six years' stint on *Madame Bovary,* Flaubert wrote to Mlle de Chantepie: "The artist should be in his work, like God in creation, invisible and all-powerful: he should be felt everywhere and seen nowhere." In the same year Trollope published *Barchester Towers* and, two years later, George Eliot *Adam Bede.* The historical significance of Flaubert's pronouncement needs no stressing; and the contrast between his novel and those of his English contemporaries is immediate and glaring. In *Adam Bede,* for instance, the novelist is all too visible in the creation; and garrulous too, busily explaining to the reader the precise nature of the creation and its inhabitants, scolding, bidding the reader admire this one, disapprove of that. Moreover, the novelist is here a jealous god, with no nonsense concerning objectivity about her. By contrast with Flaubert, she is, one might say, fussily involved in the depicted action; whereas Flaubert seems to observe his characters from a certain distance and hold them in a God's-eye view. This is most evident, perhaps, in the episode of the agricultural fete; while the degree of distance at which the novelist takes up his stance is indicated in the first paragraphs of the novel, in the description (in Eleanour Marx's translation) of the schoolboy Charles Bovary's hat:

> It was one of those headgears of composite order, in which we can find traces of the bearskin, shako, billycock hat, sealskin cap, and cotton

nightcap; one of those poor things, in fine, whose dumb ugliness has depths of expression, like an imbecile's face. Oval, stiffened with whalebone, it began with three round knobs; then came in succession lozenges of velvet and rabbit-skin separated by a red band; after that a sort of bag that ended in a cardboard polygon covered with complicated braiding, from which hung, at the end of a long thin cord, small twisted gold threads in the manner of a tassel. The cap was new; its peak shone.

The distance, the stance the narrator adopts towards the action, dictates the tone of the novel; and all the comment on the action, which in *Adam Bede* is overt, explicit, articulated by the author herself, is contained in and carried by the tone. For, as Flaubert himself says, God is felt everywhere in *Madame Bovary,* is all-powerful—and invisible; and his presence and his power are the indices of his invisibility. Through the suppression of his own overt personality, he succeeds in his novel to a degree beyond anything George Eliot achieves in hers. Tone is everything. In *Adam Bede,* on the other hand, the narrator's stance shifts, and the tone wavers and changes with it. And George Eliot's personal utterance carries less authority than Flaubert's impersonal tone, for personal utterance reveals the novelist-as-God as all-too-human, possessed of vulgar emotions like sexual jealousy. So far does the distance of the narrator from the action shrink when we are invited to contemplate Hetty Sorrel.

Something like fifty years after the letter to Mlle de Chantepie, Joyce, through Stephen Dedalus, re-stated the Flaubertian attitude in *A Portrait of the Artist as a Young Man:* "The artist, like the God of creation, remains within or behind or beyond or above his handiwork, invisible, refined out of existence, indifferent, paring his finger-nails." The statement is more ambiguous than Flaubert's; I think its tone less certain. If God is "refined out of existence," can He be said to be there at all? If He is, then certainly, as Stephen says, He *is* indifferent, "paring His finger-nails," after, one supposes, washing His hands of the whole business. The ambiguity, the indecisiveness even, is reflected in the novel. Does Joyce the artist-as-God himself know whether he is within or behind or beyond or above his creation? The consequences of this indecision are very different from those of Flaubert's more categorical statement and its dramatization in *Madame Bovary.*

The title of Joyce's novel is obviously important. The novel is not quite a self-portrait: the central character, who is "he," not "I," is in a real sense the only character in the work. And the portrait is not the only portrait of the artist possible; the indefinite article is significant—Henry James called *his* novel *The Portrait of a Lady*. The portrait Joyce paints is no doubt a speaking likeness; yet there remains the problem of the angle of vision, the stance from which we are supposed to see it. This is not a problem that arises in *Ulysses*. There, Stephen is one character among others, among Bloom and Molly and beyond them a host more, including stately, plump Buck Mulligan, who in the first pages pronounces on Stephen: "O, an impossible person!" The other characters comment on Stephen from their various points of view; we see him through their eyes as well as through his own. The other characters cut him, as it were, down to size; we have not only his own valuation of himself but that of others; he is, among other things, "the bullock-befriending bard." But in *A Portrait* there is no one to treat him with such lack of respect. We have to make our own interpretation of him, and everything exists within *his* mind; he is indeed the novel. What is in question is the nature of his mind; and in our interpretation of this, God the novelist, paring His nails in Heaven, does not help us much.

More prosaically, how does Joyce expect us, or intend us, to take Stephen in *A Portrait*? It is a question complicated by factors we don't usually encounter when reading novels. Stephen is a portrait of the artist as a young man executed by the artist himself when a slightly older man, and it is an easy temptation to read the novel as an experiment in autobiography written in the third person—in which case its value will consist largely on the light it throws on the mature artist, the man who wrote *Ulysses*. But to read it in this way is to read it as something other than a novel. The question may be put crudely: How would we interpret the novel if it had not been followed by *Ulysses;* or if Joyce had died immediately after writing it? Would we now be reading it? And if we were, would we see it, technically remarkable though it still is, as existing in its own right as a self-contained work of art? Does it, in fact, exist in its own right when divorced from its author's own life and from *Ulysses*?

The questions focus on Stephen, a very young man who, it seems, is likely to be an artist. Towards how we should see him, Joyce offers little guidance. In his earlier rendering of Stephen, in the *Stephen*

Hero fragment, Joyce the novelist is nearer in his practice to George Eliot than he is to Flaubert: on occasion, he is unambiguously critical of his hero. In *A Portrait,* Joyce follows his own way, like a forgetful or absent-minded or absent God. As one reads the novel, questions confront one. How seriously does Joyce take Stephen; and how seriously does he expect the reader to take him? Is Joyce doing no more than creating the figure of a very clever adolescent? To be more specific, what weight are we to give, for example, to the famous penultimate paragraph of the novel, in which Stephen announces that he is going to "encounter for the millionth time the reality of experience and to forge in the smithy of my soul the uncreated conscience of my race." Is this more than adolescent rodomontade? It is, of course, a diary entry, and a man may be allowed latitude in his diary. All the same, "the millionth time." In ordinary circumstances, in life, one's reaction to Stephen's assertion would be embarrassed silence or something like, "Yeah? Tell us about it, kid!" I suspect that in reading we tend to take it seriously; but we do so only because we know, from later information extraneous to the novel, that Stephen is a representation of the man who was to go on to write *Ulysses* and so conceivably was justified in talking as Stephen does.

What is lacking is evidence of Joyce's attitude towards Stephen. It may be argued that the novel is an exercise in irony. In fact, irony is seldom apparent. It is present, certainly, in Joyce's account of Stephen's discovery that he has no vocation for the priesthood, but not there at all, it seems to me, when his realization of his vocation for the other priesthood of art is being dramatized. That Stephen may be a poet is apparent from the delight and preoccupation with words that he shows from his earliest years; but we are offered only one specimen of his poetry, the villanelle "Are you not weary of ardent ways?" It is a poem of exactly the sort that could be expected of a sensitive, literary-minded undergraduate in the first years of the century, the years in which Joyce was writing *Stephen Hero.* It is too imitative of period fashion to allow us to draw conclusions about Stephen's talent as a poet. But did Joyce recognize this? Is the poem there as evidence of Stephen's promise as a poet or as evidence of his immaturity? If the latter, Joyce's intention is plainly ironic.

Or, again, there is the moment of "epiphany" when, walking along the strand and seeing the girl, skirts ahoist, paddling in the margin of the sea, Stephen discovers his vocation as an artist. The passage has been much admired—wrongly, I think, for reasons Frank O'Connor gives in *The Mirror in the Roadway*. I don't have to say that extremely skilful writing, as the passage is, can still be bad prose. Like much of *A Portrait*, it strikes me as sub-Pater. It is anything but a literal description of the girl and is intended, one imagines, to expose the nature and quality of Stephen's mind at the moment of perception. But our estimate of that will depend largely on our estimate of the nature and quality of the prose—and possibly too on the value we assume Joyce placed upon it. This last, in terms of the novel itself, I do not think we can know. If we think the prose is bad, we may if we wish assume the badness to be deliberate, and then we shall assume the passage is ironic.

Permanently fascinating though it is, *A Portrait of the Artist* can hardly be called a successful novel. Perhaps it is always the reader who completes a novel: Joyce does not give the reader bearings enough to enable him to complete *A Portrait*. This has something to do with the novelist's tone or, in this instance, lack of tone, for the tone is Stephen's, not Joyce's. Tone, I suggest, is the verbal equivalent, the verbal embodiment, of the novelist's point of view or narrative stance. In *A Portrait*, Joyce shifts his stance, on occasion telescopes the distance between himself and the action, prompts us to identify his character with himself.

His failure is the opposite of that we find in another novelist whom we see in the tradition of Flaubert, Conrad, in *The Secret Agent*. Here we are conscious of a novelist's stance that seems altogether too rigid, too inflexible, too intransigent. The irony is total, and totally crushing; and it is impossible for the reader to take Conrad's anarchists, for instance, in any way other than that in which Conrad directs him to take them. They appear at all points in the act, each with his appropriate tag—"The ticket-of-leave man," "Comrade" Ossipon, and so on. They are exhibited always and relentlessly as charlatans, con men on to a good thing; and in the end they are presented as at once ridiculous and, except for the Professor, harmless. They are absurd and contemptible. Yet the consequences of Conrad's tightness of control over his characters are not, perhaps, always what Conrad was working for. The constant reiteration of his anger and contempt may cause the reader to protest against too-muchness and to react against it. It may lead him to reflect that, as a matter of historical fact, professional revolutionaries are not necessarily like Conrad's. Remembering Herzen or Prince Kropotkin or Lenin, he may conclude that Conrad's revolutionaries cannot be taken as representative; and then the work will seem not so much a novel as an extremely powerful dramatized reactionary tract. And he may set *The Secret Agent* side by side for contrast with *The Princess Casamassima*, in which James, as between revolutionaries and the do-gooders of bourgeois society, is magnificently impartial. Conrad, we may think, is too emotionally involved in and therefore too close to the action to be an impartial witness; and powerful and brilliant though it is, the novel suffers.

Bound up with this is the notion of the autonomy of the character in novels, the strong sense we have that in some mysterious way it should be possible, in imagination, to walk round him and inspect from every angle, as though he were a person in life. I don't need to be told that this is an illusion, though I don't think it necessarily a naive one. Rather, it seems to me essential to the novelist's art; without it almost everything else he succeeds in doing will be in vain. It is clear that in *The Secret Agent* the characters are not autonomous. Conrad has over-conditioned our responses to them. Over-conditioned; for of course the novelist's control of our responses to his creations is always necessary. In *Fiction and the Reading Public*, Mrs. Leavis says that "all a novelist need do is to provide bold outlines, and the reader will co-operate to persuade himself that he is in contact with 'real people.' " It is rarely as simple as that, but Mrs. Leavis all the same is describing a rudimentary kind of character-creation which has a necessary place in the novelist's art. But the way in which we co-operate is still governed by the novelist. There is an old gentleman in the *Forsyte Saga* who may be summed up in the phrase, "Nobody ever tells me anything." He says it whenever he appears in the action and says scarcely anything else. He is a "bold outline" if ever there was one. The point is, the reader co-operates in accepting him, in endowing him with life, and does so in precisely the way that Galsworthy knew he would. We all know old gentlemen who say "Nobody ever tells me anything" or something like it, and it is from our acquaintance with them, from our experience of living, that we are able to fill in the bold outline. A vein of associa-

tion has been tapped in us, and we respond to the character as Galsworthy could count on us to do. The character may be rudimentary,
but still the author has controlled our response to it. We are not free
to fill in the outlines as we like.

The control the novelist exercises on his readers depends ultimately
on the stance, the point of view, the distance from the action, that
the novelist adopts; and on his tone, which is the verbal embodiment
of stance, point of view, distance. We know the stance is the proper
one when we feel the characters in the action are free, autonomous.
The stance may be ambiguous and shifting, as Joyce's seems to be in
A Portrait, or too rigid, as Conrad's in *The Secret Agent.* But there
are also those novels in which, intermittently and without warning,
the novelist changes his stance in mid-action, becomes too close to
the action, so that the reader complains that a specific character
"wouldn't have behaved like that." When we say this kind of thing,
are we being naive and confusing literature with life? If a character
is merely the sum total of everything the novelist has told us about
him, of everything he has said, done and felt, why should we believe
the novelist at one moment and not at another?

An instance is Thackeray's treatment of Becky Sharp in *Vanity
Fair.* If we may talk at all of characters as living, Becky must be as
alive as any in fiction. It is precisely because she is so alive, because
she gives so strong and vivid an impression of life, because, in other
words, she has been so magisterially imprinted on our minds by her
creator, that two or three times in the novel we find ourselves refusing to accept the behavior which Thackeray credits her with. We
react towards her as we would to a real person whom we know so
well that we would not hesitate to say that the report of her conduct
at such-and-such a time must be a lie, because it is so "unlike" her.
That we react in this way towards Becky on occasion is in its way a
tribute to Thackeray.

But he seems to lie about her on occasion. There is the incident in
which Becky boxes her son's ears for listening to her sing. Most of
Thackeray's critics have found her behavior here flagrantly out of
character. The phrase "out of character" goes some way towards
explaining why at this point we find her behavior incredible. Our
response to her has been very carefully controlled by the narrator,
so carefully controlled that we are totally unprepared for the behavior

Thackeray attributes to her. Here it seems useful to distinguish between Thackeray the man on the one hand and the narrator, Thackeray's persona, the puppet-master of the action, on the other. The narrator's function is to distance the characters from the author, which is why he is presented as a puppet-master; and when we are dismayed by what seems to be a lack of consistency in Becky, it is due, not to a lack of consistency in her, for she has no life except that given to her by her creator, but to a lack of consistency in the novelist. It is as though Thackeray the man has at this point intruded into the function of the narrator, taken over the distancing role and in a sense abolished it. Something personal, something belonging to the author as a man rather than as a novelist, has broken into the narration. The objective stance has collapsed; and to understand why, it is probable that we have to go back to the novelist's life, to his emotional uneasiness in dealing with the mother-child relationship. It was a relationship that one feels was almost obsessively holy to him, and it is as though, suddenly remembering that Becky is a "bad" woman, he decides she cannot be allowed the normal feelings of a mother. In analyzing his inconsistency in the rendering of Becky, we stumble against the emotional limitations of Thackeray the man that impose limitations on Thackeray the artist.

A rather different and perhaps more complex instance of the effects of a novelist's change of stance during the course of a novel may be found in *The Mill on the Floss,* in the character of Stephen Guest and his relationship with Maggie Tulliver. There is no question of George Eliot's success in creating the illusion of Stephen's reality. Dr. Leavis, who is not one to use words like "living" or "real" of fictitious characters, says that "he is sufficiently 'there' to give the drama a convincing force." Indeed, the very violence of the reaction towards him of some Victorian critics shows that he is quite triumphantly "there." One remembers Swinburne:

> The man, I suppose, does not exist who could make for the first time the acquaintance with Mr. Stephen Guest without an incipient sense of a twitching in his fingers and a tingling in his toes at the notion of a contact between Maggie Tulliver and a cur so far beneath the chance of promotion to the notice of his horsewhip or elevation to the level of his boot.

Why, then, our feelings of dissatisfaction with Guest? Simply because he is the man with whom Maggie is made to fall in love and by whom she is swept off her feet. He is the character George Eliot has invented in order that Maggie shall be faced with a moral choice: Maggie is tacitly engaged to Philip Wakem, and Guest to her cousin Lucy. In view of the way in which George Eliot has conditioned us to accept her rendering of Maggie, it is difficult indeed to believe that she could have fallen so disastrously for a man like Stephen.

The appeal here is not to life; we are concerned with imaginary beings living in a mimic world. That in life it does happen that young women of the spiritual ardor even of a Maggie Tulliver are sometimes sexually attracted to and deluded by men inferior to themselves, is irrelevant. Watts-Dunton defended Stephen and George Eliot's presentation of him on those grounds:

> Perhaps after all the novelist knew perfectly well what she was about, and intended to give an illustration of the sharp saying sometimes attributed to Thackeray, that "no woman could ever really distinguish between a cad and a gentleman."

It was chivalrous perhaps, of Watts-Dunton to make the defense; but the truth, surely, is that it is George Eliot who is deluded by Stephen, she who has failed to distinguish between a cad and a gentleman. Admittedly, there is a technical weakness in the novel. Stephen comes into the action very late, and we are insufficiently prepared for him and for the role he is to play. Nevertheless, it was, to borrow the sharp saying George Eliot uses in her analysis of Lydgate in *Middlemarch*, a "spot of commonness" in herself that led to the creation of Stephen, one she uncritically transmitted to Maggie. However convincing Stephen Guest may be as a character, in his role in the novel he is inadequate *vis-à-vis* Maggie. The upshot of the inadequacy is to force us to question whether we haven't been wrong all the time in our estimate of her, or rather—and this is as bad—whether George Eliot hasn't been wrong. In fact, it is, it seems to me, George Eliot in whom temporarily we lose faith, not Maggie, for if a novel is told well enough, we do, in Lawrence's phrase, trust the tale and not the teller.

George Eliot is guilty of a similar though less serious shortening of the distance between herself as novelist and her characters in *Middlemarch*. It is not easy to be happy about the realization of Ladislaw. By comparison with the other characters, the impression he makes is faint. He is the representative, like Philip Wakem in *The Mill on the Floss*, of the free spirit, of the values of a larger, more disinterested world; he is baffling because he seems to be exempt from the inexorable moral laws to which George Eliot's characters are normally subjected. Certainly he seems inadequate as a foil to Dorothea. As a creator of what may be called the exclusively masculine male, such as Lydgate, George Eliot has no superior, but she is much less successful with male characters she more obviously approves of. Ladislaw, one can't help feeling, would be much more convincing for the addition of a few spots of commonness. Ladislaw, one concludes, was conceived and is realised too uncritically.

One reason, then, for the shrinkage of distance between action and narrator can be the irruption into the narrator of the man behind him. Sometimes, the result is the virtual disappearance of the distinction between the central character and the narrator, with a consequent confusion of tone arising from the novelist's inability to determine or to maintain his narrative stance. This seems to throw light on the comparative failure of many novels which continue to interest and indeed fascinate us partly because their achievement does not in the last analysis measure up to our strong sense of what should have been achieved. An instance of this is Gissing's *New Grub Street*. It has always been Gissing's most popular novel, and there are good reasons why this is so. It is a work of formidable intelligence, and, as a representation, however partial, of the state of writers and writing, of novelists and the novel, at a given decade in English literary history, it is unique. It is also a study of the corroding effects of poverty at the respectable level and of the extraordinary difficulties facing the sensitive man, the artist, in the pursuit of happiness in marriage. But none of this makes the novel in the end entirely satisfactory, and this seems due to the very personal nature of the work. That Gissing was aware of the danger of this and took safeguards against it is plain from the way in which he distributes himself, at it were, and his own experience of life through so many of the characters; and the way also in which he presents what might be called possible versions of himself. His American experiences he bestows on Whelpdale; born a generation earlier, he could have been Alfred Yule; if he had been a simpler, less arrogant man, he might have been Biffen; and he could imagine his opposite, Milvain, the new "professional" writer. But the Gissing figure in the novel is the unsuccessful Reardon, "a proud, morose, sensitive man living in the shadows," to quote from John Gross's introduction to a recent edition. Reardon is not by any means a complete self-portrait, but, as Gross goes on to say, in this echoing the majority of critics who have written on the novel, "With Reardon there is the constant risk of Gissing's self-pity welling up and taking over." Gissing does not refrain from criticizing Reardon and constantly castigates his self-pity. Nevertheless, the sense of self-pity remains, together with a strong sense of identity between central character and his creator. The reason for this, it seems to me, is that there is too little differentiation between the tone of the narrative prose and Reardon's in his dialogue and reported thoughts. Both are harshly sardonic, and it is Reardon's values that pervade the novel. In other words, narrator and character are too close to each other, and the effect is that the novel appears as the powerful dramatization of a special case, Gissing's, rather than as a work that can be considered representative in the full sense.

It is useful to compare New Grub Street with the novel that immediately followed it, the less well-known but in my view finer and more successful Born in Exile. The hero, Godwin Peake, is similarly the "Gissing man," "a proud, morose, sensitive man living in the shadows." Peake's life, like Reardon's, is in obvious respects based on Gissing's; but because Peake is not presented as a novelist, there is a much greater distance between him and his creator. In the boldness and freedom of his thought, he is intellectually impressive, and this is one of the triumphs of the novel; but his greater stature, the authority he carries in himself, comes from the feeling one has that he has much more autonomy as a character than is permitted to Reardon. He is conceived of from a greater distance.

In English fiction, the master of narrative distance, the novelist whose stance never wavers and whose tone is constant, is Jane Austen. We see her characters as autonomous, and the illusion of freedom that they have for us lies in their complete accordance with the laws of the imaginary world that govern their being. It is a world in which the aesthetic order exactly mirrors the moral order. It is this that prompts our unquestioning assent and gives Jane Austen her immense authority. She is perfect, and partly so because she always writes within her limits, and limits are essential to art. They involve restriction and exclusion, and Jane Austen's are almost comically different from those of, say, Hardy or Lawrence, whom no one would dream of calling perfect novelists and yet at their best show remarkable mastery of narrative distance.

In large measure, this seems to come from the kind of novels they write. Hardy—and the contrast with Jane Austen is obvious—aims at something like the universal. Tess is not only a young woman living in a certain place at a certain time, she is also the nineteenth-century counterpart of a sequence of young women through the ages, the victim of Stonehenge, the doomed victim, of all who may be summed up in the image of the trapped bird. Hardy's characters are conceived in history. The significance of Egdon Heath in *The Return of the Native* is the stock example; but one recalls also the significance of the Roman amphitheatre in *The Mayor of Casterbridge* and the part played by classical antiquity and the association of Christminster with Jerusalem in *Jude the Obscure*. As Forster says, Hardy conceives "his novels from an enormous height." This enables him to see events at various distances as occurring as it were almost simultaneously. The opening paragraphs of Chapter IV of *Tess* provide a simple example:

> The sun, on account of the mist, had a curious sentient, personal look, demanding the masculine pronoun for its adequate expression. His present aspect, coupled with a lack of all human forms in the scene, explained the old-time heliolatries in a moment. One could feel that a saner religion had never prevailed under the sky. The luminary was a golden-haired, beaming, mild-eyed, God-like creature, gazing down in the vigour and intentness of youth upon an earth that was brimming with interest for him.
>
> His light, a little later, broke through chinks of cottage shutters, throwing stripes like red-hot pokers upon cupboards, chests of drawers, and other furniture within; and awakening harvesters who were not already astir.
>
> But of all ruddy things that morning the brightest were two broad arms of painted wood, which rose from the margin of a yellow cornfield by Marlott village. They, with two others below, formed the revolving Maltese cross of the reaping-machine, which had been brought to the field on the previous evening to be ready for operations this day. The paint with which they had been smeared, intensified in hue by the sunlight, imparted to them a look of having been dipped in liquid fire. . . .

Presently there arose from within a ticking like the love-making of the grasshopper. The machine had begun. . . .

A vision of the pristine earth in which the sun is God; a glimpse of the interior of a nineteenth-century English peasant's cottage; a close-up of a clumsy machine of the agricultural revolution: together, they convey a powerful sense of the unity, almost the oneness, of things. The sun is a god who is very much like a man; the reaping-machine is very much like an animal, even perhaps like a human animal. The prose—and it is characteristic Hardy—is not elegant. It is slow, and meditative certainly, and somewhat clumsy and uncouth; and to this its authenticity seems somehow related. It is not, I think, the prose of the novelist as God. Hardy is not God, not the President of the Immortals. The narrator of his novels is not even quite Hardy himself but is, one might say, God's observer. He watches the President of the Immortals at his sport but he is not omniscient, as the President of the Immortals must be assumed to be. His role is much like that of Tiresias in *The Waste Land* ("I who have sat by Thebes below the wall"). He has suffered all things; he has foresight and hindsight; but he has surmises rather than complete knowledge. In Hardy's novels, we are faced with a "formula of alternative possibilities," to use the phrase that Yvor Winters applied to Hawthorne. After her marriage, Tess in the carriage tells Angel, "I must have seen it in a dream." If she has, it is, according to Angel, the D'Urberville coach she has dreamed of, "that well-known superstition of this county about your family when they were very popular here." And then the D'Urbervilles themselves. John Durbeyfield seizes upon the legend of his ancestry, to Tess's destruction. But, as Hardy shows, the legend is of a kind common enough throughout rural England. "There's the Billetts and the Drenkhards and the Greys and the St. Quintins and the Hardys and Goulds, who used to own the lands for miles down this valley; you could buy 'em all up now for an old song a'most. Why, our little Retty Priddle here, you know, is one of the Paridelles—the old family that used to own lots o' the lands out by King's-Hintock now owned by the Earl o' Wessex, afore even he or his was heard of."

Hardy's narrator may know or may surmise but he does not invariably understand. And this leads to some of Hardy's greatest triumphs as a novelist. I am thinking specifically of the rendering of Sue

Bridehead in *Jude*. She is understood neither by Jude nor by Phillotson, and she does not understand herself. It seems to me uncertain whether Hardy understands her. But the modern reader does—and recognizes in her one of the most "real" characters in fiction, "real" precisely because incapable of being reduced to a simple phrase or formula. In grappling with her nature, the reader, through his efforts to understand her, endows her with life. With Sue we are in the presence of a foreshadowing of what is now a not uncommon type of woman who, in his own day, Hardy could explain only by reference to something like "the ache of modernism." It is as though Hardy, surveying the world of his fiction from an enormous height, was thereby empowered to see not only what was and what had been but also what was to be.

Something not so dissimilar to Hardy's narrative stance may be seen in *The Rainbow;* and this is the more striking because in *Sons and Lovers* there is a patent confusion, akin to Gissing's in *New Grub Street*, between the tone of the narrator and that of the central character, Paul Morel. They are altogether too close: the narrator's view of Walter Morel and of Miriam is Paul's, and we feel that justice is done to neither. The author's subjectivity has taken over. *The Rainbow*, however, which is Lawrence's most Hardyesque novel, is, like Hardy's fiction, conceived from a great height. This is clear from the first pages, which set out a traditional, almost static world, a world before the fall into industrialism when the male of the species, Lawrence suggests, lived in harmony with the soil. Then the Fall: the sinking of the mine, the cutting of the canal, and the progressive alienation of the Brangwens from the earth and the community which culminates in the experiences of Ursula. The prelude and the chapters that follow force us to take each successive generation of Brangwens in the nineteenth century as somehow representative of the men and women of their time. With Ursula we reach Lawrence's own generation. She is not Lawrence, though in creating her he must have drawn upon his own experiences of the teachers' training college at Nottingham and of teaching itself. But she is the Lawrence figure in the novel; and she is typically a Lawrence figure in that she lives through experiences which will not be understood, explained, or rationalized until after the events that generate the experiences are over. Experience, the living moment of experience, is the great thing; and she is encompassed by a penumbra of mystery, almost of inexplicability. It is in this that her disturbing actuality lies, and here she is akin to Sue Bridehead, despite the fact that Sue is seen from the outside, whereas with Ursula we are always partly within her experiencing sensibility.

The mystery—and the reality of the mystery, which the reader feels, as well as Ursula—are communicated by what we can only call symbols: the constant use of moonlight throughout the novel, the arch, whether of Lincoln Cathedral or the rainbow itself, the stampeding horses that terrify Ursula at the end of the novel. This symbolism, which seems to belong both to the characters and to the world external to them, to be the subjective rendering of an objective reality, is counterpointed against an acutely observed representation of the actual world, the world of the coalpits, the slum school, and the university college. Looking back to Hardy, one can see all this as an extension of his way of creating Tess, whose progress is lived in terms of contrasted seasons and landscapes and in terms too of an almost ritual pattern of history.

At the end, of Tess and Jude and The Rainbow alike, we are left, I believe because of the magnitude of the height from which the novels have been conceived, with the knowledge that a character is the product not simply of what he has said and done and thought but of everything else in the novel. The imagery of birds and of traps is part of our knowledge of Tess, inseparable from her, as the image of the stampeding horses is part of our knowledge of Ursula. I don't doubt that something like this is true of all successful characters in fiction: it is more easily seen in novels like Hardy's and Lawrence's than in, say, Jane Austen's. One recalls Wilson Knight's description of Shakespearian drama, a description that seems to me to cover equally well the novel, however realistic: "An expanded metaphor, by means of which the original vision has been projected into forms roughly correspondent with actuality. . . ." In a novel, when characters are "projected into forms roughly correspondent with actuality," more often than not this is a function of their creators' narrative distance and of the tone which is its linguistic equivalent.

ILLUSION, POINT OF VIEW, AND MODERN NOVEL-CRITICISM

RICHARD HARTER FOGLE

Surely more novels and more about novels have been published in the twentieth century than in all other centuries together. We have seen strong efforts to develop a novelistic theory comparable to our traditional theories of poetry and drama, and also strong and continual suggestions that the novel does not exist. How does one find his way in the confusion of this vast literature?

Assuming, perhaps brashly, that the novel does exist, I can only define it as a fictional prose narrative of substantial length, thus relying simply upon observation of the body of works that have commonly been called novels. In addition, a *good* novel is characterized by liveliness and coherence, which are the primary concerns of the critic as opposed to the mere expositor. Literary criticism—and I here avow that I am speaking with great abruptness and presumption—is made up of a relatively few traditional principles, such as unity, intensity, interest, and the like, among which "liveliness" and "coherence" are appropriate variants. Correspondingly, in imaginative literature, including the novel, there is no essential progression in the long view, although there can be a limited development; as, for example, one would not maintain that the English novel sprang full-armed from the brow of Daniel Defoe.

A good novel is, to synonymize the terms liveliness and coherence, an artistic imitation of reality that is somehow more "real" and less visibly formal than poetry and drama, though less immediate than drama that is actually presented. We observe that drama as words in a book is more formal, with more obvious and troublesome conventions, than is fiction proper. Thus novelistic imitations of drama, like James's *The Awkward Age* or the works of Henry Green and Ivy Compton-Burnett, strain the novel's generally spacious bounds, and the experiment sacrifices more in liveliness and reality than it can show as gain.

Clearly, most significant novelists have tried to express reality, and have been ambitious of breaking through old barriers to arrive at (with designed tautology) "the real truth." *Tristram Shandy* was a radical absurdist document. Herman Melville strained hard at the fictional leash, and anticipated Gide's *Counterfeiters* in his *Pierre* by writing a novel about writing a novel. His hero struggles hard to tell the deep truth, in an agonizing battle with fictional form and convention, just as Melville was doing. Neither, one must say, got very good results, but they tried. Howells presented his new American realism with a triumphant sense of revelation, as did Mark Twain in his different fashion—we remember his devastating attack upon *The Leatherstocking Tales*. Later, we recollect the sad anti-heroics of Gissing's *New Grub Street,* where honest novelists are slain by the reality they picture; and the dark polemics of naturalism, which was convinced of its unique rectitude.

Proust's reality was both strikingly new and artistically successful. His world possessed a new dimension, time, and correspondingly a new and dynamic conception of character. The Baron de Charlus, for example, is revealed to us by little and little over a period of years as he is seen and apprehended by the narrator, Marcel, a detective of souls whose inferences are sometimes wrong and need to be corrected. Meanwhile, in addition to Marcel's developing knowledge of him, Charlus undergoes a complex development in himself, which must be reckoned with. Joyce dissolved reality into flux in *Ulysses* and *Finnegans Wake,* while he abolished the barrier between reality and fiction by making language itself the ultimate reality.

Ulysses evoked T. S. Eliot's famous critique, which announced the death of the novel and of narrative itself on the grounds that significant external action is no longer possible in the modern world. Meanwhile, however, many notable fictional structures have been built: a reality of the masses by Jules Romains in his *Men of Good Will;* the music of time by Anthony Powell; the space-time word-paintings of Lawrence Durrell's *Alexandria Quartet;* and, of course, many another, down to the *reductio ad absurdum* of the new French novel, of which a recent reviewer has said, "The category of the Work is up for abolition and so is that of the Work's former owner, the Writer. Before too long, or so we must expect, the last human actor will be able to slip into the wings and leave language to get on with things on its own."[1] The last reality of all, *post quam nihil!*

The novelists have deceived us, however, with their "realities." It is, of course, their business to do so, but it is the business of the critic not to be deluded into taking their fictional worlds for realities. Criticism takes leave of the writer in the matter of final judgment, and it goes by its sense of the whole. It does not deal with the most recent theory of consciousness, or concept of the universe; the value of a novel consists in the liveliness and coherence of its imaginative world, and not in its correspondence with the latest scientific findings. It is the reader's imaginative sense of the world with which the novel must cope. As Wordsworth put the case in poetry, "If the time should ever come when what is now called science, thus familiarized to men, shall be ready to put on, as it were, a form of flesh and blood, the poet will lend his divine spirit to aid the transfiguration, and will welcome the being thus produced as a dear and genuine inmate of the household of man."[2]

As regards the legitimate concerns of reader and critic the universe may be a pint of beer, as the Devil has it in a John Collier story:

> They proceeded with the speed of rockets to the northeast corner of the universe, which George now perceived to be shaped exactly like a pint of beer, in which the nebulae were the ascending bubbles. He observed with alarm a pair of enormous lips approaching the upper rim of our space. "Do not be alarmed," said the Devil. "That is a young medical student called Prior, who has failed his exam three times in succession. However, it will be twenty million billion light years before his lips reach the glass, for a young woman is fixing him with her eye, and by the time he drinks all the bubbles will be gone, and all will be flat and stale."[3]

The passage is liberally endowed with what Henry James called "solidity of specification" and Pooh-Bah "corroborative detail, intended to give artistic verisimilitude." For Collier's fictional purposes the universe *is* a pint of beer, and he makes the reader swallow it.

The point underlying these observations is doubtless a truism, but its application is crucially important to serious students of the novel and its literature, which is vast and increasing. We need a criticism that avoids the fatal pendulum swing, as each age and fashion repudiates the claims of its predecessor and presents the new claims of fervid novelists and the commentators who are taken in by them. The problem belongs, of course, to literature and art in general, and not merely to the novelist and novels. One would be done with the recurrent brutality of fashions, manifested not merely in popular reviewing but in many well-meaning and laborious books, presenting new and distorted revelations. One forgives the individual instance, but boggles at the two-hundredth repetition of it. "Nothing is more disgusting," as Sydney Smith said of oratorios, than the cumulative impact of critical confusions.

The ideal criticism would view its subject genially[4] and comprehensively, conquering the Time-Spirit by giving him his due. It would accept the legitimate claims of each age, and assess its works by appropriate criteria. This is not to say that all literary ages are equally good, but rather that they usually have their own particular qualities. The twentieth century is unequalled in portrayals of the flux of consciousness, and the interplay of this consciousness with external perceptions. William Styron's brilliant *Confessions of Nat Turner* is anachronistic—which does not hurt it as a novel—in that no one of the narrator's time could have created the interwoven sensations, images, and emotions of Styron's fictional vision. And no one of the nineteenth century, say, could possibly have created the world of William Faulkner, with its multiple refractions of the psyche and Yoknapatawpha. On the other hand, no one today could achieve the typical solidity and centrality of the great Victorian novelists, whose characters possess the identity that we are so anxiously seeking. It may be that flux and solidity are mutually exclusive.

Henry James's "Art of Fiction" is assuredly one of the greatest documents in English on the problems of the novel, and more beneficent in its effects than the subtle prefaces to his New York Edition. It is at once graceful and decisive, "genial" and discriminating. Though addressed to writers, it is enormously helpful and encouraging to critics, and indeed to all serious novel-readers. Not even James, however, was immune to fate and the fallacy of progress. It would seem that almost all original and productive statements have potential harmfulness, and all doctrines carry in themselves the seeds of decay as well as of generation. In his rich, positive essay there is one small but dolorous stroke at the devoted head of Anthony Trollope, from which has stemmed a powerful negative influence which in turn has spawned a code of legalisms.

Organic form is the chief theme of "The Art of Fiction." A novel is a living thing, one and indivisible. Distinctions of type are superficial and inept, as for instance the familiar nineteenth-century distinction between the novel and the prose-romance: except "for the pleasantness of the thing," Hawthorne's *Blithedale Romance* is a meaningless title. In the internal structure of the novel there are no essential divisions between the elements of narrative, dialogue, and description, since each contributes to and is inseparable from the development of the others. Critical judgment should be correspondingly organic; it is born in the reader's *liking*, which grows from the inherent interest of the work. James, one would note, dismisses much as beneath or foreign to this liking, with implications for the critic, who is not called upon to discuss what is foreign to him. The novelist, on his side, must be granted his donnée, must be allowed his ground and vantage point.

The novel is by all means to be "realistic." Undoubtedly the novelist should keep a notebook for his observations, as Mr. Besant prescribes (and James urbanely agrees), but his reality must spring from his own sensibility, his intelligence, and his creative imagination. A novel should *seem* real; "solidity of specification" is vital to the illusion that it gives reality, but this solidity is a productive inference, and not of literal observation. What is fundamental is that the novelist should be "one on whom nothing is lost." Over all, then, "The Art of Fiction" is uniquely fertile and rich: but there remains the one slight cut at Trollope, the only general attack on a particular novelist in James's essay. And it opens the way for precisely the wrong kind of analytical criticism, and for James's great, undesired influence as a Mosaic law-giver of "thou shalt nots."

What is this truly horrifying utterance? "Certain accomplished novelists," says James, have a habit of giving themselves away which must often bring tears to the eyes of people who take their fiction seriously. I was lately struck, in reading over many pages of Anthony Trollope, with his want of discretion in this particular. In a digression, a parenthesis, or an aside, he concedes to the reader that he and this trusting friend are only "making believe." He admits that the events he narrates have not really happened, and that he can give his narrative any turn the reader may like best. Such a betrayal of a sacred office seems to me, I confess, a terrible crime; it is what I mean by the attitude of apology, and it shocks me every whit as much in Trollope as it would have shocked me in Gibbon or Macaulay.

James is doubtless less shocked than he pretends to be. Indeed in his memorial essay he praises Trollope roundly. Nevertheless he is vigorously chastising Trollope for destroying his fictional illusion by inconsistency in point of view, specifically by way of editorial intrusion. Now Trollope was and is still famous for his unique power in creating the illusion of reality, and I would reassert this gift from my own experience in reading him. It may be that James as a more fastidious and expert reader than most was raising the critical standard for fiction permanently by pointing out for the first time a basic flaw that no one else had noticed in Trollope and other well-reputed writers. I do not think so. He was instead establishing a rule like the famous "three unities," the observance of which is a nicety to be duly appreciated, but not a principle like unity itself.

On the contemporary evidence of Nathaniel Hawthorne, who was vitally interested in the problem of artistic illusion, Trollope's novels are "just as real as if some giant had hewn a great lump out of the earth and put it under a glass case." In 1918 Max Beerbohm said, "Reading him, I soon forget that I am reading about fictitious characters and careers; quite soon do I feel that I am collating intimate memoirs and diaries. For sheer conviction of truth, give me Trollope." ("Servants," in *And Even Now*). Hawthorne and Beerbohm were very far from being unsophisticated readers. It might be argued, contrary to the bases of my own argument, that Hawthorne was pre-Jamesian and primitive, but no such assertion can be made of Beerbohm, author of "The Mote in the Middle Distance," the finest parody of James in existence,[5] and his faithful and impassioned admirer.[6]

Despite his putative betrayals, then, many have attested that by some means or other Trollope succeeded in achieving a strong illusion of reality. Maps have been made of Barsetshire, and Angela Thirkell appropriated his characters and locale, perhaps his principal theme as well, for her own twentieth-century chronicle of English country society. We appear to be presented with irreconcilable disagreements, and for theorists it is James and the post-Jamesian critics who have prevailed, despite vigorous defense by Victorian specialists.

How this came to be is too long a tale to recount. Briefly, James went on emphasizing and refining his theory of point of view, and Percy Lubbock and others carried on the work. Norman Friedman has provided a classic summary of the process in his essay on "Point of View in the Novel: The Development of a Critical Concept."[7] The chief issue that arises devolves from the question, does the development of this concept represent an absolute advance in the novel and in criticism of the novel? Mark Schorer's well-known "Technique as Discovery" is perhaps the most memorable assertion that this development *is* an absolute advance.

With Trollope as instance, there can be a confusion between fictional illusion and the particular kind of consistency that we associate with "point of view," and the seed of this confusion is in James's "Art of Fiction." The problems of illusion are of course traditional; indeed, they are canvassed at length in Aristotle's *Poetics* in connection with artistic imitation. In the nineteenth century Samuel Taylor Coleridge evolved an elaborate theory of illusion before James, who, as J. A. Ward has shown, had decided affinities with Coleridge, particularly as an organicist and proponent of organic unity.[8] Coleridge and James agree, as perhaps we all agree, in locating value in essential imaginative truth and consistency; a work must above all be true to itself: "Nothing can permanently please, which does not contain in itself the reason why it is so, and not otherwise."[9] Coleridge's theory was, like Aristotle's, drawn from the problems of drama, although he applied it to narrative poetry and the novel as well. His views, then, were somewhat less specialized than James's. The chief difference between them is Coleridge's greater interest in "effect," the effect of a play or a poem or a novel upon an audience or reader, together with the assumptions that the latter bring to bear.

Coleridge arrives at his definition by way of dream, which he takes to represent the highest theoretical degree of illusion. Dream interposes no critical obstacles, since "its nature consists in a suspension of the voluntary, and, therefore, of the comparative power. . . . Our state while we are dreaming differs from that in which we are in the perusal of a deeply interesting novel in the degree rather than in the kind." In sleep, however, "we pass at once by a sudden collapse into this suspension of will and the comparative power: whereas in an interesting play, read or represented, we are brought up to this point, as far as it is requisite or desirable, gradually, by the art of the poet and the actors; and with the consent and positive aidance of our own will. We *choose* to be deceived." He goes on to state the consequences for willed and conscious art: "The rule, therefore, may be easily inferred. Whatever tends to prevent the mind from placing it[self] or from gradually being placed in this state in which the images have a negative reality must be a defect, and consequently anything that must force itself in the auditor's mind as improbable, not because it *is* improbable (for that the whole play is foreknown to be) but because it cannot but *appear* as such." Elsewhere he remarks that "Each part [should be] proportionate, tho' the whole perhaps impossible."[10]

Coleridge's idea of illusion thus involves collaboration between writer and reader, in which each has his role to play. Illusion is complex in other ways. As his word "gradually" implies, the experiencing of illusion need not be total or at all points of the same intensity; it is mobile and complexly organized ("proportionate"). Indeed, he strongly suggests that the most valuable illusion is a synthesis of various elements and degrees, the less probable supporting and enhancing the more probable. It is "the perception of identity and contrariety, the least degree of which constitutes *likeness,* the greatest absolute difference; but the infinite gradations between these two form all the play and all the interest of our intellectual and moral being."[11] He implies that an illusion evenly maintained would be self-defeating; illusion should arise from delicate gradations and subordinations.

Finally, Coleridge reflects that "the consciousness of the poet's mind must be diffused over that of the reader or spectator; but he himself, according to his genius, elevates us, and by being *always* in keeping prevents us from perceiving any strangeness, tho' we feel great exaltation."[12] To transpose, as seems reasonable enough, "poet" and "drama" into "novelist" and "novel," the introduction of "the poet's mind" produces questions of style, manner, and tone in the relation of the narrator to what he narrates. James would, I think, have been far from disagreeing, yet post-Jamesian criticism tends to promulgate absolute illusion, and in consequence to eliminate the narrative voice. Doubtless Joyce, with his great demands upon the reader and upon language, has been the most influential exponent of absolute illusion.

The case of Trollope is particularly apt for our problem, from the violations attacked by James and the virtues praised by Hawthorne and Beerbohm. Certainly few writers have been more confiding and "intrusive" than Trollope. He seems positively to disperse his illusion deliberately, in repeated asides to his reader. In *Dr. Thorne,* for example, he worries openly about the legal accuracy of Mary Thorne's inheritance of the great fortune of Sir Roger Scatcherd, a vital event for the plot. Even at the end of the book he cannot let it alone. "If Frank became tenant in tail, in right of his wife, but under his father, would he be able to grant leases for more than twenty-one years? and if so, to whom would the right of trover belong? As to flotsam and jetsam—there was a little property, Mr. Critic, on the sea-shore—that was a matter that had to be left unsettled at the last." He counts the moments till his job is completed. "And now I find that I have not one page—not half a page—for the wedding-dress. But what matters? Will it not all be found written in the columns of the Morning Post?" "And now," he begins his last paragraph, "we have but one word left for the doctor." We recollect, too, the story that Trollope killed off his great Mrs. Proudie in *The Last Chronicle of Barset* in response to a casual criticism he overheard in a club. All this does sound rather frivolous by the lofty standards of James.

Trollope's strengths are harder to expound than his imputed weaknesses. A common and within its limits illuminating way of accounting for the power of the great Victorian novelists is to emphasize their preoccupation and their success with living characters which strongly engaged their imaginations. Arthur Mizener says of Trollope's people that "they were all so intimately alive for him that he judged them with the sympathy most of us reserve for ourselves alone, and what he cared about most was the endless delight of their existence itself. Whenever Mrs. Proudie enters the bishop's study firm in her ignorance and her determination to manage the diocese, whenever Archdeacon Grantly angrily takes up a position even he knows he is too kind-hearted to stick to, whenever Mr. Crawley tries and fails again to control his heroic vanity, the reader feels Trollope's imagination catching fire."[13]

True, and one could enlarge the catalogue indefinitely, to include even Trollope's butts and villains. The greasy Mr. Slope of *Barchester Towers* is indomitable and entertaining to the last. Ferdinand Lopez, the dark, unscrupulous scoundrel who wrecks the happiness of a county family in *The Prime Minister,* and even George Vavasor, the "wild beast" of *Can You Forgive Her?* (a most confiding title) are shown sympathetically in their own terms as well as from outside. It is not, however, to the purpose to speak here at length of Trollope in himself, but only as an example. Briefly, his characters are at the heart of his illusion of reality, but they arise from an intricate understanding that has been most carefully and laboriously established. They are more important than their external actions, and Trollope reveals their potentialities for other actions in other circumstances— thus his tentativeness and the "violations" that so distress James. His apparent casualness is his donnée, the ground he requires to construct his illusion, in which a confessed unreality is used to enhance the reality that matters.

Our concern is with fictional illusion; yet more largely with the total criticism of the novel. We are engaged in distinguishing *illusion* from *point of view:* and in the process, perhaps unfairly, interpreting the chief issue of point of view as *editorial intrusion,* or intrusion by the author. "Intrusion" is far from a simple or spontaneous method. Fielding was its first great master in English, and from Fielding onwards many novelists took upon themselves the responsibility of acting as ingratiating and persuasive masters of ceremonies. Thackeray was perhaps unfortunate in presenting himself as puppet-master. Fielding was vigorous and graceful and, it may be, unsurpassable. Hawthorne, equally graceful, was so adept that readers were sometimes outraged to find that Hawthorne the man was much less bland than his persona. Trollope is to my mind more sure-footed than any of his great contemporaries. Thackeray sometimes hectors, sometimes whines at us, George Eliot is too steadily intense, and immoderate Dickens over-persuades. Trollope takes us along with him with seldom a slip or unevenness.

As in Coleridge's illusion-theory, these older novelists assumed a rather complicated state of mind in their readers, including a considerable tolerance of the fictionality of fiction. It has frequently been suggested that they were able to assume much more about their readers than is possible to any modern novelist. To come back, at any rate, to Coleridge, his theory was a subtle and complex reconciliation of opposite mental states. His illusion was a copula between *delusion,* in which the fiction is taken as literal truth, and *disbelief,* in which the fiction is not at all confused with truth. From this comes his famous phrase, so cautiously balanced, "that willing suspension of disbelief for the moment, which constitutes poetic faith."[14] As has been shown, he conceives of a successful illusion as a synthesis of different degrees of probability.

In "The Art of Fiction" James inadvertently upset the Coleridgean balance of writer and reader, out of his sheer ardor for fictional integrity. In context, he was of course defending the dignity of the novel as ideal history that is better than actual history, perhaps with Aristotle's *Poetics* in the back of his mind. He was assuming in the nineteenth-century reader a natural state of contemptuous unbelief, to which a writer like Trollope timidly pandered. In this, however, he misunderstood Trollope's art, and sowed the seeds of future misunderstandings and doctrinal distortions, centering upon the nature of "point of view."

What basic criticism of the novel is possible? And can there be a really objective critical approach to the works of any age but one's own? The well-intended efforts of literary history to clear the way seem frequently instead to raise insuperable barriers to understanding. Historical perspective makes criticism impossible if it lapses too far into time-relativism, from which there is no escape. From our literary experiences most of us recognize, too, the dangers of time-nostalgia, which can cause us to judge over-kindly. Forgetting that the past was once present, we attribute to it symmetries and certainties that it did not possess. We imagine an age more settled and harmonious than our own, and associate its comforts with its writers, doing them both more and less than justice.

One common way of dealing with the Victorians, for instance, is to condemn their so-called artistic faults, but to praise them for a mysterious life and verisimilitude which they nonetheless and unaccountably attained. This expedient has at any rate the virtue of registering a genuine response to their fiction. But it is suspiciously like our universal fallacy of regarding our forebears as more moral and more gifted, yet less critical and knowledgeable than ourselves, like Dryden in his "Essay of Dramatic Poesie" on the subject of the Giants before the Flood of the Rebellion and the Commonwealth. Trollope declined sharply in reputation immediately after his death, in part from the disillusioning effects of his matter-of-fact *Autobiography*. His novels then gradually regained favor, through a few critics and readers who were captivated by their "period" quality. This limited enjoyment of Trollope still persists, and has been serviceable in paving the way for a better grounded appreciation of his permanent value. A Dolphin Books paperback edition (1961) of *Dr. Thorne* proclaims on its cover that "This is Trollope at the top of his form, depicting the best of all possible arrangements in the best of all possible worlds, the English squirearchy in the English shire."

One is not disposed to quarrel with this good-natured claim, especially as it attests to the power of Trollope's fictional illusion. It needs to be added, however, first, that he created this world, and, second, that the word *possible* should be heavily accented. He was able to see around this world of his, and was not deluded into uncritical acceptance of it; his clearheadedness, in fact, is his basic claim to greatness. More important to my discussion, however, is the question, how was the illusion of his world produced? If, as James thought, he threw the game away, how does it happen that he nevertheless came out ahead?

My answer to this has been sketched in advance, by propounding after Coleridge a larger, less precise conception of artistic illusion, which will include some general notion of the appropriate state of mind of the reader, in collaboration with the skill of the writer that produces this state of mind. It may well (and even frantically) be objected that this is retrogression, a return to "effect" criticism which admits psychological imponderables into the critical process, and discards the sharp and useful tools of Jamesian and post-Jamesian analysis. As to the first objection, what was good enough for Aristotle is good enough for me: the *Poetics* is "effect" criticism. The psychological speculation involved is traditional and universal, and also experiential and practical, involving the Aristotelian assumption of a normative reader. What is intended is a general literary wisdom, as W. K. Wimsatt has well described it in formulating the critical role of psychology. It has little to do with what Professor Norman Holland has in mind as *The Dynamics of Literary Response,* which deals with a sub-literary level of responding.

To the second objection I interpose Coleridge once more, appealing to his organicist distinction between a critical principle and a rule, which has the consequence of exalting *principle*. That is, the concept of illusion is a principle, a living law, a genuine critical issue, and an end in itself. Point of view is a rule, a particular application of the principle or a means of law enforcement, the appropriateness of which must be carefully considered. In Trollope's case point of view is not applicable in our usual sense of the term. His illusion of reality, which as we have seen has been impressively attested, is reinforced rather than hindered by his authorial intrusions and apologies: his means are appropriate to his ends. As Coleridge's theory envisages, he composes his central illusion by interrelating different degrees of probability.

Thus there are various levels of relationship in the instances of "intrusion" that I have cited from *Dr. Thorne.* Trollope's confessions of uncertainty about Sir Roger Scatcherd's will effectually establish his concern for factual verisimilitude. This is perhaps an extra-literary consideration, but it supports his claims to a larger kind of verisimilitude. Here, we tell ourselves, is a writer who will not lightly transgress against the canons of fictional naturalness and (*pace* James) propriety. Further, there is the context to be considered. The will is all-important: Trollope has in actuality expended considerable effort upon its background, and his characters are closely involved with it. Dr. Thorne himself has shared his creator's uncertainties, and struggled for its verification. His battle is part of the developing exposition of his character, and his ultimate victory is the more satisfying for it.

"There's not a shadow of doubt," said the doctor. "I've had Sir Abraham Haphazard, and Sir Rickety Giggs, and old Never say Die, and Mr. Smilam; and they are all of the same opinion. There is not the smallest doubt about it. Of course, she must administer, and all that;

and I'm afraid there'll be a very heavy sum to pay for the tax; for she cannot inherit as a niece, you know. Mr. Smilam pointed that out particularly."

The final touch about the inheritance-tax is not merely factual verisimilitude, but part of the characterization. This is the way Dr. Thorne habitually thinks and talks. Furthermore, Trollope's apparent uncertainty points to an illusion so strong that it can be doubted without harming it—its exposure is in reality a reinforcement.

Norman Friedman's essay on point of view is admirably candid upon the crucial issue:

> Consistency and not cold-bloodedness is all, for consistency—within however large and diverse and complex a frame—signifies that the parts have been adjusted to the whole, the means to the end, and hence that the maximum effect has been rendered. It is, however, a necessary rather than a sufficient cause; the over-all consistency of a great but clumsy novelist may emerge *in spite of* his technical inadequacies, while the consistency of a lesser talent will not in itself produce masterpieces, succeeding within a smaller frame than that which genius may attempt. . . . But how many of our most ambitious and brilliant novels would have been even more successful if closer attention had been directed to these matters? There is surely no necessary contradiction between genius and technical mastery.

Friedman sums up in Jamesian terms: "When an author surrenders in fiction, he does so in order to conquer; he gives up certain privileges and imposes certain limits in order the more effectively to render his story-illusion, which constitutes artistic truth in fiction." These statements are admirable and undeniable. But what constitutes technical mastery? It is discoverable by the principle, and not by the rule. If point of view is identified with *consistency,* and permits of "however large and diverse and complex a frame," then there can be no objection to it. Ordinarily it has not been thus interpreted, and has been taken as a rule or as a set of rules that can be codified. So taken, it is a matter of record that it has tried to exclude authorial "intrusion," with erroneous conclusions.

NOTES

1. *Times Literary Supplement,* No. 3627 (Sept. 3, 1971), p. 1056.
2. Second Edition (1800), Preface to *The Lyrical Ballads.*

3. "The Devil George and Rosie," *Fancies and Goodnights* (Garden City, N.Y., 1951), p. 139.

4. According to Coleridge's use of the term: creatively, productively, sympathetically.

5. After its publication, "At a party that winter an admirer asked Henry James his opinion on some question. 'Ask that young man,' he said, pointing to Max who was a guest at the same gathering, 'he is in full possession of my innermost thoughts' " (David Cecil, *Max: A Biography* [Boston, 1965], p. 317).

6. In later life Beerbohm "stuck mainly to his nineteenth-century favourites: Meredith, Henry James, Trollope" (*ibid.*, p. 364).

7. Cited from *Approaches to the Novel*, ed. Robert Scholes (San Francisco, 1961).

8. See Ch. I, *The Search for Form* (Chapel Hill, N.C., 1967).

9. Coleridge, *Biographia Literaria*, Ch. XIV.

10. *Coleridge's Shakespeare Criticism*, ed. T. M. Raysor (Cambridge, Mass., 1930), I, 129, 206.

11. *Ibid.*, p. 205.

12. *Ibid.*, p. 207.

13. Introduction to *The Last Chronicle of Barset* (Boston, 1964), p. 12.

14. *Biographia Literaria*, Ch. XIV.

INTENTIONS
AND
INTENTIONS

THE PROBLEM OF INTENTION
AND HENRY JAMES'S
"THE TURN OF THE SCREW"

DOROTHEA KROOK

I

The dispute between the intentionalists and the anti-intentionalists is still unresolved, and the question is whether the problem admits of a solution satisfactory to both parties. I believe it does; and I suggest that the solution is to be approached by recognizing that there are at least three different kinds of intention (and thus three different meanings of the term "intention") to be distinguished. These crucial distinctions are up to a point implicit in both the intentionalist and the anti-intentionalist doctrines.[1] But they have not been made explicit by either, and this is perhaps the main cause of the confusions in both and the reason for their seeming irreconcilability.

The distinction directly relevant to literary criticism is that between the *author's* intention and the *work's* intention. I will call the first the "authorial," or "subjective," intention, the second the "enacted" or "objective" intention. The authorial intention is "subjective" in the sense that it belongs to, is a property of, the author's mind (the experiencing "subject"). The enacted intention is "objective" in that it belongs to, is a property of, the art-object, the created (in that sense "objective") work of art.

There is also a third kind of intention (or quasi-intention) to be recognized. This might be called the "psychological" intention—or, more properly, the psychological *motive*. An author may produce his works from a variety of motives, which are usually unconscious or subconscious, but may sometimes be conscious: when they are conscious, they may perhaps be said to operate, at least partly, as "intentions." He may, knowingly or unknowingly or part-knowingly, write his books to find relief from certain private preoccupations or obsessions; to liberate himself from particular fears, anxieties, sufferings, deprivations—the "personal and private agonies," the "private failures and disappointments" that T. S. Eliot speaks of.[2] Or it may be personal spites and grudges he is wanting to work off; or feelings of guilt about his secret crimes of commission or omission; or he may desire to justify hidden passages of his life. Or, again, the motive power for the creative effort may come from certain enthusiasms and hobbyhorses; or (less superficially) from the author's love of mankind and his desire to be of service to his fellow men; or, least superficially, from an inward pressure to magnify the beauty of the world and the greatness of man's spirit.

These motives or "intentions" are all, I think, properly described as psychological in that they are exclusively a property of the psychological makeup and history of the author. And the crucial point for criticism is that they are never the same as, and often have no connection with, *either* the authorial *or* the enacted intention. The psychological motive, or one of them, that impelled Shakespeare to write *Hamlet* may have been the need to liberate himself from a profound secret disgust with his own mother for some nameless moral crime she had committed. But this would obviously not be the same as any attributable authorial intention, either of the whole play or of the Hamlet-Gertrude part of it: say, that of writing a play (another one) about the desperate inner conflicts created for a sensitive, imaginative, intellectual young prince by his obligation to assume the responsibilities of princehood in a polity which appears to him corrupt and disintegrating; and (in the Hamlet-Gertrude story) that of showing the exacerbation of the prince's spiritual torments by the shameful conduct of his mother the queen. And if the hypothetical psychological motive or intention of *Hamlet* is different from its ascribed authorial intention, how much *more* different is it from the play's objective, "enacted" intention: the total conception or design inferrable from the play itself.

Similarly, an author like Pope may have written his *Characters of Women* from the psychological motive or intention (in this instance, fully conscious) of tearing to pieces certain living women he detested and despised. But, again, the authorial intention—say, the satirical exposure of female vice and folly—is something different from this; and so is the enacted intention of the work—that of exposing a particular complex of vices or follies in a particular way. By shifting our point of view, we may recognize here the mystery of the transmuting power of the mind that creates, which converts its own personal, private psychological "motives" into impersonal, public "intentions," first of the artist, finally of the work of art. This view of the problem of intention, as an aspect of the creative process, is something to which I shall return.

There are, of course, border-line cases. When Milton proclaims it to be his intention in *Paradise Lost* "to justify the ways of God to man," this might I suppose be taken as a statement both of a psychological motive and of an authorial intention—and, up to a point, also of the enacted intention, the design or conception actually executed in the work. However, the fact that this kind of connection, or coincidence, may sometimes occur does not prove that there is any necessary connection; and this, the absence of a necessary connection, is the important point for the analysis of our problem. It argues that the psychological motive or intention as such is no concern of the literary critic, because it lies wholly outside of both the authorial and the enacted intentions which *are* his concern.

So I return to these two kinds of intention to ask: How, in general, do we *know* each? How do we have access to it; how, in Wimsatt's phrase, does it become "available"? The answer is, we know the authorial intention mainly from extra-textual sources, we know the enacted intention exclusively from an examination of the text. To illustrate this point (and almost every other connected with the problem of intention), I take up Henry James's story *The Turn of the Screw*, whose intentions—authorial, enacted, and psychological—have been more exhaustively documented than those of perhaps any other modern work.

II

The authorial intention of *The Turn of the Screw* is stated, with the utmost explicitness, in two places: in an entry in James's Notebooks, and in his Preface to the volume containing this story in the New

York Edition of his works. The entry in the Notebooks, dated 12th January 1895, reads:

Note here the ghost-story told me at Addington (evening of Thursday 10th) by the Archbishop of Canterbury: the mere vague, undetailed, faint sketch of it—being all he had been told (very badly and imperfectly) by a lady who had no art of relation, and no clearness: the story of the young children (indefinite number and age) left to the care of servants in an old country-house, through the death, presumably, of parents. The servants, wicked and depraved, corrupt and deprave the children; the children are bad, full of evil, to a sinister degree. The servants *die* (the story vague about the way of it) and their apparitions, figures, return to haunt the house *and* the children, to whom they seem to beckon, whom they invite and solicit, from across dangerous places, the deep ditch of a sunk fence etc.—so that the children may destroy themselves, lose themselves, by responding, by getting into their power. So long as the children are kept from them, they are not lost; but they try and try and try, these evil presences, to get hold of them. It is a question of the children "coming over to where they are." It is all obscure and imperfect, the picture, the story, but there is a suggestion of strangely gruesome effect in it. The story to be told—tolerably obviously—by an outside spectator, observer.[3]

Significantly (this is a point to which I shall return), the subsequently controversial figure of the governess, the first-person narrator of the finished story, is here vague and indefinite, indeed as yet barely conceived: "the story to be told—tolerably obviously—by an outside spectator, observer." Apart from this gap, however, the author's intention is plain enough. If he writes the story, it will be a story of "gruesome effect" about the corruption of young children by depraved servants who have sole charge of the children in a big lonely house in the depths of the country. The servants will first exercise their evil influence as living creatures in daily contact with the children, then will mysteriously die, and continue their evil work as haunting apparitions.

In the Preface in the New York Edition, published 1907-09, some ten years after the story's first appearance in 1898, James reviews his story, its genesis, and some of the artistic problems involved in its composition, recalling his authorial intentions, and finding that they have on the whole been admirably executed. He mentions again the anecdote from which the story sprang, which would be "thrilling" indeed (he writes), "dealing as it did with a couple of small children

in an out-of-the-way place, to whom the spirits of certain 'bad' servants, dead in the employ of the house, were believed to have appeared with the design of 'getting hold' of them."[4] The servants are
described as "hovering prowling blighted presences" and as "abnormal
agents" on whom "there would be laid . . . the dire duty of causing
the situation to reek with the air of Evil."[5] James then discusses at
length one of his main artistic problems in this story, that of conveying in the figures of the servants a sense of absolute evil without
"weak specifications":

> The essence of the matter was the villainy of motive in the evoked
> predatory creatures; so that the result would be ignoble—by which I
> mean would be trivial—were this element of evil but feebly or inanely
> suggested. Thus arose on behalf of my idea the lively interest of a
> possible suggestion and process of *adumbration;* the question of how
> best to convey that sense of the depths of the sinister without which
> my fable would so woefully limp. Portentous evil—how was I to save
> that, as an intention on the part of my demon-spirits, from the drop,
> the comparative vulgarity, inevitably attending, throughout the whole
> range of possible brief illustrations, the offered example, the imputed
> vice, the cited act, the limited deplorable presentable instance? To
> bring the bad dead back to life for a second round of badness is to war-
> rant them as indeed prodigious, and to become hence as shy of specifi-
> cations as of a waiting anti-climax. One had seen, in fiction, some grand
> form of wrong-doing, or better still of wrong-being, imputed, seen it
> promised and announced as by the hot breath of the Pit—and then, all
> lamentably, shrink to the compass of some particular brutality, some
> particular immorality, some particular infamy portrayed: with the re-
> sult, alas, of the demonstration's falling sadly short. If *my* bad things,
> for "The Turn of the Screw," I felt, should succumb to this danger, if
> they shouldn't seem sufficiently bad, there would be nothing for me
> but to hang my artistic head lower than I had ever known occasion to
> do.[6]

Accordingly, he saves his artist's honor and solves his problem by
taking a "right, though by no means easy, short cut":

> What, in the last analysis, had I to give the sense of? Of their being,
> the haunting pair, capable, as the phrase is, of everything—that is of
> exerting, in respect to the children, the very worst action small vic-
> tims so conditioned might be conceived as subject to. What would *be*
> then, on reflexion, this utmost conceivability?—a question to which the
> answer all admirably came. There is for such a case no eligible *absolute*
> of the wrong; it remains relative to fifty other elements, a matter of

appreciation, speculation, imagination—these things moreover quite exactly in the light of the spectator's, the critic's, the reader's experience. Only make the reader's general vision of evil intense enough, I said to myself—and that is already a charming job—and his own experience, his own imagination, his own sympathy (with the children) and horror (of their false friends) will supply him quite sufficiently with all the particulars. Make him *think* the evil, make him think it for himself, and you are released from weak specifications. This ingenuity I took pains—as indeed great pains were required—to apply; and with a success apparently beyond my liveliest hope.[7]

The statement of authorial intention in the Preface obviously confirms and reinforces that in the Notebooks, the finished story (as James noted with satisfaction) shows the intention to have been fully executed, and one might suppose that here is a rare case of the triumph of intentions enacted exactly *as* entertained.[8]

However, doubts and difficulties set in the moment one turns one's attention to the figure of the governess. As the entry in the Notebooks shows, she was no part of the original conception ("intention") —certainly not in the particularized, highly developed form in which she appears in the finished story; and the author's account of her in the Preface—in which he reviews, so to speak, his enacted intention in relation to his authorial intention—appears to be far from satisfactory. He has a great deal to say about the governess; but what he says is, or seems to be, obscure, ambiguous, even evasive, or at least curiously indirect and inexplicit. He seems reluctant to say everything there is, or may be, to say; he speaks almost as if there were something he wanted to conceal. His tone nevertheless is perfectly confident, as he takes up an apparently foolish stricture made upon his treatment of the governess:

> I recall for instance a reproach made by a reader capable evidently, for the time, of some attention, but not quite capable of enough, who complained that I hadn't sufficiently "characterised" my young woman engaged in her labyrinth: hadn't endowed her with signs and marks, features and humours, *hadn't in a word invited her to deal with her own mystery as well as with that of Peter Quint, Miss Jessel and the hapless children.* I remember well, whatever the absurdity of its now coming back to me, my reply to that criticism—under which one's artistic, one's ironic heart shook for the instant almost to breaking. "You indulge in that stricture at your ease, and I don't mind confiding in you that—strange as it may appear!—one has to choose ever so delicately

among one's difficulties, attaching one's self to the greatest, bearing hard on those and intelligently neglecting the others. If one attempts to tackle them all one is certain to deal completely with none; whereas the effectual dealing with a few casts a blest golden haze under cover of which, like wanton mocking goddesses in clouds, the others find [it] prudent to retire."[9]

He then indicates what he thinks he *has* achieved with the governess figure:

"It was 'déjà très-joli,' in 'The Turn of the Screw,' please believe, the general proposition of *our young woman's keeping crystalline her record of so many intense anomalies and obscurities—by which I don't of course mean her explanation of them, a different matter;* and I saw no way, I feebly grant (fighting at the best too, periodically, for every grudged inch of my space) to exhibit her in relations other than those; *one of which, precisely, would have been her relation to her own nature.* We have surely as much of her own nature as we can swallow in watching it reflect her anxieties and inductions. It constitutes no little of a character indeed, in such conditions, for a young person, as she says, "privately bred," that *she is able to make her particular credible statement of such strange matters.* She has "authority," *which is a good deal to have given her,* and I couldn't have arrived at so much had I clumsily tried for more."[10]

From this statement we may reasonably make the following inferences: (a) that the governess' "record" (report) of her strange, terrifying experiences (the "anomalies and obscurities") is to be taken as accurate; (b) that her "explanation" (interpretation) of the anomalies and obscurities may *not* be so; (c) that there *is* a "governess story" to be told, which is separate and distinct from the children-servants story; (d) that it turns upon "her own mystery," "her relation to her own nature"—that is, has something to do with her knowing or understanding *herself,* her motives, her view of the anomalies and obscurities she records; and (e) that James deliberately refrains from telling *this* story, for reasons of artistic proportion and economy ("I couldn't have arrived at so much had I clumsily tried for more"). We are given no indication, however, as to what the governess' "mystery" actually was—what "her relation to her own nature" was, or might or ought to have been; or, most important, how her interpretation ("explanation") of the anomalies and obscurities she records was, or may have been, inaccurate.

The further, more random, statements of authorial intention contained in James's letters, in replies to correspondents who had evidently asked him questions about the story or told him what they thought it "meant," are even more ambiguous and evasive, and often downright contradictory. Thus, writing to H. G. Wells, he calls it "essentially a pot-boiler and a *jeu d'esprit*";[11] and the same to F. W. H. Myers: "*The T. of the S.* is a very mechanical matter, I honestly think—an inferior, a merely *pictorial*, subject and rather a shameless pot-boiler."[12] But to Dr. Louis Waldstein, evidently a more intelligent and sympathetic reader, he is willing to admit, it seems, that the story is a rather more serious affair. It was at least "a little tragedy," not merely "a shameless pot-boiler":

> My bogey-tale dealt with things so hideous that I felt that to save it at all it needed some infusion of beauty or prettiness, and the beauty of the pathetic was the only attainable—was indeed inevitable. But ah, the exposure indeed, the helpless plasticity of childhood that isn't dear or sacred to *some*body! That *was* my little tragedy—over which you show a wisdom for which I thank you again.[13]

But even here, as everywhere else, James gives nothing away of the deeper intentions, authorial or enacted or both, of his story: nothing of "the lesson, the idea" which his correspondent has evidently tried to extract from him. He only hints, courteously, that Dr. Waldstein *may* have read too much into it: "I am only afraid, perhaps, that my conscious intention strikes you as having been larger than I deserve it should be thought."[14]

From these various statements of the authorial intention of *The Turn of the Screw,* and in particular from those contained in the Notebooks and the Preface, two preliminary conclusions may be drawn. First, the stated authorial intention in the Notebooks—to write a story about two young children mysteriously corrupted by two wicked servants—is *not identical with* the enacted intention of the work; for the governess figure, which is an integral and vital element in the conception or design actually executed, barely exists in the original conception. Second, the *stated* authorial intention is not the *whole* of the authorial intention. The author evidently did have some intention about the governess figure he finally produced; it is only not clear from his authorial statements about her what exactly he intended.

These conclusions in turn raise a series of questions about the intention of *The Turn of the Screw* which encompass virtually all the kinds of critical question that can be asked about the intention of any work of literature.

a. What is the whole *enacted* intention of the work—the design or conception actually executed?

b. What was the whole *authorial* intention, in so far as this may be learnt from the author's statements about it?

c. What, if any, is the *difference* or *gap* between the authorial intention and the enacted intention?

d. If there is such a gap, was the author fully conscious, or only partly conscious, or completely unconscious, of that part of the enacted intention absent from his statements of authorial intention, or stated so ambiguously and unclearly, or so indirectly and inexplicitly, as to be virtually absent? More plainly: did Henry James *know* what he intended with the governess figure, and only spoke evasively because, for some reason, he wanted to conceal his conscious (known) intention? Or did he not really (that is, fully and clearly) know himself what he intended, and spoke ambiguously and evasively to conceal his own blankness or uncertainty or puzzlement, whichever it was?

Finally, e: If he did know it, why did he want to conceal his intention? If he did not know, why *didn't* he know? In other words, what hidden psychological motive or "intention" prompted him to write the story, and caused him, in the first case, to conceal his authorial intention from the world, or, in the second, to conceal it from himself?[15]

These are the questions which, in different forms, have in fact been asked about *The Turn of the Screw,* and the answers that have been attempted may be found in the collection of essays called *A Casebook on Henry James's "The Turn of the Screw."*[16] For my purpose, the paradigm is Edmund Wilson's well-known essay, "The Ambiguity of Henry James."[17] This contrives, perhaps uniquely, to give answers to *all* the questions; and the fact that most of the answers are wrong does not diminish the interest and value of its exemplary comprehensiveness.

III

Viewed in the analytic light of my scheme of questions, Wilson's answers may be broken down as follows:

a. In answer to the question, "What is the enacted intention of the work—the design or conception actually executed in it?" Wilson produces his famous hallucination theory. The governess is a sex-starved Anglo-Saxon spinster who, having fallen hopelessly in love with the children's handsome guardian, sublimates her unrequited passion by forming a neurotic attachment to the children, especially the boy Miles, and presently by having hallucinated visions of the master's dead valet, Peter Quint. Her visions, likewise hallucinated, of the second apparition, the dead governess, Miss Jessel, symbolize her jealousy of her predecessor, whose close relations both with the children, especially the girl Flora, and with her substitute-lover Peter Quint she unconsciously resents. Her sexual neurosis causes her to imagine that the children are being haunted for some hideously evil purpose by the dead servants and that it is her special task to save them. She accordingly harasses and persecutes them with her neurotic suspicions, questions, and confrontations, until she causes the girl Flora to have a nervous breakdown, and "literally" (says Wilson) drives the boy Miles to his death.

b. In answer to the question, "What is the authorial intention, in so far as this may be elicited from the author's own statements?" Wilson, in the original version of his essay published in 1934, apparently ignores, or does not recognize the significance of, James's statement in his Preface about the corruption-of-the-children-by-the-servants theme as his principal intention. Then, in the 1948 postscript to his essay, added after the publication of James's Notebooks in 1947, Mr. Wilson appears to take more seriously the statement of authorial intention in the entry about *The Turn of the Screw* (p. 356 above). But it is difficult to see why this statement should seem to him more definitive than the equally clear and explicit statement in the Preface, which was, of course, available to Wilson when he produced his hallucination theory.

c. Wilson's answer to the question, "Is there a difference, or gap, between the enacted intention and the stated authorial intention?" is clear enough. On his reading of the story, the enacted intention is *almost exactly the reverse* of the stated authorial intention. His reading minimizes almost out of existence the corruption-of-the-children-by-the-servants theme, the treatment of which the author had explicitly declared to be his principal intention, and places at the center the governess and *her* story, which the author had implicitly declared to be peripheral, or at least subordinate, to the main interest: "The story to be told—tolerably obviously—by an outside spectator, observer" (Notebooks, p. 356 above). Moreover, reviewing his story almost ten years after it was written, the author had defended his relatively perfunctory treatment of the governess figure: "One has to choose ever so delicately among one's difficulties, attaching one's self to the greatest, bearing hard on those and intelligently neglecting the others. If one attempts to tackle them all one is certain to deal completely with none" (Preface, pp. 358-59 above). Here James both implicitly reiterates his original intention of keeping the governess-story subordinate to the children-and-servants story, *and* judges that he has fully executed this intention.

d. In answer to the question about the author's degree of consciousness and unconsciousness about his intention, Wilson is again unequivocal. His recognition, in his 1948 postscript, of the corruption-of-the-children theme as a central authorial intention does not cause him to abandon his hallucination theory. On the contrary, he reaffirms it, and now pronounces James to have been *conscious* of the corruption-of-the-children intention, *unconscious* of the hallucinated-governess intention: "The recent publication of Henry James's notebooks seems . . . to make it quite plain that James's conscious intention, in *The Turn of the Screw*, was to write a *bona fide* ghost-story" (p. 145); but "the doubts that some readers feel as to the soundness of the governess's story are, I believe, the reflection of James's doubts, communicated unconsciously by James himself" (p. 146); and "one is led to conclude that, in *The Turn of the Screw*, not merely the governess is self-deceived, but that James is self-deceived about her" (p. 147). In other words, James simply did not know *what* he intended with the governess figure, and was obscure and ambiguous about her in his Preface for this reason: that he himself was puzzled to know what she was about, that he understood her no better than she understood herself.

e. As to the psychological motive or intention of *The Turn of the Screw* (what "really" led James to write the strange story, why he was so confused about his authorial intentions, why he concealed them even from himself): Wilson has a complete quasi-Freudian explanation of all *this*. James, he contends (following a hint from the Austrian novelist Franz Höllering) was a *Kinderschänder,* whose favorite theme at this period was "the violation of innocence, with the victim in [almost] every case . . . a young or little girl": besides *The Turn of the Screw* (1898), *The Other House* (1896), *What Maisie Knew* (1897), and *The Awkward Age* (1899) are the most striking examples. "The real effectiveness of all these stories," Wilson says, "derives, not from the conventional pathos of a victim with whom we sympathize but from the excitement of the violation" (p. 149). And, drawing on certain biographical data about Henry James's relations with his brother William James, he concludes: "There was always in Henry James an innocent little girl whom he cherished and loved and protected and yet whom he later tried to violate, whom he even tried to kill" (p. 150).

What are the lessons to be drawn for the analysis of the problem of intention from this test-case account of *The Turn of The Screw?* Without attempting here an extended critique of Wilson's interpretation (which I have done elsewhere[18]), I suggest the following considerations.

1. Let us grant that the enacted intention is the only intention ultimately relevant for criticism. To interpret the "enacted intention" is to interpret "the work"; to interpret the enacted intention correctly and completely is to interpret the work itself correctly and completely. Wilson was thus, in principle, doing nothing illegitimate as a critic in ignoring Henry James's authorial statement of intention in his Preface (if he really did ignore, not merely not understand, what James was saying); and he was only being inconsistent in *not* ignoring in the same way the author's statement of intention in his Notebooks. What Wilson could, and should, have argued was that *The Turn of the Screw* was an example of the triumph of intentions never entertained: Henry James *thought* he was writing a story about the corruption of two young children by two evil servants, but what he actually wrote was a story about a sex-starved hallucinated governess who destroys the happiness of two innocent children and causes the death of one of them. The author's statement of intention, in such a case, is interesting only as a proof of the fact that a work can *be* the triumph of intentions never entertained. And this perhaps is what Wilson was trying to say in a muddled way when he allowed that James's "conscious" intention had been to write the children-servants

story ("a *bona fide* ghost story," as he somewhat superficially calls it), but that what he actually wrote, by "unconscious" intention (and therefore not, properly speaking, by intention at all), was the hallucinated-governess story.

2. Now, this theoretical stand about the irrelevance of the authorial intention is generally valid; and it is valid in the particular instance *if the interpretation of the enacted intention in the given case is judged to be correct and complete.* But what happens when the account of the enacted intention—that is, the interpretation of the whole work—is judged to be *incorrect* or *incomplete?* The authorial intention, in so far as it is known, immediately acquires an important value; and the case under review is a striking example.

Wilson's interpretation of the enacted intention of *The Turn of the Screw* has been shown by subsequent investigators to be both incorrect and incomplete.[19] Proceeding by the methods normally used in literary criticism to test the validity of a critical interpretation or hypothesis, they have shown that Wilson's hallucination hypothesis fails to take account of large tracts of the *data* of the story, either by ignoring them or by explaining them in a way that explains them out of existence. Thus, for instance: if we accept the hallucinated-governess interpretation, we are obliged to treat the children-servants story as a bare function of the governess' hallucinations. But to treat it in this way is surely to falsify the literary fact. The enacted children-servants drama is executed with a fullness, a complexity of detail, which simply make no artistic sense on the bare-function hypothesis; accordingly, Wilson's reductionist account of it is an explanation that explains the fact out of existence. Again, if we accept the hallucination theory, we are obliged to ignore or (again) twist out of recognition the repeated references, implicit and explicit, to the theme of salvation: to the governess as the savior figure, the good angel, fighting to save the children's souls from being possessed and destroyed by the devil ("It was like fighting with a demon for a human soul," she says explicitly, as Peter Quint's "white face of damnation" appears at the window in the last scene of the drama). And we are also obliged to ignore certain vital *données* of the governess-figure herself, which the hallucination theory cannot easily accommodate. One of these intractable data is that she is described as a highly intelligent, charming, dignified person by Douglas, the man to whom long afterwards she tells the story of the events at Bly ("She was the most agreeable woman I've known in her position; she would have been worthy of any whatever," says Douglas). Another is that, in recording the events, she repeatedly asks herself whether she may not be "mad," proving by the very question that she is not: that she is not so mentally deranged as to be incapable of recognizing the difference between fact and fancy, and not so morally blighted (by her Wilsonian psychopathic condition) as to be incapable of feeling a normal person's horror and incredulity about the events she believes herself to be witnessing.

The post-Wilsonian critics go further, of course. Taking account of all the data of the story, and in particular those Wilson ignored or explained away, they show that the governess-story has a meaning radically different from that which Wilson proposed, and that, once this meaning has been grasped, it is no longer difficult to understand what James is saying in his ambiguous remarks about the governess in his Preface, and *why* he speaks ambiguously. They also show that the ambiguous treatment of the governess figure is only one aspect of the all-penetrating Jamesian ambiguity in this story, which is conscious and deliberate (not unconscious and inadvertent, as Wilson supposed), and, again, has a meaning entirely different from, and more profound and more interesting than, the meaning assigned by Wilson.[20] What these fresh enquiries argue is that Wilson's hallucination theory, which he proposed as a *complete* interpretation of the story, is fatally incomplete—so incomplete as to be properly described as false; and superficial and perverse, too, if we want to judge the critic as well as the theory.

The significance of these investigations for the problem of authorial and enacted intentions in *The Turn of the Screw* is twofold. First, they prove that James's "conscious" (that is, explicitly stated) authorial intention to write a story about the corruption of young children by depraved servants has been brilliantly executed, and that this part of his story is thus a triumph of intentions fully entertained. Second, they prove that the governess-story is also a triumph of intentions entertained—even though this part of the complete authorial intention was absent from the original intention or conception, the *Ur*-conception, so to speak, sketched in the Notebooks. How the complex authorial intention about the governess figure may have grown and developed will be discussed in the last section of this essay.

3. What, then, in the representative case under review, is the critical interest and value of the known authorial intention? It is obviously that of *confirmation*: the statement of authorial intention has the value of confirming the more correct and complete interpretation of the enacted intention. It can still do no more: the author's voice, as Wimsatt rightly said, can never be an "oracle," can never have a unique, or even a special, authority. And this is true even when the voice happens to be that of an author as critically self-conscious—as analytical, discriminating, and articulate, in short as thoroughly dependable, critically speaking—as Henry James. For if (as James himself insisted) it is certain that a work can be a triumph of intentions never entertained, it is equally certain that this interesting disaster may fall, impartially, upon the critically competent and incompetent among authors. But the author's voice *can* confirm the critic's discoveries; and the greater the known competence of the author as a critic, the greater, obviously, the value of his confirmation.

Moreover, in those cases—and *The Turn of the Screw* might excusably be one of them—in which the critic finds himself at a loss to form *any* reasonably complete and coherent interpretation of the enacted intention, he can do worse than turn for guidance to the author's statement of his intention if it should happen to be available. There is no need to be afraid, or ashamed, or for any other reason diffident about consulting the author about his intention, or what he thought his intention was. There is even a case for treating it with respect (though not as "oracular" or uniquely authoritative)—on the sensible assumption that the chances of an author's knowing what he was doing and having done what he intended are as good as (though not better than) the chances of his not knowing and not having done it. Accordingly, the extreme anti-intentionalist position which virtually proscribes the utilization of the authorial intention, even as a guide to or confirmation of the interpretation of enacted intentions, is to be repudiated as false and foolish: foolish, because all extreme positions tend to be so; false, because it ignores an important fact of our critical experience and practice—that we do, or may, as a matter of experienced fact, receive guidance or confirmation or both from our study of authorial intentions.

IV

The extreme position also tends to ignore, or give insufficient weight to, certain important facts of the operation of authorial intention viewed as an aspect of the creative process—conspicuously, the fact that the authorial intention may grow or change in the very process of becoming the enacted intention. The authorial intention may be one thing to start with, and become something quite different as the work advances. Or it may start as something vague and hazy, and become ever clearer and more definite as the author comes "in closer quarters" with his subject.[21] Again, the genesis and growth of *The Turn of the Screw* admirably illustrate these phenomena.

The governess, we saw, started as an undefined, featureless, characterless, sexless observer or narrator: "The story to be told—tolerably obviously—by an outside spectator, observer." Then (we may imagine), as James came in closer quarters with his observer figure, he gradually (or suddenly—we cannot know which) saw possibilities in it: more and more of them, and more and more complex ones. Invoking T. S. Eliot's distinction between "emotions" and "feelings,"[22] one might say that a dominant, nuclear "emotion" (imaginative conception, emotional image) had formed itself in James's mind, to which presently various "feelings" (other images, ideas, perceptions) attached themselves, tangling, intertwining, and finally fusing with the dominant image or emotion. Suppose the dominant image to have been that of a typically Jamesian savior-figure: a young woman brought up in a remote country parsonage, with no knowledge of the great world; by nature intensely romantic, especially about the heroic, the noble, and the brave; by nature and upbringing full of high moral ideals, in particular the ideal of service and sacrifice for others. She is terribly anxious to do the right thing, not to do the wrong thing, not to fail in any task entrusted to her; and, though naturally fearful and nervous—full of the Jamesian imagination of disaster, constantly reduced and debilitated by her fears and anxieties—yet capable of bracing herself to great efforts of courage and resolution in testing situations. She is placed, in the story, in a position of unusual responsibility for a person of her age and inexperience, that of having the sole care of two intelligent, charming, vivacious children; and then, presently, she has the further terrifying burden thrust upon her of saving the two children from the nameless evil of the two haunting apparitions of James's original children-servants story:

> The servants *die* . . . and their apparitions, figures, return to haunt the house *and* the children, to whom they seem to beckon, whom they invite and solicit, from across dangerous places, the deep ditch of a sunk fence, etc.—so that the children may destroy themselves, lose themselves, by responding, by getting into their power. *So long as the children are kept from them, they are not lost;* but they try and try, these evil presences, to get hold of them (*Notebooks,* p. 178).

So James's originally vague "outside observer or narrator" has already assumed the more definite shape of a savior figure, whose principal savior's task it will be to "keep" the children from the apparitions so that they may not be "lost." Then, as the author contemplates this basic image or conception of the governess, his catalyst's mind is invaded by other images, conceptions, perceptions, scraps of information, fragmentary sentences, phrases, even words, which the basic image somehow calls forth or draws up from the depths of his unconscious or semi-conscious mind. Something, for instance, he has read in the Reports of the Society for Psychical Research about governesses who saw ghosts, or whose charges saw them.[23] Something his friend F. W. H. Myers had told him about a Viennese psychologist called Freud who had just published, in German, some clinical studies of women suffering from hysteria, including "The Case of Miss Lucy R.," an English governess in charge of two children, whose hysteric symptoms had been traced to her having fallen in love with her employer, the children's father.[24] Something again he himself had written just recently about the Galahad figure, in the "Grail Catalogue" he had helped to prepare for the Guildhall exhibition of his friend E. A. Abbey's Holy Grail frescoes: to the effect that Sir Galahad's saving mission is defeated "at the very goal" by a "single slight taint of imperfection" in his otherwise saintly nature.[25] This brings floating into his mind the great old Faustian fable: of man brought to ruin by spiritual pride taking the form of spiritual greed—the greed to "know everything," the fatal aspiration to divine omniscience.[26] And, crowding and pressing upon and around these images, are those of remembered faces, expressions, qualities of character or personality, shades of motive (the grins, so to speak, without the Cheshire cat), which rise up and solicit him from life, or from his own fiction, or from other people's fiction. The strained face of Lady Agnes in *The Tragic Muse*, for instance, who had learnt "not to insist":[27] perhaps the governess could be someone who had *not* learnt not to insist, and would pay tragically for her ignorance? Or, stretching in a long line, his own and other novelists' studies of self-deception ("rationalization"), of self-righteousness, of moral blindness and insensibility, in the thousand forms they assume in the human spirit. Or perhaps the picture, straight from life, of small children reduced to helpless confusion and terror by the efforts of well-intentioned adults to make them "see" things—moral things, moral crimes or lapses they had been guilty of—which they, the children, had not yet the moral maturity to understand, let alone to correct or control. These are some of the secondary images that may have attached themselves to and finally fused with the dominant savior-image to produce the governess in *The Turn of the Screw*: the figure of a traditional good angel incapacitated (like James's Galahad) for her task of salvation by a fatal taint of imperfection in her moral nature, compounded by the Freudian, or pre-Freudian, sexual complications of her maiden state, and by the fascinating hallucinatory possibilities suggested by the case-histories of the Society for Psychical Research.

If this, or something like this, is the creative process by which the governess figure comes into being, it is obvious, I think, how the simplified theories of intention fail to do justice to its complexity. And what they mainly perhaps fail to recognize is the complex, elusive relation between the conscious, the semiconscious, and the unconscious in an author's intention. It is exceedingly unlikely that an author will have been conscious of every part of his intention, either before the event, so to speak, or in the process of creating the event; and if this can be true of an author as generally conscious and analytical as a Henry James, how much more true is it likely to be of authors neither very conscious nor very analytical. An author may be conscious of some part of his intention, but not all of it; or he may not be conscious of any of it, that is, incapable altogether of recognizing and articulating his intention. Yet he may, *after* the event, when he has "enacted" his intention, recognize *that* he has enacted it and *what* he has enacted (what authorial intention or intentions, conscious or semi-conscious or unconscious, have been "realized" in the finished work); and like God at the end of the third day of the Creation, he may see that it is good. This I suggest is what happened in the case of Henry James and the governess in *The Turn of the Screw;* and if the case is as representative as I have claimed, it is an aspect of the operation of authorial intention not to be ignored in any complete analysis of the phenomenon.

However (to end where I began), to recognize and articulate an intention, before or during or after the event, is a strictly *critical* act, which the author as author is never obliged to perform. If he does, so much the better; but it is then as artist turned critic that he is performing it. As artist *qua* artist, he is only obliged to enact his intention, not to articulate it, or even to recognize it; and if he is, misguidedly, pressed for an account of his authorial intention, he may justly give the Jamesian author's reply to the foolish critic in *The Figure in the Carpet:* "I do it in my way. Go *you* and do it in yours."

NOTES

1. A conveniently brief statement of the intentionalist position is I. A. Richards': "Unless we know what he [the author] is trying to do, we can hardly estimate the measure of his success" (*Practical Criticism* [London: Kegan Paul, 1929], p. 182); and, long before Richards, Pope's in the *Essay on Criticism:*

> In ev'ry work regard the writer's end
> Since none can compass more than they intend. (255-58)

The best-known statement of the anti-intentionalist position is, of course, that of W. K. Wimsatt, Jr. and Monroe C. Beardsley, "The Intentional Fallacy," in W. K. Wimsatt, *The Verbal Icon* (Lexington: Univ. of Kentucky Press, 1954; Kentucky Paperback, 1967).

2. T. S. Eliot, "Shakespeare and the Stoicism of Seneca," in *Selected Essays* (New York, 1932), p. 137.

3. *The Notebooks of Henry James,* ed. F. O. Matthiessen and Kenneth B. Murdock (New York: Oxford University Press, 1947), pp. 178-79.

4. Preface to "The Aspern Papers," in *The Art of the Novel: Critical Prefaces by Henry James,* ed. Richard P. Blackmur (New York: Scribner's, 1950), p. 170.

5. *Ibid.,* p. 175.

6. *Ibid.,* pp. 175-76.

7. *Ibid.,* p. 176.

8. James used the striking phrase "the triumph of intentions never entertained" in his Preface to *The Awkward Age (The Art of the Novel,* ed. Blackmur, p. 100).

9. *The Art of the Novel,* p. 173. My emphasis.

10. *Ibid.,* pp. 173-74. My emphasis.

11. *The Letters of Henry James,* 2 vols., ed. Percy Lubbock (London: Macmillan, 1920), I, p. 306.

12. *Ibid.,* I, p. 308.

13. *Ibid.,* I, pp. 304-5.

14. *Ibid.,* I, p. 304.

15. "Why didn't he know?" would be a silly question if asked about an author known to be not generally critical or analytical or conscious of what he was doing in his art. One wouldn't *expect* him to know, and it would be no criticism of him as an artist that he didn't know. But in the case of Henry James, an author unusually analytical and self-conscious, the question is not silly. It happens also, in this instance, to be particularly relevant, because James's consciousness of what he was doing, or of part of what he was doing, in *The Turn of the Screw* has been explicitly denied by some critics of the story, notably Edmund Wilson.

16. *A Casebook on Henry James's "The Turn of the Screw,"* ed. Gerald Willen (New York: Thomas Y. Crowell, 1959).

17. *Ibid.,* pp. 115-53. All page references are to this edition of Wilson's essay.

18. In *The Ordeal of Consciousness in Henry James* (Cambridge, Eng.: Cambridge University Press, 1962), pp. 370-81.

19. See *A Casebook of Henry James's "The Turn of the Screw"* for the reports of their findings; also my report in *The Ordeal of Consciousness in Henry James,* pp. 370-89.

20. See *The Ordeal of Consciousness in Henry James,* pp. 129-34, 388-89, 122-34.

21. Henry James uses this phrase in his Notes for his unfinished novel *The Sense of the Past:* ". . . I leave it rough and a little in the air, so to speak, for the moment. The just how and just why I can dispose of in a page when in closer quarters" (*The Sense of the Past,* ed. Percy Lubbock [London: Collins, 1917], p. 291).

22. T. S. Eliot, "Tradition and the Individual Talent," *Selected Essays,* pp. 18-19, 20, 21.

23. Francis X. Roellinger, "Psychical Research and 'The Turn of the Screw,' " *American Literature,* 20, 1949, pp. 407-12.

24. Oscar Cargill, "Henry James as Freudian Pioneer," *Chicago Review,* 10 (Summer, 1956), pp. 13-29, reprinted in *A Casebook on Henry James's "The Turn of the Screw,"* pp. 223-38, especially pp. 231-36.

25. See E. V. Lucas, *Edwin Austin Abbey: Royal Academician. The Record of his Life and Works,* 2 vols. (London and New York: 1921), I, pp. 233-34. I have discussed the possible significance for *The Turn of the Screw* of James's contribution to the Grail Catalogue in an article, "Lady Galahad: or, the Governess in Henry James's *The Turn of the Screw.*"

26. Robert B. Heilman, "*The Turn of the Screw* as Poem," *The University of Kansas City Review,* 14 (Summer, 1948), pp. 277-89. Reprinted in *A Casebook of Henry James's "The Turn of the Screw,"* pp. 174-88, especially pp. 183-84. See also my account in *The Ordeal of Consciousness in Henry James,* pp. 116-30.

27. ". . . The worn look that sat on her [Lady Agnes'] face came from having schooled herself for years, in her relations with her husband and her sons, not to insist unduly. She would have liked to insist, nature had formed her to insist, and the self-control had told in more ways than one" (Henry James, *The Tragic Muse,* chap. V., ed. Leon Edel [London: Rupert Hart-Davis, 1948], p. 61).

THE
EUROPEANS

TWENTIETH-CENTURY
TRENDS IN
CONTINENTAL
NOVEL-THEORY

JOHN HALPERIN

Continental novel-theory of the past fifty years or so has been so diverse, sometimes so eclectic, and often so original that a brief survey must confine itself to general trends. By way of illustrating as economically as possible a few of the general interests and approaches of Continental novel-theory in the twentieth century, I shall discuss very briefly, summarizing as much as possible, some of the writings of six brilliant and systematic critics of the novel whose work seems to me to be generally symptomatic of trends (and has been influential in shaping those trends), of the mood and direction of much modern theoretical novel-criticism in Europe—José Ortega y Gasset, Georg Lukács, Victor Shklovsky, Roland Barthes, Georges Poulet, and Alain Robbe-Grillet.

Modern Continental novel-theory is concerned less with the moral result of the relationship between reader and text than with the philosophic relationship between the novelist and the raw material of his craft. I choose to put Ortega first because, in my view, he is the purest of the "autonomous" critics—and also the most logical and coherent. His work is the textbook to which autonomous fiction-criticism—which I see as characteristic of theoretical approaches to the novel in this century on the Continent—may always return. Ortega's argument is lucid and relatively uncomplicated. For him, the novel is an autonomous genre which is, or at least ideally should be, incompatible with outer reality. As he says in *The Dehumanization of Art and Notes on the Novel* (1925), the novel in the act of establishing its own inner world must dislodge and abolish the surrounding one. The author must interest and entrap the reader in the autonomous world of his novel; the novel should free us from our world, allow us to transmigrate to the fictional world, and then keep us there, prohibiting us from returning. The truly "impervious" novel, hermetically sealed off from outer reality, must make us forget any reality other than that of the novel. Thesis novels and historical novels, since they do not allow us to escape from our world, are thus an inferior sub-genre—for art is judged not by its quality of "transcending consequence" or historical accuracy but by its aesthetic qualities.[1] A novel cut off from reality cannot also propagate particular political philosophies or deal obtrusively with sociology, religion, science. In establishing its own reality, however, the novel is truly the most "realistic" of genres, Ortega argues (and he always puts quotation marks around that word). For literal reality itself, as he says in *Meditations on Quixote* (1917), cannot interest us; much less can its mere duplication interest us. What can and does interest us is "imaginary psychology," the minds of the fictional personages present in the world of the novel.

Ortega distinguishes between the *form* and the *material* of a work of art. Art lives, he says, only in its form; its qualities of grace must spring from its structure, its organism, and not from its subject. A work of art is what it is only in the form it imposes upon its material or subject. None of this means, of course, that the novelist must eschew *ideas;* it does mean that his use of them must be confined within the inner world of his novel. In Dostoevski's novels, for example, religious and political ideas are not simply operative agencies within the body of the work; they appear there with the same fictitious character as the faces and the frenetic passions of the figures themselves. We must never be told, Ortega goes on to argue, what the characters' ideas are—to do so is to violate characterization and also the ideas themselves, for the ideas are buried in characterization (or should be). We must always be shown, never told. The novel's aesthetic value, then, depends essentially on the skill with which the novelist presents his characters to us. In the best novels the personages refuse to adjust themselves consistently to our ideas about them.

This makes them independent of us, makes them appear to us as an effective reality transcending even our imagination.[2] What makes Dostoevski great and Balzac mediocre, then, is that Balzac's characters are mere copies of real people, the material of life itself, while Dostoevski's are simply possible, and so suggest the *form* of life rather than its material reality.[3]

Lukács is perhaps more concerned with life's material reality. Indeed, there is a strain of the moralist in him. He sees in literature, in ideas, the potential for the spiritual regeneration of mankind. But his approach to the novel is essentially political and historical rather than moral; that is to say, his perspective is usually that of a philosophical system. In *Studies in European Realism* (1935-39) he tells us that "everything is politics" and that the realistic novel is the artistic form most suited to expressing the relationship of politics and history to life. What Lukács admires most in European realism is its ability to produce, in the protagonists of Balzac and Tolstoy, men who, as Alfred Kazin puts it, "are exceptional not because they are isolated, like the heroes of Romantic literature, but because all that is seething in the social conflicts of their time has come to dramatic consciousness."[4] Lukács's admiration of European realism in this context is again underlined, more tersely, in *The Meaning of Contemporary Realism* (1958). The central tenet of both books is that no work of art can remain impervious to the historical and political milieu in which it is written. Economic and social reality, says Lukács, always engenders a corresponding literary structure.[5] He argues constantly in his books, and most notably in *History and Class Consciousness* (1919-23), for the commitment of art and of the individual to the exigencies of political (and therefore social) conflict and the realization of the individual consciousness through the concrete historical situation. As such, as George Steiner points out, he is clearly a forerunner of modern French existentialism.[6]

The polemical thrust of Lukács's books after the mid-twenties is clearly Marxist. In *The Historical Novel* (written in stages between 1937 and 1962), for example, he explains what he terms the "decay" from realism to naturalism in nineteenth-century French fiction in terms of the corrosive effects of capitalism. As capitalism grows more oppressive, the artist feels more alien to his milieu and his grasp of reality changes to a rapacious clutching. Instead of selecting his material, the artist feels compelled, as Zola was, to describe everything. As capitalism grows more specialized and anonymous and daily existence becomes more and more fragmented and synthetic, the artist inevitably loses his grip on the particular and finds himself separated from the organic rhythms and realities of creation. Thus naturalism.

Lukács's single greatest contribution to novel-theory is his brilliant pre-Marxist study *The Theory of the Novel* (1914-20), which focuses on the relationship between the novel and time—time both as historical moment and the tyranny of the clock—and on the struggle of the individual with his own social reality. One of the things that will determine the nature and the outcome of this struggle, argues Lukács, is the fictional protagonist's quality (and quantity) of mind. Is it too narrow for his society? Too large? The novel at its epic best will close with this issue; for the epic form itself is an expression of the relationship between mind and world. Lukács identifies the epic form of the novel as arising out of the alienation of the protagonist from the outside world, a world from which God has disappeared, and based on an "autonomy of inwardness," which is the only category of existence available to the alienated hero.[7] For Lukács there is a constant and sometimes bitter irony in the fact that the author knows that his character's search for meaning, for values in his society, is vain in a society without them. The great artist knows how conventional the world is, knows the insufficiency of the final conversion if there is one, knows how idealistic his own values are. The hero of the truly epic novel is then by definition and necessity a sort of madman; he must search for meaningful values without always knowing what he is looking for or what he will find. Often he will find nothing. In the constant interposition of itself between man and his universe, clock time contributes to this process of continual degradation. The search for values in a degraded world, the opposition between a conventional society and a hero who must keep searching for what cannot be found, defines for Lukács the epic structure of the realistic novel. And yet for Lukács there is always hope, finally, in the existence of hope itself, in whatever it is that spurs on the individual in his search, hope in the promise that eventually the human mind will become conscious of its relation to abstract values, however tenuous that relationship may be. Lukács's optimism emphasizes, ultimately, the poignancy of the clash between a man with faith in a higher destiny, a higher possibility, and the society which is unequal to his faith and, eventually and inevitably, unequal, spiritually, to himself. Literary criticism written from the perspective of a particular political bias is not uncommon in our century. Much of it is distorted by the subjectivity of prejudice. Lukács's criticism is a happy example of what can happen when sense survives polemic. It should also be clear that in his discussion of the relationship between contemporary politics and society and the content of novels, Lukács is not suggesting that fiction is generated in imitation of the real world. Fiction, for Lukács, reflects rather than imitates. It is acted upon, often disruptively, by contemporary reality, which in large measure determines literary structure. We begin with the outside world and end with a novel. In traditional mimetic fiction the process is reversed—that is, the novelist begins with a fictional world which grows to resemble the outside world as the novel progresses. In George Eliot's novels, for example, we often have a sense of the novelist consciously transcribing what she sees in the manner of the Dutch genre-painters. For Lukács, the contemporary world etches itself into the world of the novel *despite* the artist's conscious intentions. As Paul de Man puts it, Lukács fress himself from "preconceived notions about the novel as an imitation of reality [in the belief that novelistic form] can have nothing in common with the . . . form of nature: it is founded on an act of consciousness, not on the imitation of a natural object."[8] Lukács is concerned, finally, less with fiction as a provider of lessons in moral conduct than with fiction as a provider of insights into the political realities of the milieu in which it is created and the effects of that milieu upon the human consciousness.

Russian Formalism is seen by some as the most influential literary criticism to surface in our century. There is little doubt that it has some connections, for example, with the American New Criticism, with French Structuralism, and with the structuralist movement in general. It was a movement that began in the late teens and early twenties with a group of Russian critics who, unlike Lukács, wished to separate literature from politics. They argued for the autonomy of art, suggested that literary criticism ignore social causes and effects, and proclaimed that Formalism and Marxism were mutually irrelevant because the former explained existence from the inside and the latter from the outside. Like the New Critics, whom they resemble in a number of ways, the Russian Formalists attacked academic scholarship, advocated the isolation of literary criticism from historical, philosophical, and sociological concerns, and sought to replace traditional critical interest in historical background, social usefulness, and intellectual content with the analysis of literary structure. The formal method they advocated was scientific, non-ideological, and concrete; its focus was always the internal relationships that prevail *within* a work of art. The chief job of the critic, said the Formalists, is to study the ways writers use words and linguistic devices; such things as ethics and psychology are irrelevant. Resisting the Symbolist movements of the preceding decades, the Formalists argued that the importance of literary devices lies in whatever value they themselves embody and not in any extraliteral "meaning" they may carry with them.[9]

Perhaps the most important member of this early group, which included Boris Tomashevsky, Boris Eichenbaum, Roman Jakobson, and others, is Victor Shklovsky, who argues in a seminal essay entitled "Art as Technique" (1917) that great art, rather than making the unfamiliar familiar to us, "defamiliarizes"—that is, it develops techniques which *impede* understanding and thus both call attention to themselves and force the reader to redouble his attempt to perceive. To focus upon specific literary techniques, says Shklovsky, is to perceive the author's universe by perceiving the author himself at work. Defamiliarization forces the reader to perceive technique by making the familiar seem strange and calling attention to its strangeness through word-play, syntax, metaphor, and other literary devices.[10]

The value of art, Shklovsky argues, lies in its enabling us to experience the artfulness of an object; the object itself is unimportant. Technique itself, not what it "means," is always of primary interest to him. The work of art, after all, need not refer to anything outside itself. Like Ortega, Shklovsky believes that art must attract and hold our attention within its own world; "meaning" will be found only within that world, never outside of it. Perception becomes, then, an end in itself; "morality" lies in full awareness, and art is the record of and occasion for that awareness. The effect of the greatest literature is to make man exceptionally aware. Art, however, teaches man less about his world than its own. It is always the literary world rather than the real one that Formalism emphasizes. As such it is patently an autonomy-oriented genre.

The current Parisian Structuralists are even more specific in their approach to structure. For Roland Barthes, Jacques Derrida, Gérard Genette, Tzvetan Todorov, and their Structuralist colleagues—difficult and dangerous as it may be to generalize—the way to an understanding of a work of art lies through analysis of its language. Structuralism in many of its manifestations today has become the science of linguistics. It is a sort of linguistic anthropology, a union of literature and linguistics. The French Structuralists advocate a return of critical attention to the fundamental categories and problems of language itself—to such things as person, tense, and voice. In its many manifestations, Structuralism may be closely tied, in its analysis of literature, to the disciplines of anthropology, psychoanalysis, or metaphysics, or it may be simply impressionistic or phenomenological. Sometimes it is concerned with literary systems or structures inspired by the exterior world. What remains constant, however, is the unbending advocacy of a return to the text, which is seen as a denotation, a distillation, of the writer's whole experience. The unity of any given work, in this genre of criticism, is defined as the psychological determination or the metaphysical choice that has given rise to that work. Since writing itself is so much a product of the unconscious mind, and since Structuralism often emphasizes the underlying foundations of structure—i.e. the unconscious mind that produces a particular structure—the Structuralist critics tend to regard everything a writer has written as an important part of his total work, and they look for signs, clues, everywhere, anywhere. Because of its interest in the unconscious obsessions of the writer, Structuralism will often fasten onto recurrent images or ideas that tend to elucidate these obsessions. Writing, then, is often seen as a system of signs, and language as an index to the author's psyche.

Roland Barthes, perhaps the most distinctive of the current Parisian Structuralists, emphasizes everywhere in his writings the idea that man can never exist prior to or separate from language, which is always his expression of what is taking place within him. In his monograph *On Racine* (1963), in a volume of *Critical Essays* (1964), in his defense of the new French criticism against the attacks of Raymond Picard and others (*Criticism and Truth*, 1966)—and even in the pre-Structuralist reply to Sartre (*Writing Degree Zero*, 1953), in which he argues, in good Formalist fashion, for the disjunction of literature and history—Barthes insists again and again that it is language which teaches the definition of man, not the reverse. Culture in all of its aspects, he argues, is a language which is itself a general system of symbols. A unified science of culture is therefore available to the critics who will study the language of literature.

For Barthes, language itself can be seen and used as an instrument for the death and disappearance of the author—one of his favorite themes. Any literary utterance is "in its entirety . . . a void process, which functions perfectly without requiring to be filled by the person of the interlocutors: linguistically, the author is never anything more than the man who writes, just as *I* is no more than the man who says *I*. . . ."[11] For Barthes, what appears in a book is not simply the voice of the author; it is a "special voice, consisting of several indiscernible voices"; literature is "precisely the invention of this voice, to which we cannot assign a specific origin: literature is that neuter, that composite, that oblique into which every subject escapes, the trap where all identity is lost, beginning with the very identity of the body that writes."[12] Language speaks, argues Barthes, and not the author—who exists "simultaneously with his text," who cannot precede or transcend what he writes, who "is in no way the subject of which his book is predicate." The multiplicities of any literary text coalesce not in the writer but in the reader, who gathers together in his reading of the book the many voices which constitute the text itself. For Barthes, ultimately, "life can only imitate the book, and the book itself is only a tissue of signs, a lost, infinitely remote imitation."[13] Here is an unmistakable expression of Structuralism's reversal of the old mimetic process, of its emphasis upon the autonomy of the work itself, which is seen as a pale imitation not of real life but of the many ingredients of which it is itself formed.

Like many of his Structuralist brethren, Barthes often deals specifically with voice, which he defines as the way in which the subject of the verb is affected by the action (the writer is seen as the agent of the action), and with person, which he views as something concomitantly personal (I-Thou) and non-personal (He-It). In studying the ways in which the personal and the non-personal are alternated and copresent in discourse, Barthes frequently distinguishes between the voices of the author, the narrator, and the persona. Whenever there is an "I" in a novel, for example, it may not be the same for the writer and the reader; and the task of the critic, says Barthes, is to explore the relationship between the "I" and everything else, "to get to the core of [the] linguistic pact which unites the writer and the other. . . . [T]he exploration of language, conducted by linguistics, psychoanalysis, and literature, corresponds to the explanation of the cosmos. For literature is itself a science . . . of human languages."[14]

Finally, Barthes is also typical of French Structuralism in his fascination with the problem of the doubleness of *time* in literature. He constantly differentiates linguistic time from calendar time, emphasizing the distinction between the temporal system of discourse (determined by the relationship between the speaker and his utterance) and the temporal system of history (the narrative, which recounts past events). His literary criticism frequently explores the structure of polyrhythmic time and its implications in the particular literary text.

Like Formalism, at least in this respect, French Structuralism is indifferent both to mimetic adequacy and the moral interchange between a literary text and its audience.

The key word in the literary criticism of Georges Poulet and that of his colleagues in the Geneva School—Marcel Raymond, Albert Béguin, and others—is *consciousness*. For Poulet, who is probably the most distinguished of the French existentialist critics writing today, literature is neither more nor less than the consciousness of the author, and to read literature is to be transported into the author's mind. In three major works—*Studies in Human Time* (1949), *The Interior Distance* (1952), and *The Metamorphosis of the Circle* (1961)—Poulet insists that the assessment of the quality of the author's consciousness is always the one indispensable task of novel-criticism. One must always search, he says, for that profound note of self-identity that is unique in each person. The great novel portrays life as a growth or extension of mind; everything else in it is of less importance. Poulet is concerned less with the aesthetic properties of fiction *per se* than with the form of human psychology. The purpose

of literary criticism in such a system is to identify that unique element of consciousness revealed in the author's work. The creative act
itself is defined as consciousness taking form, and criticism becomes
the consciousness of another consciousness, the intersubjectivity of
minds. No wonder the Geneva critics have been dubbed the "critics
of consciousness."[15]

Poulet attempts to recreate in his criticism the stages in which an
author comes to a sense of his own conscious existence. His focus is
the author's generic human experience, and he sees literature as the
best realization of that experience. In opposition to Structuralism,
Poulet recommends the critical neglect of ordinary formal objects
of scrutiny such as diction and syntax; what he as critic seeks to discover in the text is the total non-objective reality of the author as
subject.

The common experience that literature and criticism compete to
express is usually the goal of Poulet's literary analysis. Such things as
historical comparison or literary analogies, while they may be a means
toward a "point of departure" for the critic, are never ends in themselves in his criticism. Poulet is rarely if ever concerned with literary
structure *per se,* and even less with the relation of structure to the exterior world. It is true that some of the other Geneva writers go further in analyzing separate aspects of literary form. But what interests
Poulet most is the author's manner of perception when all conditions
and objects are stripped away: that is, pure consciousness.[16] Once
again we are a long way from the moral and mimetic prejudices of
the Augustans and the early Victorians.[17]

For Robbe-Grillet, literary realism is specifically and wholly the result neither of mimesis nor autonomy; while he seems to prefer the
autonomous approach over the mimetic, his view of "reality" is essentially of something simply inert and without intrinsic meaning or
fixed location. Literary realism, he believes, should therefore concentrate not on depths but on surfaces; for surface is all there is. The realistic novel may well deal with "imaginary psychology"; but it must
be sure to deal with the world the characters imagine and not the
world they are actually in—which, once again, exists only in the exterior dimension. Characters "see" only what they invent; there is
nothing else. When realism fails to be "realistic" it is because it fails

to elucidate and admit these truths. "Reality" for Robbe-Grillet is so intangible, so incapable of definition, that we cannot even call it absurd. If the material world happens to be alien to man, for example, then it is alien to man, and to say that it is therefore tragic or meaningless is to attribute to it meaning which is a falsification. Why, asks Robbe-Grillet, must everything be *something?* Why must everything *mean* something? Reality simply *is* (to make the sentence longer is to distort); and this is the way it should be portrayed in the "future universe of the novel." And, he adds, characters will remain simply *"there"* long after "the commentaries . . . will be left elsewhere. . . ."[18] For Robbe-Grillet, who mistrusts literary critics, the greatest fiction is that which continues to elude the understanding of professional readers—thus his boundless admiration for Kafka.

In a revealing comment upon himself as a novelist, however, the usually neutral Robbe-Grillet implies a preference for the school of autonomy over that of mimesis. Admitting that fiction is the inventing of a "new world," Robbe-Grillet says:

> I do not transcribe, I construct. This had been even the old ambition of Flaubert: to make something out of nothing, something that would stand alone, without having to lean on anything external to the work. . . . [Out of this] a new kind of narrator is born: no longer a man who describes things he sees, but at the same time a man who invents the things around him and who sees the things he invents. Once these hero-narrators begin ever so little to resemble "characters," they are immediately liars. . . .[19]

Since only God can be "objective," the novel by definition is a totally subjective genre for Robbe-Grillet. Man is his own narrator.[20] Elsewhere he is even more explicit in asserting the anti-mimetic credo that, to borrow a phrase from George Levine's essay in this volume ("Realism Reconsidered," pp. 233-56), all fiction is fiction:

> What constitutes the novelist's strength is precisely that he invents, that he invents quite freely without a model. The remarkable thing about modern fiction is that it asserts this characteristic quite deliberately, to such a degree that invention and imagination become, at the limit, the very subject of the book. . . . [Art] . . . is based on no truth that exists before it; and one may say that it expresses nothing but itself. It creates its own equilibrium and its own meaning. It stands all by itself, like the zebra; or else it fails. . . .[21]

For Robbe-Grillet, the artist invents "without a model," art expresses no *a priori* "truth" but only itself, and this is sufficient. Art neither imitates nor means nor teaches; it simply is.

Formal realism, perhaps the seminal ingredient of pre-twentieth-century Anglo-American criticism, is seen, in this century on the Continent, as a function and result of the interior, created world of the work of art itself, whose "reality" and effect are dependent upon the skill with which the writer creates his world out of the raw material available to any artist who begins with no particular moral-mimetic prejudices. Such criticism is perhaps more than just two hundred years distant from *Lives of the English Poets*.

NOTES

1. Cf. Flaubert's belief that the novel must be stylistically neutral if it is to achieve universality.
2. Cf. Hardy's frequent complaint (in "The Profitable Reading of Fiction," *The Forum* [March 1888], in his notebooks, and elsewhere) that the idealization of characters robs them of verisimilitude by making them too familiar to us to stimulate our curiosity or interest. Ortega's thesis also is not far removed in this context from Victor Shklovsky's concept of "defamiliarization"—see below, n. 10.
3. Ortega's work brought forth in reaction a monograph which, along with Erich Auerbach's *Mimesis: The Representation of Reality in Western Literature* (1946), represents the best of what little mimetic criticism there has been in the last several decades. This is W. J. Harvey's *Character and the Novel* (1965), which includes a long and interesting rebuttal of Ortega's views (see especially Appendix II, "The Attack on Character"). I am not including Auerbach in this discussion because, while I find his work fascinating, illuminating, and often persuasive, it is not, in my opinion, typical of modern Continental approaches to the novel, which in general are not mimetic.
4. Introduction to the first American edition of *Studies in European Realism* (1964).
5. For an approach similar in some ways to Lukács's, see Auerbach's *Mimesis*. Auerbach, however, confines himself for the most part to an examination of the ways in which an author's style interacts with, and is largely a product of, his social and historical milieu. This, for him, is the generating source of mimetic art. Lukács's version of the generating sources of fiction are, as we shall see, somewhat different.
6. See Steiner's introduction to a volume entitled *Realism in Our Time* (1957), which is one of the most incisive commentaries on Lukács's work I have encountered. Much of what I have to say about Lukács in this paragraph and the next is indebted to Steiner's essay.
7. See Paul de Man, "Georg Lukács's *Theory of the Novel*," originally pub-

lished in *Modern Language Notes* (December 1966), and reprinted in *Blindness and Insight: Essays in the Rhetoric of Contemporary Criticism* (1971).
8. *Ibid.*
9. See the excellent commentaries, of which my discussion in an expansion, on Russian Formalism in general and Shklovsky's work in particular by Lee T. Lemon and Marion J. Reis in *Russian Formalist Criticism: Four Essays* (1965).
10. It is interesting to note that Hardy and Ortega both argue against too much "familiarization" also—though perhaps with somewhat different emphases in mind. See Hardy's argument for a "disproportioning" in art, cited by the second Mrs. Hardy in her *Life of Thomas Hardy* (1962), p. 229. For an application of Shklovsky's principles here enumerated to a literary text, see his monograph, *Sterne's Tristram Shandy and the Theory of the Novel* (1921), in which he argues that Sterne uses "defamiliarization" in his disarrangement of natural sequence, which makes for the most "plotted" and least "storied" of novels and calls attention to technique as a means of elucidating the author's perspective on his world.
11. "The Death of the Author," originally published in *Aspen Magazine,* Section 3, No. 5-6 (1968), and reprinted in *The Discontinuous Universe: Selected Writings in Contemporary Consciousness,* ed. Sallie Sears and Georgianna Lord (1972), pp. 7-12. This passage appears on p. 9. I am indebted here and in the following excerpts from this essay to Richard Howard's translation.
12. *The Discontinuous Universe,* p. 7.
13. *Ibid.,* p. 11.
14. "To Write: An Intransitive Verb?", in *The Languages of Criticism and the Sciences of Man: The Structuralist Controversy,* ed. Richard Macksey and Eugenio Donato (1970).
15. See, for example, Sarah N. Lawall, *Critics of Consciousness* (1968), an excellent study of the Geneva critics that includes a chapter on Poulet. Another interesting essay on Poulet is by Paul de Man, "The Literary Self as Origin: The Work of Georges Poulet," originally published in *Critique* (July 1969), and reprinted in *Blindness and Insight* (see n. 7, above). I am indebted to both studies in the brief discussion of Poulet that follows.
16. Poulet has been particularly explicit about this aspect of his thought. An incisive account is provided by J. Hillis Miller in "The Geneva School," *Critical Quarterly* (Winter 1966). See especially the passage from a letter written by Poulet and quoted by Miller on p. 315.
17. See Introduction, pp. 3-22.
18. See "A Future for the Novel" (1956), reprinted in *For A New Novel,* trans. Richard Howard (1963).
19. "From Realism to Reality" (1955 and 1963), reprinted in *For A New Novel.* The passage quoted appears on pp. 162-63. This helps illuminate the contention in my introductory essay that Flaubert is one of the first writers to anticipate in his theories of fiction the stance and mood of much "modern" novel-theory. Flaubert talked about writing "a book about nothing . . . a book with almost no subject." See n. 22 of the Introduction.
20. See "New Novel, New Man" (1961), also reprinted in *For A New Novel.*
21. "On Several Obsolete Notions" (1957), in *For A New Novel,* pp. 32 and 45. Once again Flaubert's view on this matter is remarkably similar to Robbe-Grillet's (Introduction, n. 22). Robbe-Grillet here also sounds a bit like Barthes—see above, n. 13. It may also be interesting to compare Robbe-Grillet's

statements here and in "From Realism to Reality" (see n. 19, above) with one made by Conrad in the opening chapter of *A Personal Record* (1912): "Only in man's imagination does every truth find an effective and undeniable existence. Imagination, not invention, is the supreme master of art as life."

APPROACHES TO FICTION
A SELECT DESCRIPTIVE BIBLIOGRAPHY

JOHN HALPERIN

The following represents a partial listing of titles likely to be useful to anyone who wishes to investigate further some of the theoretical and formal questions raised by the foregoing essays. Articles and shorter pieces generally have been omitted; and the selection of full-length studies is only meant to suggest some possible further reading and is not intended to represent a comprehensive bibliographical survey of the subject.

The student would probably do well to begin with a number of relatively nonpartisan traditionalist perspectives. Among the most interesting and enlarging of these is David Masson's *British Novelists and Their Styles* (London, 1859), one of the first studies to employ in connection with fiction some of the techniques of rhetorical and formal analysis usually associated with poetry; Leslie Stephen's *Hours in a Library* (London, 1904), essays written from the late nineteenth century's perspective of instinctive mistrust of pure realism; Vernon Lee's *Laurus Nobilis: Chapters on Art and Life* (London, 1911), which expands upon some of the formal problems discussed in the essays by her cited in the Critical Introduction to this volume; E. M. Forster's *Aspects of the Novel* (London, 1927), a classic treatment of the structural bases of fiction; Morton D. Zabel's *Craft and Character: Texts, Methods, and Vocation in Modern Fiction* (New York, 1957); and Barbara Hardy's *The Appropriate Form* (London, 1964), which defines some of the radical aspects of fictional structure and then connects them through critical analyses to a number of important novels.

Other general studies written within the last fifty years which pay particular attention to formal questions include Carl H. Grabo's *The Technique of the Novel* (New York, 1928); Edwin Muir's *The Structure of the Novel* (London, 1928); Robert Liddell's *A Treatise on the Novel* (London, 1947); Bernard De Voto's *The World of Fiction* (New York,

1950); and Raymond Williams's *Reading and Criticism* (London, 1950).

Among the more theoretical·and partisan approaches to fictional form, the following ten items articulate collectively a highly diverse and thus, in all probability, a highly useful cross-section of views which should serve further as a provocative general introduction to the theory of the novel. Henry James's essays and prefaces are available now in a dizzying multitude of editions; two of the most judicious collections are those edited by R. P. Blackmur in *The Art of the Novel: Critical Prefaces by Henry James* (New York, 1934), which reprints essays by the novelist written mostly between 1906 and 1909 for inclusion in the New York Edition of his novels, and Leon Edel in *The Future of the Novel: Essays on the Art of Fiction* (New York, 1956), which includes a wise and varied selection of James's essays and reviews culled from a number of sources. In *The Craft of Fiction* (New York, 1921), Percy Lubbock applies Jamesian critical principles to a number of the world's best novels in a study distinguished throughout by clarity as well as insight—indeed, James's formal rules are expressed here by the disciple with a coherence at times more than equal to that of the prophet himself. Edith Wharton's *The Writing of Fiction* (New York, 1925) often echoes James, but is also an original and suggestive discussion of some of the theoretical groundrules of her craft. Next, four works of a more general nature which the student may well find indispensable to his study of literary theory are I. A. Richards's *The Philosophy of Rhetoric* (New York, 1936), Austin Warren and René Wellek's *Theory of Literature* (New York, 1949), R. S. Crane's *The Language of Criticism and the Structure of Poetry* (Toronto, 1953), and Kenneth Burke's *The Philosophy of Literary Form* (New York, 1957). Finally, two more recent works with a distinctly iconoclastic flavor are Alain Robbe-Grillet's *For A New Novel,* trans. Richard Howard (New York, 1965; first published in French in 1963) and Susan Sontag's *Against Interpretation and Other Essays* (New York, 1969).

Two interesting books which deal philosophically with a wide variety of novels and novelists—though in other ways very different from one another—are Ramon Fernandez's *Messages: Literary Essays,* trans. Montgomery Belgion (Port Washington, N.Y., 1964; originally published in French in 1927) and Vivian Mercier's *The New Novel: From Queneau to Pinget* (New York, 1971).

Among studies paying particular attention to literary language—often as an index to mimetic adequacy or formal integrity—the following works should repay the reader's attention. At the top of the list are two classic texts—J. Middleton Murry's *The Problem of Style* (London, 1922) and W. K. Wimsatt's *The Verbal Icon* (Lexington, Ky., 1954). Wayne Booth's *The Rhetoric of Fiction* (Chicago, 1961) provides useful vocabulary for slippery novelistic phenomena, though its literary judgments are often not to be trusted. David Lodge, in his *Language of Fiction: Es-*

says in *Criticism and Verbal Analysis of the English Novel* (New York, 1966), brilliantly applies principles of modern stylistics to the analysis of fictional texts. And finally, two classic mimetic tracts must not be ignored; these are Erich Auerbach's *Mimesis: The Representation of Reality in Western Literature,* trans. Willard Trask (Princeton, N.J., 1946) and W. J. Harvey's *Character and the Novel* (Ithaca, N.Y., 1965).

Mimetic studies specifically concerned with political, economic, and sociological matters as determining aspects of form include Irving Howe's *Politics and the Novel* (New York, 1957), and a dozen or so books by György Lukács—four of the best are *The Theory of the Novel,* trans. Anna Bostock (Cambridge, Mass., 1971; first published in German in 1920), *Studies in European Realism,* trans. Edith Bone (London, 1950), *Zur Gegenwartsbedeutung des kritischen Realismus* (Berlin, 1958), and *The Historical Novel* (London, 1962).

An excellent counterweight to the mimetic critics may be found in the work of José Ortega y Gasset, especially in his brilliant studies *Meditations on Quixote,* trans. Evelyn Rugg and Diego Marín (New York, 1961; originally published in Spanish in 1914) and *The Dehumanization of Art,* trans. Helene Weyl (Princeton, N.J., 1948; first published as *La Deshumanizacíon del arte e Ideas sobre la Novela* in 1925). See especially the essay entitled "Notes on the Novel" in the latter work.

It is often dangerous and misleading to lump together critics of different schools or persuasions who may have only one or two things in common. For the sake of convenience here, however, the next group of titles represents criticism which may be called, vaguely enough, formalism— the work of the Geneva critics, their brethren the Structuralists, and the ancestors of both, the Russian Formalists, and *their* brethren, the practitioners of stylistics.

One of the first names to be reckoned with here is that of Roland Barthes, of whose many works two volumes in particular should repay the student's attention: *Le Degré zéro de l'écriture* (Paris, 1953; trans. as *Writing Degree Zero* by A. Lavers and C. Smith, London, 1967) and *Etudes critiques* (Paris, 1964). Another extremely influential and important writer is Georges Poulet, whose most interesting books include *Studies in Human Time,* trans. Elliott Coleman (Baltimore, 1956) and *The Interior Distance,* trans. Elliott Coleman (Baltimore, 1959). Stephen Ullmann's *Style in the French Novel* (Oxford, England, 1964) and Jacques Derrida's *De la grammatologie* (Paris, 1967) provide stylistic analyses of a number of French classics. Two important collections of formalist essays are those by Tzvetan Todorov, *Théorie de la littérature* (Paris, 1965) and Lee T. Lemon and Marion J. Reis, *Russian Formalist Criticism: Four Essays* (Lincoln, Neb., 1965). Sarah N. Lawall provides an excellent commentary on the Geneva critics and others in *Critics of Consciousness* (New York, 1968), and J. Hillis Miller provides a primary text with *The Form of Victorian Fiction* (Notre Dame, Ind., 1968). An excellent introduction to Structuralism, emphasizing its early association with the sciences, is that by Jean Piaget—entitled, simply enough, *Structuralism,* trans. and ed. Chaninah Maschler (New York, 1970). Another incisive discussion of Structuralism has been written by Tzvetan Todorov—*Qu'est-ce que le structuralisme?* (Paris, 1968). Frederick Jameson's *The Prison House of Language: A Critical Account of Structuralism and Russian Formalism* (Princeton, N.J., 1972) is both a lucid survey and an excellent critique of relevant methodological prejudices and principles. In *The Languages of Criticism and the Sciences of Man: The Structuralist Controversy* (Baltimore, 1970), Richard Macksey and Eugenio Donato provide a number of interesting contemporary perspectives on the subject. Many of the most provocative issues of modern fiction criticism and theory are discussed by Paul de Man in *Blindness and Insight: Essays in the Rhetoric of Contemporary Criticism* (New York, 1971). And in *The Discontinuous Universe: Selected Writings in Contemporary Consciousness* (New York, 1972), Sallie Sears and Georgianna W. Lord have collected a number of reprints which reflect much of the originality and virtuosity of contemporary formalist criticism.

Two further studies of literary form, both of which, interestingly enough, emphasize novelistic endings, are Alan Friedman's *The Turn of the Novel: The Transition to Modern Fiction* (New York, 1966), which is uneven but often brilliant, and Frank Kermode's thought-provoking discussion *The Sense of An Ending: Studies in the Theory of Fiction* (New York, 1967).

Three more or less ungroupable miscellaneous studies the student should see are Marcel Proust's *Contre Sainte-Beuve* (Paris, 1909), which defends an anti-biographical approach to literature and criticism; Robert Humphrey's *Stream of Consciousness in the Modern Novel* (Berkeley, Calif., 1954), which includes precise and lucid definitions of many of the undescribable phenomena of modern fiction; and Northrop Frye's classic *Anatomy of Criticism,* which, despite its penchant for over-classification, will provide the student with an excellent introduction to mythopoeic criticism.

Finally, those interested in investigating further some of the possible connections and relationships between literature and cinematography may find the following volumes useful: Marguerite Gonda Ortman, *Fiction and the Screen* (Boston, 1935); Edgar Harlan Whitehead, *An Investigation of the Theory and Technique of Adapting the Novel to the Motion Picture* (unpublished, 1939; Doheny Library, University of Southern California); Sergei Eisenstein, *Film Form: Essays in Film Theory,* ed. and trans. Jay Leyda (New York, 1949); Andries Deinum, *Film as Narrative: The Affinity of Film and Novel* (unpublished, 1951; Doheny Library, University of Southern California); George Bluestone, *Novels into Film* (Baltimore, 1957); Richard Dyer MacCann (ed.), *Film: A Montage of Theories* (New York, 1966); and Fred Harold Marcus, *Film and Literature: Contrasts in Media* (Scranton, Pa., 1971).

CONTRIBUTORS

Walter Allen, novelist and critic, is Professor of English Studies at the New University of Ulster in Northern Ireland. His many works include *Arnold Bennett, George Eliot, The English Novel: A Short Critical History, The Modern Novel in Britain and the United States,* and *The Urgent West*. Mr. Allen is currently writing a book on the short story in English.

Irving H. Buchen, Professor of English at Fairleigh Dickinson University, is the author of *Isaac Bashevis Singer and the Eternal Past* and *The Perverse Imagination*. He has published extensively on nineteenth- and twentieth-century American and British authors, and has also served as President of the Northeast Modern Language Association.

Leon Edel, who recently completed his five-volume life of Henry James, is now editing the novelist's letters. He has edited many volumes of James's work, including the *Complete Tales* and the *Complete Plays,* and has also written on Joyce, Thoreau, Faulkner, Willa Cather, and *The Modern Psychological Novel*. Mr. Edel is Citizens Professor of English at the University of Hawaii.

Leslie A. Fiedler, Samuel L. Clemens Professor of English at the State University of New York at Buffalo, is the author of many works of criticism and fiction, including *Love and Death in the American Novel, Nude Croquet, The Return of the Vanishing American,* and *Being Busted*. His most recent book is *The Stranger in Shakespeare,* and he is presently working on a study to be called *What Was Literature?*

Richard Harter Fogle is University Distinguished Professor of English at the University of North Carolina at Chapel Hill. He is the author of many books on English and American literature, including *The Imagery of Keats and Shelley, The Idea of Coleridge's Criticism,* and studies of Hawthorne and Melville. Mr. Fogle was formerly Head and University Chairman of English at Tulane University.

Alan Warren Friedman, Associate Professor of English at the University of Texas, is the author of *Lawrence Durrell and "The Alexandria Quartet": Art for Love's Sake.* His essays on British and American literature have appeared in such journals as *Modern Fiction Studies, Texas Studies in Literature and Language, Contemporary Literature,* and *The Southern Review.* Mr. Friedman is now at work on a study to be called *Multivalence: The Moral Quality of Form in the Modern Novel.*

Robert B. Heilman was chairman of the Department of English at the University of Washington from 1948 to 1971, when he returned to full-time teaching there. His books include *America in English Fiction 1760-1800; This Great Stage* and *Magic in the Web* (both on Shakespeare);

Tragedy and Melodrama: Versions of Experience; The Iceman, the Arsonist, and the Troubled Agent: Tragedy and Melodrama on the Modern Stage; and *The Ghost on the Ramparts and Other Essays in the Humanities.* The last two studies both appeared in 1973.

Alice R. Kaminsky, Professor of English at the State University of New York College at Cortland, has also taught at Hunter College, New York University, and Cornell University. She is the author of *George Henry Lewes as Literary Critic* and the editor of *The Literary Criticism of George Henry Lewes.* Mrs. Kaminsky is also the author of a book on logic, and is currently completing a critical study of Chaucer's *Troilus and Criseyde.*

Frank Kermode is Lord Northcliffe Professor of Modern English Literature at University College London. He is the author of many works of literary criticism, including *The Sense of an Ending, Romantic Image, Wallace Stevens,* and *Puzzles and Epiphanies.*

Dorothea Krook, Professor of English at Tel-Aviv University in Israel, was formerly Professor of English at the Hebrew University of Jerusalem and a Fellow of Newnham College, Cambridge, and Lecturer at Cambridge University. She is the author of *Three Traditions of Moral Thought, The Ordeal of Consciousness in Henry James,* and *Elements of Tragedy,* and is at present completing an extended study in the philosophy of literary criticism.

George Levine, Professor and Chairman of the Department of English,

Livingston College, Rutgers University, is the author of *Boundaries of Fiction* and co-editor, with William Madden, of *The Art of Victorian Prose*. His critical essays have appeared in *PMLA, English Literary History,* and a number of other journals. Mr. Levine is now at work on a study of the conventions of realism in fiction.

A. Walton Litz is Professor of English and Chairman of the Council of the Humanities at Princeton University. He is the author of *The Art of James Joyce, Jane Austen: A Study of Her Artistic Development,* and *Introspective Voyager: The Poetic Development of Wallace Stevens*. Mr. Litz has also edited volumes on Joyce's *Dubliners* and T. S. Eliot and, with Robert Scholes, *Modern American Fiction: Essays in Criticism*.

John W. Loofbourow, late Associate Professor of English at Boston College, was the author of *Thackeray and the Form of Fiction*. His essays on various aspects of fiction appeared in a number of journals, including *Audience, Thought,* and *Enlightenment Essays*.

Robert Bernard Martin, Professor of English at Princeton University, has written a number of books dealing with the Victorian period and its literature, including *Charlotte Brontë's Novels: The Accents of Persuasion, Enter Rumour: Four Early Victorian Scandals,* and *The Dust of Combat: A Life of Charles Kingsley*. He is also the author of four novels. Mr. Martin has recently completed a study of Victorian comic theory.

Marvin Mudrick is the author of *Jane Austen: Irony as Defense and Discovery* and *On Culture and Literature,* and editor of the volume *Conrad: A Collection of Critical Essays*. His reviews and articles have appeared in *The Hudson Review* and many other literary journals. Mr. Mudrick is currently Professor of English and Provost of the College of Creative Studies at the University of California at Santa Barbara.

Max F. Schulz, Professor and Chairman of the Department of English at the University of Southern California, has published extensively on the English Romantic poets and on contemporary American fiction. He is the author of *The Poetic Voices of Coleridge* and *Radical Sophistication: Studies in Contemporary Jewish-American Novelists* and two more recent books on *Bruce Jay Friedman* and *Black Humor Fiction of the Sixties: A Pluralistic Definition of Man and His World*.

Meir Sternberg, Senior Lecturer in Poetics and Comparative Literature at Tel-Aviv University in Israel, has published a number of essays on the theory, rhetoric, and interpretation of fiction. He is currently at work on a comprehensive study of the principles of distribution and temporal ordering in the narrative text.

Walter F. Wright is Marie Kotouc Roberts Professor of English at the University of Nebraska. He has edited Conrad's essays and prefaces and is the author of *Sensibility in English Prose Fiction: 1760-1814, Art and Substance in George Meredith,* and volumes on James, Hardy, and Arnold Bennett.

John Halperin is Associate Professor and Director of Graduate Studies in the Department of English at the University of Southern California. He is the author of *The Language of Meditation: Four Studies in Nineteenth-Century Fiction* and *Egoism and Self-Discovery in the Victorian Novel* and the editor of a recent paperback edition of Henry James's *The Golden Bowl.* Forthcoming is a collection of bicentennial essays he is editing on Jane Austen. Mr. Halperin's own essays have appeared in a variety of places. He is now at work on a study of Trollope's parliamentary novels.